MY CONFEDERATE KINFOLK

MY
CONFEDERATE

Kinfolk

A Twenty-First Century
Freedwoman Confronts Her Roots

THULANI DAVIS

BASIC
CIVITAS
BOOKS

A Member of the Perseus Books Group
New York

Books published by Basic Civitas are available at special discounts for
bulk purchases in the United States by corporations, institutions, and
other organizations. For more information, please contact the Special
Markets Department at the Perseus Books Group, 11 Cambridge Center,
Cambridge, MA 02142, or call (617) 252-5298 or (800) 255-1514, or
e-mail special.markets@perseusbooks.com.

Designed by Trish Wilkinson
Set in 11.5-point Minion by the Perseus Books Group

Library of Congress Cataloging-in-Publication Data

Davis, Thulani.
    My Confederate kinfolk : a twenty-first century freedwoman
confronts her roots / Thulani Davis.
      p.   cm.
    Includes bibliographical references and index.
    ISBN-13: 978-0-465-01555-9 (hc : alk. paper)
    ISBN-10: 0-465-01555-7 (hc)
    1. Davis, Thulani—Family. 2. Campbell family. 3. Davis family.
4. African American families. 5. African Americans—Genealogy.
6. African Americans—Biography. 7. Silver Creek (Miss.)—Biography.
8. Yazoo County (Miss.)—Biography. I. Title.

E185.96.D285 2006
929'.208996073—dc22   2005024851

06 07 08 / 10 9 8 7 6 5 4 3 2 1

For Chloe Tarrant Curry,
Mariah Tarrant and Georgia Campbell Neal
And for all those, known and unknown,
who have fought for justice in Mississippi
"This little light"

Contents

1   **Twenty-first Century Freedwoman**   1
Fitting Two Families into History

2   **Silver Creek, Mississippi, ca. 1875**   15
Chloe Tarrant Curry Comes to
Work at the Campbell Plantation

3   **Clay Pots and a Tiger's Tooth (1850–1861)**   43
Where Chloe Came From

4   **Horses at the Door (1852–1861)**   69
Where Will Came From

5   **Behind Confederate Lines (1861–1863)**   95
The Scattered Campbells Go to War

6   **War from on the Road (1863–1865)**   127
Fighting Emancipation,
Black Soldiers, and Personal Loss

7   **"They Still Shoot Negroes" (1865–1868)**   159
In Alabama and Mississippi after the War

8   **Silver Creek (1868–1878)**   195
Chloe Leaves Terror in Alabama
for Mississippi

9   **Colonel Campbell's Constituents**   227
The Heroes and Villains of a Violent Election

10   **High Water (1880–1932)**   239
Chloe and Will and Life in Yazoo

   Epilogue   279

Notes   285
Bibliography   305
Acknowledgments   311
Index   315

Tarrant Family Tree

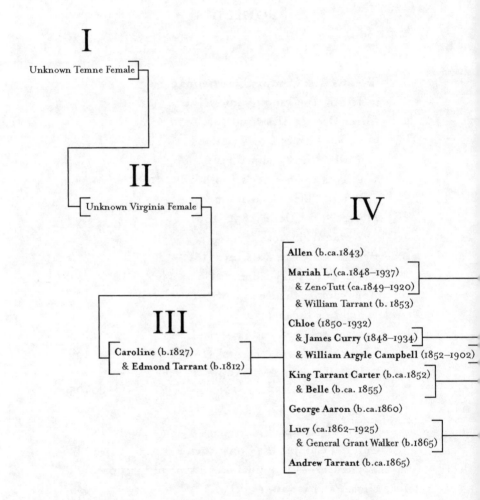

I

Unknown Temne Female

II

Unknown Virginia Female

IV

III

Caroline (b.1827)
& Edmond Tarrant (b.1812)

Allen (b.ca.1843)

Mariah L. (ca.1848–1937)
& Zeno Tutt (ca.1849–1920)
& William Tarrant (b. 1853)

Chloe (1850-1932)
& James Curry (1848–1934)
& William Argyle Campbell (1852–1902)

King Tarrant Carter (b.ca.1852)
& Belle (b.ca. 1855)

George Aaron (b.ca.1860)

Lucy (ca.1862–1925)
& General Grant Walker (b.1865)

Andrew Tarrant (b.ca.1865)

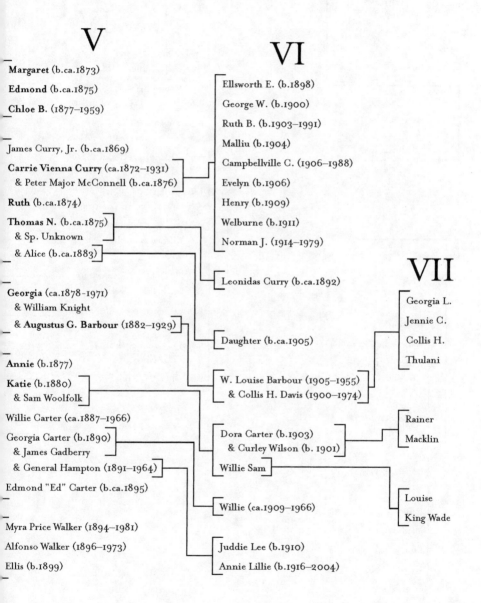

V

Margaret (b.ca.1873)

Edmond (b.ca.1875)

Chloe B. (1877–1959)

James Curry, Jr. (b.ca.1869)

Carrie Vienna Curry (ca.1872–1931)
 & Peter Major McConnell (b.ca.1876)

Ruth (b.ca.1874)

Thomas N. (b.ca.1875)
 & Sp. Unknown
 & Alice (b.ca.1883)

Georgia (ca.1878-1971)
 & William Knight
 & Augustus G. Barbour (1882–1929)

Annie (b.1877)

Katie (b.1880)
 & Sam Woolfolk

Willie Carter (ca.1887–1966)

Georgia Carter (b.1890)
 & James Gadberry
 & General Hampton (1891–1964)

Edmond "Ed" Carter (b.ca.1895)

Myra Price Walker (1894–1981)

Alfonso Walker (1896–1973)

Ellis (b.1899)

VI

Ellsworth E. (b.1898)

George W. (b.1900)

Ruth B. (b.1903–1991)

Malliu (b.1904)

Campbellville C. (1906–1988)

Evelyn (b.1906)

Henry (b.1909)

Welburne (b.1911)

Norman J. (1914–1979)

Leonidas Curry (b.ca.1892)

Daughter (b.ca.1905)

W. Louise Barbour (1905–1955)
 & Collis H. Davis (1900–1974)

Dora Carter (b.1903)
 & Curley Wilson (b. 1901)

Willie Sam

Willie (ca.1909–1966)

Juddie Lee (b.1910)

Annie Lillie (b.1916–2004)

VII

Georgia L.

Jennie C.

Collis H.

Thulani

Rainer

Macklin

Louise

King Wade

CAMPBELL FAMILY TREE

I

Robert Campbell (1724–1795)
& Jennet (1736–1799)

IV

Mary Wilson (b.1795)
& Joseph Miller

Col. Robert Bruce (1797–1852)
& Elizabeth Polk (1796–1856)

Eliza Eugenia (1800–1856)
& Abdon Independence Alexander (1798–186

Ezekiel Madison (1802–1874)
& Rebecca P. Adkins (ca.1800–ca.1876)

John Polk (1804–1852)
& **Louisa Terrill Cheairs** (1810–1866)

William St. Clair (1806–1852)
& Mildred Ann Blackman

& Sarah Nichol

Matilda Golden (1809–1870)
& Stephen H. Blackman

Junius Tennessee (1812–1877)
& Mary Ann Blackwell

Caroline Huntley (b.1814)
& ? Hardeman

Samuel Polk (1816–1835)

II

Robert, Jr.

III

William

Marguerite (b.ca.1764)

John (1788–1816)
& **Matilda Golden Polk** (1770–1853)

Robert (b.1769)

Rachel (b.ca.1771)

Polly
& Ezekiel Franklin Polk (1747–1824)

Robert (b.1775)

Martha

Jennet

Margery

Esther

Name Unknown

V

Children

n. Adkins (1821–1903)

ın Polk (1823–1900)

za Jane (1826–1859)

roline Ophelia (1828–1891)

ıry Eugenia (1830–1859)

ıtilda Golden (1832–1918)

becca Patton (1834–1868)

ıes Madison (1838–1901)

ıry Wilson (1840–1906)

bert Bruce (1843–1864)

itha (ca.1829–1848)
& Elnathon D. McKenny

ıry Frances (ca.1830–1853)
& Sam M. Sprouel

ın Nathaniel (1832–1864)
& Mary Roane Danforth
(1838–1926)

ınidas Adolphus Cadwaller
(1835–1882)
& Lucy A. McElhany
(1854–1889)

ah Rush (1837–1925)
& Jabez Owen (1831–1862)

ıes Cheairs (ca.1840–1861)

ımas Polk (1842–1862)

ıuel Independence
(1844–1872)

ınstantine (1849)

liam Argyle (1852–1902)
. Chloe Curry (ca.1850–1932)

ınidas Caldwell (1828–1863)
. Elizabeth Dodd Berry

ın Polk (b.1835)
Sue Gray

VI

Eliza

Francis

John

Louisa Cheairs "Lulu" (1848–1931)
& Frances Henry Sheppard

Laura "Lulu" (b.ca.1854)
& Thomas Merritt (b.1848)

Erskine Argyle (1857–1896)
& Ella Blythe Townsend
(1862–1940)

John N. (b.1860)

Finley (b. ca.1862)

Mary (b.1864)
& Hugh Shaffer

Robert Lee (ca.1873–1895)

Mary Frances (1855–1892)
& George T. Bryan
(ca.1855–1889)

Felix Grundy (1857–1936)
& Sallie Johnson

Sara Lucy C. (1860–1942)
& John Purdue McCammon
(1853–1931)

John Jay (1861–1889)

Georgia (ca.1878–1971)
& William Knight
& **Augustus G. Barbour**
(1882–1929)

Mary Francis

Richard Huntley

John Polk, Jr.

Junius

E. Robert Bruce

VII

5 Children

Daisy (b.1876)

Thomas Townsend (b.1892)

John (b.1894)

Mary Beatrice (b.1882–1963)

George (b. 1885)

Elizabeth Rush (ca.1889–1927)

John Purdue, Jr. (1893–1981)

Owen (1895–1954)

Lucy (1898–1991)

Wm. Samuel (b.1903)

W. Louise Barbour (1905–1955)
& Collis H. Davis (1900–1974)

VIII

Georgia L.

Jennie C.

Collis H.

Thulani

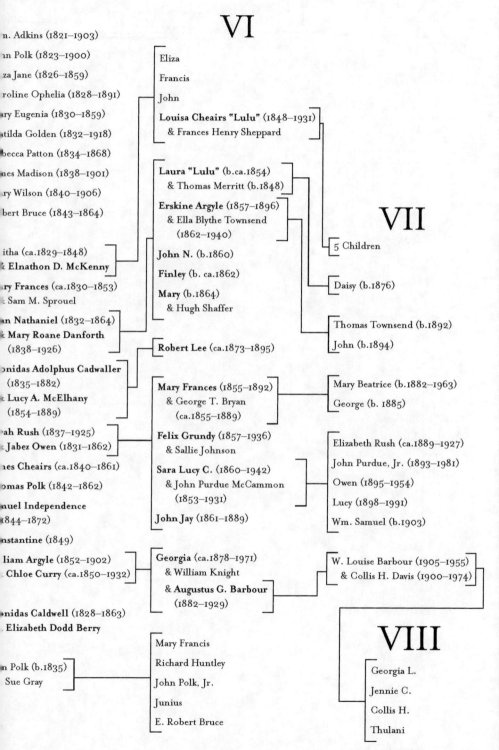

1

Twenty-first Century Freedwoman

This is a book about real people and some of their experiences from the mid-nineteenth to the beginning of the twentieth century—two families: one black, one white, many of whom never knew each other as well as some of their neighbors, folk whose families lie in graveyards next to the cotton fields they worked. In the process of trying to learn a little about a great-grandfather, I came across a sprawling extended family and a lot of classic Americana—pioneers, Midwest farmers, men who went to the Gold Rush, and southern planters. Since January 2001 when I started taking notes for what I thought would be a novel, I have added over 175 people to my family tree, kinfolk no one in my family knew a thing about four years ago. This book concerns only a few of these people; the stories their lives left behind have given me an amazing four years.

I was able to learn most about roughly two dozen people who were ordinary Americans of their time. Their journeys seem singular and extraordinary to me, yet I cannot believe they were terribly unusual. Some of the other figures who occasionally ride through on horseback, such as generals of the Confederacy, were fairly easy to look up, and the Civil War being an American obsession, there are a wide range of interpretations of such people and everything they did.

Historians have written a wealth of texts on every period in this book as well as many of the specific events, even those that may be totally unfamiliar to most of us. Some of these are engaging histories, others offer insightful analyses of the forces at work in our society when masses of people did something in concert—migrations, elections, surviving disasters—and still others have given a window on people in bondage, lives obscured by a paucity of documentation.

I have tried to stay close to the ground trod by some of the ancestors, clinging to them like a shadow and following their trails through events large and small. This sometimes involved spending five or six hours several times a month to locate where the second baby in the family was born, or dragging behind them during the Civil War, plotting on my own hand-drawn maps of Arkansas which route troops took to attack a small town from its south side. I am not a historian. The Civil War left landmarks all over Virginia, where I grew up, but I never paid much attention to the war's history. When I started my research, I knew nothing about how cotton is raised, and began to read about both cotton farming and rice farming because I was unsure which I might need. But it was cotton that ultimately ruled the lives of the people in this book, and I finally had to go look at some—not the sprigs of wood with cotton bolls and seeds one can buy in florist shops in New York City, but fields of cotton. A friend and I drove through two thirds of the state of Mississippi, and were continually awed. Even covering elections in Alabama's Black Belt did not prepare me for the vastness of the Delta's cotton fields. So many scenarios came to mind regarding the people no longer visible in those fields, who have since been replaced by machines.

I am also not a genealogist, though I am now much more agile in the face of old documents than I once was. But I am a journalist who is, like many in my trade, very curious, very stubborn, and able to push keys on a computer for very long hours. So this text is not a history nor a genealogy but built from my own great interests: how we define being American, how we deal with race, and human character.

I did not count on having to revise some of my thinking about myself. Down to the last week of writing this book I have been faced with mysteries that could not be explained, yet continued to surface. In the most recent case, a person I have never met said that one of my ancestors looked less Indian than another. There was a persistent understanding about some Choctaw heritage that ran like a loose thread through the cloth, always visible because it was out of place, but never falling away from the rest of the cloth. This thread that kept appearing but not revealing its origin made me look at the whole fabric again and again. American history as I was taught it did not prepare me for what I found, but the skepticism of my teachers in segregated schools did.

Think of any African American you know who had any family from the South or West before the Civil War and you have a person who is likely to have family ties—black and white—to the founders of the country, from those carved in marble to the unnamed soldiers of the Revolutionary War; kinship with people who were taken from their homes in the East on the Trail of Tears to designated Indian territories; connections to several different religious practices—African, indigenous American, Christian, and possibly Muslim—and at least that many languages; and ties to the American system of slavery.

I found in my own family experiences the ten prominent elements of the Grand Narrative of African American history: 1) Middle Passage; 2) southern bondage; 3) the Civil War; 4) Reconstruction; 5) Jim Crow and the rise of lynching; 6) World War I, the Great Migration, and the rise of white race riots; 7) the 1920s cultural renaissance; 8) the second Great Migration of the 1940s; 9) World War II; and 10) the mid-century struggle for full human and citizenship rights. But many items on that list are events in American history in which the white actors have disappeared. Ask a high school student the name of one politician who created Jim Crow. Ask her why people moved to Chicago in the 1940s and she is more likely to say the boll weevil than the longer lasting evil of sharecropping.

I can easily add to my list elements associated with what might be called the white Grand Narrative: the colonial period; the American Revolution; pioneering and the expansion to the Mississippi River; the U.S.-Mexican War; spreading King Cotton from the exhausted Southeast to uncleared West; the Gold Rush; the wars against Native Americans; the building of railroads and stockyards; and on and on. Ask a student to name an African American who walked from Virginia to Alabama to take cotton farming south. That person is one of my unnamed ancestors. I can say for a fact my friend Arnim's great-grandfather, Richard King, helped take cotton from Alabama to Texas at six years of age. Another friend, the late writer Buriel Clay, had a great-grandmother and great aunt who walked during the Civil War from Louisiana to Texas through the same battlefields my white ancestors fought in as Confederates. They took King Cotton there. The Campbells' slaves took it there. Because their names were not written down, we must follow those named in official papers who took cotton to Texas, whose names are now etched in monuments in small towns all over that state. There are no statues of these African Americans anywhere cotton is grown.

Naming is a powerful act. African Americans are still very much nameless as actors in American history, and our history, despite the wealth of it now available, is still considered of interest only to other black people. It may take a recognition that some of the unnamed actors of American history, from traditional heroes shot by the British in the Revolution to nameless lynch victims, are our *kinfolk*—the relatives of black and white Americans—for all of us to act when black votes are not counted. It may take the realization of kinship for the mass of Americans to say, "those votes were paid for in blood by people who might have been my grandparents, aunts, or uncles." Where compassion has failed, perhaps history can help.

At the heart of my story are people I have come to know largely by their actions. It is interesting to try to understand people without any of the reasons given for what they did. After transcribing nearly one hundred pages of personal documents for the white family, I began to have opinions about each family member—likes, dislikes, amusements, pity. Still, they rarely gave reasons for choices and stuck to stating the facts. So many issues in life were not discussed that the actions taken became the road map to the emotional life. For those who were in bondage, I have no pieces of paper that bear their thoughts. With the freedmen and women, any actions, choices, or decisions made after 1865 seemed huge. They had enormous significance if only because they could not be made before and may represent long held desires or sudden impulses, but they were all initiations of self-determination. As such, they are still compelling.

There is seldom a day in my own life when I do not try to make sure that my own power to decide has been attempted in the situations I meet. With me, that is a defining bit of character. This indulgence is not only who I think I am, but who I would like to be. I would like to have the power and consciousness to say amen to the course of my life even if I take no specific action in a given moment because I still feel the desires of those who came before me to push their own personal agency closer to their desires. That is, of course, part of life, but knowing people who lacked the power to act in their own lives brings a desire to give yourself what they were denied. As a practicing Buddhist, I spend a lot of time trying to examine my need to decide, to act, to be powerful. Fortunately, Richard King's great-grandson said to me one day, "You are a twenty-first century Freedwoman."

Yes. Though this journey has brought me many gifts, without question the greatest has been to come closer to the first generation out of bondage. I learned a great deal by exploring the white lives in this book, and learned about myself as well. The white Americans in this book went through episodes of frontier life and rugged travel across the country that seem unthinkable today. At the same time, I cannot overstate how important the lives of freedmen and women should be in the study of American history. They were the bodies on whom the effects of the Civil War were played out. Whatever ideas were in the culture about freedom, citizenship, and the right to participate in democracy—whether accepted ideas or marginalized concepts—were all tested on these people when they were suddenly emancipated from legalized slavery.

Regardless of the success or failure of those attempts to address the crisis that emerged immediately at the end of the war with this change in legal status, the people themselves pushed way beyond the intentions and limits set by those in power. Farmers in the Midwest who thought they would accept a few "refugee" servants and laborers, Freedmen's Bureau agents, and missionaries who started rural schools in the South all encountered more people than expected, met with more demands for education, participation, respect, and access to economic autonomy than anyone had bargained for. The first freed generation operated on the simple premise that their biggest problem was being in bondage, and once that was abolished, they set about shaping their own lives with results that are astounding. It is as if the spiritual waters of the culture broke through all the levees and surged forward, taking with them anything too lightly rooted, soaking the land, and ultimately enriching the ground on which we stand.

Men and women born in the last generation of bondage and the first generation of freedom invented blues and jazz, explored the North Pole, started schools, ran for office, opened businesses, created Broadway shows, and served as diplomats. They settled the West and drove the engines that became Memphis, St. Louis, Chicago, and other great cities. They wrote poems and novels, devised indispensible tools for modern life, medicine, and the study of humankind. They created justice movements, made the beds, served the meals, and polished the doorknobs. They slaughtered the hogs, delivered babies, fought in three wars, and continued to get the cotton out. If we could have bottled the air of those times and the ideas of forward thinkers after the Civil War, a most honorable human system might have been built. Our children need whatever that was, that unbounded drive to create new lives that the freedmen and freedwomen brought to the invention of African American self-determination on a mass level. The first women and men to walk away from bondage reinvented the race, redefined the terms of American citizenship, and spread that blend of African and Euro-American culture created in bondage in the antebellum South. Never has one group of people acted on such a large scale in so many regions of the country to push this society to honor its foundational principles. They taught the rest of us how to do it and yet there is no cultural memory of those millions. They are freedom's "Greatest Generation."

Like most people, I grew up knowing more about one side of the family than the other. In our family nothing was ever said about my mother's people, though we all knew there was a Mississippi plantation, and a master-housekeeper, race mixing-inheritance-squabble story. This particular mix is common, so it was *as if* we knew already the story and its meaning. My family story as a Davis was so complete, so textured, layered, and present, that when I looked in the mirror, I could connect every feature on my face with someone in my father's family. I had a Davis nose, Davis mouth, and Davis hairline. I had my Dad's hands, and might have gotten my hair from the undetailed report of blood from Madagascar or from the often heard reports of Indian blood that black folks talked about. Still, I was complete, whole.

It is just as I used to try to tell people about segregation—we weren't seeking integration because we were missing the amenities across town; we weren't going without tailors, barbers, shoemakers, gamblers, or landscapers: our world was complete. We did not enter the integration struggle to fill a void on a shopping list; we gave up one kind of autonomy in the pursuit of justice. And we all have the knowledge that our portion of humanity comes from a wholeness somewhere. I was completely explained by what I knew. If I didn't know everything, I still could explain myself completely.

As a Davis growing up in Hampton, Virginia, with no knowledge of how we came to be called Davis, my life was rich with family lore. My great-grandfather on that side of the family, William Roscoe Davis, was born in the county where Nat Turner lived and was an adolescent at the time of the revolt. He experienced a religious awakening during that same period when slaveholders decided to promote the faith among the bondpeople. Not long after, he was sold or given to an owner in my hometown, who then fled when Union troops came. My great-grandfather was able to take that opportunity to rescue his family from the farm where they were kept. I have always been aware of the closeness, the short time since slavery, because my grandfather, Andrew Davis, was born in slavery. He had told his family about seeing the battle of the *Monitor* and *Merrimac* in the Hampton Roads from a mill where the family lived during the Civil War. We weren't missing anything, and what we knew of the white ancestors was none too good.

My Uncle Arthur told me that the "furthest back" Davis ancestor was an African woman named Liza—my great-great-grandmother—whom his father had known. The family story was not that Liza was raped, that was never said, only that her son, William, was "fathered" by a British sea captain. William, in turn, was married to a woman who was a biracial person, then called mulatto, likely conceived in the same way as he, and she too had at least one child by *her* master. After he brought the family together, they raised seven children.

My hairline is not a Davis trait at all; it comes from a Scots-Irish family named Campbell. I *do* have my Dad's hands. I'm not sure about my nose. I have seen the dark circles under my eyes on photos of people I never knew existed—great aunts, a great-grandmother on the Campbell side. Looking in the mirror is quite a different experience at fifty-six years of age than it was only four years ago. That Madagascar stuff is there somewhere, I suppose, as well as at least two other unknown African heritages, the unsought input from the United Kingdom, and who knows about that Native American piece. At least now I know if I have it, more likely it's a Choctaw gene than Cherokee.

Finding the Campbell women jarred me, in part because the resemblance between us was easier for me to see on them than on the men. What spooked me though was that three of them turned out to be would-be writers: one of fiction, one of poetry, and one who wrote a memoir. Another Campbell woman built several theaters. That is a tad provocative, I thought. I started down this whole writing road to be a playwright, got snared by poetry, and realized one day that novels were something I just had to try. These are my passions. Yes, I once made a quilt with my grandmother's assistance—since it was the early 1970s, it was all fabric from old dashikis. I learned to make pottery because my mother did, and pottery is something of a family craving. All the women in the family also sew but that's where I exhibited hands that were all thumbs. But a bunch of women turning out novels and writing irate letters to the editor of the local paper—that scared me. This discovery was also disturbing simply because for so many years it did not even occur to me to look for them. Such is the barrier of imagination in a country in which racialism defies common sense.

One cannot be completely explained by anything, thank goodness, even one's lifetime of actions and decisions. But it would be easier to build selves less fictional and community less mythical if the truth of American heritage was accepted. This country has been crazy about deciding how to make people black or white ever since Thomas Jefferson thought a system should be devised and made law. From that moment, the lies began. In the eighteenth century, when most Africans lived in

Virginia and Maryland, the state of Virginia began to exile white women who had children by blacks as well as people who were "white enough" by Jefferson's standard to be free, and more lies and unspoken realities became the norm. For Jefferson, the possibility of confusion seems to have been a powerful catalyst. Toni Morrison has described the idea very well:

Africanism is the vehicle by which the American self knows itself as not enslaved, but free; not repulsive, but desirable; not helpless, but licensed and powerful; not history-less, but historical; not damned, but innocent; not a blind accident of evolution, but a progressive fulfillment of destiny.[1]

If you ask an African American where she gets her last name from, and if she has heard tales, at least in my experience, she will talk not about a one-time slaveholder but a white biological forebear. It is rare that someone tells me the family just took the name from the last owner, though that is considered the normal explanation for our names. The line I have heard most often is, "There was a Confederate colonel in there somewhere." I have heard it so many times that I still tend to think any white southerner with a sizeable plantation got an automatic rank of colonel if they submitted to service for the southern cause. Yes, there is a colonel in this book. While I remember people saying that it was rumored that (fill in the blank, Abe Lincoln or Warren Harding, for example) had "a nigger in the woodpile," no one ever said, "Yeah, so-and-so has a redneck in the woodpile." First of all, that would disparage the prevalence of rape in those family stories and, secondly, it was too common to bother about. My uncle Arthur Davis gave me his unpublished autobiography to edit before he passed, and his early-twentieth-century childhood was replete with neighbors who knew their white kinfolk, usually former masters. He has an outrageous story of next door neighbors who took in "ole massa" and how his father, Andrew, couldn't bear it. There was no mystery. But for the rest of us, folk stopped repeating all the details, and in my own childhood, for instance, the white folks' papers were kept in a segregated library I could not visit if I wanted. I know many African Americans who have their "white folks," and only one who felt the need to look for them. It wasn't strange in times past, but it is much more strange that it continues in a case like that of Strom Thurmond's African American daughter, who kept his secret.

When I was growing up, African Americans were still apt to brag about any heritage that mitigated pure Africanness, that modified black looks. People used adjectives that literally *modified* being black. "Good" hair, "aquiline" nose, "peachy" skin, mariney, cafe au lait, comely, "pretty," big boned, built not brawny, not stud-like.

And the Reconstruction period had to be ignored in order for this society to become officially segregated and to keep alive the slavery heritage as a marker for whom to marginalize, and to keep alive the romance of an elevated and gracious nineteenth century culture. In reality, this country was a fairly brutal place to live no matter where one might have been. Even as I tell people I meet today that this book deals with Reconstruction, I almost always have to define the word and to explain the "Redemption" period—the destruction of Reconstruction—I have to start by saying that Reconstruction was difficult for white southerners. The violent overthrow of Reconstruction is also part of this story.

Understanding the Redemption is central to understanding the politics of today. If I told someone tomorrow that white supremacists ran black people on their tickets in 1875 to get black people to sign on for the worst possible agenda for their lives, most people wouldn't believe me. Do we even know black people in Mississippi could vote then? If I said it happened in a northern city recently, no one would blink. These scenarios continue to be used successfully because we continue to ignore our past.

In my childhood in Virginia, I was somewhat interested in history but more interested in the latest records. I never saw the inside of the run-down plantation homes behind long driveways off the local roads. But in high school, a teacher gave me DuBois' *Black Reconstruction in America*, and it had a profound effect on me. This was one more incredible moment in history I had never learned about and one of the most fascinating. The racist textbooks of the segregated school system in Virginia painted the period as one of corruption, governed by the rise of absolute ignorance to positions of power. I'm quite sure one did not have to go to school in the South to be taught this view. This ten-year period could have changed many of the terms by which we have always lived in this country—highly racialized terms—and in the goals of the builders of Reconstruction lie the seeds of contemporary struggles for justice across the country. But when I read *Black Reconstruction*, I had no idea that in middle-age I would find myself putting my shoes in the muddy cotton fields in Mississippi and Alabama, trying to retrace the steps of people who could provide some of the anecdotal particulars of that epic study. Dr. DuBois continues to be a light on the path.

In working on *My Confederate Kinfolk* I found myself stepping into dank sinking land edged by creeks in the Mississippi Delta where the struggle people have waged has been romanticized, erased, buried, and glorified, without a sense of how personal and physically perilous it was to be thrown about a brutal countryside by the violence of what is later called history. The people in this book were forced from state to state by circumstances from sale or war, to family tragedy, the local guns of social change, and, ever so rarely, pleasure.

I have been amazed at how social change plays out face to face, at how the Campbell family went to war with brothers, friends, neighbors, cousins, and slaves. They knew well the people in battle with them. Familiarity was all. The Campbells knew family in almost all the places the war took them, fought in situations where thousands of men dug up the land for trenches and breastworks, where they hid behind hay bales, and where the fighting was close enough to use a pistol. No smart bombs. People were wounded and got sick repeatedly and went back to battle. If it was bad, and your family was able, they brought a wagon for you.

When the African American Tarrant and Curry families tried to vote after the war, they knew well the farmers who came into the fields on horseback to warn them to stay away from the polls. Their neighbors who were lynched knew the men who killed them. If any of these farm workers tried to buy land, they knew every merchant who refused them credit for supplies, or burned down their children's schools. They had been bought and sold by some of these same violent people in their midst. They had, in some cases, been concubines to the men, or fathered by them, men so often referred to by their peers without irony as "the best men in town." They lived in a world where families sold their own children because of their skin color, where most of "the best men in town" had probably, at least once, put the names of their own progeny on the inventory and had to make that decision.

When the early Ku Klux Klan members gathered in rooms in town, the carpetbagger living upstairs knew them all. Their black concubines knew to pick them up at an appointed hour, and the wives knew not to stop by during the hours after the meeting when the Kluxers and their black women often caroused before heading home. Slavery and its aftermath were much more about intimacy, all kinds of intimacy, than one learns in classrooms, or sees depicted in mainstream media. People who visit Monticello, for instance, probably seldom ponder the fact that during the many years that Jefferson built and rebuilt his home, everyone in the household slept in one room. The hierarchy of chattel slavery infers distance by way of class, power, and the physical separation of facilities between owners and chattel. The space allowed the animal stock was much more hospitable than the space allotted for human chattel who lived with no privacy whatsoever, in groups from three to six or more in a room. But the enforcement of separation came long after slavery.

My Confederate Kinfolk shares with the reader some of this intimacy of friend and foe, of slaveholder and slave, of freedwoman and employer. I have attempted to look at the communities to which people belonged: overlapping communities of choice, communities of circumstance, and communities of coercion. A handsome young black woman who might have grown up in Yazoo, Mississippi, starting life as a slave, and later—in freedom—"given" to the former master as a concubine to ensure the family's chance of making a living is a person who belongs to all three kinds of community. She has forced intimates, intimates of choice, and, if lucky, intimates who share the burden of work, or help to educate or otherwise support her. A young white man growing up in that town has more options, but, if not a planter's son, his destiny is hard work and the comradery of a male crowd that might require that any intimate ties to blacks be private. Those are just two examples, but the people in this story all had similar overlapping ties with a range of loyalties to each. The slaveholding class clearly enjoyed the expectation of loyalty and love from the majority of their ties. The African Americans knew that support from all their ties could be severed by brute force, or merely by the power of making a decision to vote or act on one's agency in any way. All thoughts of autonomy and self-reliance were dangerous, not only to one's own existence but to loved ones.

From the earliest months I spent working on this book, the characters I was discovering so fascinated me that it became a secondary matter that most of them are relatives of mine. That fact was, at first, hard to truly digest. I had already been fully shaped as an African American woman, in part by the very fact of *not* knowing most of the specific history from which my own family emerged. Like many other people my sense of self and my blackness were constructed by the living example of parents and people I knew early in life and their stories, which almost always contradicted the history I was taught. My version of blackness was also shaped by their reliance upon me to construct myself in defiance of what was said about my possibilities—and what had been said about theirs. My eight years of training in French were a defiance begun by my father when he was told his lips were too big to learn the language. He defied his instructor and became fluent (and a Phi Beta Kappa), but I also made a point of defying his instructor. My lack of shame at having no singing voice is a privilege he handed me after having to sing spirituals for his supper at Grinnell College in Iowa, and Lord knows, he was no singer either. My belief in myself was a product of family propaganda—we were told we could do whatever we chose (except perhaps play pro football!)—and learn whatever we needed to learn, and learn it fast.

And I was shaped by many people I didn't know—black American icons in every sphere—scholarship, political leadership, the arts, sports, and entertainment. They all represented some realization of ourselves still incubating. Somewhere inside my nonathletic, movie-watching body was Wilma Rudolph. Somewhere in me when the old man wasn't looking was a backup singer for Aretha Franklin. In some ways, to later find out who your own family catalysts are is to learn something you can't act on much. For example, as an African American adult who has had the chance to visit five or six African countries, I also was able to see that my idea of my Africanness was polycultural, polyglot (and polymusical), and so fluid that I could identify with most any African culture I encountered. I had no particular biases that one culture among the continent's fifty-two nations was better or worse than another. I was of all of them. I still feel that way. African Americans can do this so easily with the freedom to mix jazz drumming and African drumming as Max Roach has done, or to mix kente cloth with choir robes and leave the church with mudcloth on the head. African American weddings these days are an absolute celebration of pan-African appropriation, mixed with Baptist, Buddhist, or even Hindu flavors. In December newscasters will politely inform you that Kwanzaa, a holiday invented in Los Angeles, is a traditional African celebration. Blackness is an invention unlike any other cultural expression for its breadth of sources and its constant reinvention.

Finding out that the black women in the book, my matrilineal African forebears, are descended from the Temne of what is now Sierra Leone grounded me as a human being, even though starting out I had no idea I could even learn such a thing. In the late 1700s when my first Temne were brought here, they were rural people who raised rice and would have been astounded by a place like Charleston, South Carolina. They had probably been caught up in someone else's struggle for dominion. This bit of information arriving in the mail knocked my butt into the bottom of a boat that moved from Sierra Leone to Barbados to one of the Carolinas. Temne is very concrete.

Having the word Temne as part of my identity is in itself a new journey. Now I will mix it with the tales of those who left word of their history on these shores. The word makes me feel more like a Freedwoman, someone who knows life did not start in 1865. Someone who is still trying to stitch together a new whole on behalf of a Temne and her children, born in rice fields there, but who died in rice fields here.

2

Silver Creek, Mississippi, ca. 1875

When my grandmother, Georgia Campbell Neal, died in 1971, she had started writing a book. At the time, we thought she was about eighty-five years old, though it was well known that she was apt to lie about her age. She was more likely ninety-four. She was writing the story of her parents, Mississippi cotton farmers—one black, one white—who met near Yazoo City, Mississippi, in the 1870s. She began the few pages she wrote with a sunny image of her mother, Chloe Tarrant Curry, and Chloe's husband, James Curry, both former slaves, leaving Alabama:

> It was nearing train time. Chloe, a buxom, brown comely woman of 25, and her tall, lean husband Jim were feverishly getting their bags and baskets together to go to Mississippi, a place where they were told money could be made easily and honestly. They were leaving their four children with her father. She promised when she settled in this rich country she would buy a home for them. The distance they had to travel was just about [250] miles but to them it seemed far, far away because it took two days for the trip.[1]

Georgia Neal wanted to tell the story of how Chloe ended up giving birth to one more baby and was going to name the book after the epithet given to her in childhood, "Chloe's White Child." Just before she died, cataracts and glaucoma prevented her from writing. The last letter I received from her was in answer to a request for instructions on how to make a quilt. She drew a diagram, made a sample, and kept it simple. When she died that year her husband indignantly informed me on the way to pick up her will that my grandmother was angry with me. I could tell immediately that he was trying to let me know that, unlike the others in the car, I would not benefit from her will. He had no idea that her anger concerned a scheme in which she wanted to use me to keep *him* from inheriting all of her money, but he and I both knew my sometimes spiteful grandmother would try to punish me from the grave. After chewing me out about being a bad granddaughter, he handed me my legacy: one silver dollar from the 1920s in a tiny handsewn cotton sack that was itself quite old.

My sisters were kind enough to ask him to give me two photo albums, leather-bound tintype books actually belonging to Georgia's parents—Chloe Curry and Will Campbell—that she had once shown me. Shortly after the funeral, my sister Louise Davis Stone sent me a copy of several dozen handwritten pages of the manuscript and outline Georgia was working on. Within the pages of my grandmother's recollections there is the scent of another time and an ocean of debt, admiration, pain, maybe even guilt from a daughter toward her mother.

Looking back, I find the acts of handing me the coin and the intervention for the photos symbolic of the task of writing this book. At the heart of my task was to find what was handed from one woman to another, particularly mother to daughter, in my family—of this I was almost completely ignorant. To this day, I have no idea what my mother knew about the story written here. As my mother died when I was a child, the family story of Chloe and Will was told to me by my father. Only my father ever remarked that I looked like my mother and no one has ever told me I have anything in common with her—whether disposition, expression, or even hair color. On my own I have found our common interests in art, the tendency to grow heavy in all the same places, and go gray before forty. I didn't have to know her at all for her very existence as a woman artist to encourage me in my own dreams. I gained a whole world simply by being told that when she went in the darkroom to print pictures she did not let anyone, especially squabbling children, call her out till she had made certain the images would survive the door being opened.

In trying to learn something of the terrain from which my mother came, I found myself in the company of my grandmother and great-grandmother, whose experiences were worlds away from my own. Their inclinations toward self-sufficiency, migration, and making their own decisions resonate with me and give me a sense of roots even though I can't imagine either woman understanding my own life choices. It really doesn't matter. I have knitted together from their lives a narrative to explain my own existence that is something to pass on to whomever it may be that would like my brand of encouragement.

Silly as it may sound, it wasn't until thirty years after my grandmother died that I became curious about who the people were in the photo albums and what had become of them. There were forty-two pictures, about half of them tintypes made between the 1860s and 1880s, and the rest cartes de visite—photos glued on card stock. I had a print made of one of the photos of my grandmother and soon became mesmerized by it. I put this charming image of an eight- or nine-year-old at eye-level on a bookshelf in my overcrowded apartment, and soon I began to wonder why her outfit looked so entirely Scottish. Plaids were popular during the mid-nineteenth century, I later decided, but her shirt was the kind one wears with a kilt, the collar closed by a kilt pin, and the plaid some kind of light-colored tartan. A black girl in Mississippi done up in tartan? Her father was Scottish-American but maybe the clothes meant nothing at all. This photo was stuck in the album, and by now was turning a light brown. My grandmother's image was not actually among any of the pictures firmly fixed inside the frame pages in her mother's photo album. And that fact did not occur to me for several more years.

The people in the book were Chloe's siblings and her other children—my grandmother's half sisters and brothers. And there were lots of other faces—black and white—with names added by my grandmother in pencil, all absolute mysteries. I had no idea who the people were in Will's book, except for the clearly marked generals of the Confederacy on a souvenir photo card in the back. He had written in names, usually in ink, and the tiny book had signs of wear and tear as well as age, such as rust stains from the metal plates. The story in this book arises, in all its complexity, simply from looking for the people in those photos and trying to find evidence of the facts in my grandmother's memoir.

So I begin where she began: in 1875. As Georgia remembered it, Chloe's fateful first journey to Mississippi promised a chance to "start doing things the black folks were not accustomed to"—one of only two allusions to Chloe's previous life as a chattel slave.

> She sat back on her seat by the big window watching the landscape come up and vanish, with its fields, its houses, its winding roads with people traveling in ox carts, buggies and wagons. People she would never know and something of the old life she had lived seemed to come over and possess her. To travel for the first time in her life she felt the thrill of a traveler's freedom of heart.[2]

Ten years after the Civil War, two young adults, strangers to one another, Chloe Tarrant Curry and William Argyle Campbell, each set out to build their own lives for the first time. For Chloe, acting on her own plan for her life must have been deeply meaningful, for slavery had left room for few choices. Will's prohibition against charting his own plan was more likely his age and the destiny set for him by being the youngest in his family.

By virtue of geography, Chloe and Will had each lived at the periphery of the Civil War, though Will had camped in forests and swamps near battle grounds for a couple of months when his brothers were fighting in Arkansas. Chloe had lived in the heart of the Confederacy, not far from its capital, Montgomery, Alabama. She was probably living in Marion, Alabama, by 1861, in a world awash in army units lead by prominent men of Marion and nearby Selma. Will's hometown would be occupied by the Union army that year and, by war's end, Chloe's region was occupied after Nathan Bedford Forrest's troops made a vain attempt to hold on to Selma. Both Will and Chloe knew the extreme deprivations of food and resources that made daily life harder during the war than it had ever been, even in Chloe's first fifteen years of life in slavery. After the southern defeat, life became ever more dangerous for Chloe.

Will came into his maturity in the 1870s having buried his mother and two of his brothers as a direct result of the war, and most recently his brother Sammy, a twenty-eight-year-old veteran, who died on their Mississippi farm. By 1875 when he was twenty-three years old, Will was one of three survivors of his immediate family of twelve. Chloe's family of nine, the Tarrants, seems to have been tightly-knit like his, though they may never have lived together. While the slave censuses of 1860 give no names of bondpeople, only ages and sex, none of those whom I think may have owned the Tarrants had slaves of the various ages of all the members of that family at one time in one place. Many Alabama slaveholders listed on the 1860 slave census had large groups of able-bodied male field laborers and relatively few females. At least one of her brothers belonged to another slaveholder. In the summer of 1880, the Tarrants were all together for a visit, but it is impossible to know if that ever happened again. After she moved to Mississippi, Chloe and other family members traveled home to see their people every year in mid-summer once the cotton was in bloom.

The enormous changes brought by the Civil War to these two people who were born on opposite sides of slavery did not change their shared understandings of how the antebellum world worked—its rules, prohibitions, and, for those who enjoyed them, its layers of privilege. As daily life didn't change very much after the war, and former planters worked hard to keep it that way, what these two knew of life's rules still stood. They both understood loss and seemingly had an ability to deal with being isolated—even shunned by some people—and had a deep familiarity with the hardships of living on the land. And by 1875 they both knew what it was to have to grab the rifle to fend off creatures more deadly than deer.

At the root of these commonalities was King Cotton and, until their respective deaths, Chloe and Will stayed in the Delta, farming cotton crops and surviving seasons of floods, yellow fever, and sweltering heat, as well as suffocating humidity, boll weevils, and decades of sinking cotton prices. Farming cotton in Mississippi shaped their separate and overlapping communities, defined the goals for their families, wore out their bodies, and determined who was to be entrusted with the land itself.

Still, while these and other bonds may have been the glue that held them together through seasons of terror and violence in the Delta, enormous differences existed between them.

In 1875 Chloe Curry had been married for six years and had four children, the oldest of whom was about five. Freedom from slavery had not brought her freedom from farming and sewing for the ladies of the planter class. It had not brought her an opportunity to go to school. She had already married and begun having children before any school was established in Marion, Alabama, where she had wed. The need to work and take care of children in the evening when most adults went to school may have prevented her from doing so. She would remain illiterate and sign documents with an "X" for the length of her life.

By an odd clerical error on the 1880 census, the record states that Chloe Curry could read and that Will Campbell could not. While this is not true, Will Campbell had only a few months of schooling from the age of nine, when the war started, until 1866 when, as a fourteen-year-old, he was placed by his brother in a boarding house that served as a school. He attended this private tutoring situation and a Christian boarding school near Biloxi for a total of four years. Will Campbell, a child of a well-to-do clan from Missouri, was the least educated member of his family, including the women, who were well read. His parents' household in Springfield, Missouri, according to local histories, was the first repository of books in the town, as his father was well educated in North Carolina. However, Will was removed from that home before getting to know many of the books and, it seems, never took to reading.

Chloe Curry, though, had two obvious restraints on her ability to pursue personal dreams that Will Campbell would never experience: her race and her sex. As a wife and mother, to pursue her ambition to follow one of her brothers to Mississippi for opportunities denied by economic depression and antiblack violence in Alabama, Chloe had to convince her husband, James Curry, to take the chance. The fact that she was able to do so gave me the first inkling of the force of her character, which my grandmother, a very tough person herself, used to describe with awe. As a young woman of twenty, I was still so intimidated by Georgia that when she said she was not "half the woman" her mother was, I was, ignorantly I admit, somewhat relieved I didn't know Chloe. When a woman who knew Chloe later told me that, in her seventies, she was a "nice old lady," I got tickled. "Nice old lady" did not figure in Georgia's description. I have a better idea now that my grandmother did not simply mean she was not half as tough as her mother, which is what I took her remark to mean, but perhaps she felt she was not half as wise.

Chloe's experience as an enslaved woman—and as a freedwoman—forced her to live in the world that came to her doorstep. This remained true even after she moved to Mississippi. The racial conventions of the day, maintained by the same kind of force used during antebellum times, meant that she was subject to the harshest legalized oppression that could be devised outside of slavery. The Black Codes, put into law in 1857 and revived in 1865 and 1866 (and honored even when repealed), barred blacks from owning farmland, testifying in court, owning guns, or renting land. It is only thanks to the arrival of Reconstruction that Chloe had the hope of owning land. And it is possible that a holdover of the Black Codes forced her to leave her children in Alabama. At that time, freedmen were forced into labor contracts that were maintained by force, up to and including arrest. One aim of the contracts was to prevent blacks from leaving their county, and there was a widely used provision allowing planters to simply take away bondpeople's children on any flimsy excuse so that they would not try to leave. In planning to leave, the Currys may have had to leave their children so that their departure could be made more easily without notice.[3]

But in 1875 Chloe Curry arrived in Yazoo County at a moment when there had been a few precious years in which the Constitution and laws of the state of Mississippi had been shaped by Reconstruction progressives who were elected by the new voting majority—African Americans. In 1860 enslaved African Americans constituted 55 percent of the population of the state.[4] In 1868 black males were for the first time able to exercise the right to vote. The result was a Reconstruction state legislature holding more black representatives than anywhere in the South and a body of laws permitting people like Chloe the ordinary rights of

American citizens for the first time. On paper, they even had leeway to take to court anyone who tried to assert the life rules of the bad old days—and some did.

That Chloe and Will each chose to start their new lives along Silver Creek in Yazoo County was decided by their respective family connections. In 1875 Will Campbell lived with the head of his family, his brother Leonidas Campbell, a farmer and cotton factor with offices in Vicksburg and New Orleans, and a former lieutenant colonel in the Confederate army. Like half the planters in the county, he was addressed as "Colonel."

Leonidas Adolphus Cadwaller Campbell seemingly always tried to live up to the grandeur of his name. He definitely took to heart the association of his first name with the Spartan epitome of courage, and Cadwaller, the Celtic red dragon, may have simply been a family name but, as a symbol also linked to King Arthur, it suited the family tastes as well. In the family, he was known as "Le" or "Lonnie." As the eldest, he was the head of the family and in charge of Valley Home Plantation in Yazoo County. By 1881 the Colonel would designate one portion of the Yazoo land "Grand Oak" plantation, a name my grandmother often mentioned, but by either name, what was described was a spread of 7,900 acres, mostly still woodland, where a cotton crop running as high as 1,000 bales a year was raised. Leonidas was then living with his wife Lucy and their only child, two-year-old Robert Lee.

One of the stories in my family says that Chloe came to Mississippi after her brother King came to Yazoo with his family. Will Campbell's only surviving letter from the period says that his brother had just "sent to Alabama and got fifty Hands" and had more coming later. It sheds light on how word may have reached Chloe's brother that there was work in Mississippi. Immediately following the war, planters had sought to recruit workers when many of their former chattel slaves left for other parts. By then economic and political events also began to drive African Americans west, particularly from neighboring Alabama.[5]

Many of the planters in both Alabama and Mississippi were broke in the 1870s. Many also had difficulty adjusting to the very idea of paying wages to former bondpeople. Though several different approaches to negotiating with freedmen were tried, in time planters developed an over-whelming preference for the advantages they had with sharecropping.[6]

These issues did not weigh heavily with my grandmother, Georgia Neal, when she sat down in the late 1960s to make notes for her mother's story. Her version begins with Chloe's departure from Alabama, a joyous occasion proffering more promise than discouragement. The chance to negotiate work, a home, and a future was, for most African Americans, new. Whatever the arrangements, they seemed open-ended, full of possibility. In late 1874 or early 1875, Chloe Curry had given birth to her fourth child, Thomas, and some time later, she and her husband were able to set off for Mississippi. Relying on stories she heard from Chloe, my grandmother, late in her own life, envisioned the beginning of the Mississippi sojourn:

> There was a two-room cabin waiting for them in the Yazoo Valley where the land was rich and nothing but cotton was raised. They hoped to set up housekeeping and start doing things the black folks were not accustomed to. . . . She sat back on her seat by the big window watching the landscape come up and vanish, with its fields, its houses, its winding roads with people traveling in ox carts, buggies and wagons. . . . This was an adventure she was secretly proud of, and she said to Jim, "Why do you look so down-hearted, you want to go back?" Jim did not hear her; he was wondering what the future in that far away land would be like. An intense feeling of gloom overspread him [and] for a moment he wished he had not left Marion. There, at any rate, he was surrounded by friends, by people who had known him so long that they accepted him just as he was. . . . He was not the drifting type; he was afraid; his gloom persisted and even increased till he came to the conclusion that a man like him had no place in the scheme of things which Chloe had mapped out.[7]

Both reactions to leaving home seem reasonable, when one place is the only home one might have known, and having lived one's life during years when relocating by choice was unthinkable. My grandmother, herself an avid pioneer who lived in six states and at least two of the new all-black towns, would have disdained Jim Curry's fear of change. Still, in one sense, Jim Curry was right if he suspected that perhaps life would be the same, minus the comfort of family. My grandmother said often that the man also just plain hated Mississippi. None of us ever questioned this. No one but my mother had been there, and nothing one heard about the place would make it sound anything but sensible to keep well north of it.

The two-room cabin they were promised was on a plantation on Silver Creek in Yazoo County where the Campbells lived. My grandmother understood that Chloe and Jim first worked for Leonidas Campbell, and although it is possible she did housekeeping for him, I do not know that she did. In any case, it is important that both my grandmother and Leonidas's sister indicated that Chloe knew Leonidas.

Neal describes the Campbell lands as broken up into several parcels: 980 "much-coveted" acres belonging to Will Campbell and "several thousand" acres joining his called "Grand Oak" that belonged to "Colonel Campbell." Campbell letters clearly indicate that the Colonel had property elsewhere as well, outside of family land in Missouri. Neal's earliest recollections date to the 1890s and, by then, there being only one owner on the place, the whole of it was known as Grand Oak. Clearly she was unaware of the size of the family's holdings.

> This narrow strip of country was bounded on one side by a deep and wide creek large enough for big river boats to navigate. When the water was high, it emptied into [the] Sunflower River at a point called Campbellsville Landing, a little village of two or three hundred people, a general store, post office, a cotton gin, blacksmith shop and two lodging houses; one for white and one for colored. . . .[8]

The "Grand Oak" portion of the property along the creek, above Campbellsville Landing, had several other sizeable houses in which Leonidas and his agents lived.

The area where the Sunflower River meets the Yazoo River near Lake George and the tiny settlement of Holly Bluff is the sight of some of Mississippi's famous Native American mounds. The place was once home to Native American peoples at least as far back as 2000 BCE. The area my grandmother knew to be a steamboat port was a ceremonial center around several temple mounds. For me it is a somewhat eerie juxtaposition: slavery's massive machinery of human labor plowing the soil a few feet above one of the spiritual centers of a vast civilization that ranged from Georgia and Florida up the entire Mississippi Valley to Wisconsin.[9]

Before the war and for some years after, the geographical points of reference were quite different—the number of one's slaves and proximity to a river put a person on the map. I could almost make a roster of the "important" folk in Yazoo by simply duplicating the list of riverboat landings along the routes to and from Vicksburg. On a list of Yazoo River Landings from an 1857 New Orleans Directory, the Campbell landing is called Silver Creek. This was vital because by 1860 Yazoo County, with its 22,373 residents, was a major center for Mississippi's cotton industry. The county then "had more farm acreage and of greater total value than any county in the state and outstripped all others in Mississippi's chief product: King Cotton." At least 64,000 bales were shipped out the county that year.[10]

The farms around Yazoo didn't need docks such as were built by many Eastern plantations; the flat-bottom riverboats ran in very shallow water and simply heaved themselves upon the muddy bank till they stopped. The steamboats charged by the mile for dry barrels and wet barrels, and by hundred-pound weight for heavy goods; more was charged going upstream than down.[11]

Across the Sunflower River just in front of this general store was a saloon. . . . All day long skiffs carried the people to and from this saloon. There was nothing over there but that one building surrounded by a swamp occupied by bears, one panther, and other wild animals.[12]

The Campbell cotton gin was near this spot where the creek ran into the Yazoo River, so that once the cotton was baled, the huge bundles could be loaded onto boats. One of those boats making a regular run on a route the Campbells would have taken, the *Sultana*, became famous during the Civil War, and a picture of it ended up in Will Campbell's photo album. One of the local men who ran steamboats and also figured in the lives of the Campbells was Sherman Parisot. According to historian Harriet

DeCell, he started as a cabin boy, then became a pilot, and worked a steamer from Yazoo City to Vicksburg.

My grandmother also recalls wagons being used for local transport, perhaps because the creek dried up over time:

> Cotton was the main crop, very little of anything else was raised. It was cultivated, picked and ginned on the plantation. In the fall, wagon loads of baled cotton drawn by four, six, and eight mules, were carried to Yazoo City, a distance of 21 miles, to be sold. Cotton seeds was [sic] hauled and sold except what was needed for planting. Corn crop was not made in too great a quantity since the delta land was not adapted for much corn growing. Most years it was a failure, so corn had to be bought to supplement what was raised.[13]

Will Campbell's home was located near the gin. As my grandmother describes the house, it was classic Yazoo architecture:

> The big house where the plantation owner or agent lived was painted white with green shutters [and had] a long veranda with tall square posts. [There was] a large hall with two rooms on each side. The back hall was used as a dining room with folding doors. . . . From the dining room was a stairway to the upper half-story which was liveable only during high water. . . . The kitchen was in the back yard about 60 ft. from the house. A room next to the kitchen is where . . . [the] "Hostler" lived. He looked after the horses and mules. The big house was surrounded by pecan trees.[14]

Local homes tended to have one or one-and-a-half stories, and were smaller and less grand than the typical tourist plantation mansion. Upper stories were somewhat problematic in the fierce heat of Mississippi summers, as they would be even hotter than the lower floors, but they often did have a kind of loft story on the top where people took shelter in floods. Most of those that I have seen in Yazoo County were not large by today's standards, but certainly provided comforts unknown in the cabins out in the "quarter" where the workers lived.

From Neal's depiction of their life, Chloe and Jim seemed to work on their own, farming a patch of land, so perhaps they were sharecropping. When Georgia Neal was a child the owner at Silver Creek was Will Campbell:

> He had some who rented so many acres, some who worked on halves and some who worked by the day. The share croppers were allowed 4 lbs. of meat, a half-gallon of molasses and a peck of meal each week. They could work extras, such as cutting wood for cross ties for the railroad, which he sold and shipped by boat to Vicksburg and Yazoo City. With this money, they could by extra food such as sugar, coffee, rice, and other food.[15]

This is probably identical to rations they received in slavery. Will Campbell added one item to the post-war diet: he sold brown jugs of whiskey to his workers.

Housing for workers during slavery in Mississippi consisted of small dirt floor log cabins, or double cabins that shared a center wall and had doors at opposite ends. Beds were usually built into the walls, and laborers supplied their own mattress material, usually using straw and corn husks.[16]

These are rooms just slightly larger than the average living room rug. Any such cabin is rather what you might expect until someone points out that ten people might have lived in one. When looking at the census records, it was very often the case that a family with five or six children had boarders, almost always male farm laborers. Each time I was curious what kind of structures the people lived in, as these were households on plantation grounds even decades after emancipation.

Several years ago I called the Reconstruction scholar Eric Foner and asked for suggestions as to material I should read on Mississippi. He made several recommendations, but the first of these was a book by Albert T. Morgan called *Yazoo, or on the Picket Line of Freedom in the South*. I am still grateful for this tip as I had found some terrible old books written by men who glorified the Old South, and Morgan wrote a fascinating book about his days in Yazoo as a "carpetbagger" (a derogatory term used for a northerner who came to the South after the war). In this instance,

Morgan reminded me of something I already knew: that the people coming out of bondage had many skills we now lack, and one of these was making furniture out of available materials. He described workers on the plantation he rented, which was about half-way between Silver Creek and Yazoo City, cutting cane and gathering leaves to make bedding, stools, and tables. This also reminded me of many furnishings in ancient bungalows in Virginia, made by people who had gathered discarded army materials after the war to build homes and furniture.

Life in the Delta was ruled by cotton and the weather. I have to say I underestimated how much cotton ran life in the South. My own imagined version was shaped by growing up in an area where agriculture was diverse. Though tobacco was the main crop, farms were small by Mississippi standards, and one saw mostly corn crops and fruit orchards. In the Delta, the cycle of every year was built around what that cotton crop needed. Life centered around getting the seeds in the ground after the spring floods. Cattle had to be tended and treated for worms, ear ticks, and lice. When calves and foals were born, they required attention. Even today cotton farmers hope for the maximum number of sunny days, work with serious heat when 85 degrees would be perfect and 100-degree days mean more water is needed. A lot of rain is good and makes for improved plants; too much rain is bad and rots the roots, killing the bushes.

During the entire cycle, people working in the fields lived by the sounding of bells at the beginning of the work day, lunch, and end of the day. The bells were rung for church on Sunday and at times of alarm, such as fires, and marked the daily existence of everyone within hearing. These particular beautifully shaped Delta bells, swinging from elegant ironwork, are visible today in front of churches everywhere in the region. Early in the crop's cycle the cotton had to be "chopped," which meant workers went out in the rows with hoes to prune the shrubs and get rid of weeds. One hoped for plants with anywhere from six to eighteen nodes on each bush. The peak bloom of the cotton plants is usually in the middle of July. When the corn came up in summer it had to be harvested for feed along with hay.

October and November were spent picking cotton. Then the cotton was put through the planter's steam-driven gin where the leaves and seeds were separated from the bolls. When the cotton was baled, weighed, and then shipped, along with a saleable portion of the seeds, the pay came in for the year. Some of the livestock might be sold and some slaughtered and smoked. In the winter, the fields had to be prepared for the next crop and so the old plants were cut down and plowed under. In the 1880s the Campbells were growing cotton on slightly more than 800 acres, and producing about 400 bales, making an average of two bales from each acre.

Chloe would have had to raise vegetables for their meals, probably sweet potatoes, tomatoes, possibly cabbage, collards, and other greens, perhaps peas. Chickens would have been a staple, along with their eggs. Some people in Mississippi also raised cane and made syrup, though I have never heard of anyone in my family doing this. In the fall, vegetables were pickled and put up in jars for the winter. When hogs were slaughtered in the winter, sausage was prepared from some of the innards, lard was made and put up, and the meat would be smoked. Daily chores would have included feeding and providing water to the mules, fowl, and any other animals, perhaps horses, if they had them, or a cow, which would have to be milked. Washing involved pumping water from the well and carrying it or washing near the well. Watering the vegetable garden meant getting even more water to that patch of ground. Georgia said Chloe also kept a flower garden, papered the walls of the cabin with newspaper, and kept sewing. Quilting and knitting were necessary skills in order to provide bedding and clothing and, as Chloe was a seamstress, she may have had to construct a work table for large pieces. Periodically my grandmother continued to make soap into the 1950s, and I assume this was a skill acquired in Mississippi.

She gives a glimpse of Chloe's life by way of describing reasons she thought her mother was somewhat "different":

> She mingled little with the plantation women but she was a good wife and a good worker and was valued at her true worth by the hard-laboring farm hands. She had . . . what Jim lacked, a strange emotional affinity with this land where they made their home. Whether she was cooking over an open fire in the yard or washing clothes on the side of the cabin, washing greens at the pump, or picking feathers off a black bird which Jim had shot from the low flying armies that darkened the sky spring and fall, she was in harmony always with her task and her surroundings. . . . Hot, mosquito-ridden

summers, muddy roads, and rainy winters alike, failed to trouble Chloe. She seemed to draw serenity into her body from the black soil.[17]

Neal imagines Chloe urging Jim on with the farming, nagging him to "hook that mule to the plow," and that he would stare at her, disgusted. She thinks of him as not giving "an owl's hoot whether the patch was plowed or not" because he was "tired of being dragged into the black mire of the plantation." And she imagines Chloe not looking into his eyes because she would have known what they had to say and recognized they were "clouded with pain and with bitter bewilderment."[18]

I do not know whether this emotional subtext was supplied by my grandmother's vivid imagination or by stories related to her from Chloe. It is hard to walk the grounds of the Silver Creek plantations though without seeing that she has the right words for it. Whether behind a mule or under the gaze of the driver who waited on horseback at the end of the row where a crew worked, planting, chopping, or picking, one could easily have the feeling of being dragged through the soil by the work. And the ground is not only weighed down by wet clay but loaded with rocks. Even lacking the lash as routine punishment, the Sisyphean nature of this brutal toil would be enough to crush many. While I hear my grandmother's impatience for betterment in her description of Jim's loathing of the hot fields, her attitude comes from being long inured to doing what had to be done. It's an attitude she passed down. And yet her writing clearly shows she knew exactly why one would hate it. Still, she takes an unsparing look at Jim's real calling—preaching the Word:

His only day of happiness was Sunday. He was often asked to preach and his favorite text was "In My Father's House Is Many a Mansion, And if it Was Not So, I Would Not Tell You." He could always get an "Amen," but never a shout. Chloe said he was too lazy to raise his voice. He could not produce that moan that groan and that cry that it takes to make the church women faint and fall out. The church was near a stream of water called Silver Creek and there were cabins on each side of the creek. Boats were used to cross. When the boat was on the other side one would have to call to someone to bring the boat. This creek was wide, snake infested and muddy, fringed with cyprus, gum, willow and oak trees. On the roadside were red heart and dogwood trees which bloomed in spring.[19]

The church is still there, and many of the trees. The creek was fairly dry in the winter month I visited, and along the edge there is bamboo growing in the thickets where plantation people still bury their loved ones. Pearl Bowser, an African American film archivist, shared with me some film footage shot in the 1920s by a woman who lived on a Delta plantation north of Yazoo. In that footage, which follows the cotton cycle from planting to weaving in eastern textiles mills, the local black church, sitting next to a creek like the one in Yazoo, conducted baptisms in the water in summer months. One might otherwise wonder at building a church so close to water that frequently overran its shores. In among the trees by the New Foundation Church at Grand Oaks are grave stones bearing the last names of Chloe's friends from the 1870s, and down the road a bit, a tiny graveyard of white folks who have lived there since.

Grand Oak, whatever else it may have been, was a black world. Going into town would have brought Chloe and Jim into contact with the only urban center in the county. Yazoo City, even at its height, was a small town by any standard, but in the 1870s it was bustling. It was also a place where white men strode the streets openly wearing guns. Not unlike scenes depicted of the Old West, young men there commonly caused a small incident in the streets in order to pull their weapons. Black people who walked on the wooden sidewalks were routinely told to get into the dirt road with the horses, carriages, and livestock passing through. Black women were accosted freely on the streets, without public response.[20]

Having lived in Alabama, Chloe could easily expect that the white planters who had been powerful in the 1860s would still be powerful wherever she moved. She probably did not know that the Freedman's Bureau (officially known as the Bureau of Refugees, Freedmen and Abandoned Lands), set up to assist the enforcement of these changes, would station only one man in Yazoo, and the "important gentlemen" in town would succeed in having him removed for the better part of the Reconstruction years.[21]

The Currys came to Mississippi for opportunities that didn't exist for them in Alabama after emancipation from slavery. They had also fled violence and organized terror directed at the new black voters in their home state, which was successful the year before in driving blacks from the polls and allowing the outnumbered planter's party—the Democrats—to regain control of Alabama. This meant a return to the legalization of Alabama's version of the vicious Black Codes. The Currys were among thousands moving to the safer haven of Mississippi, "where under . . . Republican government, there was better security for persons, and more certain returns for their toil," odd as that may sound now. Morgan describes those southerners who were not ready for postwar change as "the irreconcilables," and recalled that their reaction to the black migration of Chloe's era was to deem it a "black cloud threatening the supremacy of the white race."[22]

Albert Morgan was a very unusual man for his time. I am fascinated with the idea that he and Chloe were in Yazoo at the same time, because he was one of the few there who were ready to champion the dreams of the freedmen and women. He saw in those he met what I see in my great-grandmother: energy, determination, incredible endurance, and ambition. For him the question was no longer whether they could survive outside of the dependent state of bondage, but whether whites, who had become so dependent on the slavery system, could survive competing against their former bondpeople "in the presence of the negro and while the conditions of existence were equal." Of course, people worked very hard to keep conditions from being equal, but Morgan saw the planter elite pondering their fate in very stark terms:

> The greatest minds in the State, on the "superior side of the line," were gravely debating the question, which would be the wiser policy for the white man, emigration and the abandonment of the State to the negro, or a general arming of the white race with the purpose of checking by force the "threatened supremacy" of the negro race. To such persons these were the only alternatives.[23]

The irreconcilable gentlemen of Mississippi did not leave—they armed. They decided to "redeem" the state, and their drive to take back control became known as "The Mississippi Plan." In Yazoo the leaders, like all of the planter class, were Democrats, and they had lost four elections to the overwhelmingly black Republican Party. These elections were the first occasions in which African Americans in Mississippi ever voted, and were destined to be the last for nearly all blacks for almost one hundred years. In January of 1874, the Democratic leaders outlined the plans for the next election—in the fall of 1875—and published them in the paper:

1. Organize a solid Democratic front;
2. Intimidate negroes if persuasion fails;
3. Stuff the ballot box with Democratic tickets;
4. Destroy Republican tickets;
5. Substitute Democratic for Republican tickets for illiterate Negroes;
6. If these plans do not work, then count out the Republicans and count the Democrats in.[24]

I found this completely shocking, more for having been publicly announced than for having been considered. It does convey the generalized impunity that existed within the society when it came to seizing power by unlawful means. At the same time, those whites of Yazoo County and the surrounding counties who opted for Morgan's second choice—to check African American political power by force—began to stockpile arms.[25]

In 1875 the year of Chloe's arrival, men with rifles began to break up the meetings of the Republican Party, which was made up of freedmen, carpetbaggers from the North, and a few of the courageous Union-minded southerners, known throughout the South as "scalawags." On September 1, in anticipation of the usual large black Republican turnout, several Republicans—including Morgan, then Yazoo's sheriff—were shot at during a campaign meeting. R. B. Mitchell, a white Republican, was killed. W. H. Foote, the thirty-two-year-old black circuit clerk, was wounded but survived. As Morgan, who was speaking on the platform, perceived himself to be the primary target for assassination, he got off two shots at the gunmen before jumping out of a window. Just as a point of reference, these Republican men were no young kids; most of them were roughly the same age as Leonidas Campbell, who was then thirty-eight. The youngest of those who held office was probably Morgan, who was thirty-one. All of them had been in the area at least a few years and would likely have known anyone who attacked them.

Contemporary witnesses from the other side of the political aisle reported that in order to prevent "the Radicals and their negro followers getting possession of the town," word was sent to white homes and "armed patrols were placed in every block of the streets." Rumor had it that Morgan had an organized force of armed blacks in the city area. A local headline the next day read: "A Riot in Yazoo City—The Natural Result of Radical Teaching" and, even better, the local Democrat paper reported that prior to the Republican meeting, "as the shades of night set in, beating of drums was heard for the purpose of rallying negroes . . ." and that when the shooting broke out, the blacks were panic-stricken and "the firing caused some to turn pale . . ." According to Morgan, on September 3 there was a town meeting and whites in the city agreed to buy more guns.[26]

In the ensuing days, with 300 self-appointed "militia" men in the streets, so-called White Leagues, "with Winchester rifles, needle-guns, double-barrelled shot-guns and pistols," and "carrying ropes at their saddles," all the black office holders were hunted down or run out of town. And this went on throughout the area. In Clinton, Mississippi, a little more than fifty miles south, a barbecue was attacked and "a few individuals on each side were killed, and armed whites went on to scour the countryside, shooting down blacks just the same as birds. They claimed perhaps thirty victims, among them school teachers, church leaders, and local Republican organizers."[27]

On September 11 Morgan disguised himself and escaped from Yazoo City. When Governor Adelbert Ames finally gave in to many appeals for help and arranged to send two militia units to Yazoo, so many companies of "white leaguers" set up camp, and so many reports were in southern papers that hostile forces would come from other regions, that he had to withdraw his outnumbered men. In the following weeks leading up to the election, almost twenty African American men were killed, and the black office holders and activists in the county were either killed, burned out, or driven out by armed posses. Morgan remarks that the description "hung by parties unknown" became a common citation on the official records. He also reports that sometimes other blacks were forced to take part.[28]

Perhaps the most famous lynching at the time of this reign of violence before the election of 1875 was on the Campbell plantation at Silver Creek. When I came upon this incident in Morgan's book, I was very shocked. By this time, I had read all the letters of the Campbells in Mississippi, talked to several people who are very much acquainted with the family's history, and spoken with three members of the Campbell family, and not one of these encounters had given me any clue that such a thing had occurred. I was almost sickened by reading a description of the lynching, and further dismayed by a piece of the newspaper documentation that made it certain that one of the Campbell men was there. This clue led me to the certainty that, in fact, Leonidas Campbell had permitted a posse to lynch a man outside his home.

Having followed Chloe's path to Mississippi and this farm on Silver Creek, while at the same time following the trail of the Campbells from Missouri to Texas, to Mississippi and through the Civil War, it was totally astounding to me that their paths may have met during this violent season, forever marked by the most gruesome of American traditions. I also became personally grateful to Morgan for writing it all down, especially the deaths of every man he heard of being killed, and for reminding me that those of us who write have this same duty to tell what may not be otherwise saved. He documented these events before there was an organized movement to track such events, published them himself, and went to the U.S. Senate to ask for help. His life in Yazoo thus became folded into my great-grandmother's story, as an observer of her world, and as a man to be remembered in his own right.

On October 19, according to local newspapers, an African American man was shot while in his bed at Silver Creek. Word went into town that the murder was arranged by another black man, James G. Patterson, a teacher who lived at Silver Creek and a Republican member of the

Mississippi House of Representatives. Papers said that Patterson had a fight with the murdered man over politics and that Patterson had him killed because he was a Democrat. The murder victim's name did not appear in the newspaper clips that I have seen, most of which were saved by Morgan. The newspapers themselves, all of them from the Reconstruction era, are no longer among the archives in the Yazoo City library.

One paper reported that Patterson had paid another Silver Creek man, William Thomas, fifty dollars to kill "the Democrat." An unnamed person who signed a letter to the editor, "Democrat," informed the *Clarion* that Patterson's "friends swore he should not be arrested. The negroes being numerous, it was thought best to send to this city for assistance, and a company left here this morning to arrest the assassin. . . ."[29]

Most provocative of all, another dispatch to the *Clarion* the following day came from someone who signed their name only as "Campbell." It gives a highly suspect account of the disappearance of Patterson:

> The deputy sheriff and posse who left here [Yazoo City] yesterday to arrest Patterson, who, it is supposed, murdered a negro on Silver Creek because he was a Democrat, have just returned. They report that they captured Patterson and another negro who is implicated in the murder. Patterson paid this negro fifty dollars to do the deed.
>
> The deputy and posse were returning to this city with their prisoners, when they were met by an armed body and Patterson taken from them. They report him lost in the swamp. The other prisoner was brought to this city and placed in the county jail.—Campbell.[30]

This was most likely Leonidas, the man who called the posse out to the creek.

One man who later testified before a Senate Committee investigating the violence of that fall reported:

> He was hung on Silver Creek, in the eastern portion of the county, close by the residence of Col. L. A. Campbell. I think that Colonel Campbell sent over for assistance. He claimed that there had been a murder committed

there and that he wanted the matter looked into. There was quite a body of white men over there, and while they were there this man Patterson was hanged. I don't know who was there from my own knowledge.[31]

The rather numerous party that came to Campbell's farm stayed at least two days before bringing one prisoner into town, whom they soon released, at least for a time. Patterson was killed the first night. One has to assume they were Leonidas's guests for the remainder of their stay.

James G. Patterson, known to friends as Jim, was lynched that first night of the posse's two or three day visit, September 20, 1875. Born in Mississippi, he served in the Mississippi State House from 1874 to 1875. Yazoo's African American Chancery Clerk, James Dixon, later testified about the event before the Senate committee and said that Patterson "was a school teacher down on the creek at the time when the legislature adjourned; between times he would teach school."[32] Morgan describes Patterson as "my friend, an intelligent cultivated, orderly, peace-loving man . . . I knew him personally and well." He adds that he knew Patterson was holding Republican meetings out at Silver Creek, and had continued to do so in spite of threats. Morgan added that Patterson's body was left hanging there as a warning to "all other Republicans," until "the buzzards came and picked it."[33]

James Patterson, about whom so little is now known, was the hope of once-enslaved African Americans all over the South and the North. He was already an embodiment of freedom that Chloe, as an illiterate and not yet enfranchised woman with four children, probably never hoped to be—a teacher, a voter, and a representative of his people. And yet, like her, he worked cotton, lived in a cabin, dined on fatback and greens, cornbread and molasses. People who would never know his name shared the belief that they could learn to read and write at the freedmen's schools, as Patterson may have done. In every town where such schools were set up, men, women, and children packed the one-room facilities at night after work to learn basic language and math skills. He represented the fulfillment of the hope that blacks could take their places alongside the New England school marms teaching their children. He embodied the aspiration to save money from paid labor, perhaps to buy land and build a more secure livelihood for the family.

Most of all he represented the widely accepted idea that once a legally-binding, enforceable equality was established by law, African Americans—despite the handicaps of illiteracy, ignorance of some of the fundamentals of capital, and society's repugnance at their equal standing—could and would achieve self-reliance and fight for the "greater good." James G. Patterson was an instrument for social change and one of those who, had he lived, was prepared to bring the South to a point it did not reach till the latter part of the twentieth century.

But he didn't live. When he was strung up on that pecan tree and silenced along with all the other African Americans who dared to vote and lead, all the hopes of freedmen and women, such as Chloe and James Curry, were put back into chains. Every person who saw or heard of the violent Redemption of the South had to wonder if legislated freedom would mean anything at all. And one of the most devastating legacies of the overthrow of Reconstruction was that there was no second generation of blacks in electoral politics, no political power or bases of power in the South.

When Patterson and his fellow Reconstruction activists were strung up, drowned, shot, and run off, the progressive agenda of those who tried to carry forth the ideas of Reconstruction also died and, one could say, the modern civil rights movement and people like Martin Luther King, Jr. and Fannie Lou Hamer were born. Had the James G. Pattersons lived, history teachers would more likely have been giving classes on a widespread *nineteenth-century* movement across the land—but begun in the South—for justice in the courts, economic parity, gender equality in the workplace, integration of schools, and public transportation and accommodations. This is not something people like Chloe and Jim did not understand; they knew full well who James Patterson was.

And the attack on Patterson was neither the first nor the last of that election season. The first was the shooting of Foote, the local Republican Party secretary, which he survived, only to be assassinated later; then Horace Hammond, whose connection to the Republicans, if any, was as a voter, was hanged; Augustus Taylor, an election activist, was hanged;

Hilliard Golden, a county supervisor, had his house burned down; and Chancery Clerk Dixon was threatened, along with State Representative Walter Boyd and Yazoo Justice of the Peace, Major Harris.

Henry M. Dixon (unrelated to James, as far as I know), a local white man who headed up Patterson's lynching posse, was honored by his fellow Democrats in "humble appreciation of his brilliant services in the redemption of the county from radical rule in 1875." But he was a scoundrel and, after the turnover in government, when $2,800 was immediately stolen from the county treasury, Dixon got into hot water with his own pals. It came out that he might have stolen that as well as all of James Patterson's $1,500 in life savings. He claimed in an open letter to a local paper to have used Patterson's savings to "defray current expenses for the eventful campaign of 1875." And another $3,000 was used to bribe people to stuff ballot boxes. And he got a receipt, and a key to any stuffed ballot box! In his defense, Dixon claimed his action was "indorsed [sic] by all Democratic citizens." In this last point, it seems he was quite right. In 1879 Henry Dixon was shot and killed on the street by a double-barrelled shotgun. But in 1875 Dixon certainly was not the only man to be rewarded for his assistance to the Democrats.[34]

Leonidas Campbell was awarded a nice quiet election to James Patterson's seat in November 1875. If I had found any record of his holding another local office, I might have thought that Leonidas always had his eye on such a political perch. I have no sure indication that he was even on the ballot prior to the lynching. These facts don't mean that he hadn't held office before or was not on the ticket at the outset of the campaign, only that I have not seen evidence of either. Would he have ridden with one of the local militias? I think so, though again, I have only seen the names of one or two groups that Morgan documented and did not see Leonidas listed. In any case, Leonidas faced no opposition whatsoever as the Democrats captured the few white Republicans in Yazoo and forced them under threat to sign a pledge not to put up any slate of candidates at all. Blacks stayed home in droves, and it is safe to assume that at Silver Creek *no one* who worked for Leonidas tried to put in a ballot voting against him. On those terms, he probably could have stayed in office the rest of his life, had he so desired.

The state representatives of Yazoo county for the 1876–1877 session were: L. A. Campbell, A. M. Hicks, and R. S. Hudson. These three were all former slaveholders and Hicks had been a member of the all-planter board of police that ran Yazoo in days past. Hudson, though, was a special case: he was the author of the infamous Black Codes in Mississippi. Bad times were definitely back.[35]

The violence of that election had long lasting effects: the black vote was suppressed there and all over the state until the 1960s when the Freedom Summer workers came to the Delta. The violence of 1875 also brought an investigating committee from the U. S. Senate to town, a body that was openly defied by local officials. Their work had almost no impact on Yazoo, but did leave a record from those who lived through it. According to the testimony by African Americans who spoke, the violence brought new bitterness and fear to the harshness of sharecropping in Mississippi. This must certainly have been true along Silver Creek.

That "Colonel" Leonidas Campbell may have risen to statewide office on the heels of having permitted a man to become carrion for display on his land is reason for him to be loathed by anyone at Silver Creek. That he was a political partner of the author of the Black Codes is salt in the wounds. Will Campbell was most likely there as well when the lynching occurred, and his actions and feelings will likely never be known. Not having served in the war and therefore not exposed to the violent death throes of men being killed, I can only conjecture that witnessing the hanging must have been as traumatic for him as for any anyone else. At least, I would hope so. His sister's many folders of saved letters include none from either man from 1873 to 1881.

If Leonidas went to the capital in 1876, he evidently didn't take to politics, or politics didn't take to him. According to the *State House Journal* of 1876, L. A. Campbell was present on the first day of the session. In the *House Journal* of 1877, L. A. Campbell is listed as a member but was absent at the beginning of the session, as were many of the members that day.[36] For the next two terms after his tenure, Yazoo had only two representatives instead of three. I found no mention of his year in office in family papers. Nor have any of the articles from his hometown papers mentioning his presence at the local centennial ever cited that he was a state legislator in Mississippi. Curious.

A year after Patterson's lynching, while Leonidas was at the State House, William Thomas, the alleged fifty-dollar hit man, was found guilty and sentenced to life in prison. According to a newspaper story of December 15, 1876, entitled "A Court House Scene," when asked if he had anything to say, Thomas jumped up and began to rant, proclaiming his innocence. Evidently he denounced the witnesses who appeared against him, and it would be interesting to know who they were as it seems there were no eye-witnesses. When he began to speak of his wife and two children, "a loud clapping of hands was heard near the doorway, and presently his wife began to shout, and this shout was taken up by fifteen or twenty more colored women. . . ." The women carried on shouting prayers and calling on the Lord for help and stopped everything cold with a deafening uproar. The bailiff tried unsuccessfully to stop them.[37]

The fact that the women of Silver Creek burst into the main floor of the court seems surprising given the severity of the repression in which they lived. That they turned out the proceedings was heartening, and yet also completely in keeping with the consistently courageous behavior of blacks in Yazoo throughout the Reconstruction years. Given the harshness of the consequences meted out for their political organizing, voting, and election to office, the open defiance displayed in the county struck me as history I had not been taught. That my great-grandmother may have witnessed any of these events or could have been in the courthouse is, of course, fascinating to ponder. If the people of Silver Creek judged William Thomas to have been framed when innocent, this certainly would have been grounds for another grievance against Leonidas Campbell. Even if they judged Thomas to have been guilty, the trial surely opened the wound of the lynching and the overthrow of anyone who might act officially for local African Americans.

For reasons that are unknown, Leonidas and Will's sister, Sarah Rush Owen, would later accuse Chloe Curry of having harbored a grievance against Leonidas that, in Owen's estimation, led Chloe to take tragic action. Her mention of Chloe's rage has the quality of a much more personal wrath. All the same, if it is true, I wonder if the roots of her anger are in the events of 1875. It is my best guess that she and Jim would have arrived by the harvest and that the election violence was the horrific welcome to their new home. Other possibilities for her ire that come to mind are a labor dispute or something indeed personal.

After they had gotten settled at Silver Creek, Chloe Curry was approached by Will Campbell's ailing housekeeper to see if she could work at his house. When she took the job as cook on Will's place on the south side of the Colonel's farm, her life became one for which there was no precedent in her past experience. Everything one might think on hearing mention of Mississippi and the bad old days, probably happened in some form at Silver Creek.

3
∞

Clay Pots and a Tiger's Tooth
(1850–1861)

Chloe Tarrant was born in bondage about 1850 on a plantation in Alabama. I can't say for sure if that plantation was in Marion in Perry County, where she seems to have lived most of her first twenty-five years, or elsewhere. It took me one trip to look at the Mississippi census at the National Archives office in New York City to approximate her birth year, and four years to find out *where* she *might* have been born. After four years, I can also say for the first time that I know the names of her parents—no one among my living family had ever known them—and I can say she was the third of seven children though, until this year, I thought there were only six.

I have never seen any trace of letters from the Tarrants and didn't expect to find any as most of Chloe's immediate family did not read and write. My grandmother did send cards to her mother, some of which have survived and ended up in my mother's possession. Any letters in my grandmother's possession were probably tossed long ago.

I had originally started with a family tree from a cousin in Denver, and Chloe's photo album, dated 1877, with names my grandmother had written on most of the pages. The album, very thick compared to Will's, contains multiple images of Chloe's children (except for her youngest son and my grandmother), Chloe's siblings, and perhaps her parents. There are also a few white faces, two or three that repeat over a span of years. And it contains a few odd commercial, religious cards and a rather wacky carte de visite for a female performer with the P. T. Barnum circus—one Zaluma Agra, "Star of the East," who played a rescued white slave. She had written a note on the back and signed it.

I might never have found Chloe's entire family at all had I not sent to the Alabama Department of Archives and History (ADAH) for a marriage certificate. Unknown to me, the Tarrant name had been garbled in the federal census indexes and, miraculously, the good people of the ADAH sent four pages of the 1880 census that covered the entire household in which my great-great grandparents were living—twenty-one people were there that day! The household had all of Chloe's siblings, along with the spouses of those who were married and their children, as well as the Tarrant elders, Caroline and Edmond Tarrant.[1]

Just to illustrate the fragility of such scant family information, let me point out that no one knew the names of Chloe's parents despite the fact that my grandmother probably knew both of them and stayed in their home, and absolutely knew Chloe's father. I myself could have asked my grandmother about her grandparents sometime before she died when I was twenty-one years of age. That their names disappeared is the result of inexcusable negligence on the part of my family. To locate a family that was in captivity, one has to start with the last name taken in 1865, which at best only points to the possible last owner of the head of the family. Even if one knows the slaveholder's last name the process is the same. In the end after having nearly given up on finding Chloe's family, it was a search for one of Chloe's married siblings that turned up the parents and, indeed, the whole family.

The first time I received any piece of paper containing the name of any Tarrant was when I received the marriage license of my great aunt Mariah. As it turned out, on several occasions when I hit a wall, or was simply dragged away from my work by other concerns, a piece of paper would arrive from Alabama with Mariah's name on it. It's one thing to form an impression of the personality of a person whose letters and loan papers are available; it is another thing entirely to create an impression from someone who is known only through bureaucratic documents. So I became somewhat reluctant to tell people that I felt the "shade" of a freedwoman almost unknown to me was sitting on my shoulders. With the census attached to her marriage license I pieced together the Tarrant family.

Edmond Tarrant, the family patriarch, told the census taker in 1880 that he was sixty-eight and was born in Virginia in about 1812. His wife, Caroline, said she was then fifty-three, born around 1827 in North Carolina. I did find later though that Chloe and one of her sisters repeatedly reported on census records that both Edmond and Caroline were from Virginia, and this was also recorded on Mariah's death certificate by her niece. Edmond gave his occupation as farmer, and Caroline said she was keeping house.

Their first child, as far as I know, was Allen, a farm laborer born in 1843 or 1844 in Alabama. He would have been born when Caroline was sixteen or seventeen, and his birth in Alabama means that she had been brought to that state by the early 1840s. All of the other members of the family were also born there.

The second child was Mariah Tarrant, born about three years later, in either 1847 or 1848. On the 1880 census she is listed as a "washwoman," married in 1873 to Zeno Tutt, a farm laborer. This couple had three children at the time: Margaret, a son Edmond, whose name was totally unknown to me before, and Chloe B. Tutt, who became a familiar figure in my family as she seems to have been close to her namesake, Chloe Curry. I have never talked to anyone who knew Allen, but Mariah is the eldest of the three Tarrant siblings who were supposed to have "Indian blood," according to people I interviewed. This caught my attention from the first time it came up in the 1970s because no one said all of them had this heritage. When I mentioned this recently to a man who is a descendant of one of the three part-Choctaw Tarrants, he laughed and said, "Well, you know how things were." That has finally always been the explanation. I'm going to be happier when I know more precisely "how things were." Mariah's photograph in my album did raise the question for me: It was not labeled with her name and it took me several years to decide that she was in the family. She definitely looks more *something else* than her siblings.

Chloe was the third Tarrant child, born about 1850, and listed on the 1880 census as a seamstress. Though I never heard she was a seamstress, her trade was unsurprising considering my grandmother's sewing skills, but I had thought for some years that she worked as a cook, primarily because of the housekeeping job at Silver Creek. She was married to James Curry in 1869 in Marion. Ten years later they had five children: James Curry, Jr., Carrie Vienna, Ruth, Tommy, and my grandmother, Georgia.

The fourth Tarrant of that generation was King Carter, born about 1852, a farm laborer and at the time fairly recently married to a woman named Belle, who was born in South Carolina around 1855. According to his great-grandson, Reverend Rainer Wilson, both King and Belle had a different owner and thus got the name Carter, but in 1882 King Tarrant appeared on a list of workers owed pay by Leonidas Campbell.[2] They had two children at the time: Annie and Katie. I already knew from King's granddaughter, my cousin Annie Lillie Coleman, that they later had other children and she spun a few tales that were new to the rest of us, among them that King was "a Choctaw Indian, never assimilated." She didn't have any explanation for that and, after four years of digging, I can't say that I know from whence any Choctaw background springs. As for the name Carter, slaveholders in the Yazoo area named Carter held many slaves who later lived there and used the name.

The fifth Tarrant child was Aaron, born around 1860. That summer of 1880 he was a twenty-year-old farm laborer. My grandmother recorded his name as George Aaron. Aside from this census and a photo, I have never found any other items pertaining to his life.

Chloe's younger sister, the sixth child, was Lucy Ann, born about 1862 and called Nunnie. Lucy was then a seventeen-year-old student at the Lincoln School in Marion. I looked for the man she later married in records for a long time under the name Grant Walker. It was only when I received Lucy's death certificate from the State of Alabama that I learned his name was *General* Grant Walker—a true freedman name!

The youngest Tarrant sibling, Andrew, was born about 1865 and was the seventh known child. At the time of the census, he was fifteen years old and working on the farm. I have yet to learn any more about him.

One of the misleading issues on the census records that one still has to pay some attention to is the racial description. Sometimes the listing of a person as "mulatto" means only that to the recorder's eye, the person in question did not look African. Likewise, the census taker may have deemed as black someone who was a mulatto because they looked African and the question was not asked. Sometimes the color designation is a reported fact from the respondent or reported though not true. I mention this because the records on this family give different racial descriptions at different times and places. In 1870 both Chloe and her husband were listed as mulattoes. In 1880 in Mississippi they were listed as black. In Alabama in 1880 the census taker created a mix that is confusing. Edmond and Caroline are listed as black. Their eldest son, Allen, is listed as black. The rest of the Tarrants are listed as mulatto.

If some of the Tarrant offspring had a different parent, there is still a mystery as to whether they had another father or mother. Allen could have been the child of a first wife for Edmund or a first husband for Caroline. On the other hand, the rest could have been the child of a white man, a white woman, my mysterious Native American heritage, be it male or female, or just a different color. Chloe's photo album displays a family retaining the coloring, hair, and features of West African heritage, and yet any and all of them might have been biracial. This is one of the common problems in tracing freedmen and women.

There is one photograph, a tintype really, of an older woman in Chloe's album. There is no name on it and for a long time I assumed it was an image of Chloe's sister Mariah. At a point, I realized, especially after learning when they were born, that this woman looked much older than a sister born two years before Chloe. Around 1880, Chloe still looked quite young. The older woman also had a more serious mien, perhaps just from the awkward requirements of photography at the time—long periods of sitting still and the need to take the occasion as the creation of a formal record. Still, she is a woman whose hands show the damage of field work rather than sewing or washing. Her hair is fixed as Chloe wore hers in a photo some years after the war, with a braid across the crown and fresh flowers. The rest of her hair seems gathered in a net or snood, such as women wore in the 1860s. A pin sits at the neck of her blouse, dark, in the shape of a shell—I have never made out exactly what it might be—and she has a tiger's tooth on a chain around her neck as well. These bits of adornment spoke to me of a taste in material objects quite different from my great-grandmother who sported traditional Euro-American jewelry in later photographs. Perhaps this is Caroline. Even if Caroline was a mulatto herself, the heritage of her mother seems clear on her face. The tiger's tooth inspired a bit of wishful thinking that there are not too many more generations to the first African of her line. Her grandparents, I suspect, were people who came through Middle Passage.

When I looked at the birthdates of the seven Tarrant children, my first thought was that there may have been two periods of separation for the parents. There were as many as four years between Allen and Mariah, and there is an eight-year span between King and Aaron, and five years again between Aaron and Andrew. The siblings all favor each other very much, so I am inclined to think their parents were separated more than once.

When I could not find any of the people except Chloe and Jim in the 1870 census or Alabama's unique 1866 Colored Census, I began to suspect that many were stuck in working situations where they were not made available to record takers and perhaps did not even know they had been liberated. Also, by 1870 a noticeable number of the whites of Perry County's planter class were gone from their antebellum homes. I have found no other census record in which Edmond and Caroline appear.

By the time I found their names I had already been tracing the migrations of white farmers named Tarrant for a good long time, but on learning Edmond and Caroline's birthdates, I realized I had to look for an earlier generation of white Tarrants. Of course, this might tell me simply where Edmond lived, and would tell me about Caroline's experience only if she happened to come into the hands of a Tarrant before marrying Edmond. What was new for me to deal with was that Caroline said she was born in North Carolina and that her parents were from North Carolina as well. Edmond said he was born in Virginia and that his parents were from Virginia, which made sense, as all the Tarrants I had found have their roots in Virginia.

∞

When I did searches on the name Tarrant, and the names of the white people in Chloe's photo album, I inevitably came up with dozens of items relating to the same families in three and four southern states. This caused me to follow every son and daughter from a Tarrant family in Virginia, for instance, to outposts where cotton was raised in South Carolina, Alabama, Mississippi, Tennessee, and Texas.

For example, the family of a Leonard Tarrant of Virginia went through the Revolution in their home state, and then moved to Abbeville District, South Carolina, where cotton was raised, and the next generation had several members who later moved to Jefferson County, Alabama, and what is now the Birmingham area, and some then moved on to Marion, Alabama, where Chloe lived. These seemed fruitful paths to follow for several reasons, some concrete, some instinctual.

First, if one follows cotton, one is going to end up in certain places. (If one follows rice, she ends up in other spots.) If looking for someone who worked in cotton, in South Carolina there is a strip of counties where that crop was viable. Abbeville District is one of those areas. I also had this other hunch that I should look for the places where pottery was made because, despite the protests of some in my family, I thought pottery making was something of a family tradition that nowadays is expressed as a family-wide habit of buying pottery. On my memory that my grandmother made or painted pottery, I followed the clay. If one traces where the clay is in the South, where bondmen and women actually mass-produced pottery and many people might have had the skill, one will discover the Abbeville-Edgefield area. The most well-known enslaved potters lived in that area. The whites who began setting up shops to make large containers for farmers to buy moved to areas where the soil was rich in clay.

These two work hand in hand though, as cotton farmers worked the land till it gave out for that crop, and moved on to land being settled by sons or nephews elsewhere. Many of the cotton farmers who were in the clay-rich districts of South Carolina had younger family folk who settled in the blackbelt of Alabama.

According to federal census data, in 1850 there was a small number of white Tarrants scattered around Alabama, the largest number in Jefferson county around Birmingham. They started out in Virginia, went to South Carolina, and then settled in Alabama. The earliest Tarrant was in Alabama by 1820. By 1850 there were five Tarrants in the town of Marion, in Perry County: one young widow and four children.[3]

In 1860 there were three Tarrant households in Perry County. W. R. Tarrant, a physician, held two bondwomen; Mary Ann Tarrant, a thirty-six-year-old widow, owned twelve men and women. Larkin Young Tarrant, who had two residences, held thirty-two enslaved people in town, twelve more on his farm in the Seviere area of the county, and fifteen in Mississippi. I also looked at two other slaveholders: Julia Tarrant Barron and her brother-in-law, John Barron. All of these people were related. Larkin and Julia were siblings, descended from Leonard Tarrant of Virginia and born in South Carolina. Mary Ann Tarrant and John Barron were their in-laws.

The Tarrants moved from Virginia to Abbeville, South Carolina, where they raised cotton in the 1780s. The Barrons came to South Carolina from Ireland about the same time. Members of both families then came to Alabama, where they bought land in several areas. In looking into those Tarrant settlers I found Julia Ann Tarrant, who married a man named Barron and moved to Perry County.

William C. Barron moved to Marion with his brother John in 1820. Both were born in the York District of South Carolina and later moved to Jefferson County. William opened one of the town's first stores. Julia Ann Tarrant, born in Abbeville and raised in Alabama, became a widow four years after her marriage. Thereafter she developed into a well-known philanthropist, remembered for trying to give away most of her money. Perhaps, I thought, she brought one of Chloe's parents with her from Jefferson County to Marion when she got married.[4]

In 1850 Julia Barron was a wealthy fifty-four-year-old widow with twenty-nine slaves on a property in a place known as Rascoes in Dallas County, which lies next to Perry. In that year, she was not the owner of any bondpeople who were the right ages or sex to be my ancestors.

Her next door neighbor was her sister-in-law, Mary Ann Smith Tarrant, widow of Julia's brother, Colonel Felix Noble Tarrant, who died in

1848 at twenty-seven years of age, leaving her with money, cotton land, and slaves. Mary Ann had in 1860 $28,200 in real estate and $64,900 in other wealth (in today's dollars somewhere between $2 million and $25 million). I have not found any military record for Felix, but I would guess by the date of his death that he may have been among the many Alabamans who went to the U.S.-Mexican War. In 1850 Mary Ann had thirty-two slaves. Four of them could have been Caroline and all the children she had at the time. In 1860 she held twelve people in Perry County from a three-year-old girl to a forty-five-year-old man. Three of them were roughly the same ages as Edmond, Caroline, and Mariah. As it happens, when I found Chloe Tarrant and Jim Curry on the 1870 census, they were listed as domestic servants living next door to Mary Ann Tarrant and, I would guess, on her property.

By 1860 Julia was worth $15,000 in real estate (at least $330,000 today) with personal assets of $30,000 ($660,000 to almost $8 million depending on the index by which you convert it) and had eight slaves in three cabins at her Marion home. (Julia's son, John Thomas Barron, was listed in 1860 as a physician and had six slaves who do not seem to fit the profile of my family.) I did not find the Rascoes farm under her name for that year. If either Julia or Mary Ann owned members of the black Tarrant family in 1860, one would have held the mother without her two youngest children—eight-year-old Chloe and one-year-old King—and the other would have held these two children. The same would be true if Julia's brother Larkin had commandeered the older members of the family and left the two babies with Julia. While this is not unheard of, the psyche, of course, seeks a more comforting set of facts, such as the situation presented by John Barron's bondpeople—several people of each age, offering the chance of an intact family.

This possibility of separation brought up another interesting question that occurred many moons after I learned the names of Edmond and Caroline Tarrant: Among those I've found, no one else in the family was ever named after Caroline, with the possible exception of Chloe's daughter Carrie. Edmond's name was carried on by three of his descendants. It is intriguing.

Julia Barron was a devout Baptist, who by most lights became rather powerful in the church for a woman at that time. According to several local histories, she was a member of Siloam Baptist Church, gave the land on which the church building stands, and was instrumental in the 1838 founding of Judson College (then Judson Female Institute) and in the 1840s, Howard College, now Samford University, both schools with strong Baptist roots. Along with her pastor, W. H. McIntosh and the educator Milo P. Jewett, she began *The Alabama Baptist*, a denominational newspaper. A librarian at Samford told me that Barron brought Jewett to Alabama and put him up when they started Judson, and indeed, Jewett, who was also a founder of Vassar College, was Judson's first president.[5]

Julia's brother-in-law, John Barron, was quite a successful planter. In 1860 he was married with one daughter and worth $64,000 in real estate and $88,295 in other wealth ($3.4 million to $40.5 million today). He became a politician as well, serving as a Whig in the Alabama legislature from the late 1830s into the 1840s. He held seventy-four people in sixteen "slave houses" at a farm in the Scotts area of the county. He may have had the whole family with some slight errors on ages or, possibly, just Caroline and most of her children. And one has to assume that the family moved people around at will.

Larkin Young Tarrant, another of Julia's brothers, also moved to Perry. He was there in 1840, and although I could not locate him in 1850, by 1860 he held sixty-nine slaves in Perry County. He was, in the main, a building contractor and also designed several of the local buildings, and he farmed as well. In Perry County, Larkin had females of the ages of all the Tarrant girls and women; the males held by him of the correct age to be the Tarrant men are among his slaves in Mississippi, an all-male contingent probably breaking in new land in that state. This could account for at least one of Edmond's absences.

Siloam Baptist, Julia's church, was a real gentry church. The slaves of these white families attended and sat in a separate section to worship. At the end of slavery, the blacks of Siloam departed to start their own church, and it is said that Siloam aided the development of the black church, Berean Baptist. Neither Siloam nor Samford University, where the church's old papers are archived, have records from the 1860s. And I have found no papers for the Barrons in any Alabama archive, and none for the Tarrants that were helpful. Yet I had two more reasons for trying to pursue a connection between Julia Ann Barron and my great-grandmother Chloe: Barron's pastor, W. H. McIntosh, was the man who married Chloe Tarrant and James Curry, and I have several tintypes from Chloe's photo album that seem to resemble a portrait I have seen of Julia Tarrant Barron.[6]

In the 1870 census, the first federal record to show blacks by name, ninety-four African Americans named Tarrant suddenly emerged onto the rolls of official documents: forty in Dallas County, fifteen in Jefferson County, and twenty-one in Perry, along with a handful in three other counties. Most of these people were born in slavery in Alabama, like Chloe and her siblings, and likely got their name from Alabama Tarrants. Edmond may have gotten the name from early Tarrants in other places, or they may have been owned by Mary Ann Tarrant's folks, a huge clan of Smiths!

Chloe's husband, James Curry, was also from Marion, and I downloaded an old map of the Scotts precinct in the county, where many of the local farms were, and found the white Curry family had a farm next door to John Barron's farm. This may be how they met. The Currys had many people in bondage and people by that name were once very numerous in the county. The first time I put the names Tarrant and Curry into an internet search engine, I came up with living people from local phone directories. This caught my eye because there were only six Currys and one Tarrant. The one Tarrant was an older woman who told me her family was from Detroit, but after we talked a while, she said her mother was from "down Uniontown" there in Perry County. I knew her mother's name because it had appeared on a website listing the graduates of the Lincoln School. I don't know if her mother was related to me, but I have seen her records and those of her parents as I explored Perry County time and again. One of the Currys on the list lived at an address provided by my Denver cousin as the only contact information he had for any of our people in Marion. I called her.

Minnie Curry, a retired school principal, was kind enough to explain everything she knew about her grandfather, James Curry. She further told me the family had been written about before and directed me to a book already on one of my bookshelves, *Climbing Jacob's Ladder: The Enduring Legacy of African-American Families* by Andrew Billingsley. Her story and the more elaborate version in the book proved to be rather puzzling. She told me "Jim" Curry, born in 1848, was her grandfather, and he was "out of Mississippi." Billingsley reports that "his only wife," Sallie, was born in 1842 and had also been in slavery in Perry County. (Minnie recalled that Sallie's maiden name was Laird.) The couple had six children, of whom only three survived into adulthood.

> Reflecting the high level of literacy in antebellum Perry County, James had emerged from slavery with the ability to read and write. His grandchildren recall him as the resident intellectual, always collecting books, magazines, and newspapers and helping them learn to read them. He worked after slavery for a white family on Polk Street in Marion. He later purchased property from them and built a small house next door at 310 Polk, which still stands today in modernized form. The Polk Street house would be the center of life for the Curry family for more than a hundred years.[7]

The James Curry I knew about was a preacher and, from my grandmother's recollections, abhorred the drudgery of farm work. Minnie was kind enough after the first conversation to send me his picture, which was the very image of Chloe's son James, Jr. Minnie's father, Irving, was born in 1895. This also caused confusion.

Chloe and Jim Curry married in 1869, and their children were born for the most part in the 1870s. It seemed unlikely that a couple born in the 1840s—Jim and Sallie—would not have had children until the '90s. The records make it clear that Chloe's husband had a second family in the 1890s after he and Chloe divorced. It was in fact a second marriage for both Jim and Sallie, and she was a somewhat young wife for him, which at least puts all that child-bearing she did into a clearer perspective.

In subsequent conversations with Minnie, I finally had sense enough to ask what church the family attended. She remarked that they had always gone to Berean Baptist, and Jim had even preached there on several occasions. But she knew nothing about a woman named Chloe.

Having found my great-great grandparents Caroline and Edmond Tarrant without expecting to, I did wonder if I could find *their* parents. I have not as yet and I think that will take a lot of luck. They would have been born, by my guess, during the revolutionary period—anywhere from the 1770s to the early 1800s. At that time, there were Tarrants in South Carolina and one or two in Virginia. And of course, if Edmond and Caroline's respective parents were African Americans, then the African generation—if I am lucky—would have been their grandparents, born maybe twenty to thirty years earlier, brought here roughly in the mid-1700s.

I happened to be in the library of Columbia University one day in 2004 looking through indexes of government documents while a somewhat imperious librarian insisted on checking for a report I needed without my assistance. As I sat staring at the reference books in front of me, I spotted a book about the Virginia slave trade. This short, broad book was a list of slave ships and owners coming into Virginia from 1698 to 1775. I learned several things from reading this book, one of which was that slaves coming into Virginia were sometimes reported at a customs house in my home town. Again, never heard about that.

But the following items appeared: In 1739, the sloop *Ruby* brought in two slaves from Barbados to Hampton, Virginia. The master of the ship was a William Tarrant. The man who had bought the slaves was a John Tucker. To have moved from getting in the Atlantic slave trade by way of owning a ship to buying land and owning slaves was, as far as I know, common enough. Looking at the year 1810, I found four people who might have held Edmund's mother around the time of his birth: Richard, Lucy, Francis, or Carter Tarrant.[8]

Here I want to relate an interesting coincidence. First of all, it has been my experience whenever I am working on a project that my life becomes prone to a whole series of coincidences that crop up as leads to information that I might need. There are a few such events in this book. Sometimes though, I have been blind to what the coincidence might offer. When I was writing my first novel, *1959*, set during the time of my childhood, I named the central characters Tarrant. I picked this seemingly remote family name because I liked the sound of it, and also because of a coincidence. I had heard somewhere that the first African American child born in Virginia was a boy born in my home town named Caesar Tarrant. This resonated with the theme of my book, which had to do with how blacks at mid-century felt ownership of the town and were easily motivated to exercise boycotts as a means to integration in 1959.

Caesar Tarrant was *not* the first African American child born in Virginia, or even in my home town, I'm sure, as he was born 120 years too late for that—around 1740. There is a school named after him now because he was a local hero. While enslaved he became a boat pilot, expert in the local waterways, and he served heroically in the navy during the American Revolution. Afterwards he was returned to slavery. He was so gallant under fire, however, that the white pilots who performed the same service during the war petitioned for him to be honored with his freedom and the state legislature made it so. It then took him decades to get his one or two members of family out of bondage and they, in turn, had to carry on the effort to liberate the others into the next century, decades after his death. One son, Sampson Tarrant, probably never made it out and a grandchild was left in bondage.[9]

The point of my story is that I never looked beyond the coincidence of the names. I never knew there was a Tarrant farm a couple of miles from my home that later became a school district. Never thought to look at these Virginia Tarrants as possibly having a connection to my mother's Alabama/Mississippi family. Thus in 2004, seeing the state of Virginia as Edmond Tarrant's birthplace, I had to root among the slaveholding records from Virginia for people named Tarrant, including the one who owned Caesar.

The man who owned Caesar Tarrant was dead by 1810, but he had left his property to his wife, and it was to then go to his son Francis. There

were only four heads of household in Virginia named Tarrant: Richard
Tarrant, of Caroline County; Lucy Tarrant of Hampton; Francis Tarrant
of Norfolk; and Carter Tarrant, a farmer then listed in Norfolk, but who
also lived in Hampton. This last man may be another son of the man
who owned Caesar Tarrant. Edmond's mother could have been the property of either. (Neither of these men named Carter Tarrant is the famous
abolitionist of the same name, a Baptist minister from Virginia, also a son
of Leonard Tarrant. Rev. Carter Tarrant moved to Kentucky and fought
slavery all his life.) In 1820 there were no Tarrants listed in the census in
Virginia, most having relocated to South Carolina. Edmond, if in the
hands of any of these people, probably spent time in South Carolina.

People rarely think of Virginia as cotton country. Even though it is my
home, I never knew people raised cotton there. Cotton came here with
the settlement of Jamestown in 1607. Simply put, the colonists needed
fiber for their clothes, though in time it was learned that this particular
bush has more uses than most plants on earth. In 1793 when Eli Whitney
finished Yale and moved to South Carolina, it took one slave sixteen
months to separate the seeds from the fiber for a five-hundred-pound
bale of cotton. Farmers did not consider it a profitable crop. Some time
that year, he came up with the model for a gin that would do the separation, and raising the fiber plant became an entirely different enterprise.

Needless to say, this is why my great-great-great grandparents found
themselves on the East Coast of the United States sometime around 1800.
Cotton was farmed in Virginia, particularly in the same region my Davis
relatives were brought to—what is now Smithfield ham country. This part
of the state is flat, low-lying ground spreading from the south side of the
James River down to the more rolling country around Emporia. Fiercely
hot in summer, it was also a misery of mosquitoes and other pests in the
areas near the James or along the many local creeks. The Tarrants I found
on the 1810 Virginia slave census lived near the port of Norfolk, a few
miles east where the James flows into the Hampton Roads and then into

the Atlantic. The Tarrants I saw on the Alabama records nearly all hailed from a family in Henry County, west of Emporia, near Martinsville and the Blue Ridge foothills.

Realizing the plant did best in the southernmost regions, cotton farmers bought land south and southwest of Virginia. In 1800 South Carolina produced 60 percent of the nation's cotton crop. In the next two or three decades most of the cotton producers moved further west and south into areas occupied by Native Americans.[10] From the 1814 defeat of the Creek people of what is now Alabama until 1835, the inhabitants of Alabama—Creeks, Choctaws, Chickasaws, and Cherokees—were driven out to make way for white settlers. One of the men assigned to oversee Creek removal from the Eufala, Alabama, area was a Tarrant, who later became an Indian agent.[11]

Throughout the search of these roots of mine I used some of my gut feelings—such as my pottery idea. Likewise, reading about Alabama and West African quiltmakers encouraged my interest in this craft connection between past and present, and sent me searching through my own memory of which quilt patterns Georgia favored. This seemed a lot more tenuous, as so many people had to quilt their bedding. My grandmother's own personal sewing quirks, such as adorning all the linens with appliqued flowers—which appealed to few of us when I was young—tantalized me as a habit from some unknown station in her much-traveled life.

One feature of Americanness that can haunt a genealogist is the fact that old country ways were so disparaged, ignored, and forgotten. Trying to recall them forty years later is vexing, and more so if you begin to suspect that the lace curtains someone was sewing for the white ladies down south had a meaning as to where a woman may have been born. For someone as compulsive as myself, food culture, hairdos, jewelry, and household arts become tantalizing as secret repositories of unrecorded pasts. If you tell me the folks in your family like okra, I will think something much different than if you tell me you could never stand the stuff because it's slimy. That rocking chair was made by your grandmother's brother? Had he been enslaved? I'm all in your family tree.

So, with my own recollections, it seemed important that my grandmother was proud of some of the porcelain items in her house that she had either made or painted, or that she had made a huge metal tray I own that is etched with vines. As Georgia had the much-disdained habit of making everything possible by hand, even when she could afford to buy them, her household practices have sometimes kept me awake nights.

African American roots, being the mysterious mix of clues that present themselves in each of our families, make for endless fascinating conversations among friends about the possible origins of the family specifics. My college roommate Christine has kept me intrigued for years with a family lineage of women who worked in textiles across generations and migration, as well as her uncle, the fire-eating, Koran-reading spiritualist and performer. When she describes his costumes—mixing animal skin, tinges of Orientalism, and more than a whiff of northern nightclub—I both giggle and wonder. When she quotes him on his meditation practice, I am in her grasp. Where does it all come from? These days, one hardly ever encounters someone who is fashioning a persona that is not on television somewhere. Black folks who came into adulthood before the emergence of mass media seem to hold clues to cultural encounters that the scholars are only now beginning to document for us. When Joseph Jarman told me his father raised horses in Louisiana and that all the men in his father's family had also raised horses in the Texarkana area as well, I was riveted because it told something specific about their origins. Years ago, a drummer of mixed black and Native American background told me that growing up in Oklahoma, where some of his people were on a reservation, he had been confused that his parents ate rice as a staple when there was none in the state. He later learned they had come on the Trail of Tears from the Carolinas.

The fact that my mother continued some of her mother's ways—growing certain vegetables on the side of the house, eating pig brains scrambled with eggs, giving us molasses every morning, sewing like crazy, making clothes, school theatrical costumes, and doll outfits—didn't mean much in the 1950s when people I knew were becoming crazy for "store-bought." Now it seems so entirely logical that she made craft games for birthday parties, collected Juba dances and other "plantation" dance forms, loved Fats Waller, and moved from taking photographs, like her mother, to developing and printing them. This mix of country ways and aesthetic passions was not part of the culture of assimilation or the conformity urge of the Eisenhower era. Being a woman artist was just as "different" as hanging on to a taste for chittlins among people who had never tasted them.

Women have seldom been taught that these skills of their mothers were important, and now it seems to me they are the memory banks for family history with their recipes and quilting stories. Of course I routinely meet young women at the grocery check-out counter who do not know what my collard greens are, so let me not get carried away about food practices being handed down. Much more concrete is the work of some scholars now investigating what Africans knew on coming here, and how that knowledge was mixed with what they learned in those rice and cotton fields.

During 2004 I wondered how I could get closer to information on where Edmond and Caroline may have come from or their parents. I decided to try a DNA test I had read about, available from a firm called African Ancestry. With these tests one can trace one's paternal or maternal line for African ethnic identity. Any given individual can only test for the ancestors of his or her same sex. I decided to trace the DNA of my mother's line. I later asked my brother to take the paternal test, but the company offers an interesting caveat for the male test. According to interviews with the head of the company, there is a 30 percent "failure" rate with the male test—that is, a failure to find African roots in the male line. This is attributed to the impact of rape and the concubinage of African women. I will be anxious to see if this percentage holds up as they are able to test many more thousands of African Americans, because it tells a tale always maintained by black people—that millions of us are mixed, that plantation rape was not a marginal phenomenon, and that most of us are mixed on the male side of our lineage. As the Davis family story includes exactly this kind of incident, of a child born of an English sea captain, I cautioned my brother that we might be spending several hundred dollars to find out what we already knew—and indeed that turned out to be the case.[12]

That fall I received a certificate stating that Chloe's maternal line is from the Temne people of what is now Sierra Leone. I did not know anything about the Temne, yet I had a feeling of enormous satisfaction, a sense of being grounded. After years of hearing about the Scots-Irish planters in southern African American heritage, and knowing only fragments about Liza, my father's French-speaking great-grandmother from Madagascar, the Temne ancestry seemed to have solidity. The Temne journey to America fits the contours of the grand narrative of black history, and ties me to great swaths of our collective history. Suddenly I could fill out some of the story that I cannot yet build from the slim threads remaining of Liza's story. And all the stories are connected.

According to what I have since read, most of the people taken from Sierra Leone went to Barbados before being brought here. My notes and xeroxed copies from the Minchinton study of the Virginia slave trade show many boats arriving with slaves by way of Barbados, like the *Wray Galley*, which arrived in 1771 and caught my eye, not because of the Tarrants but because the captain was one of many English captains named Davis. As I gazed down at a two-page spread from the spring of 1739, there were three other boats that brought Africans from Barbados to Virginia. For the entire period of the statistics in that book, there are dozens of such slave ships that may have held Temnes. Without an owner's name or a solid date, I would go no further.

The idea that at least three different branches of my family tree might have come through the same Virginia ports, maybe even my home town, was almost disturbing. It's not like having several sets of grandparents coming through New York harbor or even Baltimore; this is a much more humble gateway through which small groups traveled and were bought by relatively few people. And it was disturbing to me just to realize—having searched records kept in New York, Alabama, South Carolina, Missouri, and Mississippi, with a few digressions into Choctaw and Creek family lists, and libraries all over—that the records of those unknown Temnes, Ibos, or East Africans in my history may be a two-minute walk from where I was born.

Like most other Americans of my age, and probably even those younger, I learned virtually nothing of African history in my education. In college, I took a newly minted class in modern African political systems (it was the

1960s) because I was very interested in Pan-Africanism and African independence movements. Other than that, my familiarity with any historic African political entities was next to *nada*. So in reading up on the Temne, when I saw mention of something called the Futa Jallon jihad, I did not know whether Futa Jallon indicated a people, a place, a leader, or a movement. It is a regional name, homeland of several groups of people and, when you add the word jihad (roughly, holy war) to that name, you have one of the reasons there are today so many African Americans with Sierra Leonean heritage. The conflict, which began in the 1720s, lasted for six decades, providing a long-term devastation to people in the area who lost thousands to captivity. The heaviest human trafficking came in the second half of the 1700s and sent nearly 400,000 people into the hands of slave traders. Lastly, Temnes were much more likely to be sold to farmers in South Carolina and Georgia than to slaveholders in Virginia. Now, looking at Caroline's place of birth, and even her name, I have come to assume she or her mother started out in South Carolina rather than North Carolina.[13]

My female Temne ancestors came from a patrilineal society, but one of greater gender equality than they would have found here. They were rural people who raised rice, usually primarily farmed by women, as well as yams, groundnuts, millet, cotton, and other crops, while men were responsible for hunting and fishing. They also brought with them pottery, ironwork, and weaving traditions; their basketmaking skills, which will be familiar to anyone who has been to Charleston or the Sea Island area, are passed from mother to daughter. Just as a point of levity, I will mention that though my mother collected baskets, and in fact had a large, round rice-winnowing basket hanging in our hallway, I learned basket weaving in the Girl Scouts from a kit.[14]

A point made by historian Michael Gomez in his study, *Exchanging Our Country Marks: The Transformation of African Identities in the Colonial and Antebellum South*, gave me a new insight into the impact of Middle Passage. He writes about the lack of contact these coastal rice farmers had had with any of the urban cultures of the time, or with the situation that created the conditions of their lives in Africa and the Americas. These folk were utterly unfamiliar with urban centers, trading with other centers, or literacy. Far from being urbane, tolerant, and comfortable with people from other cultures, they were more likely to be hide-bound about their own practices and, in Gomez's language, "provincial." I laughed out loud when I read this, as being provincial was, by the 1960s, an insult in my family.[15]

I look at their isolation in terms of what it gave, rather than what it withheld. A culture devoid of traded and manufactured goods is a culture that teaches complete self-sufficiency within the village. Such a culture would produce people who could, having somehow successfully absorbed the trauma of violent transplantation, survive in a system that provided less than what the village needed. In my mind these are people who might have been spiritually broken by separation from home, but also people who, if they survived the crush upon the spirit, were otherwise well-suited to living in pioneer communities. Though I think of myself as pretty broad-minded, I am grateful for the Temne provinciality also because I see it as the engine driving preservation of the cultural ways of their home. I would even go so far as to say that saving money may not have been the only reason that my grandmother would go shopping and simply look, then go home and just make what she had seen rather than buying it. My sister Jennie recalled Georgia doing this in the 1940s when Jennie showed her a fetching wide red leather belt in a store, only to later watch her whip one up, having gotten some red leather from who-knows-where.

Still, a lack of awareness of the rest of the world is a disastrous background for kidnap, imprisonment, and the forced transnational journeys of Middle Passage. The psychological impact of learning of the rest of the world behind a whip seems both devastating and complex. Without knowledge of literacy, the impact of the typical propaganda meted out by slave handlers concerning white supremacy, the dominance and superiority of western societies with their literacy, economies, and Christianity would seem to force people into a conflict running to the core of their individual and collective being.

One barrier to the intrusion of the slave handler's worldview, or perhaps, a means for processing the conflict of worldviews presented by being forced into slavery, may have been the regeneration of the so-called "secret societies" of the coastal people of Sierra Leone within the confines of chattel slavery in the United States. Along with their neighbors, the Mende, the Temne people became known among westerners for these so-called "secret societies." According to Gomez, they served many functions having to do with health, family life, and self-governance.

The Temne societies of the eighteenth century were gender-based and, within those groups, men and women trained the youth in gender roles and expectations, as well as assisting in transitions from youth to adulthood, from single life to married life and through the universal rigors of adulthood. Women in the societies of that area held political power within their cultures, although Gomez points out that this was a fact primarily among the elite of those societies, and that it was a tradition put under considerable pressure in this country.[16]

It may take me years to forge real connections between what I learned of these people, what I may learn of my other African genes, and any facts concerning the people who were my actual ancestors. Many of the characteristics of the Temne given above would be easily recognizable to most African Americans I know. All of us would recognize holdovers of the secret societies in fraternal organizations and the one-time dime savings clubs to the many gender-based groups inside our institutions, and even the considerable number of such groups that any one person might join—church groups, brotherhoods, sisterhoods, sororities, women's clubs both civic and social, movements such as the Garvey Movement or Father Divine's service organization. Our famed ability to improvise in situations where resources are scant certainly did not come purely from any culture as much as the culture of necessity. The endurance that I feel I got directly from tough-minded tutelage was also enforced by experience. Having somewhere specific to look for clues, though, is consoling.

The search for African American genealogy is an incredibly frustrating ordeal. Little wonder that so many of us were elated by the very idea of Alex Haley having succeeded in mapping generations of his forebears who not only were found, but who had passed on some fragment of African identity that was specific to a culture somewhere among the continent's fifty-two countries. Though questions have been raised about whether he really did trace his line all the way back home, it absolutely can be done. And for many, the DNA test will remove the need. While in my youth we were told we did not know who we are and where we came from, and that our history had been taken away, mine will be the last generation that needs to have that sensation. The scholars have already told us quite a bit about the history we were not taught. With computers my task took four years, where it might have taken twelve years if I had tried it in the 1970s without the Internet. One can get to rough percentages of all the complex heritage for any African American through science. But locating the stories—that will take stubbornness, boundless curiosity, and luck.

I can attribute some of my own frustration to my lack of training to dig up history. But nothing has caused as much distress as trying to find any simple paper verification of the existence of members of my family, some of whom I could see on tintypes saved for over 100 years. After two-and-a-half years of researching everyone in the book, I began to work exclusively on this group of nine Tarrants and their children. Soon I began to have episodes of lights flashing in my eyes that would last up to forty-five minutes. Two trips to eye doctors informed me that I was having a form of migraine that does not bring a headache, just blinding light effects and a subsequent "sick" feeling with several symptoms. My next door neighbor, a therapist, asked me if this was a metaphor–in other words, what was I not seeing?

What I was not seeing was any sign of the existence of tens of thousands of people who built the places I could see, and nursed the children whose names are present in some records throughout the length of their lives.

Because Will Campbell's father was founder of Springfield, Missouri, there are papers about the exact location of the family home, and even one news article on when the family home was lifted off the ground and moved to another location. The black Tarrants worked for a family that spread out from Virginia to Texas, where Tarrant County, surrounding

Fort Worth, was named after one of the clan who is credited with running the Native Americans out of the area. Some of the black Tarrants left no traces in the annals of this country except in slave inventories now lost. My dogs have more documentation of their existence than most of my forebears. Considerably more.

What I *did* see were page upon page of records of enslaved people in the slave schedules of the nineteenth century with lines drawn through the space where a name should have been written. Pages of human beings, mostly men, marked by M for males, F for female, B for black, a number for the age, following in columns after the name of a white planter, usually a man, who needed only the number of slaves and their sex and ages to determine their worth, and hence his own cumulative worth. They were lists of bank deposits, if you will, that added up to more wealth in the 1860s than was held by any single population on the planet at that time.

On several occasions, after one or two hours of looking through numbers for a nameless person of the right age on a farm in the right county, I had to get up, turn off the microfilm machine, and leave the National Archives office, abandoning work for the day because I had become so depressed. I had a student assistant a few years ago who I sent to the National Archives to look for the family of a friend. Afterward she begged me not to ask her to go there again. She had found the family but was so disturbed by the process that she could not take heart from having found the needle in the haystack.

My student had the kind of experience that any African American might have looking through the records left behind by slaveholders in that many of us, in the absence of our stories, are very much susceptible to all the stories. This is why Alex Haley's *Roots* was so affecting. I remember a woman in Washington—"Sugar," a neighbor of a friend of mine—telling me I would especially love digging through the Freedmen's Bureau records in the National Archive. She was doing her family history and she was so enthralled by the material there that she described the brown envelopes with red ribbon wrapped around them in which the agents' records had been filed, and said as she sat there day after day it was all she could do not to read everyone's papers. "There are so many stories in there," Sugar said. And now, people who do look at original documents tend to post them on the internet because they know so many are desperate to know.

Still, when one is looking for one's own family's traces there is a fear, not only that the facts are gone, but that if they are found, they might tell something awful, prove some harm came the way of those missing ancestors. During the time I was doing my research, my Aunt Lenne used to sometimes say she wished she could find information on her family. Once, she remembered the name of her family's "Colonel"—a Colonel Bridges in North Carolina. She said that he had had children by two sisters, of whom her great-grandmother was one. I found them both living next door to the thirty-five-year-old former colonel in 1870. I almost did not want to call my aunt, who is in her eighties, because on paper these two women seemed to have been caught in such an ugly situation: The eldest, age twenty-four, had six children from the ages of three to thirteen years old; the younger sister, age twenty-three, had seven children, from the ages of five months to twelve years old. While it is possible the census taker got both women's ages wrong, it is also possible they told him their correct ages, which would mean they were both raped as children. Eight of the children were born in the same years, and they each had several more children before 1880, by which time he seems to have died. My aunt's line—nine children—finally left the town, the state, and the name behind. When I told my aunt her great-grandmother may have become a mother at age twelve, she said, "I'm not a bit surprised."

I have been extremely lucky, and luck is important, yet sometimes I have had to just cry when five minutes on the internet can turn up over 500 Mississippi lynching victims on one site, and days of research can result in no information whatsoever on the individuals who were lynched.

Thus, while I will tell you now how Will Campbell came up and fared until the Civil War, I have to ask you to imagine Chloe Curry in the 1850s. If she was fortunate, she knew her mother and perhaps her father as a young child. Her parents were then still young enough to work in the fields and may have even been taken to another farm, along with her brother Allen, to clear an untilled piece of land, or plow fields, plant, or pick. If she was fortunate, she may have known one of her grandmothers, an older woman from Virginia, or South Carolina, who may have hated a new home in Alabama, missing her own ties on the Eastern Seaboard. She may have heard that one of her grandparents was Choctaw or Creek, or indeed, even a parent who had "folks" who were pushed even further west before Chloe was born. If she was not fortunate, she may have only learned sketchy details from her older sister Mariah, or realized something about plantation parentage when her mother became pregnant again when she was a toddler, or later still when the war was on.

By the time she was a ten-year-old black girl, she would have been bringing meals in buckets during the noon hour out to people in the hot sun of an Alabama cotton field, helping to pick the bolls and put them in sacks in late summer and fall when the heat was the same as July. A bell would have rung to signal the time when she should hustle out of the kitchen with her load, and a bell would have rung again when she needed to stop talking to whomever she met in the rows and she would have to hustle to pick up as many buckets as she could carry before the overseer appeared in her path to holler out an order to move faster.

We can know that in 1861 the whites she knew may have expected the war set off in Charleston to be brief and victorious for their side. What she may have made of this we will never know. She was surely told nothing will stop the work. There, near the capital of the Confederacy, the idea that the war could free her may have been remote, the idea that she would live another life without the masters, unthinkable. As it was, we know five years after the war—maybe ten—she was still with the family that probably had a tax form filed for owning her.

4

∞

Horses at the Door
(1852–1861)

William Argyle Campbell was born on March 12, 1852, in Springfield, Missouri, the last of the ten children of Louisa and John Polk Campbell. He would never know his father because near the time of Will's birth the forty-eight-year-old John Polk was waging a losing struggle to keep his own life. As I originally heard it, the father suffered malnutrition and scurvy while crossing the Oklahoma prairie trying to make it back home, and died near Tallequah in the Oklahoma Territory. This tale turned out to be not exactly as told, and perhaps by family elaboration took on a mystery that mirrored the most widely believed story of the demise of his own father, the first John Campbell. Will's grandfather, John Campbell of Virginia, is said to have disappeared fifty years earlier, probably on the Mississippi River, traveling in ill health. Will would grow up with the legend of his father rather than the man.[1]

Will was born in the comfortable home of Springfield's founding father, a structure that went on to have its own storied life. At the time of his birth though, the house was new and the family had just moved in. John Polk Campbell died on May 28 of that year. The father's legend was one that glorified valor in battle, heading for the new frontiers, staking claims where new lands opened up, building homesteads, and keeping the wealth within the blood lines. It was a lot to emulate.

I began my search into Will's life with his little album of sepia-colored photographs. I looked into each of the images in the small picture-frame pages, and began to find people from Missouri and Mississippi, people in the livestock business, farmers, one map-maker, a steamboat that blew up with hundreds of prisoners of war aboard, a card of Confederate generals, and the photo of one teenage girl who remained a mystery for several years.

In the early twentieth century, some wise citizens of Springfield, Missouri, had a series of dinners to which they invited surviving pioneers or their children to come and tell their stories. They recorded what was said. It was primarily through one of those histories that I was able to determine that Will Campbell was my great-grandfather. A first-person narrative of 1907 by Will's older sister, Sarah Rush Campbell Owen, listed the names of the Campbell children. She told the story now taught to school children in Springfield as the history of its origins: How John Polk Campbell, accompanied by his brother Ezekiel, came out to Missouri in 1829 from his home near Columbia, Tennessee, and found a freshwater spring in the southwest part of the state, near which he "blazed" an ash tree with his initials—an accepted method of claiming property at the time. The site is now near Founder's Park in downtown Springfield, on what was once the Kickapoo Prairie.[2] According to an 1883 Greene County history, there was a Kickapoo settlement of "100 wigwams" in the area that is now Springfield, as well as Osage and Delaware settlements.[3] The Tennessee pioneers returned in 1830 with a group including several Campbell brothers and others like Josiah Finley Danforth and William Fulbright, whose family names are now synonymous with the Midwest. The town was founded in 1831, and Campbell gave fifty-three acres of land for its development.[4]

Campbell's granddaughter Lucy McCammon wrote in 1929 that John Polk Campbell was a younger son in a large family, and therefore unlikely to inherit much land, so he had to look elsewhere for his living. He had become a deputy lawman in his twenties, when "Tennessee was trying to rid herself of a noted band of thieves and murderers, and proved himself so resourceful and courageous that a wealthy Nashville man offered him a large sum to hunt his only child, a boy who had wandered off with an unprincipled man." Apparently while on this mission with his brother Ezekiel, they were looking for good places to settle where land was freely available. In this manner they found the spot in southwest Missouri with four springs of fresh water that they came to claim. They got logs to start a cabin and, after finding the missing boy, returned him home.[5]

There are several stories about Campbell and the Kickapoo—one in particular about a chief's son down with a fever, who was aided by Campbell and restored to health. The grateful chief was kind enough to give the white man from Tennessee permission to stay on the land where, over time, he built thirteen cabins and a host of friends and family formed a settlement. While this may be true, we have definitely seen that movie.

Another version holds that the sick nameless Kickapoo recovered and went with Campbell and his brother back to Tennessee, then guided them back to the area that is now Springfield. He became a cherished member of the household and had occasion to save the life of Campbell's wife Louisa. "He killed an Osage who was pursuing Mrs. Campbell. Mrs. Campbell twisted her foot, fell and fainted as she reached her own door. The Kickapoo felled the Osage, carried Mrs. Campbell into the house . . ." and then hugged her little baby, "returned her to the nurse and was gone." They never heard of him again.[6]

While I believe that the Tennesseans may have begun settling in Springfield without incident, it was the 1830 Indian Removal Act that really made that possible. In one legislative blow, Andrew Jackson declared nonexistent all Indian land rights east of the Mississippi. This in effect gave primacy to white settlers everywhere and certainly would have lent a sense of impunity to settlers west of the Mississippi who tried to force Native Americans out of settlement areas. At that time, the Kickapoo and all other Native American groups—notably the Cherokees, Chickasaws, Choctaws, Creeks, and Seminoles—were rounded up and driven West on a forced march. I did not find numbers for each group, but the first to be removed were the Choctaw, 4,000 of whom went west, followed by 2,500 Muskogee, and the Chickasaw, of whom 500 died from smallpox. The Cherokees suffered the most. At first 2,000 went peaceably, but at least 14,000 resisted and, along with 2,000 enslaved African Americans, were marched at gun-point across the country, resulting in 4,000 deaths. Rice growers were packed into the same territory with nomadic peoples from the North, to-bacco and maize growers from the eastern seaboard, and people from cot-ton regions in the Deep South. Some Native people claim that this caused them to give up some two million acres of land in Missouri.[7]

It would have been unavoidable in the year 1832 in Springfield to be unaware of the removal of all these people. It would also have been hard not to notice that by 1835 people driven on the Trail of Tears from points south—Cherokee people from northern Alabama and Georgia—were brought by two primary routes through Missouri: some marched from the Missouri River south to Arkansas through Southwestern Missouri, and others cut across the state right through the region in which Greene County was established.[8] (Just over the state line in what is now Okla-homa were survivors of the Indian Removal from the Miami, Cherokee, Potawatomi, Osage, and other peoples, including those taken all the way from New York.) The Campbell pioneers in Missouri were among the many white settlers in the South and Midwest in a position to have a firsthand view of one of the greatest tragic upheavals in our collective history, and although many gained from this mass relocation, these pio-neers benefited directly.

John Polk Campbell came by his pioneering instincts from the previ-ous two generations of his family. His first American ancestor was Robert Campbell, who came to the outskirts of what is now Charlotte, North Carolina in the 1700s, probably from Scotland, perhaps by way of Ireland and Pennsylvania. The Campbell journey from Scotland may in fact be known to some of the hundreds of Campbells who do that genealogy work, but I chose to pick up their history during the 1700s here in the United States. The ancient Campbell history, according to the Clan Campbell Society of North America, goes back at least to the legendary first ancestor, Smervie or Mervyn, son of Arthur, also known as "the Wild-man of the Woods," in the eleventh or twelfth century. The name came into use in the thirteenth century. Not wanting to work my way from there, I decided I would let the reader look elsewhere for that part of their story. I hope the MacCailen Mor (the Chief of Clan Campbell and the 13th Duke of Argyll) will forgive me.[9]

John Polk's father, John Campbell, was the third of Robert's twelve children and he married Matilda Golden Polk. His marriage to Matilda created a labyrinth of associations between the Campbells and the large tribe that produced James K. Polk, eleventh president of the United States. (Matilda was his aunt.) The Campbell and Polk families managed to settle near each other and intermingle their names across the South and Midwest, from Tennessee to Texas.[10]

So when the second John Campbell was born in 1804, he received the middle name Polk, and when he was about five, the family moved to Maury County, Tennessee. The area was settled by men who received land grants there for service in the Revolutionary War. He and his first cousin James Polk were raised together there. John Polk met and married Louisa Terrill Cheairs, born in 1810, who came from a prosperous slave-owning family in Tennessee of French Huguenot and Scots heritage. They had made their own claims to history, having several men who fought in the Revolution.[11] According to an article written by his granddaughter Lucy McCammon, John Polk Campbell had such a love of Scots lore, music, poetry, and such that the family joked about it. "Mr. [James] Polk remembered this, and at the time of his inaugural instructed his secretary to arrange with the orchestra that was to play at the Inaugural ball to strike up 'The Campbells Are Coming' as John Polk Campbell entered."[12]

It is interesting enough for a middle-aged black woman to have discovered the breadth of this family connection on a website called "My Confederate Kinfolk," but it is almost funny to have been told by any number of people met in the past three years, "You know, you are a sixth cousin to President Polk." The heritage of enslavement being what it is, one does not get surprised so much as amused at having these connections. So many of the founding fathers and early presidents and Supreme Court Justices, for that matter, were slaveholders that they doubtless have scads of black descendants. In the world I grew up in, being eligible for membership in the Daughters of the American Revolution (DAR) would be a joke. The DAR was reviled by African Americans like myself for preaching an elitist version of who built America, and practicing racial exclusivity. The group earned much scorn for refusing to allow African American contralto Marian Anderson to sing in its Constitution Hall in 1939. I am sure though there were many Campbells who were proud that the Springfield, Missouri, chapter of the DAR is named after Matilda Golden Polk. The only value in making the connection between such organizations and their members' black relations is to highlight the hypocrisy of their longtime policy of discrimination.

At the History Museum for Springfield-Greene County, Missouri, there is an interesting photograph taken the day Will Campbell was born in 1852. It is a picture of the exterior of his parents' two-story home in Springfield, and with almost a dozen men, women, and children, white and black, attending eight handsome horses, mostly unsaddled and not tethered to any posts. When I first saw it, I thought this somber formality perhaps attended a funeral. At the same time, the horses seem to be the subject. The window shades of the house are up except for one upstairs bedroom. This is an image not of things as they usually were or of visitors at a prominent household, but a fleeting hour before the horses would be taken back to the stables. It is the only view remaining of a life the Campbells would try to put back together after they were scattered and cast into harsher lives like domestic steeds let loose on the prairie.

Before Will was born, John Polk Campbell had arranged for the construction of the house and hoped to have built a replica of his father's home in Tennessee. The spot he picked was next to a peach orchard that had been part of the Indian settlement. He asked for six rooms, twenty-feet square in dimension, with a fireplace in each room and a central hall. The builder, not being a plantation man, probably did not grasp the grandeur Campbell had in mind. The upper and lower porches did not stand behind stately two-story-high columns as in Tennessee. Evidently when he finally saw it, Campbell was "greatly disappointed." But John Polk Campbell was unable to supervise its construction because he had moved his family to Texas.

This is where the local lore, as told by a Springfield paper in the 1930s, takes on the distasteful reek of nostalgic hokum for antebellum days. The article spins a tale in which Louisa Campbell comes from Quaker stock and is opposed to selling slaves. "When Mrs. Campbell's father died, Mrs. Campbell, here in the west, inherited the family slaves, which were movable—her brothers and sisters in Tennessee inheriting the land and such property." The only problem was that the bondmen and women "were prolific, and she soon had an amazing number," and this became an almost unbearable expense, so Campbell devised a way to keep the people "busy" and let them contribute to their expenses. The story goes that in 1847 he bought large land holdings in Texas to put them to work. This tale ends with a priceless detail: "In Texas, they noticed a film of oil on some of the spring waters—never guessing that years later their land would furnish some of the richest oil wells of the world."[13]

I will come back to that bit about oil later. The pity is not so much that this was printed in 1932 as the truth, but that it lasted so long that someone repeated it to me a year or two ago. In the version I heard, the Campbells started with only four or five of these prolific Negroes. Court documents in the Springfield County Archives tell the story of a family that had no problem with slavery, jealously guarded their slaves, and even sued in-laws to get them back or be paid for them. The most astounding event is in court papers from 1836, when John Polk Campbell was charged with kidnapping. The papers state that on April 1, 1836, John Polk Campbell, "with force and arms, unlawfully and forcibly did seize confine and kidnap a Certain free woman of Color, Calley Easter . . . with the intent to cause the said Easter a free woman of color . . . to be sold as a slave against the will of . . . Easter." The inference could be made that he didn't have nearly as big a problem with selling African Americans as he did with seeing them free.[14]

In 1850 Campbell was holding thirty-three slaves in Texas, while local lore has the number at ninety. Texas land grants suggest he was homesteading land that had recently become available at a cheap price in Cass County in the northeast corner of the state. The Campbells had with them five of their children, one grandchild, and three white hands. On the 1850 census, Campbell valued his real estate in Texas as worth $7,000, a value that today could be put anywhere from $154,000 to $1,800,000 depending on the yardstick.[15]

Cass County was settled by slaveholding cotton farmers from other states, and though it may not seem now like the most direct route, people and goods came to northeast Texas by steamboat from the Mississippi and Red Rivers east of there. The county seat in antebellum days was the booming port of Jefferson on the Big Cypress Creek, where boats pulled in from St. Louis and New Orleans. One of the main streets there is named after President Cousin Polk, and its denizens still have quite an affinity for the bad old days of southern culture—the town boasts a Gone With the Wind Museum, and a "Tara in Texas" weekend when many of the white women in town get out their hoop skirts.[16]

According to a letter written by Sarah Rush Owen and published by a popular historian, William Elsey Connelly, John Polk Campbell did trade in Texas and Northern Mexico, and at about the time Texas became a state, took work laying out a road from white settlements into the Mexican state of Chihuahua. For this work, Campbell expected to receive a land grant in Texas. Owen said her father "spent much of his time on the plains, which he crossed and recrossed many times."[17] In 1846 Missouri Governor John C. Edwards asked Colonel Alexander Doniphan to head up troops for war with Mexico, and Campbell went with them. He took with him a family slave named Ab. Of course it was John Polk Campbell's cousin President James Polk who decided the United States should send troops to support the new state in battles with Mexico.

This regiment marched 3,600 miles from Fort Leavenworth into Chihuahua. That journey sounds pretty daunting in any description one can read. Owen says her father fought in the February 1847 Battle of Sacramento, though the enlistment contract for the Missouri men had expired by then. Indeed Campbell's participation is mentioned in Doniphan's official reports. On March 1 the U.S. troops took control of Chihuahua. While most of Doniphan's men headed home by marching east through Mexico to Monterey and took boats to New Orleans, Campbell was reported to have returned—safely—overland through Texas.[18]

This account contradicts Owen's dramatic story of her father's demise, which Connelly printed as a footnote on Campbell's life, and has become part of his myth. I quote it only because I could not do justice to this spin-off of the first Kickapoo tale:

Father reached the Texas frontier in a starving condition after leaving Colonel Doniphan, having been continually pursued and harassed by hostile Indians. He was finally rescued by a Kickapoo Indian, whom he had many years before saved from freezing to death, but who had killed a Delaware Indian and fled to the wild western tribes. He recognized my father instantly, furnished him and his party with food, and guided them safely to the Texas frontier settlements. In the hardships of this trip, he contracted scurvy, from which he never recovered, and from the effects of which he died . . . [19]

Campbell made it home at least once to where they lived in Texas, as Owen recalled him returning with various Mexican souvenirs, including a gift from a wounded Mexican officer whom, she said, he saved from being trampled to death. (Campbell seems to have been saving people's lives on a "right regular" basis.) The enslaved body man, Ab, also made it back. Campbell was also home in Texas long enough to be counted in November on the 1850 census and to father his tenth child, Constantine, who was born and died there in 1849. By this time, their eldest son, John Nathaniel Campbell, then 18, had gone to Yazoo County, Mississippi, to start farming land the old man had bought in land grants dating back to 1841.[20]

Here the Campbell mythology picks up the tale about moving the slaves to Texas and carries it forward as a rationale for sending John Nathaniel to Mississippi. According to the 1932 article, John Polk Campbell's health was broken by the war and he wanted to return home, yet he did not want to "abandon" the bondmen and women. "So he bought large plantation lands in Mississippi, sent two of his sons, John and Leonidas Campbell to manage them." I can only imagine the gratitude of the "servants."[21]

These kinds of stories are both fascinating and unsettling. The fact that so many facets of the myth of this pioneer (and by extension, his family) are based on his relationship to the "other Americans" shows me how much these issues are woven into American identity, at least for this generation. No one asked then, "How did you treat the Native Americans? Where do you stand on the issue of buying and selling human beings?" I have taken the time to explore all of the myths surrounding Will Campbell's father because most of the interpretations made of his life that became the myth were propagated by his children and grandchildren. They are important figures in this process because they lived in Springfield, where they were called upon annually in the 1920s and 1930s to contribute to the celebrations of the city's founding. Their role in the creation of these fictitious one-dimensional relations to their "social inferiors" was shaped by too many influences for me to discuss here in any meaningful way. How the Campbell children may have integrated these family stories into their own lives though bears directly on how they may have dealt with Chloe, who acted on her own notion of family valor. These are some of the fairy tales of the American past. The mix of ownership entitlement and victim ideology that arose from the lore of an amiable racial past positioned the rest of us as a menace on the loose without the controls of reservations or de jure slavery. And to some of the Campbell children, the menace was real.

By the fall of 1851, Louisa and the rest of the children were back in Springfield and she was pregnant with Will. Her husband wrote to her on September 4 from Van Buren, Arkansas:

> My Dearest Louisa, I arrived here this morning at 8 o'clock. I'm a little over four days from Springfield. My health has much improved. My arm is well or nearly so. I have nothing to write of importance. It is very dry here. Water scarce on the road.... Your affectionate husband, John P. Campbell[22]

Perhaps he made it home but he journeyed again into Texas. In Owen's papers in Springfield I found a letter written to Louisa by her father, dated October 28, 1851, and posted from Texas. He says he had met up with son John Nathaniel in Vicksburg, Mississippi, and they had done well with their sales—"about 40 mules & horses." He was headed "down [the] Red River" and expected to be in Springfield by December. He signed the letter, "Your affectionate husband till death separates us," a bittersweet note as this was his last journey.[23]

I have never seen any family business records from that period, but from this and other letters I learned that on the Missouri farm they raised mules and horses for sale. Sarah later added hogs to her own business, and perhaps the father had also raised them. Whether John had cotton to sell yet is not clear. If I have correctly transcribed his letter, Campbell and his son had been to Washington, Mississippi, just outside Natchez. One newspaper ad I've seen from 1858 announces the sale of mules from Missouri at the Forks of the Road marketplace in Natchez, Mississippi, indicating at least that the livestock needs of the huge Delta farms attracted Missourians. The Natchez market, one of the country's largest slave markets, offered slaves, cattle, mules, and poultry in one space. "During the winter—slave-selling season—the market resembled a sprawling prison camp, with anywhere from 100 to 500 [human] 'stock' for sale."[24]

When Campbell did reach home, he entered a long period of illness. There is one last story that he went to a mineral spring in Oklahoma and died there, but it is fairly certain he died at home in the new house that had failed to please him on May 28, 1852. His granddaughter Louisa McKenny Sheppard remembered that from his deathbed he called her "Mammy" to him and told her to take care of little Louisa. "She obeyed as long as we were together," Sheppard added.[25]

When I reflect on the horses shown outside the Campbell house the day Will was born, most the same size and all of the same coloring, they seem to be part of one of the Campbell journeys to market. Likely raised by the Campbells, they are lined up and standing still for a photograph, perhaps before venturing the hazards lying between Missouri and the ports of exchange.

By 1853, Louisa Cheairs Campbell had buried not only her husband, but her first two children—both married daughters. Mary Frances Sprouel, who had been an invalid, died in 1853. The eldest child, Talitha McKenny, died in 1848 giving birth to her only surviving child, Louisa Cheairs McKenny. Her father, Elnathon D. McKenny, Springfield's first newspaper editor, moved to Texas and the baby was brought to live with the Campbells. Louisa McKenny became known as "Lulu," which is also how I shall refer to her. Three years older than Will, Lulu still called him Uncle, and sometimes called him her "Uncle-brother."

Lulu was the second secret writer I discovered, after my grandmother. In 1892, under her married name, Louisa McKenny Sheppard, Lulu wrote a memoir of her grandmother and of her own life during the Civil War. She entitled it *A Confederate Girlhood*. (Imagine my files. Two manuscripts by two women who were cousins: *A Confederate Girlhood* and *Chloe's White Child*.) Lulu's fifty-five-page saga was sent to me by another John Polk Campbell, great-grandson of John Nathaniel. I was elated when I saw at the beginning that Lulu had known where Will Campbell was during the length of the Civil War. Even more, she had been part of his childhood.

One scholar has recently shown that during the turn of the century the United Daughters of the Confederacy (UDC) influenced many white women who were Civil War survivors to write down what the group still terms "the truthful history of the War Between the States." The Daughters has origins in Missouri and Tennessee, so I would wager Lulu Sheppard learned of the group early on. Whether or not this initiative gave any motivation to Sheppard beyond leaving a story for her children I do not know, but the manuscript was a Godsend for me. To my knowledge, the manuscript was never published, although I did come upon a recent novel for young readers inspired by the story. I'm not surprised, as an unusual adventure is told in her memoir.

Lulu describes her grandmother Louisa Campbell's family as having brought her up in "comfort and ease." She writes that late in life Louisa told her of her intense loneliness once the Campbells set out to build "a white settlement in the Ozark Mountains, 240 miles from the nearest town." Despite having to adjust to frontier life, which had a variety of privations including substantially fewer slaves, Louisa is described by her granddaughter as a woman whose stories were usually "of the lighter side" of her earlier years.[26] She describes candidly her then forty-three-year-old grandmother, who had borne ten children, though Lulu is obviously very impressed with the elder woman's resilience. Lulu paints a portrait of a woman who was loved by many for very different reasons—

by some for her forbearance and kindness, by others for her frankness and stubbornness.

A young bondwoman named Ann was in charge of Will and Lulu, the two youngest children in the household. When Lulu came to Will's home both of them were toddlers. Ann was charged with teaching them how to behave. Their childhood, Lulu says, was happy and uneventful. When they were school age, they were taught by various "New England schoolmarms." In their free time, which she says was "abundant," they seem to have been able to roam the farmland on their own. Calling herself a tomboy, Lulu says she played with Will and his brothers, probably Thomas and Sam, who were closest to them in age. They all played with the African American children their age. She learned to ride, at first sitting in front of one of the boys in the saddle and, by the age of nine, was "riding wildly about the country on my own pony." She rode with Will and his brothers to check the traps they had set in the woods, and went hunting with them. Judging from his letters, Will remained an avid hunter. He seems to have loved riding and being in the countryside. In later moments, it is easier to see him as the baby of the family and very attached to his mother, but in the early pages of her manuscript, the boys are treated as a group. As the war approaches, though, and the other boys become teenagers, Lulu and Will are still young and still very much under Louisa's care.[27]

The Campbell household had about fourteen bondpeople, ranging in age from two to eighty years of age. Lulu describes her grandmother treating them "with unending patience and consideration." Those for whom I have seen names—Ann, Henry, Ab, Eve, Marina, Mary, and Ellen—had a long-term presence in various Campbell households. The only man listed on the 1860 slave schedule who was old enough to have gone to the U.S.-Mexican War is a forty-seven-year-old male, who may have been Ab. Another man, Wash, turns up on family papers as a runaway, along with a Henry, who may or may not have been the one mentioned above, but there were only two males young enough to have taken off: a twenty-three-year-old and a sixteen-year-old.

The Missouri countryside where Will Campbell was growing up was in bitter division over slavery. This was, after all, the land of many veterans of

"bleeding Kansas." There, in the mid-1850s, John Brown and other abolitionists, known as "jayhawkers," and proslavery "bushwhackers" had a series of murderous clashes before Kansas became a "free" state in January
1861. Many of the white owners of small farms in the counties along the
Missouri River across the state line from Lawrence, Kansas, were embit-
tered by the loss of Kansas, and anxious about abolitionist activity in Missouri. When the war came, many of the young men of these families—like
Jesse James, a contemporary of Will Campbell—ran off to join Confederate forces in whatever ad hoc units they could find, and were widely feared
for their deadly guerrilla raids. However, in the run-up to the war the
Campbell family, having greater wealth than the likes of the James family,
was following the pattern of many planters with the wherewithal to scoop
up land deals in various states and begin setting up homesteads and cotton farms. This was not an entirely new venture for the Campbells. Their
family in Tennessee ran slave-based plantations and Louisa's family, the
Cheairs, were cut from classic planter cloth.

In the 1850s the Cheairs family of Maury County, Tennessee, were in
their heyday and, from that time, Louisa's brother, Nathaniel Cheairs IV,
stands out as the most notable. While he later became known in Tennessee, in part for his Civil War letters, he is something of a figure today
in the state tourism business. His home, Rippavilla Plantation in Spring
Hill, was bought and restored by the Saturn Corporation when it moved
there to make cars. The first time I encountered the story of Rippavilla,
I learned that Cheairs had the walls taken down three times because
the bricklaying did not suit him. This tale seemed to me to epitomize
one kind of misery encountered by the enslaved people who were doing
the work.

The homepage for the plantation tells a longer version of the story in
which Nathaniel's father objected to the younger man's choice of a bride
because her name was Susan. (Cheairs men only married women named
Sarah!) To make the offer of his daughter more enticing, William McKissack II said he would supply for free all of the bricks and slave labor required to build the couple a home. The offer was accepted, and the
father-in-law also gave the couple $5,000 in gold, and the slaves began to
put up the house. With the work more than half done each time, Cheairs

decided first that the walls weren't straight, then that the mortar between the bricks did not please him, and finally, during a winter season, Cheairs thought some of the mortar had frozen. Rippavilla is available for weddings and special events. I noticed the lavish menu for this year's Grandparents Day included a few items that one doesn't often see: Apricot Congealed Salad, a Relish Tray, Chicken Lombardy, Pork Loin with Peach Chutney, Corn Pudding, Summer Squash Casserole, and, naturally, sweetened tea.[28]

I have been to a least a dozen such places now. While this menu has a savory sound to it, and my memories of unusual vegetable concoctions and exquisite baked goods in southern places are dear, the taste for antebellum romance in this country seems a bottomless pit. What is being served up is not only nostalgia for a life of luxury built on chattel slavery enjoyed by precious few people at the time, it is in many respects just fantasy. The fantasy is in part about a cultural refinement that may not have been genuine in any way, but is certainly suspect when you remember that in many southern states laws prescribed the lash for any dispute or disagreement with the enslaved labor force. It is a little hard to consider someone who rises from their Chicken Lombardy dinner and steps outside to whip a screaming human being till her back is raw flesh as having refinement.

The landmark homes I saw in Vicksburg, Mississippi, were becoming flooded on the rainy day that I arrived there. As flooding is a way of life in the Delta, it seemed somewhat lucky to see that reality at work. The homes were soggy outside and inside, dank with the smell of mold. One home on the Vicksburg history route, a National Historic Property that advertises itself as having been voted "Best Antebellum Home" in that town and "A Top Ten Most Romantic Place," boasts a tiny cannonball in the wall from the siege of Vicksburg. I picked up a brochure for accommodations at this faded-grandeur bed and breakfast whose rooms start at $130 in the off-season. You can rent Jeff Davis's room, or "Prissie's Suite," or Robert E. Lee's for that price, but the "Belle Whatling Suite" will cost you more. In Natchez, according to one article, Monmouth Plantation, "just up the hill" from the city's one-time slave market, has been turned into "a luxury hotel where guests can sleep in 'garden cottages' with minibars modeled on slave cabins."[29]

When Sarah Rush Owen married Jabez Owen, they first moved to the Owen's home near her mother in Springfield and then to Tennessee, his home state. There she became accustomed to plantation life. Her in-laws had fifty-eight slaves in 1850. She lived near and was likely a visitor to her uncle Nathaniel's Rippavilla. In 1850 he held fifty-two people in slavery. She also frequently stayed with her aunt, Nancy Cheairs Perkins in Spring Hill. Aunt Nancy, Louisa's sister, was married to Constantine Perkins, a farmer who, according to the 1850 slave census, owned about 106 slaves.[30] In a 1900 chapbook Sarah published, she recalls:

> ... the negroes' rations on the old plantation: The great ovens of nutritious corn bread; the great squares of salt pork, with sweet potatoes packed around it [sic] tight, and covered close; New Orleans molasses, and gallons of buttermilk.[31]

Weekly food rations for slaves were hardly a bounty when they reached the cabins: roughly three to five pounds of salt pork, and a peck of cornmeal. Sometimes there was an addition of sweet potatoes, molasses, and buttermilk, and occasionally some game. Some were allowed to keep vegetable gardens, which certainly would have been needed, and owners and slaves alike fished and trapped. The largest meal of the day was the noon meal, which workers took in the field, from buckets brought by children.[32]

In the early 1850s, the eldest Campbell son, John Nathaniel, was in no such showplace in Yazoo, Mississippi. He had married Mary A. Roane Danforth and set up house, calling his cotton plantation "Valley Home." They had also become the guardians of Mary's younger brothers, James and Josiah Danforth. (Their father had gone to the Gold Rush and died out West.) The homes in the Delta were a lot more modest than the palaces of Tennessee or Natchez. It seems to have taken each of the Mississippi Campbells some time to even furnish their homes, I would guess owing to their distance from the shops of fine cabinetmakers and the like. One of my sisters has told me that when she was a child in the early 1940s and she heard that her grandmother grew up on a plantation, her only reference was *Gone with the Wind*, and Georgia had to disabuse her of the notion that her Silver Creek home was grand. She described something quite normal, perhaps smaller than her own Kansas City house, with one bedroom, a sitting room, and a separate kitchen. John Nathaniel's home likely had more than one bedroom but was probably built on the standard story-and-a-half "dog-trot" model of the Delta.

Though old man Campbell may have sent his son to Mississippi for the "benefit" of the slaves, there is no mystery as to why John Nathaniel might have been willing: Cotton plants were creating millionaires in the Delta. By the 1830s more than half of the country's cotton was raised in Alabama, Mississippi, and Louisiana. Natchez, the capital of King Cotton's showy excess had, by 1860, "more millionaires per capita . . . than any other town in the nation."[33] If they were taking mules to market anywhere on the southern end of the Mississippi River, the Campbells would have seen for themselves the riches being reaped from cotton.

Slaveholders were moving into Mississippi at this time in great numbers. The empty blocks and storefronts seen today on Yazoo City's one-time main street, rising up a gentle hill from the former steamboat landing, belie what was a small but fast-growing center of commerce and shipping when cotton was king. In the decade when John Nathaniel Campbell moved there, the county was becoming one of the richest in the state (contrasted with later years when it became one of the poorest), and in 1860 it produced more cotton than any other county in Mississippi. That John Polk Campbell already had land there must have seemed good fortune indeed.[34] "From 1830 to 1860, the slave population of Mississippi rose from just over 65,000 to more than 435,000, an almost seven-fold increase."[35]

Despite the lore that the Campbell parents could not condone selling slaves, John Nathaniel and Leonidas did sell them. John Nathaniel either gave his people some "prolific" pills or bought some because he amassed a considerable number—always over fifty and sometimes over one hundred—as he built his plantation.[36] John consulted Leonidas on setting prices for slaves when they were going to sell some. Though John was the oldest, like the other siblings in the family, he consulted Leonidas in business matters. Leonidas was the worldly businessman who, according to family papers, kept an office in New Orleans for decades and traveled much of each year on various enterprises ranging from cotton to railroads. Lulu Sheppard says that he was usually away at "other plantations" (I'm not sure where) and traveling to New York City, and even Liverpool, "in the interest of his cotton business in New Orleans."[37]

John Nathaniel was the more typical antebellum cotton farmer who spent most of his time at the farm, leaving annually to take his family to watering holes in the worst heat of summer. He homeschooled the Danforth boys and rewarded good work with days to hunt ducks and squirrels. Still, both men seem to have been sufficiently fashion-conscious to shop in larger towns and cut the kind of figure described by Margaret Mitchell some eighty years later. Both were handsome, and John's appearance and letters show he was concerned with image and style.

John's correspondence sometimes attempted descriptive flourishes, not always successfully, and in one 1853 letter to Aunt Nancy, he poked light fun at the affectation of Yazoo citizens mixing new styles with old items in their wardrobes. His spelling is awkward but I think the meaning is clear:

> Our little community is once more radiant with life & gaiety[.]
> the summer fugitives have returned to their homes . . . with new
> fashions new Equipage & the last touch of the Parisian manors in-
> troduced in to Yankey Land—But if you ever spend a few weeks
> here, in Miss[issippi], you will say, indeed Miss has changed very
> much—alas! I must say No! although we hav [sic] a great fancy for
> the last touch of the fashion. . . .[38]

He describes himself and his wife as "plain people" with the odd ending that they were always "glad to see our neighbors & visit our friends at a reasonable distance." I think this last bit was a joke, but it's hard to tell.

Much of the mail the siblings exchanged during this time has to do with the probate of their father's will, which caused all of them as heirs to be besieged with claims for years to come. While they waited to be able to sell some of his land or otherwise exercise their rights as heirs until after the Civil War, they dealt with an endless stream of cases that pulled one or the other into court in Missouri and Tennessee.[39]

This situation may have precipitated an arranged marriage for Sarah Rush Campbell to Jabez Owen in 1855. She was seventeen, and he was about twenty-three years old.[40] Sarah is the third writer I found. Years after her marriage she started writing stories and wrote a novella with a main character also named Sarah, and built the background for the character around facts similar to her own. The manuscript suggests a tale of young marriage that perhaps was not shared with her siblings. In the novella, a family friend relates that Sarah was married off in an arrangement "concocted by her mother to prevent a lawsuit," which then "closed up without judge or jury. The suffering caused them both could well have been dispensed with [had they not been forced together]."[41]

In another manuscript chapter, written in Owens' hand in a sermon composition book, the character Sarah recalls a trip with an uncle and perhaps an aunt, presumably to middle Tennessee. The story says, "One of the saddest things about her going down to the [iron] Furnaces—was the fact, she was taken for the purpose of making a match, between she and the young manager."[42] In this romantic novella the young lady fell in love with someone else but, on her return, her mother's mind was made up. "I had been at home only a short time, when my Mother began urging me to marry Phillip . . . I hated Phillip. . . . My Mother continually upbraided me; talking to me of things I could not understand."[43]

The novella describes a young woman unable to abide her husband because of his "coarseness," who tried to "refine him," though it was hopeless because he had been "indulged, uncontroled [sic] naturally grew idel [idle], tyrannical and vicious."[44]

There are some grounds for believing she may have married someone with a vicious temper. Owen's father, also named Jabez Owen, was head of a sprawling household that lived in an interesting 1808 house called Forge Seat. Now a large, handsome national historic landmark, the Owens bought it sometime in the 1850s. An article from a local Tennessee library says that after the Owens moved in, "Jarvis" Owen stabbed his brother "Big Dick" to death during a family quarrel. Is Jarvis a corruption of Jabez? I have not been able to find a Jarvis Owen, but in 1850 the eighteen-year-old

Jabez did have an older brother named Richard, then thirty-three, who was dead two years later. The library document on Forge Seat luridly reports that "the blood stains on the floor are still visible."[45]

As a new bride, if she discovered that her husband was indeed capable of such rage, it is easy to imagine this Campbell teenager becoming furious with her mother Louisa over pushing her into such danger. It goes a long way to explain the fact that, as a writer, she had scathing criticism for the heroine's mother, unmitigated by any warm relationship shown elsewhere in the story.

All of this, which I found long after reading the family papers, made more interesting one of John Nathaniel's 1855 letters to their Aunt Nancy, full of ruminations on the marriage. First, he says that Sarah married without speaking to him about it, and that if she has "don badly," he does not have the added burden of feeling he abetted the match. He is impatient about hearing any "sighs" over it until he has learned the facts. One of the most amusing lines in the letter is his feeling that Sarah was, in a sense, "of age" when "most Ladies of other times marry & indeed if they are not at school nor are authorists I can't see but Little else they can do." While it does suggest that, to his knowledge, there were plenty of women authors, which is cheering, one can certainly see in his conclusion why a women's movement was aborning. He admits to not knowing Jabez Owen, but by some southern extra-sensory perception, judges him to be a gentleman:

> This short acquaintance is decidedly the worst feature I can see in
> the affair—So far as my acquaintance with Mr. Owen will allow
> me to judge I take him [to] be a gentleman who has been . . . in
> respectable & independent circumstances. He is decidedly a man
> of elivation & dignity of manner & I was led to infer he was a
> man of pasible education & an independent fortune—I take
> Rush to hav some discretion & much good sence . . . [46]

In the same letter, he apologizes for the fact that creditors were dunning Nancy's husband for debts claimed against his sister, but pleads that he is unable to pay them. He says he was in a situation of "great stringency in monetary affairs." One problem already plaguing his prospects that spring was a lack of rain during one of the driest years he had seen in Mississippi. The next year he writes about trying to get money due their mother from Texas, though it is not clear whether this was rent or cash from a crop or land sale. In any case, the Texas land continued to be an asset.[47]

Sarah may have felt it useless to complain to anyone but her aunt Nancy. It's hard to say she made her peace with her situation though. In Owen's novella, the character Sarah suffers guilt for her indifference toward her husband, calls her marriage "sacreligous," (sic) and makes several references to being forced "too soon" into motherhood, and "the horror of . . . unwilling motherhood." This last item, like her anger at her mother, seems out of step with mainstream sentiment for the Victorian era when the novella was most likely written. I have to give her credit for being able to face her ambivalence at the birth of most of her children.[48]

Sarah Owen's first child, Mary Frances Owen, was born in 1855 in Missouri, according to the census records. The Campbell Family records put the date a year later. Felix Grundy Owen, her second child, was born in 1857 in Missouri. The fictional Sarah wanted nothing to do with each of her first two children when they were born. "When the baby came I refused to look at it, or have anything to do with it. I refused to take medicine, and often nurishment." [sic] The fictional father also rejected at least the first child in a rage over its "coloring."[49]

Political issues rarely appear in the Campbell family letters, but it is worth mentioning that as they exchanged letters in 1857, a court case that came to be known as the Dred Scott Case was decided in their home state of Missouri. It gave greater impunity to the Campbells to take their slaves wherever they wished—which they did regularly—without fear of having to lose them by entering free states. The case determined that blacks were "beings of an inferior order," had no rights that "white men were bound to respect," and were subjects for commerce—property. The nationally known case articulated a world view that dominated life in Yazoo County and Mississippi throughout the lives of Will Campbell and Chloe Curry.

Along these lines, in 1856 and again in 1859, Louisa Campbell went to court to get back two of her slaves or their value in cash. And in addition to these suits refuting any notion that she had a repugnance for the selling of slaves, they suggest she didn't worry much about getting along with either of her sons-in-law. First she sued Dr. Samuel Sprouel, her late daughter Mary's widower, over a fourteen-year-old mulatto girl named Margaret. His statement to the court was that he and his wife had been given this girl by John Polk Campbell when they married in Texas (in 1849), and that his father-in-law did not say the girl was on loan. Margaret had been in his home for five years. Louisa's claim was mainly based on the fact that she was her husband's heir, and she said she was owed $1,000, though the young woman was valued at $800. It didn't seem to me to be much of a claim, and I believe it was thrown out, but I was struck by Sprouel's account that Leonidas rode out to Sprouel's farm and then snatched up the girl while she was on an errand and put her on his horse. Sprouel took off after him, caught him, and got the girl back.

Three years later Louisa sued Jabez Owen, who was married to her daughter Sarah, over another fourteen-year-old enslaved girl, Puss. Owen responded that he had gotten the girl three years earlier, a year after his marriage. This case seems very strange as Sarah and Jabez lived practically down the street from Louisa. All of these handwritten documents were very difficult to read, but it seems as though Louisa won this one. I think it only fair to say that unpleasant as Owen may have turned out to be, as a latecomer to Springfield he must have been at a political disadvantage against the founder's widow.[50]

In Mississippi, John Nathaniel must have had some good crops since the time he was claiming financial distress. In 1860 he reported to the census that he had $40,000 worth of real estate and $70,000 in other personal assets. By today's standards, he was certainly one of those made rich by cotton; the land now would be worth conservatively $880,000 and his bank account anywhere from $1.5 million to $18 million. At the time, farmers in the Delta were still trying to clear land for cotton. In 1860, only 28 percent of the privately held land such as the Campbells' had been cleared. Among farmers, perhaps the most common dread (though only one of many) in the area was flooding. There were few levees to slow down the spring overflow of all the Mississippi's tributaries across the plowed and planted fields on the Delta's alluvial plain.[51] In June 1859 Leonidas wrote about planting corn in a flooded section after the water had gone down three-and-a-half feet on the creek. Though that sounds like a pretty serious flood, he happily reported having 400 acres of good cotton coming up. The Campbells sent many letters then by steamboat captains rather than riding the twenty miles to the Yazoo City post office. This loose-knit, free-delivery system and other improvisations would stand them in good stead when all postal service ceased during the war.[52]

With the election of President Abraham Lincoln, seven states seceded from the Union—South Carolina, Georgia, Louisiana, Mississippi, Florida, Alabama, and Texas. Southerners began to set up a provisional government in Montgomery, Alabama. An undated Campbell letter that seems to be from this period concerns selling some of the bondpeople as well as some land. It is hard to know if the intended sale is simply a part of the end of the year routine with the Campbells, as with many slaveholders, or a transaction in anticipation of war coming. In any case, John wrote to his brother Leonidas in Springfield with two lists of bondmen and women selected for sale. John seems to have advocated selling as few slaves and as little land as possible:

> Dear Le
> This is an old list I drew off last year to giv in taxes & other purposes the alterations I have made in it makes it rather unsightly but I think you will understand it—Whether you send me a list of all the names with their respective value attached, or the aggregate amount you are willing to take for all the Negroes specify what you are willing to take per acre (& not the [w]hole tract) for the land & what you are willing to take for the 37 Negroes. . . .
>
> Your Brother
> JN Campbell[53]

The larger list holds ninety-four people: forty-six males and forty-eight females—including almost all of those on the list for sale. Their list of thirty-seven people for sale confused me because several of these people definitely were not sold. They include fifteen males and twenty-two females and range in age from one to fifty-five. The sale group contains at least four whole families, and the preponderance of women are either at the end of their childbearing years or, seemingly, without children. At best there are only three males that are in their prime working ages, and they all seem to be part of the four families. So clearly they weren't selling their most highly valued people to raise a lot of cash in a hurry, but I wonder what kind of money they were trying to raise because this group would still have brought in a sizeable sum.

John wrote his mother, apparently after she visited for the Christmas holidays of 1860. The fact that he describes a hunt for four runaways is not startling. What is surprising is the fact that this flight and the search occurred during an extraordinary snowstorm. On the first night, when the men left, it sleeted so heavily that the limbs of trees were breaking throughout the night. John and the overseer went out in the weather and searched till four in the morning. When he awoke at eight A.M. there were four inches of snow on the ground, and the snow continued until it reached eight inches deep. I would think this is almost unheard of in the Mississippi Delta. He and the overseer went after the runaways:

> "[We] hunted till night with the hope of finding the tracks & then all night again & the next day & the next & could hear nothing of them & I gav [sic] them as lost. . . ."
>
> They all came in yesterday pretty well worn out by the cold & hunger They seem now to be quite satisfied to go to work & behave themselves. I hope if they should ever runaway again, that they will take better weather for it, or at least choose a time at which I will not feel so much uneasiness for them to get my toes frost bit as is the caise [sic] with my self & Overseer both.[54]

The fact that Campbell did not find the four men was par for the course. According to historian Stephanie Camp, owners often made unsuccessful searches. "Alone or in teams and sometimes with dogs, planters pursued truants ruthlessly. . . . generally such 'hunts' had 'no Luck' in locating their prey. So long as they stayed within the parameters of their local knowledge—as fugitives to the North could not do—truants were surprisingly successful at evading capture."[55] Campbell's comment that he "could hear nothing of them" may indicate checking with the common sources of information: the patrols of white men who monitored the roads around plantations for runaways; other blacks, who often helped to sustain truants with food; or favor-seeking blacks who used information on truants to their advantage. An example of this last resource is the man who betrayed James Patterson to the posse at Silver Creek. Nevertheless, most people who took off suffered both from exposure and hunger, such as Campbell reports of the men who left his place. And all of these flights into the local area informed people about their immediate environs, information that became essential for successful escape.[56]

The storm was followed by rain and more snow. John complained that the weather had cost him three-weeks work, that the women had not been out of the slave quarter in two weeks, and that the men had only worked about three days in that amount of time. Even before the snow, he said, he had been working in mud and water "laying off ditches" and had suffered chills and colds all winter. I was amused to read that he thought acting as if immune to the effects of exposure was a facet of the stubborn Campbell character. Evidently he traveled to New Orleans each year at that time in order to get his pay for the crop and then sent his mother, and possibly others in the family, a share of the income.

When John wrote to his mother, he was anxious to hear whether she had made it home safely, given the weather. Presumably sometime after Louisa's return, her sixth child, James Cheairs Campbell, then twenty-one years old, had a bad fall from his horse and died from the injuries. I've learned nothing of James except that he seems to have been the basis for a minor figure in Sarah's novella. Louisa Campbell was just that much more handicapped in taking care of her family without this grown son. She had at home now two adolescents—Tom, eighteen, and Sam, sixteen, and two youngsters, Lulu, twelve, and Will, who was nine.

On April 12, 1861, the first clash of the Civil War took place at Fort Sumter in Charleston, South Carolina, and the news must have spread through the streets of Springfield by many an anxious local. The communities of Missouri were already experiencing division over what they would do when that day came. The state government was completely divided. The Campbells seemingly had little debate over the issue, as Louisa's brother-in-law Junius was the only Union man in the clan.

Louisa's brother, Nathaniel Cheairs IV, formed the 3rd Tennessee Volunteer Regiment for the Confederate side, and near St. Louis, General Sterling Price formed the Missouri State Guard with the hope of assisting the Confederacy as well. Louisa Campbell must have known she would have two teens ready to ride off any day. The presence of Union soldiers coming into St. Louis presented her with another problem: the bondmen and women in her household may have been thinking there was a chance for freedom if they could get to that city. Since it was the family's habit to take several of the "servants" on trips east to St. Louis and Tennessee beyond, at least one or two would have been familiar with the roads.

In June two of the bondmen took off. In all likelihood, she first mounted a search with her sons. Immediately though, she made a draft for a wanted poster or newspaper ad. The first missing "boy" was a thirty-year-old named Wash, said to be about five-foot-ten-inches tall, 160 lbs. and of a "light copper" complexion. She said he had "rather heavy hair inclined to be busy," and described him as a person with a sad demeanor. The second, Henry, twenty-two, was five-feet-four-inches in height, heavy set with a dark copper color. The ad states that a six-foot, twenty-six-year-old bondman named Luke belonging to William Fulbright was probably with them. This episode may have guided her thinking on getting her bondpeople out of Missouri, which, as a border state, was going to be a difficult place to try to hold on to them.[57] Within weeks, Springfield was under siege as U.S. troops marched into town. Will's childhood in his hometown came to an end that July.

5
∞

Behind Confederate Lines
(1861–1863)

On a Sunday in July 1861 in Springfield, Missouri, Will was at an all-day "basket revival" at the Christian Church with his mother, Louisa, and her granddaughter, Lulu, when Federal troops appeared in the streets. The children had only recently seen soldiers for the first time when local men formed a Union Home Guard and marched in town with fife and drum. The youngsters greatly enjoyed these summer revivals because of the picnics held afterward in a grove next to the church where everyone feasted from picnic hampers. That morning they were still in church when soldiers in blue uniforms were seen through the open window and at the open doors. "Two men of the congregation arose, and silently pointed out every man present who was a Southern sympathizer," writes Lulu later. "I had not, at the moment, a very clear understanding of this scene, nor that these two men, our friends and neighbors, were now our enemies. Then a tall officer stepped forward with a paper in his hand which he read aloud. . . . All Southern sympathizers, men and women, were directed to come to the public square."[1]

The men who had been pointed out were put under guard and their families followed them. At the square the people were told they would have to sign an oath of allegiance or be taken prisoner. The signing went on until nightfall, when the soldiers decided to let the women and children go home. It was dark by the time Will, Louisa, and Lulu got home.[2]

At the house, Ann, one of the "servants," came running out to inform them that Sam was gone. "Mother showed no surprise and asked no questions," Sheppard recalls, but "went calmly into the house and into her room and closed the door." Ann said that Sam had come running home and asked her to fix a roll of his clothes, and have his horse, Telegraph, saddled. He took "ole Marse's gun off'n the wall" and rode off. The next day Tom packed his horse and left as well.[3]

Lulu describes Sam as a "a sweet-natured, open-hearted youth," who was also impulsive, with a "reckless, daredevil courage." She says he resembled most of the Campbell men with a stocky build, ruddy color, and what she regarded as blunt features, though I have to say they all look tall, slim, and angular in their photographs. This is more like her description of Tom, whom Lulu says, was "tall, hawk-nosed and handsome, like his Mother." Whereas Sam seemed to have left without speaking to his mother, perhaps not to let her forbid him from going, Tom waited to tell her and, according to Lulu, left with her blessing. Tom was a more contemplative sort, regarded as "the brainy one of the family; bookish, quiet, very reserved." They were equal, she said, in possessing "absolute fearlessness," a trait she thought was characteristic of all the Campbell sons. If Louisa Campbell was upset that the boys went to war, she reconciled to it quickly.[4]

Political events had been heading to this moment since January, when Missouri's proslavery governor, Claiborne Fox Jackson, a former bushwhacker leader, had announced at his inauguration that Missouri should join the Confederacy. Months later when a state convention met to decide on seceding or staying in the Union, it voted down the would-be Rebels. Jackson set up a pro-South militia and asked Jefferson Davis for arms.[5]

The man who would try to stop Jackson's organizing was Captain Nathaniel Lyon, who was in charge of the Federal arsenal in St. Louis. He had fought Jackson during the border wars, and now recruited regiments from the German-American population of St. Louis to surprise Jackson's camp and take his militia as prisoners. But a riot was triggered when the southern sympathizers were paraded through the streets.[6]

Some Federal officers defected to support the Confederate States of America (CSA), notably General Sterling Price. Price, a former governor of the state, got his military title serving with the Missouri troops in the U.S.-Mexican War, and may have known the Campbells. Will Campbell carried a souvenir picture of him in his photograph album. Price was first put in charge of the Missouri Home Guard, which Sam, Tom, and Leonidas joined that month. These three fought under Price for the length of their service in the war.[7] In June all sides had tried to avoid armed conflict by sitting down together. Jackson and Price offered to disband the militia and defend the state against the CSA if the Union would do the same with its occupying troops. Lyon, who seems to have had a real temper, stormed out, declaring war. He came after Price's troops and drove them into southwest Missouri. This was probably the first episode Sam and Tom fought in after joining their cousins and friends in the state guard.

At the time troops came into Springfield, Leonidas, who was away on business, evidently returned and went straight to join Price's troops without seeing the family. Louisa's daughter Sarah Rush Owen and her little family, who had lived nearby, moved to Jabez Owen's home in Tennessee. Owen does not seem to have signed up to fight. At the end of July, a letter from John Nathaniel's wife, Mary, in Mississippi, reached Sarah in Tennessee:

> We cannot but deplore the circumstance and necessity that drives you from your homes. We do not hear any thing at all from Mo. or any of the family. . . . We are in a deplorable condition the whole South but how much better off are we than down trodden Mo. & Md. . . . we must submit to many privations and sacrifice and fight the same Battles and from the same cause as did our Fore Fathers before peace can again reign over our devoted land. . . .[8]

In describing their home situation, Mary says that John was adding on to the house to accommodate more people and that she had been successful in raising both poultry as well as vegetables and sugar cane. She thought they also had sufficient corn and wheat to last for a while. This would be important, she points out, in surviving without supplies they would usually purchase. "Mr. Lincolns Blockade wont hurt us bad. we wont starve at least." She refers to the president as "old Dabe twaddle."[9]

Mary Campbell's optimism that they were better off in the South, her faith in Jefferson Davis, and the comparison she makes to the Revolutionary War are typical of the writings of women at the outset of the Civil War. She also mentions a recent Confederate victory that would seem to be the Battle of Bull Run, an early southern triumph that stunned the North. It's hard to know what news she would have heard by July 28, 1861, when she wrote the letter, but Bull Run was the news driving Union troops in Missouri.

Having pushed Price's army west beyond Springfield, Lyon's troops, numbering about 5,500 according to historian James M. McPherson, occupied Will's hometown. Lulu Sheppard recalls the German-American soldiers under Franz Sigel coming to town and becoming "so troublesome" that Louisa Campbell complained to General Thomas W. Sweeney. Sweeney said that if she would give rooms to two of his staff officers, they would see that her property was protected. A Colonel Mills and a Major Spencer showed up almost immediately, and Spencer befriended Louisa. By the beginning of August, a battle in the Springfield area had become inevitable. The day before that battle, which was at a place called Wilson's Creek, the colonel brought the infamous Nathaniel Lyon to dinner:

> General Lyon was a rough-looking man with good manners. He sat at Mother's right and opposite to me. During dinner he raised his wine glass to Mother, and said, "Madam, you wish us success?" "Sir," she answered with grave dignity, "I am a Southern woman." He looked at her in utter amazement, then said, "And have you sons in the Confederacy?" Mother's fine grey eyes were dark with trouble, as she made answer: "Four," then with a sudden flash of spirit, "and I wish they were fifty and I were leading them."
>
> Some at the table smiled and our friend, Major Spencer, twinkled at me, but General Lyon arose and took her hand as he said: "I hope no trouble is at hand for so brave a woman.[10]

Lyon was killed the next day, the first general to fall in the war.

Louisa had received word by then that John Nathaniel, now twenty-nine years old, was a captain with Mississippi troops and that Leonidas was with Price's army in Missouri. In fact, Leonidas had sent for Ab, known to Lulu as "Mother's colored foreman, a fine trustworthy man," and the man who had gone to the U.S.-Mexican War with John Polk Campbell.[11] At the outset of the war, many southern "gentlemen" officers took "body servants" to do their cooking and washing. According to historian Ervin Jordan, the bodyman's duties included getting up before dawn, preparing breakfast, cleaning uniforms, polishing boots and swords, and maintaining the weapons and quarters of the planter. In many places, these men were expected to sing and provide entertainment and, more important, "body servants . . . tended their wounded owners (or escorted their bodies home) and occasionally fought in battles."[12]

Later on the day of the dinner with General Lyon, Lulu and Will were sent several miles out of town to their Uncle Junius Campbell's farm for safety's sake, as it was assumed fighting would be very close by their own home. Junius home was five-and-a-half miles from the battle, and when they heard the first cannon the next morning, August 10, everyone ran outside. During the confusion, Will, Lulu, and several other children slipped away. From atop some small haystacks they "watched the dense columns of smoke as they arose," and listened to the thunder of the cannons. The two barely spoke until, Will exclaimed, "I reckon Brother Lonnie is shooting those cannons." Though Lulu says Leonidas had attended military school, I have not seen any clues as to its name or location. Despite the fact that Lyon's forces were outnumbered two to one, he attacked, making the further error of dividing his troops. At about four in the afternoon, a cloud of dust began to roll toward the Campbell children and they ran to hear if there was news. A rider on horseback came along "hoarsely shouting . . . Hurrah for Price! Hurrah for Price!"[13]

Will and Lulu returned to Junius's home to find huge food preparations on and a makeshift hospital in the making. Each side had about 1,300 casualties. When Sam showed up, his head was "tied up in a bloody rag," but he was "gay and elated." He had been grazed on the head by a saber but was not seriously hurt. At sunset, Leonidas and Tom arrived in search of their baby brother, Sam. Their aunt took linen, bedding, and other first aid help into town. That night, she and Louisa went with an ambulance to the battlefield. They picked up as many wounded as could be carried to the Campbell house, "and did not return until morning."[14]

When Will and Lulu returned to their own home the next day, the scene was much the same, the house having become a hospital. "I do not know how many men we had, but there were cots and pallets everywhere, filled with Union and Confederate men, many of whom were past all aid. I was given my duties at once," Lulu recalls. Many of the dead were buried in and around the Campbells' peach orchard and in their family cemetery.[15]

At the same time that war arrived in Springfield, a controversy was brewing across the country about whether slaves could be confiscated as property by northern troops to hamper the South, which used slave labor to continue agricultural work, build fortifications, and eventually to do the industrial work. Two unexpected developments complicated this picture for southerners in general, and for the Campbells in Missouri.[16]

In Hampton, Virginia, in May of that year, several slaves had escaped a plantation and took refuge behind the Union lines at Fortress Monroe, commanded by Major General Benjamin Butler. When the owner appeared and asked for their return, Butler declared them "contraband of war," refused to return them, and assigned them work in the camp. This led to a flood of fugitives coming into the camp from all over that part of the state, and later, when they could no longer be accommodated inside the walled fortress, they camped on the beach outside. This is a story that I grew up with, as my own great grandfather, enslaved in that town, was able at that time to escape, rescue his wife, mother, and children, and get them to the fort. This was the story of my community's ancestors and an integral chapter in the building of my hometown. Its relevance to the Campbells is that the frustrated Union General John C. Fremont, who Lincoln had put in charge of the Western Department (mostly Missouri), under fire for the loss of Wilson's Creek and half of Missouri, declared martial law, promising execution for guerrillas caught behind Union lines, freeing the slaves of southern supporters, and claiming the right to confiscate their property.[17] While this edict turned out to be the worst kind of political bomb for Lincoln to have to defuse, it was the first of several unusually volatile edicts issued in Missouri.

Louisa's response was immediate. About the same week, she packed off Will and Lulu and fourteen slaves to Mississippi. Given her two earlier runaways, she probably did not want to take the chance that her household staff could simply walk out of the house and go to the nearest soldiers to be liberated. She kept only Ellen and Aunt Eve with her. Lulu calls Ellen "a strong dour woman, not a general favorite," and says that she taught the woman how to read and do arithmetic. Ellen worked as a nurse after the battle of Wilson's Creek and was later taken by the Federals to be a nurse in an army hospital. Then the Campbells lost track of her. Aunt Eve fits the slave census description of an eighty-year-old bondwoman held by Louisa, who some months later sent the woman to her daughter, allowing her to retire, temporarily. When Louisa returned after the war, Ellen came to work for her again and was still living in Springfield in the 1880s, at more than one hundred years of age.[18]

Fremont's Missouri proclamation, even though it would be rescinded by Lincoln in September (and Fremont removed from command), made very tangible an outcome of the war that both sides tried to deny—freedom for African Americans in captivity.[19]

Louisa accepted an offer to take the children and slaves south from a "cousin" by marriage, Major Daniel Dorsey Berry, a merchant and farmer, and the richest man in Greene County. Berry's first wife was one of the Campbells' Polk cousins, and his second wife was the widow Letitia Danforth, John Nathaniel's mother-in-law. Major Berry, who was transporting several dozen of his own slaves as well as dozens of horses and mules to his plantation in Arkansas, offered to take Will and Lulu that far. Will's brother Thomas and their cousin Wallace Blackman obtained leave from Price's troops to escort them.

> So we were hurriedly gotten ready. Mother, as usual, was bustling and cheerful, and it was not until she put her worn old willow mending basket in my luggage, and said, "Lou, take care of Will,["] that I realized something of the heartache of her parting with the last of her children. I was

heartbroken over leaving her myself, but no loss of self-control on my part seemed possible in the face of that calm acceptance.[20]

Lulu says, though, that the "colored people" carried on. They must have, not only to be parted from Miss Lucy, but also from a chance of freedom, as well as everything and everyone they knew. Yet, for most of them, this was probably not the first time they were taken from a home. Lulu and Will rode in Major Berry's carriage, reportedly also loaded down with some of the family silver and "the best quilts." The two teenage soldiers followed on horseback, and the blacks rode in covered wagons. Soon they crossed the White River at Forsyth, Missouri, near the Arkansas border and camped there for several days in order to make tents and better organize their caravan. The trip seems to have taken somewhat more than a month. They camped several times. At other times, particularly if the weather was bad, they paid a household for some of them to sleep in the home. They carried chickens, eggs, and butter, supplemented by game shot by Will, Tom, and Wallace, and Lulu's "mammy," Mary, cooked. Their route took them through many swamps and across muddy creeks. At least once they suffered a wreck when the mules slipped on an old wooden bridge that broke, and sent the animals a long way down into muddy water. Fortunately, the mules survived.[21]

During the days of riding Lulu learned that Tom Campbell was studying the law with hopes of going to New York City to continue his law training in 1862. On Sundays, Berry read to everyone from the Bible and "the negroes would sing their old spirituals."[22]

On September 18, 1861, Price's men fought in the Battle of Lexington in Missouri. They achieved a victory by using hemp bales as mobile fortifications, rolling them forward while under fire, thereby gaining close proximity to Union troops. Some of the Confederate re-enactors claim this to be the first occasion when land mines were used. I spent a foolish amount of time unsuccessfully trying to check this out because Lulu Sheppard's memoir says that during this battle when "my uncle was seriously wounded by the blowing up of a mined embankment, Ab [the Campbell bondman] went out under fire and carried his unconscious master to safety."[23]

By the end of 1861, there was no more federal mail service in the South, so when any of the Campbell brothers were injured, family members would not hear of it sometimes for months. The letters have only scant mention of these events, and while this family continued to be consistent about writing letters, a once-a-week habit in peace time, the letters went by circuitous paths to their destinations. From 1861 on, the Campbells posted their letters on steamboats for as long as the South had access to the Mississippi. After that, they gave the letters to travelers who dropped them at businesses in different towns, where they were later picked up by relatives. In September and October of 1861, if Leonidas was still in Missouri, it would be possible for his mother to hear of his condition fairly quickly, but they soon both moved south of the Union line.[24]

Will and Lulu journeyed on with the Campbell slaves and their teen-age escorts through Arkansas to the Mississippi River.

> We crossed the river at Memphis. The first city I had ever seen, and the first trains and boats. When we were nearly at our journey's end, my little colored foster-sister, Marina [her "mammy's" daughter], and I managed to lose ourselves. . . . We loitered and picked flowers, so when we came out on the road there was no one in sight. . . .[25]

With some assistance, they managed to get back to their group. Reading this, I was wondering what it must have been like to see Memphis, and trains and boats, for the first time. Though she does not remark on it, to me this presents the moment when Will and Lulu would have had their first glimpse of the enormous scope of this war. They would not only have seen boats, but likely a harbor clogged with boats and material for troops. The next day, they continued south, and were met by their uncle "Jack." John Nathaniel took them to his plantation, "Magnolia," which I think was another farm he had in Carroll County, north of Yazoo.

I did not recognize the name of this plantation from any of the family papers, though I do not think it a fictional name created by Sheppard. Her location of the farm puts it, at the least, on the north end of the Yazoo property and, at the most, closer to Silver City in what is now Humphreys County. This is only slightly north of their main property;

however, that is something like 150 miles south of Memphis. Putting these two facts together, I am inclined to think John had another property much farther north at that time.

The day after they arrived at John's plantation, John Campbell and Cousin Wallace left to return to the army. It was the last time Will, Lulu, or John ever saw Tom. John left also, returning to his unit, probably in one of Mississippi's so-called twelve-month regiments. The men's departure may have hit Will with some force, as he was now no longer with any family that he knew well except Lulu. I imagine he must have been impressed by his brothers-turned-soldiers, proud and maybe envious. It undoubtedly added to the sense of exile that he and Lulu found themselves under the care of an obviously very unhappy Mary Campbell. Her situation is easy to grasp also as this woman was suddenly in charge of the farm, seven children, and seventy-five to one hundred hands. Not to minimize the amount of assistance she had, it still seems easy to imagine that she did not feel up to the task.

Less than three weeks later, on October 25, Springfield was again occupied by the Union army. The home guard was driven out of the town and the Campbell house was commandeered as a Union headquarters. In late September, after pro-Union legislators had refused to secede and disbanded the legislature, pro-Confederate legislators had had a separate convention and declared secession. According to Sheppard, Louisa was forced out of her house altogether and moved in with her brother-in-law's family. She was evicted suddenly, given only a few hours to get out. The records of the Union Provost Marshall of Missouri state that Louisa was informed on October 2, 1862, that the house was being commandeered as a hospital. She was told to take "only personal effects and be out by 8 A.M. the next day." Clearly this suggests she was around Springfield for another full year, or at least back and forth, and that the house was used twice by Union forces. Lulu says a Union general who was a longtime family friend sent two wagons and that she was helped by an elderly African American soldier named Musick who had stayed with her. They put her furniture in the wagons and sent it to friends and relatives. Lulu writes that "a little handful of my own mother's [Talitha's] table silver she carried in her saddlebags until after the war, and I have it to this day."[26]

Years later a local paper in Springfield had a much more colorful version of this eviction. The 1932 rendition claims that Louisa would have been left in her home "unmolested," had it not been "for the articulate patriotism of a vivacious young woman who was staying with her," one Miss Fanny Smith. The story paints a picture of northern soldiers marching past the house and "the irrepressible Miss Smith," standing on the front porch, waving a Rebel flag, "shouting, 'Hurrah for Jeff Davis!' Of course that invited invasion. . . ." The soldiers decided then and there to take the house for a headquarters. Louisa's brother-in-law Junius is in this scene, cautioning Louisa not to say anything. In irritation, she defies him, and exclaims,

> "I don't care if you are a soldier—you are a coward, too, to come way out here and take a widow's home, when there are a lot better houses that are owned by men!"
>
> "Throw her trunk out here," the furious officer told his men, "and let her get what she can in it, and get out." It was a little cowhide trunk, with the hair on the outside. It wouldn't hold much. And so she left her home.[27]

That little cowhide trunk is straight out of a movie from the 1930s. I don't believe a word of it, but I was very glad to have found the clip because it was a bit of melodrama, and a clue to who Fanny Smith might have been. Smith, then twenty years old, is a frequent character in the family letters, and I finally was able to discover that Louisa considered her like another daughter. Clearly they shared vehemence about the southern cause. Smith came to Springfield from Tennessee with her wealthy banker father. Her mother had died, and she was said to have adopted Louisa and on several occasions came to the aid of Louisa and the family. The eviction forced Louisa not only out of her house, but also out of Missouri. She was unable to get a pass to cross the Union lines despite several attempts because she never signed the loyalty oath. The same general who had sent wagons to help her move told her the only solution he could suggest was for her to take "papers of exile from her state" and leave. She gladly took the papers and left the state. That month her brother-in-law Ezekiel Madison Campbell had many run-ins with Union officials; he signed an oath but refused to promise not to help the rebels.[28]

In November the Confederate States of America admitted Missouri, in spite of its divided status, and in December General Price reassembled his troops, set up a winter camp, and converted the Missouri State Guard into the Missouri Volunteers of the CSA. A feud Price had going with Confederate Brigadier General Benjamin McCulloch resulted in Jefferson Davis forming the Military District of the Trans-Mississippi on January 10, 1862, and appointing his friend Major-General Earl Van Dorn to command the Trans-Mississippi. Van Dorn would have charge of the Campbells' fate for the next stretch of the war. Samuel I. Campbell enlisted as a private in the Trans-Mississippi (the 3rd Missouri Company) on January 10, 1862. Thomas signed up, also as a private in the same company, on March 1, 1862, in Cove Creek, Arkansas. According to records in the National Archives, Leonidas went in as a major in the 3rd Missouri, soon being promoted to lieutenant colonel, and John became a captain in Company I of the 30th Mississippi Company.[29]

As the New Year began, Louisa left Missouri and headed for Searcy County, Arkansas, where some of the Springfield families had moved. In Arkansas, she visited the home of Major Berry, who had two sons fighting with the Campbell boys. I have often wondered if Lulu meant to write that Louisa went to the *town* of Searcy in the eastern part of the state, rather than Searcy County in the western half. The county by that name was famously divided over the war and was often considered traitors' ground by the Confederacy. More important, it was a dangerous place to live during the war, frequently suffering raids from bushwhackers who looted and pillaged the county. The Berrys, whom she was visiting, lived in the eastern Delta region of the state, holding two plantations in eastern counties. Whether she traveled across the state to the Berry home or lived nearby, she had a meeting of the minds with Letitia Berry. The two decided to pack up whatever medical supplies they could and travel to the Missouri men's battle sites with their tiny makeshift hospital.[30]

Will and Lulu had no word from Louisa, and would hear no more of her for two years. Sheppard later says this part of the war was the hardest for her to endure. "Will and I were left very much alone, and we were a desolate little pair," says Sheppard. "We did not hear from Mother and, as time went on, we ceased to look for her." The bondmen and women who had come with them to Mississippi were sent to "distant quarters," which I would assume to be Yazoo. Mary Campbell did not let Lulu run around being a tomboy. Will was allowed to roam freely on his own, and so he saw a lot less of her. Still, she said, they "clung to each other as closely as we could. Whenever the weather was good, we used to sit under the big Chinaberry trees and talk. I grew expert in making up stories to entertain him."[31]

As the other members of this family found themselves scattered by the war in different directions, by fate Sarah Rush Owen was also kicked out of her new home. In January 1862, her husband, Jabez, died of pneumonia at age thirty in Maury County, Tennessee. She was twenty-four and had just given birth to John Jay Owen, her fourth child. As soon as she was able, she fled her in-laws' home. A published letter from 1907 includes her account of this period.

> I was left a widow at the age of twenty-four, with four children, the eldest six years of age, the youngest a few days old, five hundred miles from my beloved Ozark mountains, all my possessions being twenty dollars in Confederate money. For many months I lived in a lonely farm-house between the Federal and Confederate lines, always treated with courtesy and kindness by both armies.[32]

If the novella she wrote based on her life is any indication, her husband borrowed liberally from her aunt and left his plantation deep in debt. Sarah took sanctuary on a piece of property in the mountains that belonged to her and her aunt. From what is said in the novella and in her letters from the period, it seems to have been something of a cabin in the woods—perhaps a family home before the Cheairs family became prosperous.

In February Price had to abandon Missouri and head for Arkansas. At the same time, Louisa and Letitia may have started for Crane Creek in Barry County, Missouri, near the Arkansas line, where there was a skirmish. Almost surely unknown to her then, her brother Nathaniel Cheairs IV (he of the thrice-built Rippavilla Plantation) was part of a force of 12,000 Confederates left by General Albert Sidney Johnston to defend Fort Donelson in Kentucky during a retreat. They were soon surrounded on three sides by the army of Brigadier General Ulysses S. Grant. When Fort Donelson surrendered, Major Nathaniel Cheairs was taken as a prisoner of war and sent to Fort Warren in Boston, Massachusetts. A century and a half later, tourist sites in Tennessee would advertise that Cheairs was given the "honor" of handing over the white flag to Ulysses S. Grant.[33]

When I first read of Louisa Campbell and Letitia Berry traveling from battle to battle, it seemed somewhat dramatic, like one of the heroic tales they might have read. I, of course, had no idea what the terrain of Arkansas would have been like or the weather. They clearly knew that what they were getting into would be no tale of horseback adventure to save their boys. Another Springfield wife, Mary Whitney Phelps, also fitted out a wagon with supplies and went to the men's first major battle in Arkansas. The first fighting was near the Boston Mountains, and it was winter. They had to deal with fording icy creeks, even if it didn't snow. And it did snow.

Price's army fought daily on its way out of the state of Missouri. After the February 14 skirmish at Crane Creek in Missouri, they crossed into Arkansas and started moving southwest, with the Union army of Brigadier General Samuel R. Curtis on their tails. They rode through snow, sleet, and rain, and the cavalries, of which the Campbells were members, fought another skirmish two days later. By February 20 Price's men had had to give up their temporary headquarters at a place called Cross Hollows, burn it, and then march "in miserably cold weather" to a Confederate supply depot at Fayetteville, Arkansas.

Unable to remove the tons of military stores because of a lack of transportation, McCulloch made everything available to the passing troops. The disorganized system of distribution soon degenerated into looting. Homes and businesses were ransacked and vandalized. The situation grew even worse the next day when McCulloch ordered all remaining supplies destroyed. Unsupervised soldiers set fire to warehouses, some of which contained ammunition. The resulting explosions spread the fire and several city blocks burned to the ground.[34]

During this time, the commander of the Trans-Mississippi, Van Dorn, had to cross Arkansas because he had set up his headquarters in the eastern part of the state. When he got to the mountains he ordered each soldier to carry "only his weapon, forty rounds of ammunition, a blanket, and three days' rations." Ordering a fast march, he left all else and did not account for moving additional supplies. Three regiments of Native Americans from the Five Civilized Nations, mostly Cherokee, joined them.[35]

On March 4 the army—now over 16,000 strong, and much larger than the Union force—marched out of the mountains and northwest toward Bentonville. But the fast pace could not be maintained. "That same day, a late winter blizzard swept across northwestern Arkansas, dropping temperatures and covering the road with ice and snow." To make matters worse, Van Dorn had a wrong-headed battle strategy that could not be implemented. As hundreds of men literally fell out Van Dorn began to lose his numerical superiority.[36]

Union scouts, evidently including "Wild Bill" Hickok, picked up on the Confederates' movement and, on March 7, they suffered in a fierce fight with Union troops. Leaders of two flanks were killed and their men scattered. The Native Americans were shelled by artillery and scattered. Price's troops, including the Campbells, had better luck several miles to the east, pushing back the Union at a junction identified by the Elkhorn Tavern. The next day, however, with all men near the tavern, Van Dorn's army got trapped and ran out of ammunition. The flanking movement had put the Union army troops "between them [the Rebels] and their ammunition wagons" twelve miles away. Major General Franz Sigel, the same man whose troops had occupied Springfield, led 7,000 men onto the field, and the southerners "turned tail and ran."[37]

The two-day battle, now known as Pea Ridge, produced, according to McPherson, about 1,300 casualties on each side. Historian William Shea estimates the Confederate numbers at possibly more than 2,000 and asserts that Van Dorn lied about his losses "to hide the magnitude of his defeat." One of those injured was the Campbell boys' cousin L. C. Campbell (also named Leonidas). It was two weeks before the Confederates could reassemble, after going back through the Boston Mountains to a camp near Van Buren, Arkansas. Van Dorn was then ordered to bring his army across the Mississippi River to back up defense of a major rail crossing in a small town called Corinth, in northwest Mississippi, a journey of about 400 miles by my rough guess. They made at least part of this trip by river. Shea reports that the head of the army began to board steamboats on the White River at Des Arc, Arkansas, on April 6. Had they been able to get there sooner, they would have provided back-up for the southerners at the battle of Shiloh, but they did not.[38]

Living in Mississippi, Will and Lulu are apparently uninformed about specific battles going on in other states. Lulu Sheppard wrote of this period of their exile in Mississippi in an idyllic reminiscence of plantation life. Top on her list of delights was African American song:

> As evening came, we would wait for the first twang of the banjo from the quarters, then the high sweet notes of the fiddles, followed by the deep organ tones of the African men's voices, mingling in the delicious unison with the softer treble of the women. The innate instinct for vocal harmony is a marvelous racial trait. The tiniest shaver can strike in and "counter," as they call it, with no training at all. I can still hear the rich volume of those two hundred or more voices in such songs as "Roll Jordan," "Dem Charmin' Bells," "Travel on, for de day's most gone," and the indescribable weird pathos of: "Go down in de lonesome valley, Go down in de lonesome valley, my Lawd, Go down in de lonesome valley, to meet my Jesus

dere." This last will haunt my memory forever, seeming as it did to express, and at the same time, console my desolate homesickness.[39]

I'm not sure it matters, but I have trouble believing that there were 200 voices singing, and it set me reeling when I read it. The mere size of the choir is a signifier of the worth of one's possessions and, even more, of the affection held for the master by the slaves. I can't help but think of the choir conducted by Jester Hairston that turned up outside Massa Clark Gable's door when da place done burned in the horrid, torrid *Band of Angels*. Even when I was a child seeing such movies on a tiny octagonal black and white TV, I did not believe that such music would occur impromptu. Nevertheless, the less skeptical people in the country did learn from such scenes to expect fine singing from African Americans depicted as slaves. In any case, though my information is limited, I have not seen any record that John Nathaniel Campbell had that many slaves. In 1860, he is listed on the slave census as owning fifty people. Still a good-sized choir.

Lulu's comments on the race's innate "instinct for vocal harmony" and the ability of a little child to participate ably "with no training at all" simply show the prevailing ignorance of the day concerning what were longtime vocal traditions. Just as she picked up the words (and presumably the tunes) and held onto them for life, surely a child hearing them daily from birth would be "trained" in the rhythms of call and response.

What is more important to notice about Sheppard's recollection is her continued passion for the songs. Thirty years later she can summon up the sound and words of any number of tunes and finds affecting words with which to pinpoint the emotional tone of the music. She is able to describe how that music spoke to her of emotions she felt that she shared with the singers and, like them, had rare occasion to articulate. This appears, along with her relationships to the black nannies, to show an abiding attachment to the antebellum era as one that provided deep emotional succor for a child of privilege.

I cannot say whether Will Campbell had these same emotional ties to black music. My grandmother did not say or write much about him, and none of it had to do with sentiment about African Americans. That the music may have offered him solace is believable, but he left no trace of such feelings. He spent his life living among African Americans, so I have to say that this period forced him into his first immersion in plantation culture, and perhaps that society became an emotional home for him.

One of the most pervasive and enduring legacies of slavery in the United States is the paternalism that emerged from the system. Some scholars maintain that slaveholders during the Colonial period were operating out of patriarchalism, as opposed to paternalism. I have never personally used the word patriarchalism, so I sought some clarity on how it differs from paternalism.

According to historian Stephanie M. H. Camp, writing in *Closer to Freedom: Enslaved Women & Everyday Resistance in the Plantation South*, early slaveholders "viewed bondage as a 'necessary evil' and demanded obedience while expecting resistance and opposition, [but] antebellum paternalists argued that the institution was a 'positive good,' beneficial to both the master and the slave. In addition to obedience, paternalists demanded loyalty and at least the appearance of consent." She says that the nineteenth-century planters, unlike their predecessors, were "often surprised, even shocked, by the occasional acts of organized rebellion, such as Nat Turner's 1831 slave revolt, or the escape of thousands of enslaved people during the Civil War." This helped me to understand the phenomenon among the people holding slaves in the 1860s of being simultaneously afraid of their slaves, and yet unable to imagine their slaves revolting against them. While their fathers and grandfathers had laws passed against any uprising by captives, the latter day planters made illogical excuses for resistance that came to their attention.[40]

One premise of this strange mindset is that enslaved African Americans would not act in their own interest. The loyal slave theme takes as its primary assumption that slaves would always consider the masters first. This is a constant thread in Lulu's interpretation of events that occur in the Campbells' lives during the Civil War. Camp points out that "paternalism was also influenced by the early nineteenth-century ideal of affectionate family life. . . . Planters desired the affection and allegiance of their underlings, imagining an intimacy with their slaves that patriarchs had not."[41]

I wonder if this was purely a matter of imagination. I would assume that by the nineteenth century slavery had evolved in such a way as to provide a great deal more actual intimacy—and loyalty too—than during the earliest days when captives recalled a homeland, did not speak the language, and had not given several generations to the care and feeding of the planters. Families like the Campbells lived in slave-operated villages where the kinds and numbers of services provided by slaves had no doubt increased over time, where dependence on slaves expanded from agricultural labor to include a plethora of daily, domestic, and intimate services such as nursing, grooming, dressing, waiting at the table, door opening, fireplace tending, bed changing, child care, sex, and companionship. A friend told me that one of his ancestors had the childhood job of cleaning the boots of anyone coming in the door of an Alabama plantation. Clearly, slaveholders developed more and more "needs" for slaves to meet. If loyalty was imagined, it at least makes some sense that a person would *want* loyalty from someone changing one's bedpan and wiping one's feverish brow. That they assumed the enslaved person would put loyalty above personal liberty, though, is difficult to understand.

Still, all the restrictions of movement and attempts to prevent Africans from meeting without supervision for any purpose, including religious practice, were kept in place and enforced because common sense must have told them bondage is an undesirable condition. The delusion that the content slave would not rise must have been very powerful. During the Civil War, whites spread innumerable rumors of slave risings. To have the belief that the men who enforced bondage could march off to war and leave their families on farms where there might be fifty to one hundred enslaved people and two or three whites and all would remain as before is to dig deep into delusion. Such foolishness displays the belief that African Americans would not utilize a practical opportunity, as well as a conviction that the enforced intimacy of the slave system engendered esteem for the slaveholder.

Belief in the loyalty of one's slaves, of course, affirms one's own goodness and innocence. The assumption of loyalty presumes a mutually beneficial relationship, shared experiences perhaps, and possibly even mutual affection, and it denies the true coerced nature of most facets of the relationship. It is an interesting expectation: We all want to feel worthy of loyalty, and if owning slaves logically would deny that one should have loyalty, something is taken away from one's own self-esteem. From that vantage, it seems much easier—less of a confrontation with the self—just to assume the captive likes the master.

Lulu Sheppard trusted the solace she received from the plantation hands, regardless of whether it was offered or just part of the 24-7 job description. Secondary to the comfort provided by the "servants," she regarded John Nathaniel's books of Shakespeare and the romantic novels of Sir Walter Scott as consolations for being ripped from her parents and grandmother. From these writings she fashioned her own stories to tell Will. She says he did "not care to read himself," but never tired of her stories.

During that spring of 1862, the ideal world of people like Will and Lulu was being dissolved by political means in small, somewhat painful steps. Lincoln and his generals continued to wrestle with crises arising from African Americans fleeing farms to take refuge with Union army forces, and the efforts of the various generals to both stop returning them to masters and employ them as laborers. Congress passed a Lincoln resolution offering assistance to states that would begin a gradual program to end slavery within their borders. Then Congress worked on legislation to confiscate Confederate properties—obviously including enslaved people. In May the commander of the Union forces for South Carolina, Georgia, and Florida declared martial law and summarily—without telling Lincoln— ended slavery in his jurisdiction. The president countermanded the edict, but on the South Carolina and Georgia coast, where many owners had fled, the edict became reality for thousands of African Americans. The treatment these newly liberated bondmen and women received at the hands of Union soldiers, who were not trained to aid thousands of refugees, was a mixed bag.

McPherson points out that "only a minority [of northern soldiers] in 1862 felt any interest in fighting for black freedom." He describes "indifference, contempt, or cruelty" as a "more typical response" than compassion to encountering the people who stood to be freed by the war. In Port

Royal, South Carolina, where a much-storied long-term encounter between northern liberators and newly escaped bondmen and women
occurred, according to McPherson, a shameful episode took place. A private described an 1861 incident after Union forces captured Port Royal:
"About 8–10 soldiers from the New York 47th chased some Negro
women but they escaped, so they took a Negro girl about 7–9 years old,
and raped her." A Connecticut soldier wrote from Virginia that some
men of his regiment had taken "two niger wenches . . . turned them
upon their heads, & put tobacco, chips, sticks, lighted cigars & sand into
their behinds." Even though slaves were encouraged by white southerners
to fear northerners, it must have been shocking indeed to find that representatives of the nonslaveholding North held them in such contempt and
loathing.[42]

Chloe Tarrant would have had no chance to go near Union lines in
central Alabama. At that time Chloe Tarrant was a twelve-year-old, probably in Perry County, Alabama, where 60 percent of the population was
enslaved. The county was knee-deep in Rebel fever; according to Perry
County history, Alabama's "'Secession Governor,' Andrew Barry Moore,
hailed from Perry County, and the 'Stars and Bars' Confederate flag was
designed and sewn in Marion." It was not until the spring of 1862 that
Union forces came into Alabama, occupying the northern portion of the
state. In May Union soldiers burned and looted Athens. Later that month
the Confederacy moved a large arsenal operation to Selma, twenty miles
from where she lived, making the city a Union target.[43]

In April 1862 and unknown to the Mississippi Campbells, the Missouri
troops crossed the Mississippi River from Arkansas to the east side of the
river. Van Dorn had evidently stripped the Trans-Mississippi operation
in Arkansas of all "troops, weapons, equipment, stores, machinery, and
animals." The governor protested to Jefferson Davis. Still this all took
two months, too long for the Arkansas troops to assist their comrades
in Tennessee. On April 6 and 7 Confederates of the Army of Mississippi

under General Albert Sidney Johnston met the forces of Major General Ulysses S. Grant and the Army of Tennessee at a place now known as Shiloh for the small church standing there.[44]

General Pierre Beauregard, a Louisianan who seems to have had a few nicknames, among them "the Little Napoleon" and "the Little Creole," helped Johnston pull together 42,000 men at Corinth. Grant was twenty miles north with 40,000 men. They expected to surprise Grant on April 4 before an additional 35,000 Federals arrived with General Don Carlos Buell. But the march did not go as planned and they did not arrive until the night of April 5. Beauregard became discouraged and did not want to attack, assuming Grant now had 75,000 men, which, as fate would have it, he did not. Grant did not believe he would be attacked and had not moved the men to his location. Johnston insisted on an attack and managed to surprise the Union forces, first encountering Grant's most inexperienced troops, who were nearest the South's position, then hitting the troops of William Tecumseh Sherman, who had also misjudged the situation. Grant had to rush from breakfast to the front.[45]

According to McPherson, both sides lost many men in this terrifyingly huge battle and had to shore up their lines throughout the day. In doing this himself, Johnston was killed. By day's end, the southerners had driven the Union back a couple of miles and captured 2,200 men, but the next day Grant had gained all his additional troops. On April 7 Grant's numbers were seriously higher—and in better shape—than those of the Little Napoleon. This time Beauregard was taken by surprise, and the Rebels were pushed back to where they started near Corinth, Mississippi.[46]

The sheer size of the engagement was new for this war. According to McPherson, "the 20,000 killed and wounded at Shiloh (about equally distributed between the two sides) were nearly double the 12,000 battle casualties at Manassas, Wilson's Creek, Fort Donelson, and Pea Ridge *combined.*" Sherman's description of it is, by now, famous, but well worth repeating: "piles of dead soldiers' mangled bodies . . . without heads and legs. . . . The scenes on this field would have cured anybody of war."[47]

Both sides began amassing even greater numbers of troops. A few days after Shiloh, John Nathaniel, now thirty, signed up with the 30th Missis-

sippi Infantry regiment, also known as "Buckner's Rebels," which was organized around Grenada, about 110 miles southwest of Corinth and 60
miles north of Yazoo. By the beginning of May, Thomas and Samuel
Campbell would have arrived at Corinth. Beauregard had 70,000 men
around that town. Union forces numbered over 100,000. John Nathaniel
was in charge of ordering supplies and he requisitioned camp equipment
on April 15, and received ordinance at Corinth on May 16. As Leonidas
was also in Van Dorn's army, it is likely that all four of the Campbell
brothers were at Corinth in May. This was the only time during the war
when they would all be in one place. I imagine they would have expected
to meet up, and made sure they did. The brothers, along with the thousands of others, were there for nearly a month, to their detriment. Many
of those who had been at Shiloh were recovering from their wounds, but
the water supply, which was apparently insufficient to begin with, became
tainted and thousands contracted typhoid and dysentery. Thousands
died, as many as had been killed at Shiloh, according to McPherson; that
would put the deaths at about 3,400. Thomas Campbell most likely contracted one of those diseases while camped at Corinth.[48]

On May 9 according to their military records, Samuel, eighteen, and
Thomas, twenty, fought in a skirmish under Van Dorn in Farmington,
Mississippi, a few miles east of Corinth. This was part of an unsuccessful
larger attempt to break some of the Union hold slowly building around
Corinth. Beauregard backed out of Corinth on May 29, moving fifty miles
south to Tupelo, costing the South a vital junction for transportation. The
southern gentlemen can be rather amusing sometimes: evidently, Beauregard claimed both Shiloh and the fall of Corinth were victories. But Beauregard's sense of privilege evidently even got on other southerners' nerves:
after Corinth, Jefferson Davis got rid of him.[49]

John was transferred to Chattanooga. By June 7 he was engaged in battle there. At the end of June, a G. N. Beaumont wrote to Louisa Campbell,
who must have inquired about her sons. He says he has had no chance to
ask anyone where her sons might be, and knew only that his own unit was
headed to General Price, who was about seventy miles south of Corinth.
On July 1 the day after Beaumont wrote the letter, Thomas Campbell was
"discharged for disability." And a few weeks later, sometime in August,

Thomas Polk Campbell, age twenty, died of exposure near Okolona, Mississippi, roughly the location Beaumont had given for Price's army.[50]

On July 13 their brother John was probably in battle again in Tennessee. Nathan Bedford Forrest led a successful attack on a Union garrison in Murfreesboro, not far from Spring Hill where John's grandparents lived. His sister, Sarah Rush Owen, was in Brentwood, also not far away. An August letter to her Aunt Nancy at Spring Hill suggests she was probably unaware of any news of the previous month; the information contained in it seems to date from at least three months earlier. Inside her own letter, she passed on another letter from a cousin near Memphis. Sarah reports that her children had been sick, one with jaundice, and one of the bondwomen had had a miscarriage. Without rain, Sarah had been hauling water from the well to feed her livestock. Evidently she had to present herself regularly in Nashville to get a pass to move around, and on the most recent trip, she had been asked to sign the loyalty oath.

> I had to plead hard upon *conciencious scruples* [sic]—until the tears came to my eyes and the clerks too, before he would give me a pass out of town with out the oath—much less one for thirty days—so ended my fine play . . . [51]

John Nathaniel does seem to have gotten home to Mississippi some time that summer. Sheppard's memoir has a vivid recollection of another Edenic scene on his plantation at the occasion of the corn harvest. When the harvests were in, the hands from a number of plantations went from farm to farm and participated in a kind of feast during which people shucked the corn.

> The unshucked corn was piled in great mountains in the barns, and bins lined with zinc or tin stood empty to receive the stripped ears. Atop of these mounds stood the shuckers, who stripped and tossed the ears into the waiting compartments, with all the exact speed of a machine. These men worked in relays, and there was singing and dancing and refreshment going on meanwhile. Great banks of roasted sweet potatoes and pork and other delicacies were consumed all night.

At midnight came the big feature of the festival when two strong men approached the "Big House" to fetch "Mahstah." Uncle Jack was blind-folded and carried to the barns on a pack saddle. Then round and round the busy scene they carried him, to the accompaniment of shouts and cheers. At last his bandage was removed and, after expressing great sur-prise, he made them a speech.[52]

John allowed Will to be carried out as well (on the back of someone called Big Jim), and Lulu rode on the shoulders of a man called Yellow Ike. Before leaving to return to the front, John engaged a governess for Will and Lulu, but she met with universal disapproval, "being high-tempered and sentimental," and they ignored their schoolwork.[53]

By September 10, 1862, Louisa Campbell had somehow acquired a pass from the Springfield, Missouri Union headquarters to cross the Union line into Confederate territory—one of several she managed to obtain during the war. One may wonder why she even needed such papers if she had gone to Arkansas. Apparently, to get supplies, she continued to return to Missouri and then, with a loaded wagon, headed back south. Where she was going that September, I do not know. She did not turn up at the plan-tation in Mississippi. However, on September 14, Price's army of 15,000, including Samuel, still struggling in Mississippi, succeeded in pushing Union troops out of a small railroad hamlet named Iuka in hopes of mov-ing northward toward Tennessee. Price fought troops coming at him from the south on September 19 and escaped. So perhaps this is where Louisa got to after receiving her friend's letter. At the beginning of October, at a time when Mississippi still had 90-degree temperatures, Price attacked the troops holding the recently lost Corinth with some success against the much larger force. The next day, however, they were whipped from dehy-dration and exhaustion and had to flee. Louisa may also have headed for Tennessee where John Nathaniel was bedridden and "absent with sick leave" through September and October.[54]

During these weeks of private suffering for the Campbell family, Lin-coln made up his mind to emancipate the black southerners in bondage. On September 22 he brought the matter to his cabinet and it was ap-proved, and the edict given that as of January 1, 1863, slaves in the states still in rebellion would be freed. On December 1 in his State of the Union address he said:

> In giving freedom to the slave, we assure freedom to the free—honorable alike in what we give, and what we preserve. We shall nobly save, or meanly lose, the best hope of earth.[55]

Over the next weeks word spread into the South but probably *very* slowly to the enslaved. What the Campbells made of the news is nowhere evident in their papers. I have to assume that they judged their bondpeople to be too far from enemy lines to be in jeopardy of being lost. And certainly they would have hoped the war could still go their way. Prominent abolitionists hailed the decision, while others decried the fact that it only applied to the Confederate states. Democrats howled that horror would follow. In a December 1 message to Congress, Lincoln recommended gradual emancipation for all slaves not freed by the war.

For many reasons I have come to believe that many of the African Americans in this particular story did not learn of the end of chattel slavery for some time after it occurred. And it is not at all hard to imagine that life continued for the Campbell clan as it had the month before Lincoln decided emancipation would be necessary. Sheppard's account describes a bout of severe illness striking the family in Mississippi during October. Lulu and John Nathaniel's sons Argyll and John came down with typhoid fever. John Nathaniel, still on sick leave, came home and helped nurse the children. Lulu succeeded in getting the Campbells to send for her "mammy" Mary, and recalls in great detail the woman's ministrations—being rocked, sung to, and having her hair brushed. Underlying Sheppard's own devotion to her nanny's memory, I believe, is the awareness that neither the kindness nor the obedience could be taken for granted. One might take for granted that a mother was tender during a bout of typhoid, but Sheppard's description of these mercies is similar to one that might be given to an unexpected kindness.[56]

At that time, Leonidas Campbell was playing his part in what became known as Marmaduke's Expedition from Arkansas into Missouri from December 31, 1862, to January 25, 1863. From January 2–6, they were in skirmishes in Arkansas and Missouri, and on January 8 they fought in the Campbell hometown of Springfield. In a January 20 report filed by Porter's Brigade on the events of January 9–11 around Hartville, Missouri, Leonidas and his cousin of the same name are cited. "The detachment of Colonel Greene's regiment was gallantly led by Lieutenant Colonel [L. C.] Campbell, assisted by Major [L. A.] Campbell." On January 11 they were caught by surprise by Union troops and forced back into Arkansas.[57]

That fall John Nathaniel had returned to his regiment in Tennessee and was still there in November and December. In the days following Christmas, up until January 2, southern forces in Tennessee tangled with Union soldiers around the Stones River near Murfreesboro. Southern soldiers suffered a horrible artillery barrage during a foolhardy attempt to drive Federals off a hill, and 1,500 Rebels were picked off in an hour. The most vivid image in accounts of this fight describes men pulling cotton from the fields to stuff in their ears during deafening fire. John Nathaniel's various military medical records, suggest that, in addition to fighting illness since Corinth, he may have been wounded at Stones River. He was listed as sick in his tent through most of January and February.[58]

Stones River was a devastating loss for the South and an important but devastating win for the North. According to Bruce Catton: "The casualties had been shocking. The Federals had lost 13,000 men and the Confederates 11,700 or more—in each case, about a third of the army's total strength. Few Civil War battles ever cost more or meant less."[59]

On January 1, 1863, Lincoln followed through on his emancipation promise and signed the formal Emancipation Proclamation, announcing that "all persons held as slaves within any State or designated part of a State, the people whereof shall then be in rebellion against the United States, including the military and naval authorities thereof, will recognize and maintain the freedom of such persons, or any of them, in any efforts they may make for their actual freedom." Lincoln termed the liberation "a fit and necessary war measure" and "an act of justice." He followed through on the logic of encouraging bondpeople to aid the North by allowing the enlistment of African Americans in Federal forces. Though he intended to have blacks serve in a labor capacity, rather than to be armed, before long, black troops were a reality in several places. Still, African

American abolitionist leader Frederick Douglass told an audience in
Rochester, New York on December 28:

> It is difficult for us who have toiled so long and hard to believe that this
> event, so stupendous, so far reaching and glorious is even at the door. It
> surpasses our most enthusiastic hopes that we live at such a time and are
> likely to witness the downfall, at least the legal downfall of slavery in
> America.[60]

The reality that emerged—black men fighting—proved too much for
the likes of Price's troops in Arkansas.

That January, Louisa Campbell, who was back in Springfield and
therefore probably heard news of both the proclamation and the fighting
in Tennessee, headed across the Union lines again. The pass she received
recorded that she was permitted to transport some domestic goods,
cakes, three yards of linen, ten yards of gingham, a pair of "small shoes,"
and vials of camphor and other medicines. The officer in charge of contraband goods reported that the articles were for her own use and for use
by her children in Mississippi. But Louisa did not appear at the plantation in Mississippi for another six months. General Grant's men, however, came awfully close. During the first months of 1863 Ulysses Grant
kept trying to find a route to Vicksburg that would allow him to arrive
east of the city and have support for his army. He tried several means of
using the tributaries of the Father of Rivers by digging a canal, widening
an outlet from a lake, blowing up a levee, and lastly, sending a flotilla of
gunboats through bayous and narrow overgrown water routes. When his
troops blew up a levee near Helena, Arkansas, to flood the Yazoo Delta's
rivers, the fighting and the flooding came near John Nathaniel's plantation in Mississippi, and worse came when the standard spring flooding
took place.[61]

At the beginning of February, John was still in Tennessee, still sick, and
still doing his job for the regiment. By February 27 a doctor's report said
that he was "laboring under . . . pneumonia . . . with chronic laryngitis &
bronchitis and has also a predisposition to Phthisis [tuberculosis]." The

unit surgeon said the problem had begun seven months earlier, "since which time he has been fit for duty but a few days. I further certify that in my opinion he will *never* be able to stand field service and his continuance in the same would prove fatal, and I therefore recommend that his resignation be accepted."[62]

In March of 1863, the floodwaters came to John's farm and, according to his company muster roll, John resigned his post with the 30th Mississippi at Shelbyville, Tennessee, and headed home. According to Sheppard's memoir, John's house was on a rather high bank immediately above the Yazoo River. At the beginning of the high water, bondmen and women living at the lowest land level, as well as livestock, were moved three miles inland. "We woke one morning to find the murky water swirling two feet deep beside our porch . . . "

Animals were prodded to higher ground by men in dugouts. Shortly after, "two federal gunboats with transports for troops" came through the cut levees at Yazoo Pass and into the Yazoo River. There was a fight not far from them at the tiny Confederate Fort Pemberton. One of the boats was sunk. When the water subsided, the place was wrecked. The crops were ruined, the bondpeople's cabins were destroyed, and "everything covered with mud and slime." Soon people got sick, and many died.[63]

At the same time that spring, John's connections in the Confederate army were trying to get him a plum job. Colonel G. F. Neill, one of the commanders of the 30th Mississippi, wrote to Confederate Congressman O. R. Singleton in Richmond, Virginia, in an effort to get John Nathaniel Campbell appointed as one of the "commissioners" of Mississippi. He promoted the idea that Campbell could be helpful in the implementation of impressment. Along with the much despised draft laws (including the "Twenty-Negro Law" exempting planters with large holdings of enslaved people) and tax hikes in the South, came impressment of goods. This caused food riots in some localities, especially Richmond. In an attempt to stem complaints and problems caused by impressment, the Confederate Congress created commissions to regulate prices. This then is the work for which Colonel Neill thought John Nathaniel would be well suited, even given his illness.[64]

In late March Nathan Bedford Forrest captured Union troops guarding the railroad where Sarah was living in Brentwood, and on April 10, Van Dorn fought a few miles away at Franklin. During his sojourn near Franklin, Van Dorn, who had led the Campbells so disastrously in Arkansas the year before, managed to involve one of their uncles in an episode that became one of the more infamous sidelights of the Civil War.[65]

Van Dorn set up headquarters at Spring Hill, where Louisa's family, the Cheairs, still lived. He also took up with a married woman whose much older husband was often out of town. The woman, Jessie Helen McKissack Peters, was sister-in-law to Nathaniel Cheairs. The woman's frequent visits to Van Dorn's office became the subject of so much gossip that the locals demanded he move. Another of Louisa's brothers, Martin Cheairs, offered Van Dorn space at his home. It was there that, on May 7, Jessie's husband, Dr. George B. Peters, burst in with a gun and killed Van Dorn.[66]

The siege of Vicksburg began on May 17 and lasted into July. During that time life was affected all around the Mississippi environs. At John Nathaniel's plantation, the residents had to move to higher ground twenty miles away. They lived in a meeting house, while the bondmen and women lived in tents and cabins nearby. Will and Lulu began to get their lessons from John Nathaniel:

> One day in July, as we sat in the front room at our lessons, little John [Jr.] came in and said, in his funny old-man way: "I believe my granma's a-comin'." We thought nothing of this, but his father went to the window and looked out. On his exclamation of surprise, we followed him and, here, riding up on a big bay horse, was MOTHER! I was shocked with Joy. I did not move a step to meet her, but Will went out of that room like a shot from a gun.[67]

Evidently Louisa had recently been in Arkansas with her sons Leonidas and Samuel. Leonidas had arranged for an officer to go with her to Mississippi and, having left Arkansas some time in June, she got to John's plantation during July. Crossing the well-guarded Mississippi River had been difficult and they had spent quite a bit of time waiting for a good opportunity to get across. The officer paddled a dugout while she held the reins to the horses swimming behind them.

She stayed only a few days. When she announced she was leaving right away, Will Campbell put up quite a protest. After two years of separation, the eleven-year-old became indignant enough to speak vehemently to his mother and to contradict her, surely a taboo in those days. According to Lulu, he said, "NO, MA'AM, you aren't going to leave me." He announced he was going too, if he had to hang on her horse's tail. It's all too easy to imagine the frustrations amassed in his chest over the previous two years, the sense of helplessness, and grief.

Louisa said it was impossible to take him and Lulu, that Leonidas and Samuel were living in the swamps in Arkansas where many were sick and she was going there to take medicine and clothes. But she changed her mind.[68]

6

War from on the Road
(1863–1865)

During the first three days of July 1863 the Battle of Gettysburg was fought in Pennsylvania at a human cost of at least 46,000 lives. Robert E. Lee lost nearly a third of his whole army. Confederate dead lay strewn across sites whose names are now associated with the slaughter of this conflict—such as Cemetery Ridge, Little Round Top, or the Peach Orchard. On July 4 after a siege that brought continuous bombardment and starvation to the city, the Confederates surrendered Vicksburg, fifty miles downriver from the Campbells. Two years into the war, its course had turned definitively against the Southern cause, but even as these moments came and passed, the remaining two Campbell soldiers were fighting in Arkansas in the Battle of Helena, an attack originally intended to divert Union forces pressing Vicksburg, as well as to capture a southern garrison.[1]

Now part of Marmaduke's Division, the Campbells had been in Arkansas through most of the spring—except for going on Marmaduke's failed 2nd Expedition into Missouri—and in June they camped near what is now Forrest City (after Nathan Bedford Forrest). The Campbells' command then moved toward Helena for an assault at daylight on July 4. Helena, a busy port with a white population of 1,024 and 527 enslaved African Americans, was now jammed with thousands of Union soldiers as well as several thousand emancipated bondpeople. A three-pronged Rebel attack was at first successful but then collapsed against the well-prepared if outnumbered garrison. The Confederate commands failed to act in concert, leaving each wing without assistance as their situations eroded. Major General Benjamin Prentiss of the Union forces reported that Price's men, though late in charging, came at a Federal battery, "Yelling like so many fiends let loose from the bottomless pit," and showed "a courage and desperation rarely equaled." But the battery they captured was useless. By 11 A.M. it was all over, and the Union soldiers had defended their position against Rebels twice their number. The U.S. had 206 casualties, the Confederates 1,636. Apparently the Confederate men heard the news of Gettysburg and Vicksburg after their defeat.[2]

A Confederate soldier summed up the reaction to the other losses:

This Department is now fully cut off from the Eastern portion of the government, and we must stand or fall alone. No helping hand can be extended across the Mississippi River to aid us . . . [3]

Two days after the fall of Vicksburg, Louisa Campbell had made new plans to leave John's plantation and head north to cross the Mississippi, taking not only her son Will and granddaughter Lulu, but the dozen bondpeople she had shipped south with them in 1861. I am curious what the thought was behind taking so many people, and can only share my guess that she may have had intentions to get her "servants" to Texas, and therefore even farther from Union troops. Her initial goal though was to take them to Little Rock, where her sister Nancy Perkins had moved when the war came to her door in Tennessee.

I came to read Lulu's account of these adventures after looking through many records for any sign of what had become of Will Campbell during the war. I learned early on that the Union army had taken the Campbell home in Springfield and that four of his brothers fought in the war, but at the time, lacking even his correct birth year, I had no idea if Will had joined the Confederacy himself as a teen or lived with relatives. At work one day I received an email from a man named John Polk Campbell. This was a little eerie since the only person I knew to have the name was the patriarch of the Campbell family, who died in 1852. This John Campbell turned out to be a third cousin of mine. (I had to look on a kinship chart to figure this out!) Jack is a great-grandson of my great-uncle John Nathaniel Campbell and was trying to find out about the Mississippi Campbells.

Jack Campbell and I had an interesting and amusing conversation about similar health traits we thought we had inherited from the Campbells, among other things. It turned out we were both at Columbia University at the same time in the 1960s and that I might have become acquainted with his wife while at an artists' colony some years ago. Sometime later he sent me a photo and I responded by sending him a picture of my brother, who is his age and definitely looks like his cousin. I was intrigued that we could have met and easily never discovered we were related. One usually doesn't have reason to mention one's great-great-grandparents in early conversations with a person and, until 2001, I would have had no idea who any of mine were.

Law professor Patricia J. Williams touches on this kind of coincidence in her memoir, *Open House: Of Family, Friends, Food, Piano Lessons and the Search for a Room of My Own*. She writes that one day in class she spoke of a white family that had owned and had children by women in her family in the slavery era, only to be told afterward that a young man in the class was descended from those slaveholders. Some even accused her of purposely embarrassing him.[4] It may happen all the time that people are in the same room, unaware of shared history. I remembered one of my sisters informing a federal judge from Mississippi at a dinner one night in the 1960s that they might be related, and the red-faced brush-off she said he gave her.

My own recent encounters with this phenomenon have been more enlightened. In Mississippi, a man who is related to that judge walked into a room where I was going through old records and, being a southerner, came over to greet me and my friend and ask what we were researching. We talked for a while and he assisted us. I later told him my mother was born in that town and had the same last name as he did. He asked if it was spelled the same way, as there are two local families with that name but different spellings. He didn't blink when I spelled it the same way he does. We talked a bit more and returned to our respective work. A little while later he came over and remarked, "A lot of people don't even come into this room because they are afraid they might find out about some relatives they don't want to know about." I laughed and said, "Luckily, I don't have that problem." I probably should have said, I couldn't afford to have the problem since so much of a family tree—black and white—is a surprise in the first place. He helped me for two days, though I have to say that I was not researching his family at the moment. We may only be connected by the ownership of a relative who kept the name, or we may be third cousins like Jack Campbell and I. If I had been sure, I would have mentioned it to him. He was kind enough to help me do my Campbell research, tell me how to get to Grand Oaks, and offer me his card. Perhaps one day if I find out the details I will give him a call.

Sarah Rush Owen recalled after the war that she felt fortunate during the war to have family ties to prominent families all around the South. It amuses me to be able to say that most of us black folks with families from the South have those same kinds of ties. Slavery was such a corrupt institution that any black woman like myself whose family was in slavery can look into their four sets of great-grandparents and find ties to anywhere from one to eight slaveholding elites. I am related to three that I know about and, if I go back a generation, there are more, not fewer. At the same time, reading Edward Ball's *Slaves in the Family* made me realize that a man like Ball, descended from generations of slaveholders, has many more African American relatives than most African Americans.

A few weeks after our first conversation Jack Campbell sent me a copy of the Sheppard memoir, *A Confederate Girlhood*, which solved the mystery of what had become of Will Campbell during the Civil War. He has since sent copies of letters Will wrote to his family, as well as much other helpful material. Still, except for a few letters and records of the battles in which the Campbells fought during this period of the war, I have had to depend on Sheppard's narration to relate the events of 1863 to 1865. Lulu describes herself and Will as exuberant over leaving with Louisa. "Having exhausted every expression of delight, and talked about our coming trip until there was no more to be said, we now exchanged grins of joy whenever our eyes met," she writes. The night before they left, Will and Lulu ran "hand in hand" in the rain down to the slave cabins "built on each side of a narrow bayou with bridges across it here and there."

> We went last of all to visit old Aunt Nellie, a very aged blind woman. All the others followed us from house to house until, by the time we reached Aunt Nellie's, there was a crowd accompanying us. The old soul took my hand in hers and began to call down blessings on us, and to tell the tale of her long life with our family. Now and then she held my hand to her withered cheek, all wet with tears. I cried like a baby, and I think Will was hard put to keep from joining me. As the old woman grew more vociferous in her song of praise, the others at the door took it up and before we left there was a regular camp meeting over us. I asked them to sing some of the old songs for the last time and, as Will and I trotted back to the Big House, we heard more and more faintly the strains of: "Sound, sound de trumpet, dont you grieve after me; Oh, sound de silver trumpet, dont you grieve after me; Oh, sound de trumpet, Gabriel, dont you grieve after me; I dont want you to grieve after me."[5]

I just wanted to holler "Oh Lord" myself after that gem. First, I am sorry Lulu did not write down the content of Aunt Nellie's griot moment recalling her own life. And I am intrigued that she identifies Nellie's ritual as a praise song, a demonstration that an African custom was still being practiced far from where it started in the 1860s. The custom itself sounds lovely, the kind of hospitable treatment people receive in Africa still today. When such a practice is offered in a racialized slaveholding society, it becomes a marker of white privilege, as the lines get blurred between an owner's wish and an owner's command. In addition, a slaveowner does not need to be part of the African community to receive the benefits of belonging. After all, when asked for a song, could the folk in the slave quarter say they weren't feeling it that night? Equally, the blurred lines probably allowed Will and Lulu to feel themselves part of the community in the quarter, even if no one would have encouraged it. This too is a privilege when you think how little Lulu's manuscript reflects any knowledge of the people in the slavequarter.

Sheppard's recollections never include the slaves' work or its connection to her well-being. I had to read it several times to pinpoint which young "servant" might have been the child of another older one. Did she ever walk the cotton rows and feel the rocks underfoot? Imagine what it was to lift the hand-sewn sacks of cotton once they began to get full or shuck hundreds of ears of corn? As a person hungry for information I am still grateful she wrote down as much as she did, and disappointed she did not write more.

On July 6 Louisa, Will, and Lulu, along with perhaps a dozen bondpeople, said good-bye to John Nathaniel, who was still ailing. They rode north along the river "bottoms" and took roads that were still damaged from the flood. It took eight days to get to a place in northern Mississippi where they might cross to Arkansas. By an odd coincidence, they took shelter with a family who had left in their room "towels, brushes, and a trunk marked, "L.A.C., Yazoo City, Mississippi." Lulu explains that this was Leonidas's address before the war. As it turned out, Leonidas had been seriously injured some years earlier when a steamer he took blew up and sank in that area. The trunk had been part of the wreckage. Unable to get across at that location, the group kept going north along the river and, in time, ran into Will's brother Sam, who was looking for them. They eventually were sent to a man with a large scow who would help. On July 16 the men took their "carriage," horses, wagon, and mules across. Louisa, Will, Lulu, and the rest of bondpeople were to wait.

> Unfortunately, after they had crossed over, the scow somehow got adrift and was found by one of the Union vessels patrolling the river. Our new friend who was helping us was already suspected of giving aid to blockade runners and, when this further evidence came to light, another boat, the "Covington," belonging to the ironclad ram, "Eastport," was sent to make investigations.[6]

According to the Naval Historical Center of the Department of the Navy, the *Eastport* and the *Covington*, both former side-wheel steamboats, had recently returned from other locations to the Mississippi River that July. Just at the moment when the *Covington* appeared, some of the bondmen on the Arkansas side of the river took the mules to water them at the river. The Union navy men took them to be bushwhackers, and fired on them. The Campbells heard that at least one of the men was killed.[7]

On the Mississippi side, where Will and Lulu were watching, the ferry owner's wife further confused matters by becoming so alarmed that she tied a white sheet onto a stick and ran down to the shore waving it. The *Covington* thought this was a distress signal and sent boats ashore. Will and Lulu ran up to the house yelling at Louisa that the Yankees were coming. They dashed out the back of the house, over a fence, and into the woods to hide. At this point, Louisa was trying to get the bondpeople to hide in the woods but was unable to do so before the men had landed. This amuses me because Sheppard says "it was slow work to collect the frightened darkies." I guess so. While the "darkies" may sensibly have been frightened after an armored boat started shooting down other black people across the river, they may have also been reluctant to flee. First of all, they may have known they were free. Hiding as Mistress Campbell asked was to commit to remaining in the condition of being her property. Second, they may have wanted to see for themselves what the Union soldiers were saying. Third, running from armed whites while still in plain sight may not have seemed sensible to people accustomed to violence being directed at them and to being hunted.[8]

The first scene they would have witnessed would have been Louisa lying to the soldiers. Whatever she said to try to deflect suspicion that she was moving free people to another slave state did not work. The Campbell party was put on the small boats and carried to the *Covington*. They had to manhandle Will to get him to go, and carried him bodily while he was "fighting like a wild cat." While the officer in charge appeared to them to be stern, the other seamen apparently looked openly tickled. Not understanding the new realities concerning freedmen, the Campbells thought their group should have been taken aboard the *Eastport* as prisoners. However, liberating the freedmen and women from the Campbells seems to have come first. The sailors took everyone to Helena, Arkansas. There, Lulu recalls, they "were marched from place to place about the town for no reason that we could understand. I was exhausted and near fainting." I would guess they were looking for a freedmen's camp (earlier called a "contraband" camp) that could take the dozen blacks. The camps in Helena were quite crowded and the whites were probably the sailors' secondary concern. Strangely, when Louisa became concerned that Lulu was not well, she "stopped in her tracks and asked if there was a Mason present." Sheppard does not explain this one, and I have to say it stumped me except for reminding me of Ishmael Reed's novel *Mumbo Jumbo* in which all the white folks with power share in the mysteries of the Masons. Nevertheless, "a tall officer came forward and Mother talked with him. Just what he did I never knew, but the result was that the three white people were put in a conveyance and taken back to the wharf and aboard the *Eastport*, where we were given our dinner and treated very well." I guess Reed was right.[9]

I do like this story. The following day, July 18, the "three white people" were taken to another boat, the *Hamilton Belle*, and carried back to the ferry owner's house in Mississippi and dropped off with "orders to go back home, or at least, stay on the Mississippi side of the river."[10]

The last paragraph of this episode in Sheppard's memoir deserves a close reading. On its own, it is an amazing window into race in America. Seemingly oblivious to the fact that the people are free, Lulu recalls being allowed to go under guard to visit "our servants."

They were in a big stockaded yard with cabins along one side. They seemed dazed and apathetic, and apparently did not realize what was happening. After we were outside the fence, going back to the wharf, I heard a whisper beside me of "Coonie!' and looking down at the stockade, saw a brown hand trust [thrust] through a wide crack. Then Mammy's voice, saying; "Take it, Coonie," and a small roll of bills was thrust in my hand. . . . It has always seemed to me the most touching thing in the world. This devoted negro giving her savings to her white child in trouble. Dear Mammy! That brown hand was my last sight of her. After the war I corresponded with her, when she was living at Memphis, and every arrangement was made for her to come and nurse my children, when she took yellow fever and died. The Union authorities transported these servants of ours to a concentration camp for slaves in Iowa.[11]

First of all, being curious about the stockade camp, I did investigate where the Campbell workers would have been placed. By 1863 there were contraband camps in any number of regions, particularly cities to which freedmen could flee on their own, such as the one in Virginia in which my Davis ancestors took shelter. In Arkansas, it happened that, following the Emancipation Proclamation, Union General Samuel R. Curtis was liberating Africans as his army came into the state from Missouri. When he got to Helena, he set up refugee camps for the freedmen, presumably in an attempt to see that they were treated properly.[12] Getting food on one's own must have been difficult due to the fact that the Federal forces were appropriating livestock and other foods for the army to live on. The camps turned out to be horrid places.

The contraband camps were usually located next to Federal army garrisons or camps. Once African American men were allowed to serve in the Union army in 1862, mostly women and children were left in the camps, which were, more often than not, overcrowded, under supplied, and unclean. The government put them to work.

The military . . . removed slave women, children, and men unfit for military duty from the contraband camps and placed them on abandoned plantations. They there became part of the first major experiment with non-slave labor in the South. These plantations were run either by Northern white men or by Southern planters who had taken a loyalty oath. In many areas, the employers had to promise not to whip the freed workers or use physical punishments against them.

These free laborers were supposed to be paid, but often they received very low wages or no compensation at all. . . . Also, food and clothing were usually in short supply. Adult workers were charged for their food and that of their children.[13]

The Campbell "servants," though no doubt grateful for their freedom, probably had a difficult time in the camp in Helena. There were extreme hardships in the freedmen camps. People may have had bedding, but no furniture or cooking tools. The housing of the camp was actually "old, dilapidated houses in town, or tents and cabins in Ethiopia encampment, not averaging a room to a family." All those freedmen in the town who were taking rations from the camp but living elsewhere were required to move inside the camp to continue getting food. The diseases that struck in the camps were likely the same ones wreaking havoc among the soldiers, both Union and Confederate: typhoid, dysentery, malaria, and, due to a lack of vegetables in the diet, scurvy.[14]

The very fact that the camps were constantly receiving new people brought about a debate in white society about where to put its emerging southern black society. This was not a discourse that involved the freedmen and women themselves; at worst it was purely logistical and, at best, paternalistic. "Where do we put them?" Education materials from Arkansas's Old State House Museum claim that within two months in 1863, the year the Campbell bondpeople were detained there, "at least one thousand" freedmen had gone North, "four fifths by government transportation. The larger portion left at St. Louis." Indeed, according to later letters from the former Campbell bondpeople, some of them were taken to St. Louis, some stayed in Arkansas, and others, as Sheppard says, were sent to Iowa.[15]

"Some 4,000 African Americans, mostly women and children, relocated to the upper Midwest during the Civil War," according to historian Leslie Schwalm.[16] Two of those who would end up in Iowa were the loyal Ab and a woman who shared his household, Maryann, also formerly held by the Campbells. The black population in that state increased 337 percent between 1860 and 1865, from 1,069 to 3,603. Before the war, laws were passed in the Upper Midwest to restrict blacks' liberty. "Midwestern territorial and state governments . . . circumscribed black freedom by disfranchisement, prohibiting blacks from testifying against whites in court or serving in state militias, segregating schools, and prohibiting interracial marriage."[17]

At the end of Sheppard's account of losing the "servants" she describes Mary as, "this devoted negro giving her savings to her white child in trouble." This is really disturbing given the conditions of the freedmen camps. Even if Mary did not yet know all of the privations that might await her, she may well have been giving the money to Lulu for safekeeping. Why give it away having just been informed that she is now going to need money for everything? Seeing that Lulu had been released, she had reason to expect that Lulu could better protect it. Had Lulu written that she told Mary, "I'll keep it for you," I would assume Lulu had a sensible appreciation of Mary's peril in a freedmen camp. Her use of the term "concentration camp" is interesting in itself, beyond suggesting Lulu later learned something of Mary's situation. Looking that up taught me something. Only the earliest use of the term—applied to Spanish military prisons during the Cuban Revolution of 1868–1878—had occurred when Sheppard initially penned the memoir. Soon after she completed her memoir the term was used for military prisons run by the U.S. in the Philippines between 1898 and 1901, and those run by the British during the Boer War during roughly the same years. As all of these usages involved putting brownskin people under guard, she certainly picked an apt term.[18]

Lastly, Sheppard's effort to bring Mammy to her home to care for her own children rankles as a response of gratitude to a beloved nanny, and all the more so, if she thought the woman had been confined to a concentration camp. Again, if perhaps she had said simply that she tried to bring Mary to live with her, one would be left with one impression, but to specify she wanted her to work as a nurse leaves the impression that Mammy was always viewed as a servant. Lulu may have sent her assistance, and I certainly hope she did.

A disturbingly similar "concentration camp" solution to a very different problem was unfolding that summer in Missouri. In August an extraordinary civilian crisis began. During the spring, the state saw an upswing in attacks by the border guerrillas. According to McPherson "the guerrilla fighting in Missouri produced a form of terrorism that exceeded anything else in the war."

> Jayhawking Kansans and bushwhacking Missourians took no prisoners, killed in cold blood, plundered and pillaged and burned (but almost never raped) without stint. . . . Guerrilla chieftains, especially the infamous William Clarke Quantrill, initiated the slaughter of unarmed soldiers as well as civilians, whites as well as blacks, long before Confederate troops began murdering captured black soldiers elsewhere.[19]

In the summer, General Thomas Ewing, Union commander in Missouri, decided to deprive the guerrillas of their civilian support by arresting the wives and sisters of Quantrill's raiders. The families were taken to Kansas City and kept in a building that, on August 14, collapsed, killing five women. This enraged the guerrillas into uniting into one force of 450 men to attack Lawrence, Kansas, a target from their earlier border wars. Leading the band, Quantrill ordered them to "[k]ill every male and burn every house." In three hours they murdered 192 men and boys and torched 185 buildings.[20]

Ewing retaliated by issuing "Order No. 11 for the forcible removal of civilians from large parts of four Missouri counties bordering Kansas. Union soldiers ruthlessly enforced this banishment of ten thousand people, leaving these counties a wasteland for years." No doubt many Missourians were horrified, but General Sterling Price sent compliments to Quantrill for his endurance and gallantry. Getting Missouri back had been a cause with many of the Confederates since Price was run out of the state at the beginning of the war. Encouraged by men I would call white supremacists, members of a group McPherson terms the "shadowy" Order of American Knights (later the Sons of Liberty)—Price decided to invade his home state. Still, he had to get through Arkansas to do so.[21]

Sam Campbell crossed the Mississippi from Arkansas presumably in hopes that his mother, brother, and niece would be released by the Union patrol. Sam was with a fellow soldier, Colonel Price (a cousin of the general, of course) and Link, the only former Campbell bondman left. He had not been captured because he had been on the first ferry trip from the Mississippi shore. Link is a fascinating figure. His number on the Campbell inventory was 31. No age, no last name, just Link, number 31, with an X after his name, suggesting he was among those John and Leonidas considered selling two years earlier. I assume he was at one of the farms in Mississippi. I have no idea if it was his good fortune not to be sold in 1861. It was definitely the Campbells' good fortune (as with Ab), for they were the beneficiaries of his heroism. I found no trace of

Link in the 1870 census, nor of several others. In fact, I'm pretty well convinced that less than a half-dozen of those last owned by the Campbells took the name even though that was common practice and helped people find each other.

Sam and Colonel Price had seen the capture of the Campbells while hiding at the river's edge and two days later came over to the Mississippi side of the river and found them. Price had had to restrain Sam by force to keep him from being caught with his mother, brother, and niece. Louisa intended to stick with her plans, and so late at night under a full moon they waited for clouds to pass in front of the moon and attempted to get across again, this time in a skiff. After a close call crossing between the passing of two gunboats, they landed on a sandbar, waded in, and were nearly caught one more time before making it into the woods, where they slept. In the morning, they found Link waiting at a designated spot with their wagon, carriage, and luggage. Lulu specifically remarks that he could have run off but did not because he was only concerned for their welfare. And she recognizes that with the detainment of the other blacks, he had lost his family, friends, and the girl he was to marry. They decided to head for Major Berry's plantation, and on the way ran across a Dr. Peters, another old friend of Louisa's from Spring Hill, Tennessee. In 1860 a G. B. Peters, a slaveholder from Tennessee, had a plantation at Walnut, Arkansas, near Helena. What is tantalizing about the Campbells having breakfast with him is that he may have been the same Dr. George B. Peters who killed General Van Dorn in a jealous rage three months earlier at the home of Louisa's brother. One of D. D. Berry's farms was also in Walnut, about eight miles from Peters' place, and he had another in the area called Spring Hill. They stayed with Berry a few days.[22]

I have often looked at a map of this area, wondering exactly where they did all this crossing of the Mississippi. Clearly, at the outset they were trying to cross near Helena, Arkansas. Just north of Helena, the river loops around a number of peninsulas that look like sensible places to cross, but I do not know if that is true. When they left Berry's, they must have gone south and had to cross the St. Francis River north of Helena. A white guide Berry had provided took off, stealing their best mule. They returned to Berry's, regrouped, and started out once more. At the river, they saw the *Hamilton Belle* was again on patrol but succeeded in getting out of sight. They heard that the boat was delivering supplies to Union forces about to lay siege to Little Rock, where they were headed. They stayed camped in the cane breaks on the St. Francis for more than a week.[23]

One day Will and Lulu were left alone at their camp while Sam and Link went to find fodder for the animals, and Louisa went to a mill for meal. The two sat leaning against a tree with a fire going while Lulu made up stories. When it grew dark they discovered a growling panther overhead in the tree. Will backed him off with a flaming log until Sam showed up and shot the animal.[24]

Unknown to the others, Sam and Link were building a raft, and they used it to get the party and their vehicles across the river. Once on the other side, they heard that the Federals would be on the road to Little Rock the next day. Sam was not willing to leave them, so they had to change plans and head for Searcy County. They took the main road that night until daybreak, and then used trails through the woods running parallel to the road. Soon enough the Federal troops were pounding along beside them, so to speak, and continued to be present on their route for three days.

It is hard for me to guess which way they were attempting to go around Little Rock to Searcy County, which lies northwest of the city. Seemingly unknown to them, the Union forces approached Little Rock from two directions. Brigadier General John W. Davidson, the man whose troops they saw, came toward Little Rock from the northeast and Major General Fred Steele, commander of the Army of Arkansas, marched on the north side of the town. Coming from the Mississippi, they could have run into either Federal army. While on an errand to get food, Lulu encountered several Union soldiers, including a young man she knew from Missouri, but she escaped without raising their suspicions. Once in Searcy County, Sam returned to his regiment. They also saw Musick, the old gentleman who had helped Louisa when she was evicted. Lulu recalled how he "gladly came back to work for us," and that Link was the "mainstay" of their little household. Louisa and Letitia Berry decided to once again take medical supplies to the "boys."[25]

On the morning of September 10 Steele attacked the Rebels camped on the north side of town and, as those troops under Davidson came toward Little Rock, he ran into Greene's regiment, led by Leonidas Campbell at Bayou Fourche on the east side of Little Rock. Davidson pushed the southerners back into the town. The idea that Louisa may have been there watching her eldest remaining son lead that charge shows her fearlessness. I can only think that the first times she did this must have been transforming, such as happens to anyone in battle. Perhaps numbness protected her, but I doubt that any of the Campbells were immune to the constant defeat. The Battle of Little Rock was won by the U.S. that evening. Leonidas and his men were ordered ten miles south—basically back the way they came.[26] The Confederate colonel in charge, William L. Jeffers, wrote of the retreat:

> On the morning of the 11th, I was ordered to continue the march, Major Campbell's regiment acting as rear guard. At 10 A.M. the enemy drove in his vedettes [mounted sentinels]. Retiring slowly by company, making successive formations, Major Campbell fought the enemy for 7 miles, drew them into an ambuscade, and completely checked them for the time . . . [27]

I cannot resist mentioning that two Confederates at Little Rock made their contribution to the colorful Rebel sidelights of the war: Four days before the battle, General John Marmaduke, with whom the Campbells fought, killed his superior, General Lucius Walker, in a duel. Marmaduke had insulted Walker when he accused him of having endangered the men by not showing up for an earlier battle. Walker supposedly forgave him before dying, and Marmaduke went on to become governor of Missouri.[28]

I have never been a student of military battles so this may be way off base, yet it seems to me there was a pattern in the military careers of the Campbells in Arkansas and Missouri: Not only were many battles lost, but most began well for their side. Despite a variety of commanders, they lost several battles where they had a numerical advantage, several where they took some strategic location and lost it, and seemingly often met better prepared or better entrenched Union soldiers. And they had their share of little Napoleons and dueling men of "honor." I am not pained that they lost, nor do I have any sympathy for their aims or cause. I just wonder that they did not suffer the disillusionment that we associate with more recent conflicts when leadership became disastrous. Unlike the Campbells' cousin Leonidas Polk, who was part of the southern victory at Chickamauga that September, these men in the Trans-Mississippi had no experiences for another soldier to envy.

After Little Rock, Louisa Campbell decided to take Will and Lulu to Texas. Lulu's father had been disabled in the war and had somehow sent word that she should come live with him and his new wife. Louisa planned to leave Will with an aunt in Waco. Leonidas was said to be in Arkadelphia, Arkansas, which was on the way, roughly speaking. First, Louisa left Will and Lulu in Clark County, south of Little Rock, and rode toward Arkadelphia. The two kids were camped near the house of a family friend. At this farm Lulu had a fall that dislocated her shoulder and elbow. While the shoulder slipped back into place, there was no one available to try to reset her arm. She was given the drug laudanum and put into bed. Will, who was normally a "bold, high-spirited and restless boy," took seriously the task of taking care of her, stayed by her side, and patiently entertained her while she was bedridden. It was a week before Louisa reappeared. She packed them up and moved on, riding southwest toward the Texas border. I'm not sure what Louisa had in mind about Lulu's arm, which not only out of place but twisted backward.

Had they not run into a retired physician near the Red River, I wonder how long Lulu would have suffered before getting help. Lulu was sent to a home they saw to see if the people were friendly. When the gentleman there saw her arm, seemingly without saying a word, he took hold of it, pulled, and snapped it into place. She passed out. Louisa was quite indignant when she came to find out what happened. The doctor, had to apologize for not coming to ask her first but he thought she might not want a stranger to touch it. Evidently it took a little while before her anger passed. I didn't quite know what to make of that. Fortunately for the fourteen-year-old Lulu, the doctor kept them there for two weeks.[29]

By the middle of October, Louisa, Will, Link, and Lulu crossed the Red River at a place called Miller's Ferry, near Texarkana, and then rains set in. Lulu describes the terrain as the "black waxy lands" of northeast Texas. They crossed vast prairies with few houses except the occasional shanty. Lulu then came down with malaria and became delirious. They went on through a howling storm and Louisa sent Will ahead to find shelter, giving him a roll of cotton with which to mark his trail. The house Will found was in fact the home of Lulu's father and his new wife and child. Lulu was put to bed by a fire, given quinine, and slept for several days. When she awoke, she was neither prepared to see Elnathon McKenny, nor to embrace him. Louisa explained that McKenny had left it up to her when Lulu should come to his home, and she thought it best for Lulu to stay in his home. Despite much pleading from the teen, Louisa left her there and went to Waco. Lulu, who turned fifteen while crossing the prairies, behaved so badly at her father's home that after three weeks he packed her up and took her to Waco where, soon enough, Louisa left both children. Will and Lulu were once again each other's only family.[30]

The Sheppard manuscript made me feel very sympathetic toward Will and Lulu with regard to nurture. Louisa seems, even in this adoring memoir composed in her honor, almost unable to contend with nurturing Will and Lulu once the three were alone. Her actions really raise questions not only about how driven she was to see about the two sons who were soldiering. They make one wonder how much she had relied on the "servants" to take care of her children. Sarah Owen seems similarly detached in raising her young children. I don't wonder that Lulu lionized her "mammy" and was the most avid letter writer in the family for years after the war. She lived in many different homes and several schools and tried to keep all the strands of her life intact. I can't be surprised either that Will was able to accept isolation from Sarah and other family members over the presence of Chloe in his life. He had spent very little time with any of them really. After the age of nine, he no longer had much family life. Having grown up without a mother myself, I know what it is to expect that attachments may not survive and to accept such separations with an unbending attitude of self-reliance. My instincts kept intimating to me that Chloe was separated from her mother and, therefore, stubborn independence was a quality she shared with Will Campbell. As Will came of age during this four-year trek away from the places and family he had known, he must have begun to develop the muscles of others who eventually learn to do without the succor of those who brought them into the world.

On the morning of October 25 near Pine Bluff, Arkansas, a company of Union cavalry ran into the troops of the dueling General Marmaduke. A little shooting ensued and the Federals retreated to their garrison in the town with the Rebels after them. In what may have been a typical use of the Union's African American soldiers, about 300 of them were ordered to roll cotton bales out of warehouses to build barricades. The Confederates, with a battalion commanded by Leonidas Campbell, failed to get past the Union's four howitzers and other heavy artillery behind the cotton, or to burn the Federals out of the town square. After five hours Campbell and the other Rebels retreated to the position they had held in the morning. Commander Colton Greene commended all his troops, in particular Leonidas: "Major Campbell had his horse killed under him, and acted with the greatest coolness and bravery during the day." Marmaduke settled for destroying some commissary supplies and ordinance and capturing "about 250 mules and horses, about 300 negroes (men, women, and children)." He left the women and children.[31]

The report filed by Powell Clayton, the Union commander, presents quite a contrast. First of all, he states, "the fact that so small a [Union] force kept four times their number at bay for five hours, and finally drove them from the field, bespeaks for the whole command greater efficiency and gallantry than words can do." He wrote at length about the fire.

When the fire was raging, the mules were cut loose to keep them from burning, and 62 of them are missing. The enemy also burned one ware-

house, containing over 200 bales of cotton. In setting fire to these buildings, General Marmaduke committed the gross and barbarous deed of
burning some of his own wounded. Several of his own men, who were
wounded, were burned to death, and almost entirely consumed by the
flames he kindled. . . . There is scarcely a house in town that does not
show the effects of the battle. The enemy plundered every house he could
get to, and stole every horse and mule from the citizens that he could lay
his hands on.[32]

Also, the superintendent of the contrabands in Pine Bluff reported
that when African American volunteers formed a bucket brigade to help
put out the fire, the southerners began shooting at them. Fifteen other
freedmen who had weapons were able to hold another site for the Union
forces. On November 1, Leonidas was ordered to a place called Munn's
Mill. On November 19 his cousin, Lieutenant Colonel Leonidas Caldwell
Campbell, with whom he had fought for two years, was killed in action,
according to his military record.[33]

Will, Lulu, and Louisa spent the Christmas of 1863 in Waco at the home of
Louisa's aunt Nancy Sedbury. In January Lulu was sent to stay with a
schoolmaster's family forty-five miles north in Hill County. Will stayed in
Waco a while longer and then was also sent to the school. Sometime in the
New Year of 1864 Louisa's brother Nathaniel defied the terms of his release
as a prisoner of war by rejoining the Confederacy and went to fight with
Nathan Bedford Forrest. Sarah Rush Owen was still in Tennessee, where
sometime in January she received a letter from L. C. Campbell's widow,
Elizabeth "Lizzie" Berry Campbell, that caused me a good deal of anxiety:

> I saw your Ma in Sept and heard from all your brothers Lately all
> are well except your bro Jack[.] His health is not good. He is in
> Texas with his servants, your Ma's all went to Helena Sam, Loulu,
> and Willie, are with your Ma.[34]

There is no mention in Sheppard's memoir of John Nathaniel going to Texas with all of his now free "servants." The very idea that he would transport all of them to Texas suggests that he had not only failed to shift to a wage-earning basis with them, but moreover that he may have kept from them the information that they were free. And this letter was also my introduction to a conundrum presented by the fact that various Campbell family documents record that John died that spring on April 7, 1864, in Carrollton, Mississippi. It seems more likely that he died in the fall of 1864, probably of the tuberculosis diagnosed in Tennessee.

Lizzie's letter and another from Leonidas mention John Nathaniel as still alive for several months after April 7. A letter from Leonidas dated August 13, 1864, has John doing pretty well, and also says he was living in Texas: ". . . Brother J & family all well a month since they move out to Texas this fall—all of his Negroes are now out there . . ." John Nathaniel's Confederate grave registration muddies the waters by giving his date of death *and* date of discharge as April 7, 1864. This is curious given his 1863 resignation. Then there is his gravestone in Mississippi, which simply says 1864. Sheppard's memoir, which proved reliable for facts up to the spring of 1864, says that John died just before the end of the war, which is not quite right either. Sheppard's error is somewhat easier to understand given that family letters from the summer of 1864 begin to anticipate the end of the war, perhaps expecting it to come earlier than it did. Sheppard may have simply recalled John's death (which none of the Texas group witnessed), or heard about it as occurring during the winding-down of the war. Lastly, John's will, which was not probated until 1865, gives no date of death.[35]

In any case, on December 9, 1864, Leonidas wrote that he was getting a leave to go to Mississippi "to attend to Brother's affairs and his family."[36]

Most curious to me is the possibility that John and Mary moved to Texas without anyone in Waco knowing or visiting the dying John. As events turned out, Louisa would not have seen John in either Texas or Mississippi. That John Nathaniel was able to move himself, his family, and any sizeable number of his former bondmen and women seems quite a feat.

∞

In Arkansas that spring the two remaining Campbell soldiers, Leonidas and Sam, were part of what is now known as the Camden Expedition. In April they fought at a place called Elkin's Ferry, near Okolona in the southwest of the state. According to their Confederate commanders, the Campbells' units were "not actively engaged" in this skirmish, but "constantly under fire and behaved well." Reports list Leonidas leading Greene's Regiment in fighting from April 5 to April 7. At this time, Louisa heard that Samuel was not well in Camden, Arkansas, and packed to leave. She took Link as a bodyguard.[37]

> She did not let Will and me know her plans until she had started. Before she left all the relatives had the usual sewing and knitting "bee" to provide as much as she and Link could carry with them for the soldiers. Mother made some beautiful socks for Uncle Lonnie from the best grade of cotton. Before spinning it she cut up and raveled an old silk dress and mixed it evenly with her cotton. This, when spun, made a lovely yarn and knitted with very fine needles made the softest and finest of socks.[38]

Here Sheppard's story starts to confuse as to time. I have pieced together her memories with the historical events, which at least I could verify. Louisa would have left in April, though I am dubious about Lulu's recollection that she did not return until January 1865. When she got to Arkansas, according to Lulu, she heard they were at the Battle of Poison Spring, and headed there.

The Battle of Poison Spring, Arkansas, was on April 18, 1864. It was caused by orders from Union General Fred Steele, whose men were in dire need of food, for a foraging party to confiscate a supply of corn stored near Camden. The Confederates were nearby and on the lookout for Union foragers, and that was how "a force of nearly 3,600 men, including about 1,200 Arkansans and nearly 700 'hungry, half-clothed Choctaws,' and twelve guns commanded by Marmaduke got between the forage train and Camden." The fighting that took place when divisions led by Marmaduke and Brigadier General Samuel Bell Maxey attacked the wagon train became a tragedy for a unique unit, the First Kansas Colored Infantry regiment.[39]

The 400 men from the First Kansas were traveling with some 200 cavalry to bring back the corn, which had been loaded into nearly 200 wagons. The First Kansas Colored Infantry was organized at Fort Scott, Kansas, in August 1862, by abolitionist James Lane, with men who were then-fugitive bondmen from Missouri and Arkansas. They became the first African American troops to fight in the war, and one of their number was the first black to die in combat in the war. They had fought some of Marmaduke's men the previous week at Prairie D'Ane. When the Confederates attacked and overwhelmed the wagon train on April 18, the African American soldiers were at the center of the assault and took the worst of it. Half of them were killed in "little over an hour of fighting," not by battle fire alone.[40]

> Once penetrated, the Union line collapsed rapidly. Threatened with envelopment when the cavalry screen on their left flank was beaten back, the remains of the First Kansas broke and ran. This proved to be their undoing. Pursuing Confederates, enraged as the Rebels usually were when the Federals used blacks as combat troops, showed no mercy. They continued to fire into the fleeing ranks, and many wounded blacks were murdered as they lay on the ground. Other black troops, hunted down and trapped in the surrounding swamps and woods, were executed when they attempted to surrender. . . . A few blacks, realizing the vengeance being reaped on their comrades, feigned death by lying motionless on the field. After dark, they crawled into the woods and made their way back to Camden. Kirby Smith, who arrived from Louisiana on April 19, admitted that of some two hundred captured Federals, he saw "but two negro prisoners."[41]

Leonidas had been following the wagon train the day before, and was at first ordered to attack it but was pulled back. The next day, April 18, Leonidas charged the train. Colonel Colton Greene, commander of the brigade bearing his name, wrote in his report, "I marched with Greene's regiment, commanded by Lieutenant-Colonel Campbell." He reported that about an hour into the fight:

> . . . The left and center were hotly pressed, when I advanced at the double-quick with loud cheers, passed the line, delivered several well-directed vol-

Chloe Tarrant, taken in Selma, Alabama, circa 1870s. From Chloe's photo album, along with all pictures of her family. Collection of the author

Possibly Caroline Tarrant, Chloe's
mother, Alabama, ca. 1870s.
COLLECTION OF THE AUTHOR

Allen Tarrant, Chloe's older brother,
ca. 1880. PHOTO BY W. R. WORKS, SELMA,
ALABAMA. COLLECTION OF THE AUTHOR

Mariah Tarrant, Chloe's older sister, ca. 1880.
COLLECTION OF THE AUTHOR

King Carter, Chloe's younger brother,
ca. 1880. COLLECTION OF THE AUTHOR

Belle Carter, Chloe's sister-in-law. ca.
1880. COLLECTION OF THE AUTHOR

ucy Tarrant, Chloe's younger sister,
a. 1880. COLLECTION OF THE AUTHOR

George Aaron Tarrant, Chloe's younger
brother. COLLECTION OF THE AUTHOR

The Campbell family home in Springfield, Missouri, on the day Will Campbell was born in 1852. THE HISTORY MUSEUM FOR SPRINGFIELD-GREENE COUNTY, MISSOURI

William Argyle Campbell, ca. 1870s. THE HISTORY MUSEUM FOR SPRINGFIELD-GREENE COUNTY, MISSOUR

Possibly John Polk Campbell,
Will's father, ca. 1850.
The History Museum for
Springfield-Greene County,
Missouri

Louisa Terrill Cheairs Campbell, Will's mother, ca. 1850s.
The History Museum for Springfield-Greene County,
Missouri

Mary Danforth Campbell & John Nathaniel Campbell, ca. 1850s.
THE HISTORY MUSEUM FOR SPRINGFIELD-GREEN COUNTY, MISSOURI

Mary Frances Campbell Sprouel, Will's
oldest sister, ca. 1850–53. THE HISTORY
MUSEUM FOR SPRINGFIELD-GREEN
COUNTY, MISSOURI

Leonidas Adolphus Campbell,
ca. late 1850s. THE HISTORY MUSEUM
FOR SPRINGFIELD-GREEN COUNTY,
MISSOURI

Louisa Cheairs McKenny Sheppard, ca. 1890s. THE HISTORY MUSEUM FOR SPRINGFIELD-GREEN COUNTY, MISSOURI

Sarah Rush Campbell & Jabez Owen on their wedding day, ca. 1855. THE HISTORY MUSEUM FOR SPRINGFIELD-GREEN COUNTY, MISSOURI

Josiah Danforth, Mary Danforth Campbell's younger brother; possibly Samuel I. Campbell, ca. 1861. COLLECTION OF THE AUTHOR

Carte de visite of Confederate generals from
Will's album. COLLECTION OF THE AUTHOR

The steamboat *Sultana* docked at Vicksburg. It blew up two days later on
April 26, 1865, at Helena, Arkansas, killing nearly 700, mostly former
prisoners of war. From Will's photo album. COLLECTION OF THE AUTHOR

Chloe Tarrant Curry in Mississippi, ca. late 1870s–80. COLLECTION OF THE AUTHOR

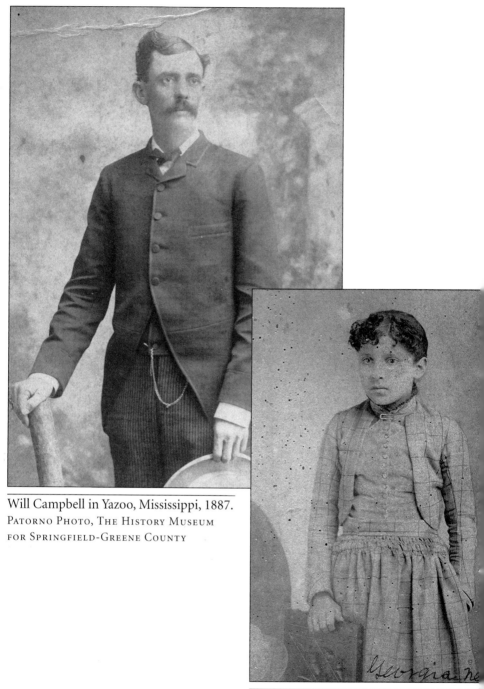

Will Campbell in Yazoo, Mississippi, 1887.
<small>PATORNO PHOTO, THE HISTORY MUSEUM
FOR SPRINGFIELD-GREENE COUNTY</small>

Georgia Campbell, at about 9 years old,
Yazoo, Mississippi, 1887. Taken in the same
studio as Will's photograph, this may have
been taken the same day. Note the hat on the
table, and the hat in his photograph.
<small>PATORNO & COOVERT PHOTO, COLLECTION
OF THE AUTHOR</small>

James Curry, Sr., Marion Alabama,
ca. 1930. COLLECTION OF MINERVA CURRY

James Curry, Jr., Alabama, ca. 1875.
COLLECTION OF THE AUTHOR

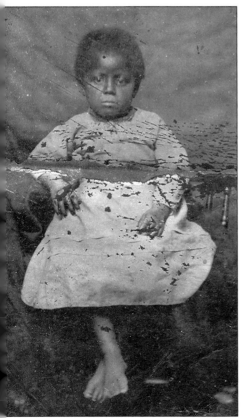

Carrie Curry McConnell, Alabama, ca. 1875.
COLLECTION OF THE AUTHOR

Ruth Curry, Alabama, ca. 1875.
COLLECTION OF THE AUTHOR

Menu from the Anchor Steamboat Line, ca. 1882. THE HISTORY MUSEUM FOR SPRINGFIELD-GREENE COUNTY

arah Rush Owen and her children, from left: Jay Owen; Sarah; Fannie Owen Bryan; hotographer, possibly George Bryan; Felix Owen; Lucy Owen McCammon, ca. 1885–89. ℋᴇ Hɪsᴛᴏʀʏ Mᴜsᴇᴜᴍ ғᴏʀ Sᴘʀɪɴɢғɪᴇʟᴅ-Gʀᴇᴇɴ Cᴏᴜɴᴛʏ, Mɪssᴏᴜʀɪ

Robert Lee Campbell, son of
L. A. Campbell, ca. 1876.
THE HISTORY MUSEUM FOR
SPRINGFIELD-GREENE COUNTY

Georgia Campbell, ca. 1898. PATORNO & COOVERT PHOTO
COLLECTION OF LOUISE D. STONE

Augustus Garfield Barbour, Chicago, 1920s.
COLLECTION OF LOUISE D. STONE

Louise Barbour Davis, 1950s. Reuben Burrell
photo. COLLECTION OF THE AUTHOR

Edgar Barbour, Chicago, ca. 1930.
COLLECTION OF JENNIE D. BROWN

Chloe at the flooded Grand Oaks Plantation, late 1920s. COLLECTION OF THE AUTHOR

Grand Oaks Bell, 2004. COLLECTION OF THE AUTHOR

leys, and charged the enemy through burning woods and a dense smoke. He gave way, closely pressed, but reformed under cover of his train. Upon this position we advanced firing; charged the train, with great slaughter to the enemy; who abandoned his artillery on the field and again formed behind the huts, fences, and timber of an adjoining plantation. . . .[42]

Marmaduke's own report concluded there was a "federal loss about 400 negroes killed, some 60 whites killed, and about 125 prisoners." He commended Brigadier General William Cabell (later mayor of Dallas, Texas) for a "cheap and quick victory," and Leonidas Campbell was given special mention: "Though painfully wounded, he did not quit his regiment until the engagement was over." Lulu's memoir says that Louisa found him slightly wounded. Confederates reported taking only four black prisoners. Marmaduke's numbers have been lowered by later historians to 300 casualties, some giving just over 200. Even by 1959 though, it was accepted that wounded African Americans were shot.[43]

This incidence of Confederate vengeance against freedmen and the refusal to take them prisoner occurred less than a week after an episode at Fort Pillow, Tennessee, when the troops under the command of Nathan Bedford Forrest (possibly including Louisa's brother Nathaniel) slaughtered dozens of the 262 black men holding the fort. The numbers still vary wildly according to the source: originally reported at 300, many sources today report that 62 of the blacks survived, and 200 died.

One survivor, Sergeant Benjamin Robinson, interviewed by a congressional committee and cited in McPherson, reported being bullied to hand over money, shot, stripped and dragged up a hill, laid on his stomach till night, and then carried off to an old house. He crawled his way out and down the hill. Asked if he was shot after he surrendered, he replied, "Yes sir; they shot pretty nearly all of them after they surrendered. . . ." Eli Carlton reported being shot in battle and taken to "a little hospital."

I was in the hospital when they shot me a second time. Some of our privates commenced talking. They said, "Do you fight with these God damned niggers?" they said, "Yes." Then they said, "God damn you, then, we will shoot you," and they shot one of them right down. They said, "I would not kill you, but, God damn you, you fight with these damned niggers, and we will kill you"; and they blew his brains out of his head. . . .[44]

These events did send a shock wave through the North. The issue of the treatment of African American prisoners had been brewing for over a year, and after Fort Pillow many wanted to take an eye for an eye. From the time of the Emancipation Proclamation, the Confederacy took the position that captured African Americans should be regarded as insurrectionists and orders were given by the southern army to execute blacks even before black enlistment in the Union army was official. In 1862 Confederate Secretary of War James A. Seddon ordered black soldiers to be killed without trial. In the spring of 1863, the Confederate Congress had authorized this, but for the most part, it was not enforced. In response, the Union war department had suspended prisoner exchanges. And it goes without saying that from this point on, black soldiers would have thought it advisable to fight like hell in any battle on the assumption that murder would await them if they lost. Many went into subsequent battles having taken oaths to avenge their brothers, and even civilians called for vengeance.

This kind of preaching to freedmen must have increased the dread among Confederate soldiers already hungry, battle weary, and scared of dying. The armed former slave with vengeance in his heart was the signal horror driving much of the animus in the first place. The image drove rumors of uprisings and kept the widows company—whether the secret sharer come to slit the white's throats silently as they slept, or the screaming warrior charging with musket or bayonet. A letter written in July 1864 by a white soldier cited in McPherson claimed: "the Johnnies are not as much afraid of us as they are of the Mokes [black troops]. When they charge they will not take any prisoners, if they can help it. Their cry is, 'Remember Fort Pillow!'"[45] Mokes. That is definitely what I would call an "old school" term. I had no idea it was THAT old. The liberal use of these epithets really brings home what black people were up against—a year-and-a-half into freedom, even their allies were still calling them mokes, and most everyone used the words nigger and wench.

I have taken this detour through the massacres of the spring of 1864 to impart some of the background behind Poison Spring, an aptly named spot as it turned out. Also important is to know that African Americans had a reaction to discovering the rules of war had no application to brown skin, and that the decision of these men to continue to fight was informed by awareness that there was no such thing as just getting wounded or being taken prisoner. It was victory or death. And with Poison Spring as part of Leonidas Campbell's history, it is easier to see that he would allow a lynching at Silver Creek in response to African American voting power.

I do wonder what Louisa Campbell saw after riding from Camden to Poison Spring. Perhaps she thought it entirely necessary to kill these former slaves. I then wonder what reaction she had as a woman, being guarded at the time by a freedman like those lying on the field. I can imagine the peril Link realized he was in just being present at the battle and then going forward in his life. I do not imagine them discussing it as they rode away from the scene. What Lulu recorded was that Louisa found the citizens of Camden were starving under Rebel occupation, as well as the soldiers, and that the southern army was in bad shape and in dire need of quinine for widespread malaria. And she learned from her sons that their cousin Robert Bruce Campbell lost his life during the Camden Campaign. Riding with Link again, she went east toward the Mississippi, where she could get a steamboat to Missouri. What a pair they must have made. Louisa was a fifty-four-year-old woman making at least her third trip on horseback across the state of Arkansas. I have tried to guess at Link's age by looking at John Nathaniel's chattel holdings for 1860. The males ranged from the age of fifteen to forty-five, most in their twenties and thirties. He only had about two young adolescents and about four men in their forties. Sheppard doesn't help by using the word "boy" for all. So, I can only assume John sent with his mother a bodyguard fairly young, very able, and loyal.[46]

The Campbell men carried on in other battles of the Red River Campaign through April. At Marks' Mill, on April 25, the Rebels punished Union General Steele enough to convince him to give up fighting in the Camden area and try to get away. On April 29 at Jenkins Ferry, the Confederates were beaten and it was their turn to retreat, in part due to the effort of the Second Kansas Colored Infantry, who came at them full bore under the cry, "Remember Poison Spring."[47]

As a precaution, I suppose, Louisa left Link on the Arkansas coast and got a riverboat. She made her way to St. Louis, presumably avoiding situations where she would have to present papers. She went to the home of her brother-in-law Junius, who assisted her once more.

Louisa's trips did not go unnoticed. I don't know if she stayed until July on this particular journey but a military telegram was sent to the Union Provost Marshal on July 18, 1864, stating that Louisa "left Springfield via Sedalia to St. Louis. Believes she is carrying letters which will be sent to the South." Three days later the Federals decided she should not be compensated for the use of her property and there were requests made to investigate "what portions of property are owned by her sons, serving in the rebel army."[48]

According to Lulu, in Missouri Louisa had the medicines "quilted" into her clothes, and then retraced her steps to some riverboat stop in Arkansas, where Link was waiting. She rode back across the state and was able to find the troops and deliver the medicine.[49]

Leonidas and Sam spent May and early June on the west bank of the Mississippi River in the southeast corner of Arkansas, firing at Union gunboats and large transports. Colton Greene's report claimed they had "engaged 21 boats of all descriptions, of which 5 gun-boats and marine-boats were disabled, 5 transports badly damaged, 1 sunk, 2 burned, and 2 captured."[50] In Texas, cut off from news and unaware of most of the events of the war, Will and Lulu were in school in a county north of Waco. They were still making socks, bandages, and clothes for soldiers, but they had run out of cloth and had to make homespun. There were no shoes available, no coffee (they made a substitute of ground grain or dried sweet potato), or white sugar (they used molasses or coarse ground brown sugar). The monotony of the young people's rural lives was only broken that summer by two tornadoes, a flash flood, and a wedding.

At some point during the last part of the war Sarah Rush Owen learned that the family home in Springfield was occupied by squatters, mostly immigrants from England and Ireland. She would have to delay plans to return to her mother's home. On August 14 Leonidas wrote from Monticello, Arkansas, that the family in Texas was doing well, and that Louisa had hoped to go to Tennessee but could not. He expected her to wait out the rest of the war in Texas, and it is at this time that he says John Nathaniel was doing pretty well in Texas as well.[51]

Louisa must have been gone most of that summer, and the months-long absence of that trip began to take a toll on the now twelve-year-old Will Campbell. I have no idea if they got letters from Louisa when she was away, but I assume not, so it's easy to imagine that one would just worry. Perhaps he suffered a depression or a period of prolonged anxiety. Surely he must have worried that he was in jeopardy of losing the remaining members of his family to the war, particularly after each of his remaining brothers had both been wounded and had gotten sick. As Sheppard describes him, it is hard to know if his anxieties took the form of depression or anger or both.

> Just at this time Will, who was growing very fast, became quite delicate and was really unreasonable about Mother. Certainly I, after my performance at my father's house, could not criticize Will in this respect. I think our two years in Mississippi had left on our minds an indelible impression of horror at the thought of being separated from Mother even for a short time. However, Will was better by fall and went to school with me at Dr. Church's in September and stayed there until the school broke up about Christmastime, owing to the illness of Dr. Church.[52]

At the end of summer, General Sterling Price tried yet another invasion of Missouri, this time intending to take St. Louis. According to McPherson, Price expected the white supremacist Order of American Knights to alert the populace to rise up and support his army, but the Knights turned out to be all mouth and no legs; they were arrested by Union officers, who discovered the Knights really had no organization. The Missouri Campaign [August 29–December 2] seems to have been a miserable affair, and from testimony at a later inquiry into its conduct, Price's army was at its worst by this time, with more men who were given to depredations and resistant to discipline. According to one soldier who was asked about out-rages committed by the army, "[t]he soldiers commenced plundering at Arcadia, and from there throughout the whole expedition. Wherever sup-plies were to be found there was more or less plundering. . . . All kinds of property was taken." Many of his troops were raw recruits, and a third of them had no weapons at all. This is one reason Price decided to go after the Union arsenal at St. Louis.[53] Near the end of September, delays had slowed Price down and allowed the Union a chance to send support to St. Louis, so he decided on what he thought would be an easier target, Fort Davidson at a place called Pilot Knob, south of St. Louis. Price had 7,000 men, Campbell's being among Marmaduke's several thousand. The Union garrison had 1,000–1,500 men, and seven guns behind an earthen fort and moat, and they blasted away at each charge of Price's men. Price had failed to position his own artillery to be successful against the Union guns. He took at least 750 casualties and the Union soldiers slipped away from the fort during the night.[54]

Price's army had some bad elements, of which he was quite aware, wreaking havoc around Missouri, namely William Quantrill and "Bloody Bill" Anderson. "Through August and September," writes McPherson, "An-derson's band struck isolated garrisons and posts, murdering and scalping teamsters, cooks, and other unarmed personnel as well as soldiers." The day Price attacked at Pilot Knob, Anderson was northwest of St. Louis.

The climax of this [Anderson's] saturnalia came at Centralia on September 27. With thirty men including Frank and Jesse James, Bloody Bill rode into town, burned a train and robbed its passengers, and murdered twenty-four unarmed northern soldiers traveling home on furlough. Chased out of town by three companies of militia, the guerillas picked up 175 allies from other bands, turned on their pursuers, and slaughtered 124 of the 147 men, including the wounded, whom they shot in the head.[55]

The rest of Price's Missouri Expedition was more disastrous than the start. Union forces pushed Price away from his objectives, first St. Louis, then Jefferson City, and then drove him further west. Evidently Price's men plundered the whole way. For nearly the whole month of October, they had armies coming at them from the back and the front. The usual route south to Arkansas was cut off and they were forced into Indian Territory and then Texas in order to get back to Arkansas. Anderson was killed, and when Quantrill took off east thinking he could kill Lincoln, he was also killed.[56]

There is an ironic symmetry to this ending for the Campbells' war of rebellion. Price's army was driven back to its origins in the bloody border wars back and forth across the Missouri-Kansas Line. The appeal of Price's mission itself fell back upon the violent white supremacist ideology of the bushwhackers. (And Price became one of those who fled to Latin America after the war to set up little Confederacies, and recapture the dream of antebellum slaveholding life.) The James and Younger boys survived and became the James and Younger gangs, terrorizing northern Missouri. And lastly the army was driven through Indian Territory, the same stretch that was the land of John Polk Campbell's fabled death, if not his real demise, and then into that northeast corner of Texas that had been their first hope for the expansion of the Campbell cotton lands.

In late November Confederate General John Bell Hood marched into Spring Hill, Tennessee, and Nathaniel Cheairs's plantation Rippavilla became part of the killing ground of the Battle of Spring Hill. Both armies camped there at one time or another. Some skirmishing took place there and both armies marched through as they progressed toward the Battle of Franklin on November 30. If Louisa was on the war front in the fall, she returned by November. She may well have been in Texas that fall, though Louisa recalls her absence until winter. Leonidas was back in Camden, Arkansas, by then, and wrote to Louisa in Waco.

> I wrote to you on yesterday—Since that time I have made application & obtained a 60 days leave—I start tomorrow to go to Mississippi to attend to Brother's affairs and his family. I shall make my

stay there as short as possible & Come on out to see you & the children—I shall try to Induce Mary to Come to Texas with her family as soon as the roads through the bottoms will permit—I wish Rush & her family of Children was down—The Children must go to school. If I have to Rob to pay their tuitions try & impress it upon Lulu & Willie's Minds that they must learn as fast as possible while they have an *oportunity* [sic] tell them I shall be out there in January & will see how fast they have improved—I shall take Samuel with me to Mississippi tell John Blackman to make every edge cut in the trading line—My love to all—

your Son
LA Campbell[57]

Why John Nathaniel and his wife, Mary Danforth Campbell, returned to Mississippi, I do not know. Leonidas does seem to have been successful in getting Mary to move out to Texas at some time near the end of the war. The several women in Texas, as well as Will and Lulu, likely all spent the Christmas holiday together. I found a fragment of a letter Mary wrote from Texas to Sarah in Tennessee.

Ma sends her love to you and Aunt and says she would be much pleased to have the railroad completed especially if the good fortune would bring a visitor whom she could welcome as she would "Cousin Louisa" sister, and hopes the day is not far distant. . . .

Sammie [sic] tells me Lee [probably Leonidas] had the gin house with 35 bales of cotton burned just before he left; cotton is very low now five cents in Waco I hear__ I seldom see a paper, have lost almost all interest in the politics of the day Mr. Lambeth [their lawyer in Yazoo] writes me from Miss affairs there are too horrible to speak of entire stagnation in all business had I the means this country would not long contain me I would go to England any place rather than South__ I never yearned so for wealth as now. . . . Write soon you will find me no tardy correspondent. . . .[58]

By the spring of 1865, Will and the family no longer knew where Leonidas and Sam were. When April came and Lee surrendered on April 9, the Campbells did not hear about it. Nor I guess did they hear of the assassination of Abraham Lincoln on April 14, though I doubt that it would have disturbed them greatly, being as consumed as they were by their own sacrifice. They only learned weeks later that the war was over when the first returning soldiers showed up. They were "ragged, half-starved, and nearly all them were sick," recalls Sheppard. This must have fed their fears for how the Campbell brothers were faring. Louisa set herself to nursing again. By then she showed signs of wear from her last trek in Arkansas and Missouri. At long last, Leonidas wrote that he was recuperating from wounds and "a serious illness" at the farm in Yazoo, Mississippi. He wanted his mother to bring the family there. It must have been August before they received the letter because the Trans-Mississippi did not surrender until May 26, and Leonidas did not sign his surrender and loyalty oath until June 11 in Monroe, Louisiana. Sam and another cousin were coming to get them, he said. These two apparently appeared shortly after the letter came. Lulu recalls the occasion as the only time she ever saw Louisa shed a tear. Probably all of the Campbells had long been ready for their exile to end. Sometime close to October 1, they were packed and ready to make the lengthy trip back to Mississippi. Sam was now a twenty-one-year-old man, Lulu was seventeen, and Will was thirteen years old.

> So, we took the road again. Mother, Sam, Will, June Blackman and I, with our faithful Link, who paid not the slightest attention to his freedom, and would not hear of being left behind. . . .[59]

7

"They Still Shoot Negroes" (1865–1868)

Just before the end of the war, in March 1865, African Americans in Alabama finally had the Union army heading their way. In the last weeks of the month, Major General James Harrison Wilson marched and fought his way through Alabama with about 13,500 men in three cavalry divisions. On March 28, his forces had a skirmish with Confederates at Elyton, Alabama, where a number of the white Tarrant families had their homes. On March 30 he clashed with General Nathan Bedford Forrest for the first time at Montevallo, Alabama.[1]

On April 1 the two armies fought at a place known now as Ebenezer Church, a few miles east of Marion, where Chloe was probably living.[2] The intrepid Forrest told his men to draw their six-shooters and stand their ground, no matter how many Federals rode at them. They got off one volley with their rifles and then drew pistols and rode toward the enemy. The Union men had drawn their sabers. Lieutenant George Cowan, who was in Forrest's personal escort, wrote an account of that day's events. Forrest had a close call:

I saw General Forrest surrounded by six Federals at one time, and they were all slashing at him. One of them struck one of his pistols and knocked it from his hand. Private Phil Dodd was fortunately near and spurred his horse to the general's rescue, and shot the Federal soldier who was so close upon him, thus enabling General Forrest to draw his other pistol, with which he killed another of the group, who was still persistent in his attack upon our commander. General Forrest and Captain Boone, of the escort, were both wounded. Although Federals rode through us and over us, those that survived were beaten back, and we did not leave the field until we saw their main column advancing later.[3]

Forrest took a slash to the head that must have left quite a scar. The Confederates fell back to Selma. The Battle of Selma took place the next day over part of the twenty miles of terrain between Selma and Marion. While Wilson's invasion of Alabama must have been welcome news to African Americans, this first experience of a battle nearby must also have been terrifying. Two Union cavalry divisions routed Forrest's 5,000, costing him 2,700 casualties.[4] It was the last hurrah of the war for Forrest, the self-made cavalry commander known widely by then for some brilliant maneuvers in battle and for the slaughter of blacks at Fort Pillow. After the war, the Mississippi planter became a founder of the Ku Klux Klan and Grand Wizard of the Empire. Jefferson Davis gave the oration at his huge 1877 funeral. The same day of the Battle of Selma, April 2, 1865, Davis and his cabinet were fleeing Richmond, Virginia, and President Abraham Lincoln is said to have dreamt of his own death.[5]

During those last convulsive days, a Methodist chaplain with the 7th Minnesota Volunteer Infantry came to Alabama's black belt. Elijah Evan Edwards, later president of several colleges, kept a wartime diary, complete with many sketches. He recorded that in the days after the Battle of Selma throngs of blacks swept into the town and also that many were routinely murdered by angry whites.[6]

During the previous year Edwards's unit had been among those chasing Price's army, including Leonidas and Samuel Campbell, across Arkansas. In the last months of the war, his regiment was fighting in various skirmishes from New Orleans to Mobile Bay, through Alabama to Selma, where he was camped all summer in 1865. He gives a ground-level view of how life proceeded in the area where Chloe Tarrant lived at the end of the war. It is my assumption that most, if not all, of the Tarrants were still in

Perry County or in Selma's Dallas County at the war's end, as they were still there several years later, and because it would have been difficult for them to leave. "For a great many slaves," writes historian Steven Hahn, "the course of the war made flight from slavery exceptionally difficult. Substantial sections of interior Virginia, North and South Carolina, and Mississippi; almost all of Georgia, Alabama, Florida and Texas; and sections of Tennessee and Louisiana remained in Confederate hands at least until the war's last months."[7]

Chloe had been thirteen years old when she was emancipated by Lincoln and, at the end of the war, probably not at all liberated from her situation, she was now fifteen. Her parents, now forty-three and thirty-eight years old were probably grateful to be as young as they were when the armies appeared, for they could hope for many years to enjoy "freedom," whatever that might come to mean. If one remembers that Chloe was roughly Lulu's age, and then compares what is known of their two lives in the Civil War, it is easy to see the vacuum that frustrates the construction of a narrative putting the two together. Perhaps it will help to look at it in the most simple way: Chloe might well have been moved around from place to place like the Campbell bondwomen or, more likely, without any threat of troops nearby, she may have been working in the cotton fields and living on increasingly scarce food, consisting mainly of vegetables from the garden for these four years. For every day that Lulu traveled or lay sick in bed with malaria or a dislocated shoulder, Chloe probably worked sunup to sundown and beyond. As the Union troops came into Dallas and Perry County, Alabama, Chloe would never before have seen such a sight, and probably had never been out of the state. She likely knew nothing of the world beyond the local farms.

Elijah Edwards, who had by then seen a great deal of the war and a number of states beyond his own, arrived in Alabama literally as the war ended. As the Minnesota troops marched north through the backwoods of Alabama, Edwards says, "The negroes crowded the roadsides to see us pass. They were delighted. They had been told that our soldiers had . . . a horn on the forehead and one eye just underneath. 'Bress God, it was no such a ting' One sable Goddess, Diana or Dinah shouted to our grinning boys. Some of the soldiers got caught up in the merriment of a soldier who tied a cowhorn to his head, and when the joke was revealed, many blacks followed along with the army. In consequence a small army of darkies swarmed on our flanks. . . . They had a general idea that they were going north to be free."[8]

The next day, a messenger "rode galloping along our lines shouting at the top of his voice, "Peace, peace, Lee has surrendered." The march stopped, "guns were thrown upon the ground, the flags were all unfurled. Men rushed frantically about cheering, hugging, handshaking, weeping." They saw white flags hung out, and met up with some Rebel soldiers who said they were glad it was over and they just wanted to go home. As they neared Montgomery, he says, "the soldiers behaved generally well," but a few ran off "grubbing and stealing." Edwards deemed it "their last chance for plunder." Three never returned, records Edwards, having been "killed by rebels who saw no good reason why they should be robbed in time of peace." (As the occupation began, there were continued problems with Union men looting and robbing in the area. Some were turned in to their superiors, some were just killed by their victims.) When the troops took Montgomery, they flew the Union flag from the dome of the capitol. Throngs of blacks and poor whites came to greet them. Around the first of May, they heard about Lincoln's assassination. "It is well for the people of the south that the news of this tragic event was not confirmed at once but dawned on us slowly. If the soldiers had been at first convinced of its truth it is probably that no power could have prevented scenes of violence."[9]

Early on, a few blacks established themselves in the camp, entertaining and doing chores in exchange for something to eat. Edwards, having his first real encounter with African Americans, was taking notes every day on blacks he saw in the area. He was particularly astonished by the fact that the black women could balance loads on their heads while walking, "the most difficult being to balance a tub of water, which the wenches were able to do apparently without effort." His drawing of one of these women has stayed with me since I first found it, being a kind of glimpse back into Chloe's time and place, and unlike other sketches I'd seen from the time.

Of course, while it seems logical that my great-great-grandmother Caroline, Chloe's mother, may have carried loads this way, I wouldn't know. Despite seeing women do this everywhere I've been in West Africa, and seeing pictures of women in the Sea Islands carrying loads this way, I have to say I had never really envisioned my own family members walking around balancing loads on their heads in Alabama. Maybe they did. Certainly it was not part of any known family lore. But then, if everyone could do it, why would any of our aunts or uncles have mentioned that Grandmother Caroline carried the wash on her head? Besides, people would have learned to be ashamed of a skill that specifically said Africa.

There are a thousand such habits new to a white chaplain from the Midwest in 1865 that would have been consciously dropped in the coming years. So many that our own art and literature have failed to take many of them into account, even as we have tried to reimagine changes when families moved to cities and to the north. What needs to be shown is not just sweeping the yard with a broom, cooking bread in skillets, keeping fetishes, and praying to the living forces of nature, but how people walked, the colors they wore. Edwards remarks on some of the hairdos, fashioned with the natural hair, not in braids, not straightened, but in shapes that may have signified styles or meanings not seen in photos of African styles today. A book I read on archeological digs at plantation sites commented on the profusion of blue bead necklaces worn by women; and another book remarked that blue beads were linked to Muslim religious practice. It sends the mind reeling for lost clues about blue beads. My cousin Joan used to remark that all the women in my family wore cuff-style bracelets—her grandmother, her mother, my mother, me, and my sisters. She associated this with our African past and what the women in the family wore one hundred years ago. She and I once pondered one that was supposed to be 150 years old in a Charleston antique market—we both thought its floral engraving reminiscent of her grandmother's ever-present silver cuff, and concluded a white lady would not be wearing such a large band in the 1850s. What is intriguing about our conversation is that the bracelet was clearly not African. We just thought that it would have been *worn* by an African-American. It is as though those habits that were *labeled* African were dropped, and those that were not specifically labeled that way remained. Joan is no longer here but the bracelet sits on my dresser.

On May 9 Edwards's outfit received orders to move by boat to Selma and to maintain a garrison there until order and peace took hold. He describes the burned buildings of Selma still smoking. He was told that the army of Major General James H. Wilson, who ran Forrest out, behaved "in a style worthy of Quantrill," though Edwards thinks it a "doubtless exaggeration." He writes the locals told him Wilson's men ransacked houses, stripped jewelry off women, and searched their bodies for hidden valuables. In condemning "such barbarousness" in his diary, he specifically mentions rebel horrors at Andersonville and Fort Pillow.[10] Within two weeks, Edwards was ensconced in a camp at Selma. At this point, he says, "the story . . . of rebel atrocities is slowly coming to our ears and it is chiefly in . . . regard to the treatment of freedmen both before and since the truce to hostilities."

Soon as it was definitely known that Lee had surrendered the murder of negroes commenced. It seems as if the defeated could by turning upon the unhappy cause of all their reverses and shooting them in this way revenge themselves and keep up their feeling of superiority. The negroes have been shot down at sight in some neighborhoods. The policy of their murderers is to kill them since they cannot retain them as slaves. Hundreds of terrified negroes have fled to this military for protection and some of their assassins have had the coolness to come in to town.[11]

Killers were sometimes arrested by the military, according to Edwards, who thought this meant troops would need to be in the South for a long time, but for the most part it seems to me that they did nothing about it. A week later he writes:

The people are slowly bending to the new order of things, but not gracefully. A few labor under the impression that the government has surrendered to them. . . . Some try to hold on to their slaves, and have murdered some for asserting their freedom. Their theory seems to be that by surrendering their arms they have placed the government under obligation to restore their human chattels. Meanwhile the negroes uncertain of their status continue to come in. The black and ebony tide threatens to overwhelm us. What to do with them is the question. Those that are able to make terms with their former masters are sent back. The others are corraled in a large pen where they are fed and cared for by the government.[12]

I have no way of knowing if Chloe's family found themselves in one of the contraband camps, though the camp where Edwards was chaplain may have been the one nearest to them. Edwards found everyone, both black and white, near starvation, and the army gave out rations daily for the entire time they were in Selma. I assume the Tarrant family did go to the Union army for food, but after some of the soldiers' behavior toward freedmen and women became known, black ministers started advising people against spending any time at the camps. People who came into the bigger towns certainly seem to have been worse off for shelter than those on farms. The *Montgomery Advertiser* reported at the time that some people lived on an old fairground there, and that thousands were "living in shanties, old furnaces, boilers, and at the ruins of the arsenals' foundries, and under shelters on the banks of the river and other such places as they can squat upon and remain undisturbed." That many never went back to the plantations, even in winter, speaks volumes about life in slavery. My grandmother recorded in her memoir that once Chloe came to work in the Campbell kitchen in the 1870s, one of the differences she enjoyed was the plentiful supply of food. Edwards writes that the army regarded some of the refugees coming to the camp as a nuisance, "especially . . . some of the wenches who hang about camp pretending to be cooks and washer women and begging, stealing." Some of these were arrested, and then "some of the rougher class of soldier amuse themselves by the . . . sport of tossing some of these poor creatures in a blanket."[13]

That summer the area had a profusion of magnolias, hollies, laurels, willows, mimosa, and mulberries. Also growing were apricots, plums, dewberries, and strawberries, which freedmen and women "sold in the streets at cents a quart." I was amused by the fact that the foliage that so charmed Edwards in June, had him complaining by mid-July when the heat was "torrid" and he was gasping from the scent of the "dense mulberry foliage" and the "heavy, penetrating almost sickening odor of a jasmine hedge nearby."[14]

Edwards says that planters were hiring some of the freedpeople in the camp but left the aged and sick, and he guesses that three quarters of the freedmen and women there would find work. The fact that the planter elite was leaving behind the old retainers contradicts all the sentiment in the mainstream culture about those old loyal dependents who were practically part of the family. Popular culture was definitely at a remove from the facts as Edwards was finding them in Alabama. Indeed popular publications were well on the way to producing a proliferation of caricatures pertaining to the newly emancipated Negro that would do as much to keep us in our "place" in the North as the repressive laws of the former Confederacy would do to keep blacks down in the South. In "The Contraband's Return," published in *The Richmond Whig* in 1864, a popular Southern theme of the return of the former slave who has been disappointed by freedom is couched inside a plea to return to the old plantation.

> *I never knew the old plantation*
> *Was half so dear a place to me,*
> *As when among the Yankee nation*
> *The robbers told me I was free!*
> *But when I looked around for freedom,*
> *(We thought it something bright and fair)*
> *Hunger, misery and starvation*
> *Was all that met us there. . . .*
>
> *O, Massa William, see me kneeling!*
> *O, missus, say one word for me!*
> *You'll let me stay? Oh! thank you, massa;*
> *Now I'm happy! Now I'm free!*
> *I've seen enough of Yankee freedom,*
> *I've had enough of Yankee love!*
> *As they have treated the poor negro*
> *Be'st done to them above.*[15]

Reminiscent of some Stephen Foster songs of the 1850s such as "Old Folks at Home" (Suwanee), and "Massa's in the Cold Cold Ground," where fond memories dominate the slave's lyric of longing, this poem merely represents an extension of the imaginary refuge of slave affection, a denial of the elite's despotic control over the southern black population. In the postwar period the privilege of unquestioned control came under assault from anyone who upheld the reality of emancipation. What Chaplain Edwards was in fact encountering was the violent reaction some had when the freedpeople in their midst did not get on bended knee, as in the lyric, and ask to return to bondage.

On one occasion Edwards makes a sketch of a woman that he labels, "a white contraband." The picture is of a woman who definitely appears to be white, in a wide brim hat with wavy hair pulled back underneath. Edwards had been told that the "octoroon" came in that morning pleading for her life and asking protection from her master, whom Edwards learned was "a sort of Southern blue beard." Edwards describes her as "whiter than many white women."[16]

> She reported that her master had stripped her naked and burned her with red hot tongs, and she offered to exhibit the scars, but the gallant captain would not permit the exhibition. The story is generally believed. The master's character makes it probable.[17]

The master's name, Tom Walker, caught my eye because Chloe's younger sister later married a black Walker. The single, wealthy, fifty-eight-year-old Thomas Walker owned 102 slaves in Dallas County in 1860, and was the only planter named Walker in the census. In Perry County where Chloe's family lived, a T. A. Walker held thirty-eight slaves. Presumably, the army assisted the woman.[18]

During this first month of Edwards's encounters with the former bondmen of the area, he continues to note their intense joy at being freed from chattel slavery. He describes those kept in the corral as dancing and fiddling all night, and seems to find curious that they would siesta in the middle of the day "when the hot sun shines upon them with all its fire." He also is struck by their naive trust in all the Yankees.

On his first talk before a black congregation, Edwards was taken aback by the reaction. "The mere reading of the 14th chapter of St. John set them wild. They were consequently in a very receptive mood afterwards at the close of the service they gathered around me and indulged in the most exhausting handshaking demonstration. I distributed some books among them to those able to read." Days later he witnessed a group of about twenty African Americans performing a baptism by immersion in the Alabama River, which greatly impressed him not only because everyone was so demonstrative, but because those baptized actually felt they had been cleansed. I felt badly for him that he had so long ministered to people who failed to demonstrate the depth of feeling that so fascinated him. And, of course, the music got hold of him—the "most mournful, most musical" singing—and he would pursue this music elsewhere during his Alabama sojourn.[19]

Two months after arriving there, Edwards felt the potential for anarchy was still real and that violence in Alabama was still on a hair-trigger.

> They still shoot negroes and try to force others to work on their plantations asserting that there has never been any emancipation proclamation. . . . There is a class down here radically contumacious and barbarous.[20]

Edwards began to speak to more black congregations and to perform weddings. So captured by the music, he also began to write at length about it, even noting down the lyrics, the fact that some were called jubas, and commenting on the overwhelmingly sad nature of the music. This preoccupation reminded me a great deal of Lulu's recollection of lyrics. In his case the intellectual interest seemed to mask an emotional reaction perhaps akin to the solace Lulu took from the sorrow songs. In turn, I am fascinated that Edwards documented the miserable experiences of freedmen and women and yet he was startled at the depth of pain expressed in the music. One African American minister visited Edwards "for advice as to what he and his brethren should do." The black congregants wished to separate themselves from the church and connect to the northern wing of the denomination. They were holding meetings in the basement of their former owners' church. He writes that people asked, "If we are brudders in Christ Jesus what for de whites occupy the upper room and we worship God in the basement?"

This scenario also took place in Marion with two former planter churches, one of them Siloam Baptist Church, whose black membership included the Tarrants. They began the Berean Baptist Church and laid the cornerstone of a brick and mortar church in 1873.[21]

According to my friend Christine Clark-Evans, a professor at Pennsylvania State University, African Americans just out of slavery gathered to hear African American preachers and build their own churches for one simple reason: "African Americans worshipped a different God; they worshipped a God both just and merciful."

Edwards and his regiment left Selma on July 20 by train, and he describes the departure: "The heat was excessive. The men on the open cars sheltered themselves with boughs from the trees till the train looked like a moving forest, not unlike the wood of Dunsinane." At Demopolis, Alabama, they caught a steamboat down the Tombigbee River to the next station, where they caught a train into Meridian, Mississippi. Edwards found Jackson, Mississippi, "worse battered . . . than Selma, being in fact a mass of ruins." Moving on to Vicksburg, "we traveled all night over rough roads and through ghostly scenery. The entire route looks as it had been the theater of a battle rout and is yet somewhat perilous to travel. The night before a traveler had been robbed . . ." In Vicksburg, a pickpocket stole a diary he carried containing two years of battle notes and a picture of his wife.[22]

At the beginning of the fall of 1865, the Campbells were still in the midst of transition as well. Shifting to their situation, there is a drastic change of tone from Edwards's observation of Alabama. The problems of these planters, who were among the elite in Missouri, Texas, and Mississippi, were quite different from those of ordinary people in Alabama, where the Tarrants lived. Whatever means Leonidas used to jump start the family income again were not communicated in the letters I have seen, all of which were addressed to the women of the family who may have known little about the family's finances. So, their day-to-day concerns were much more about reestablishing the material comforts of life enjoyed before the war and trying to resume progress toward the expectations they had then. When the Campbells set out toward the Mississippi around the first of October, they were in high spirits to be together again.

The first leg of their journey took them through a drought-stricken area, but after that they had no problems. They rode to Shreveport and then went on to the tiny town of Enterprise, Louisiana, where they met Leonidas. He tried to convince Louisa to come to Mississippi, but she insisted she wanted to go to Springfield to reclaim her home. The family patriarch had decided Will should go to school in Yazoo, and Lulu to a school in St. Louis. It was arranged then, over much protest from thirteen-year-old Will, that he would be sent on to Mississippi with Sam and Link. Leonidas's housekeeper was to look out for them at Valley Home, and Louisa promised to send for them as soon as she got their home repaired. This was the last time Will ever saw his mother.[23]

Louisa, Lulu, and Leonidas went by boat down the Red River and then by a larger vessel to New Orleans, where Lulu was to get school clothes and Leonidas had business. They went to the St. Charles Hotel, which was evidently a grand edifice on the polite western border of the French Quarter. Then they went shopping. As Lulu described both her humble Texas clothes and her New Orleans finery, some terms, like "Garibaldi waist," eluded me. When I was a kid some older people used the word waist for shirt. When I put the Garibaldi variety into a search engine I discovered the incredible world of "affordable authenticity" in Civil War-era garb. Yes, you too can acquire a nipped waist, balloon-sleeved, Nehru-collar Garibaldi waist, even in women's size 28. Well, I thought, I've seen antebellum homes, food, monuments, battlefields, and re-enactors, how could I forget clothes? The outfits designed for re-enactors are, of course, exactly as they would have been—no Velcro. At seventeen years old and after a war, Lulu undoubtedly did not need the larger sizes of on-line catalogs, and was treated to clothes assuredly more exquisitely made and fitted to her figure.[24]

Here again I am tempted to compare the end of Lulu's war with the end of Chloe's; for two southern girls there could hardly be more contrast. Chloe would have been hard put to acquire fabric to begin with, as Lulu was in Texas, but that is only where one might begin. The fact that Lulu's uncle sent her north for a formal high school education, and then college, and wrote her frequent letters insisting that she out-perform the other students, not only speaks to his interest in some aspects of modernity, but indicates Lulu's uncommon privilege. Chloe would never receive even an elementary education.

Albert Morgan observed during his years farming and serving as Yazoo sheriff that black females had little chance of not being abused on plantations and in town. Having seen students return to the freedmen's school after being raped by a "gentleman," and having had a desperate parent offer him one of her daughters, he found that girls Chloe's age were only able to stand up in pride and safety in church and school. They were at risk, he says, everywhere from their parents' homes to places of employment, "almost always upon the streets, or in the fields." Given that they were "at all times liable to the grossest vulgarities and obscenities from white youth and men, and from black, too," he found it amazing that more were not raped. "The fact is, the aspiring young colored girl, black or light complexioned, has always had to contend with such a multitude of obstacles that those who have conquered them are entitled to wear a crown in this world, as well as in the next." One young woman who was the victim of rape by a local gentleman of the elite told him, "ain't no use for me to try, I'm nothing but a nigger anyway." Chloe surely understood these realities, as so many of her family may have been the products of this common form of assault. This may have happened to her mother. That Chloe was always so determined to move on is a tribute both to her own sense of self and to those in her family who gave her that sense of worth. The fact that Lulu and Chloe led such divergent lives and may have even known each other really intrigues me. Would Lulu have seen in Chloe another "foster-sister"? Somehow I think both would have seen more of the differences.[25]

Lulu met one of Leonidas's lady friends, of whom Lulu remarked, "[s]he had perfect taste," and also the woman's daughter. They assisted her in shopping for a black silk alpaca school outfit, a grey silk dress "for the street," russet button boots, coat, hat, and a soft white nun's veil—the last item required for formal wear at her Catholic school. She also acquired a white frock "with a creamy frill of old lace," slippers, gloves, and fan. Returning to the St. Charles Hotel, she marveled at herself as only a teenager can. That evening, no doubt they dined well, and Lulu received flowers from her uncle.

They all decamped to hear Adelina Patti at the opera to recover from the rigors of the day, the trip, and the war. The glamour of New Orleans must have refreshed them. Louisa did not join in. I can well imagine that hotel bed was good enough, and at the same time, that nothing would ever be enough.[26]

In Alabama, the Tarrants may have gone for more than food from the occupying Union army of which Edwards was a part. I cannot imagine that with all the celebration going on among the new freedmen and women they would not have gone at least once simply out of curiosity. If they went for assistance about working for wages, they would have been advised to first negotiate with their former owners. In hindsight, it is easy to see that the real arrangements might not have involved wages at all. If they accepted a situation where they worked for food and lodging, they would have been too hard-pressed for cash to move anywhere else. Rumors circulated around the South that the Federal officials would distribute land confiscated from Confederates to former slaves. The rumors arose in part because General William Tecumseh Sherman did exactly that in January 1865, doling out forty-acre allotments in Georgia and Florida—hence the expression "forty acres and a mule." That arrangement was only to last for a year, but the idea of land redistribution spread like wildfire. That being the case, people like the Tarrants might also stay put in hopes of receiving some of the land they had already worked.[27]

By late that year, the newly formed Freedman's Bureau (formally titled the Bureau of Refugees, Freedmen and Abandoned Lands) had field offices throughout the South to assist people newly out of bondage with labor issues, legal issues, and education, among other efforts. At this time the bureau agents specifically advised freedmen and women that land would *not* likely be given to them, and that they should make work contracts for 1866. Most of these contracts ran for a year and, by several means, kept the laborers wherever they were located for at least that year. The bureau also attempted to keep track of what it called "outrages" against African Americans in each district. Reading even one month's entries in the Alabama records is chilling, including many incidents of maiming violence against laborers inflicted by "employers" and events in which freedwomen or men were assaulted by small groups of white males on the road or hauled out of their homes and assaulted, in some cases for refusing a labor contract.[28]

African Americans had several reactions to the sudden rise in violence against them and the conflicting reports on being awarded land. By Christmas of 1865, there were rumors that African Americans were planning an uprising January 1 to take what they considered their due. DuBois writes that in Alabama African Americans making moves to defend themselves against the violence fed the fear.

> The negroes were disappointed because of the delayed division of lands. There was a natural desire to get possession of firearms, and all through the summer and fall, they were acquiring shotguns, muskets, and pistols, in great quantities. In several instances, the civil authorities, backed by the militia, searched Negro houses for weapons, and sometimes found supplies which were confiscated.[29]

That fall was when Albert Morgan and his older brother, Charles, arrived in Yazoo, Mississippi. In 1861 the two brothers from Wisconsin had planned to go to Oberlin College but chose instead to join the Union army. By 1865 Albert was a twenty-three-year-old survivor of Bull Run, Gettysburg, and the siege at Petersburg. He had grown up in an abolitionist household and during the war his parents belonged to a Freedman's Aid Society. After recovering from malaria in Petersburg, he and his

brother went west looking for a place to make their own, and finally decided instead on Mississippi, where they leased a farm in Yazoo County.[30]

When the Morgans first landed in Yazoo and while they were still being
welcomed and tutored by their cash-poor landlord, Colonel J. J. B. White,
rumors began to spread of a Negro insurrection. Rumor had it that the
rising was based in Vicksburg. In reality the rumor was probably part of a
single panic spreading across the South. Morgan found the rumors to be
sketchy and unbelievable and thought that the talk might be an excuse to
rearm. (It would be the first of many such maneuvers he would witness in
Yazoo.)[31] Hahn explains the widespread nature of the panic:

> This has come to be known as the "Christmas Insurrection Scare of 1865,"
> and its resemblance to earlier slave insurrection panics . . . was not fortu-
> itous. It came at a time of heightened tensions and anxieties, of political
> division and social unrest; it inflated episodic resistance and discontent
> into full-blown conspiracies; it implicated outsiders; and it served to in-
> spire greater vigilance among whites and greater repression against blacks.
> But whereas previous panics tended to be localized and somewhat brief,
> the 1865 scare proved more protracted and far more extended in scope.
> And together with the rumors of property redistribution that circulated
> among freedpeople, it came to be a weapon of direct struggle over the bal-
> ances of power in the countryside.[32]

According to Hahn, one upshot of the Christmas scare was that blacks
in various places in the South refused to make labor contracts until
sometime in January of 1866. For some this meant that planters who
paid wages were willing to pay a little more once they became anxious
about being short of labor. Southerners of the old school were quick to
contact the Reconstruction governors about needing militias and kept up
pressure to have African American soldiers removed from their areas.
One such tiny group of black soldiers was stationed in Yazoo City. The
letters to governors were very effective and black soldiers were all called
back over the next year and a half.[33]

∞

Sometime in late fall, Louisa and Lulu boarded the steamer *Missouri* but had to get off at Cairo because of ice in the river. They went to St. Louis by train, arriving in January, when Lulu was to start school. According to one letter, they arrived in St. Louis on January 13, 1866. She was to be there for two years to make up for what she missed of high school studies. In St. Louis they evidently did "a good deal of shopping." Louisa probably had to outfit a wagon with all that she might need to camp out at her occupied and damaged Springfield home. There is no mention of any fear of an uprising in their letters. Oddly, in a letter from there to Sarah, Lulu says at the beginning of the letter that Leonidas was incredibly improved in his health, weighing 182 pounds, and had left New Orleans after their departure to go "up the Washita." Then at the end of the letter she said he was doing poorly. This is a puzzle I cannot explain, as well as why he would have gone up this Oklahoma river.[34]

The icy trip Louisa and Lulu had to St. Louis took place during a particularly brutal winter. Evidently the winter of 1865–1866 was an extremely cold one even in the South. Freedmen and women in places like Alabama faced the dual threats of cold and starvation.

> With the onset of winter, food became scarce for blacks and whites alike—so much so that an estimated 200,000 Alabamians stood in danger of dying from starvation. Reports circulated of circumstances that forced whites and blacks to resort to stealing hogs, chickens, and stray animals. Freedmen's Bureau agents issued rations to more than 70,000 destitute persons in November 1865 alone. . . . Between November 1865 and September 1866, Bureau agents issued 3,789,788 rations to about 166,589 white and 72,115 African American indigents.[35]

In 1866 the state of Alabama undertook a "colored" census but I have been unable to find any of the Tarrants on that census. I have never solved the mystery of where these almost two dozen people were at this time.

The contrast of the situations of planters such as the Campbells, who seem to be quite well off during this time, and the conditions facing the people raising the cotton is startling. Considering that some significant portion of these workers were also the kinfolk of the planters, this seems one of those moments when the eyewitnesses of the time saw the ugly result of America's peculiar institution at its most raw: the homeless, starved four million—scarred, illiterate, and primarily skilled at farming—roaming the towns and cities in search of food and shelter.

By March Leonidas had decided to send his brother Samuel to school in Tennessee. This was most likely the La Grange Military Academy, which according to the town's website, was operating in the late 1850s and early 1860s, later replaced by an institution called the La Grange Male Academy. The school was in the tiny town of La Grange, Tennessee, "La Belle Village" according to locals, a reportedly idyllic antebellum town of gracious homes with tall columns and green lawns. Apparently it is unchanged today, except for the shrinking of its population to 167 souls. For those ready for another pearl of Confederate lore, the village boasts the home of the so-called Queen of the Confederacy, a young lady whose image graced the Confederate dollar bills. Lucy Holcombe Pickens married well and had her first baby in the winter palace of Alexander II, Czar of all the Russias. He and the Czarina were the child's godparents, and this obligation evidently fell to their son after the father was blown up by a revolutionary's bomb. The website coyly refers to the incident as a fatal explosion in the dining room, making it seem rather more culinary. During the Civil War, Pickens' husband was governor of South Carolina and her grand life continued.[36]

Will Campbell had to wait for months for his uncle to return to Mississippi. At the end of January, Leonidas wrote Sarah from a steamer somewhere "below Vicksburg" to say he was headed up to Yazoo for a few days and then on to Memphis with fourteen-year-old Will and twenty-two-year-old Sam. He suggests sending his mail to a man there. Clearly, at this point Leonidas resumed the whirlwind of business travel and socializing with the planter elite that consumed him before the war.[37]

But he missed Sarah's letter in Memphis and found it waiting for him in New Orleans where in March he was once again escorting ladies to the sights—this time eligible wealthy southern girls.

> Mrs. Hall [from Yazoo] came down with me & I am also an escort
> for about 7 other ladies all of them as beautiful as eastern *Houris*

[Persian, voluptuous maidens with whom the blessed live in Paradise], If I had ? met with one of the young ladies I don't think I could have withstood the temptation of courting one of them as it is I cannot decide which to take__& then I am paying *devoted* attention__to a young little widow from Louisville Ky__ the most charming lady__I have ever met__rather small__with eyes & Hair as black as "night" & the sweetest looking little mouth imaginable only 2 children & worth 26,000 dollars & I seem to be the most forward *Richmond* in the field [the suitor at the head of the line] Would you not be surprised to hear of me marrying a widow— I am going, going, & nearly gone . . . I cannot comply with your terms of marrying Miss Fanny [Smith] or of being a *bachelor. Seriously,* I shall never marry Miss Fanny__ for a long time I was seriously in court but she treated me so outrageously, that I now could not think of reviving the engagement__ Nor would I retaliate upon her__ that is one of the things of the past__ Never to be brought to life again . . . [38]

Two weeks later Leonidas was in Memphis to settle some business affairs that had apparently given him some earlier "apprehension," and there he cancelled plans to see Sarah and wrote that business requiring his immediate attention forced him to take a train for New Orleans. Other than his frequent vehement lines about how he will never marry Fanny, his letters sound like something you'd expect from a business executive today. The pace and distance of his travels seem out-of-step with the leisurely travel of the people they knew.[39]

While her son was in the midst of this round of trips between Louisiana, Mississippi, and Tennessee, Louisa Campbell had made her return to Springfield, and Fanny Smith returned from Tennessee and accompanied her to the homestead. They had difficulty getting into the house as people were living there, and finally secured as shelter Louisa's own kitchen, a separate building at the rear of the home. General Marmaduke, under whom her sons had fought, had used the house as a hospital on one of his failed incursions in Missouri. After the army had left, the same Mary Phelps who drove a supply wagon to the Battle of Pea Ridge had used it as a home for war orphans. Sometime after the end of the war the house had become the sight for a treasure hunt owing to a rumor that "a fortune was buried somewhere on the Campbell place and large holes were dug around the foundation, under the floor and out in the orchards." No treasure was found. Still, she had been extremely fortunate in one regard: her Union-supporting friends in Springfield had paid the taxes on the land so she wouldn't lose it. Her former bondwoman, the eighty-six-year-old Eve, came and worked for her to help get the house in repair.[40]

Lulu had started school at the Academy of the Visitation in St. Louis, savoring her stay with the nuns so much that she later converted to Catholicism. Louisa wrote her about the damage and filth in the house and the repairs she was making. In mid-May, Lulu was expecting Louisa and Sarah to come to the school, and was irritated that Leonidas had said he would not get there until July. "Every letter I get he postpones coming. The first thing I know he will be wanting me to stay during vacation . . . I have not been home for five years . . . and I am anxious to get there." Louisa had promised Lulu that the family would all be together that summer "in our own home." But Lulu would be left there at school at least till the next month. One day in May, the Mother Superior called her but was unable to prepare her for the news that her grandmother was dead.[41]

Louisa Terrill Cheairs Campbell died on May 29, 1866, at fifty-six years of age. She had developed pneumonia and lived only a few days after taking sick. She passed too quickly for any of her family to be reached. Louisa had given birth to ten children from the time she was nineteen until her forty-second year and, despite the fact that only one died in infancy, she had outlived six of her children. Her journey had taken her from a settled existence among the gentry of her Tennessee home to a pioneer life, which in turn had equipped her rather well to live on the road throughout the Civil War. Never having secured her home from the squatters, she died in the kitchen building she probably seldom used since the household cooking had always been the work of her slaves.

Of all her surviving children, Will certainly knew her least. He was raised by her only for his first eight years, and then was set on his own solitary path by the guns of the Civil War. When she died, Will Campbell was waiting to come home from Mississippi, but now, at fourteen, he was planted in the Delta for life.

Several weeks after Louisa's death, Sarah Rush Owen wrote a letter from Springfield to her oldest daughter, eleven-year-old Mary Frances, who was in Tennessee with Sarah's other children. I don't know if Sarah was trying to shield her daughter from the tragedy but the letter noticeably lacks the expected sentiment on arriving at the scene of her mother's death.

> I do not know now when I will go back to Tennessee, as soon though as I get through my business__ I will go down to St. Louis . . . and it may be I will go on to Columbia, If I do, your Cousin Lu will go with me I will stop for you or send up immediately after getting to Aunts __ Your Cousin Lu is quite an elegant young lady__I saw her when I passed through St Louis . . . I expect you will go to the Convent with Lu next session. . . .
>
> Miss Fanny [Smith] sends a great deal of love to you__ Some robbers broke into the Bank and stole Eleven thousand dollars from her Pa (old Mr. Smith) the night before I got here__but he has thousands left__ and the loss dont hurt him. Miss Fannys house is nearly done, she is going to house keeping soon, We are staying at your Grand Ma's house until her's is finished Every body was very kind to your Grand Ma during her sickness she died with Congestive Chills__only lived three days after she was taken.
>
> Her place is nearly all refenced and there are eight families living on the place, making in all about fifty persons__five families of them came over from England last May.
>
> Our Lands will sell very high and I hope we will soon have money enough to settle down in a little home of our own. . . .[42]

Sarah did not soon get to settle in a home of her own or to move back to Springfield. Leonidas sold some Missouri land to his future father-in-law that July, but I do not know if that is the deal she thought would bring her money enough to move. He was planning to sell more Missouri land in the fall. In July Leonidas took the now twenty-two-year-old Sam to see the school in Tennessee, and was then planning to take Sarah's daughter Lucy to Lulu's convent school. He had heard from Yazoo that the crops looked "encouraging" and that Willie was well. Back in Mississippi in August, he had decided Will was to go to a school in Yazoo and board with a local family. In the fall of 1866, Leonidas paid tuition for Will to attend the Trinity School for Boys in Yazoo City.[43]

The Trinity Church had actually been burned down, so when the boys' day school was set up in 1866, it was held in the local Baptist Church. His tuition, board, and book expenses for the one month from October 17 to November 19 were $24.65. (That may sound good by today's standards, but it was a fair amount then.) He paid for the adolescent to be boarded at the home of Mrs. Oceana Hyatt, a forty-three-year-old widow who was raising her three orphaned nephews—Willie, Harry, and John Quackenboss. She had also raised their two older sisters, but these three boys, ages thirteen, fifteen, and eighteen, would take their place several years later as friends in Will's photo album. Another photograph in the album portrays a teenage girl named Margy Corbett, whom he must have met at this time. She also lived in town, and like the others had lost her parents; both Corbetts died in a yellow fever epidemic in the 1850s. If Will was now to be boarding in different homes and schools till he was old enough to have his own place, at least he began his journey among other children not only uprooted by the war but wounded by death at home.[44]

Around the same time in Marion, Alabama, according to local stories, a wounded Union soldier who had remained in Alabama began teaching black students in Marion, Alabama. This soldier is assumed by the school's historians to have been among the federal troops under Wilson, who fought near Marion or one of those in the occupation forces like Edwards. "In 1866–67 the newly freed people of Perry County—approximately sixty-six percent of the population—drew up a petition for the incorporation of [the] Lincoln School in Marion, Alabama, in honor of recently assassinated President Abraham Lincoln. Pooling their resources, the former slaves erected buildings for the school on land donated by a white man and appealed to the American Missionary Association for teachers from the

North." Chloe became a staunch supporter of this school, though she seems never to have been able to take classes there.[45]

A. T. Morgan, at Tokeba Plantation in Mississippi, began his education in the situation of freedpeople as he hired workers for his farm, offering the fairest wages he could and, in some cases, finding people would work for him simply because he was not from Mississippi, and treated people with decency. Thus began the alienation of his southern "hosts."

One of the first things he noticed was that African Americans were attempting to be hired in family groups. This is particularly understandable given the numerous accounts of freedmen and women making vigorous and extended attempts to reunite with their families after the war. Hahn writes that freedpeople began organizing themselves into "squads" made up of kinfolk, with one person as "head." The squads were mostly men, as women began to refuse fieldwork. I was interested to learn this, as I had noticed that in about 90 percent of the southern black households I pored over in the census records, the wives and mothers reported being full-time housekeepers. This struck me as something of a luxury, and at first I assumed this to be an indicator that there were more ample supplies of necessities—which was definitely not the case.

Some observers of the time reported that women were lazy and wanted to emulate their former mistresses, and others held that the male heads of household wanted to emulate white households by keeping the wives at home as a full-time mothers. Full-time mothers would have been a boon to the community, but I doubt if this motivated the change. From what I have read of the outrages committed against freedpeople, particularly in Alabama, staying out of the fields was *safer*. The dangers against women were almost greater than those facing men as exposure to menacing males was a daily occurrence.

Together, these observers described a virtual "withdrawal" of freedwomen and children from farm labor. What they failed to see was a process of reorganization and renegotiation designed to limit the discretionary power of employers, better protect vulnerable family members, and redeploy the labor force to the advantage of freed households. . . . There can be little doubt that black women, and especially those attached by kinship to able-bodied black men, performed less field labor immediately after emancipation than they did as slaves. But freedwomen "withdrew" not so much from field labor in general as from *full-time* field labor under the supervision of white employers and managers.[46]

Among the Tarrants, staying home was not possible for most. Only Caroline was keeping house. The rest worked, some at home as seamstresses and washerwomen; others worked as domestic servants or farmers from 1865 at least until the 1880s. In addition, the dozens of black households I looked at from the 1870s through 1900 invariably had one or two single black males boarding with them who worked as farm hands. This seems to me to be an indication that to fill out a squad, family units took in extra males.

Morgan hired the whole families and immediately began to learn that the protections for women and children took hold at his farm. The wives stayed at home to attend more fully to what had previously been a much-limited "private" life. All hands seem to have come into the fields at harvest time, but children among freedpeople had some opportunities to attend school (such as were available) and women were able to more freely see to food gathering, preparation, laundry, clothing, etc. Morgan observed at the time that sexual exploitation of young African American girls was to some degree expected from the "masters."

By the time Morgan was setting up a gin and a lumber mill at Tokeba, the old political structure was pretty much back in place in Yazoo County. Robert S. Hudson, author of Mississippi's infamous Black Codes, was a delegate to the constitutional convention, and soon after, the state enacted a somewhat modified version of the codes. Across the South members of the former ruling elite were elected.

However much it [the Mississippi legislature] may have modified Hudson's recommendations, it enacted one of the most severe Black Codes produced by any of the provisional legislatures called into session during the fall of 1865 at the conclusion of the various state constitutional conventions. The

Mississippi code prohibited its black citizens from owning farmland or guns, renting land, or testifying in court against whites. To force African Americans to labor for white planters, the legislature placed so-called black minors under the control of their former owners and compelled every adult to sign a contract for employment.[47]

The lone agent of the Freedman's Bureau in Yazoo pleaded for help from the federal government—to little avail—after receiving a number of depositions from freedmen and women documenting violence done to them over labor contracts, or simply because former masters insisted they could do as they pleased, including killing blacks. "Alarmed and bewildered by the mounting violence, Freedman's Bureau agent Charles W. Clarke begged headquarters for guidance. Although he hoped his superiors would at least curtail the new state laws . . . the bureau challenged only the prohibition against black farmers leasing land and let all other provisions of the laws stand."[48]

In 1866 the Morgan brothers were making a go of it although the first crop was poor because they started late. But farmers in the area had lost two crops in 1864 and 1865, and living in debt was seemingly universal. Albert Morgan had a dispute with the Colonel over the fact the Morgans treated the black workers as people with rights. When Albert had insisted "a large share of a laborer's hire is respectful consideration from his employer," he made an enemy of the colonel.[49]

According to John C. Willis, some of the longtime planters in Yazoo decided to do something about those farmers like Morgan who had adapted to the new order when it came to hiring freedmen. "Along the Yazoo 'an organization of men whose avowed purpose is to discourage freedmen and moderate planters' attempted to resurrect slaveholders' hegemony," writes Willis. "Their tactics: 'a concerted system of persecution by murdering negroes at work upon the plantations' of honest planters."[50]

∽

President Andrew Johnson tried to accommodate former Confederates during 1865 and 1866, and had allowed them to begin putting the old power structure back in place with impunity. In the spring of 1866, the U. S. Congress stepped in, refused to seat the all-white representatives, and began hearing testimony on events in the South. Northerners were not only hearing that the old boys had put themselves back in power but that they were exacting vengeance on African Americans. Trying to see what kind of environment Chloe and her family were living in I checked the website dedicated to publications of the Freedmen's Bureau information. The site gives lists of some of the incidents reported to the bureau by freedmen seeking assistance. Planters who could no longer count workers as assets had no compunction about maiming workers who would not accept the old work conditions of food, a shanty, and no pay. For Alabama there are two lists for 1866 totaling fifty-three incidents, including at least twenty murders. These contain items from sites near the Tarrants' home: a freedwoman killed with an axe in Montgomery; a woman hauled out of her house in the middle of the night to a swamp, whipped and beaten; a man taken to the woods and hung until nearly dead to find out who robbed a store; another killed for refusing to sign a work contract. Near Tuscaloosa several were hung; a man who protested his wife being beaten by an employer was dragged out of his house and whipped nearly to death "with a buggy trace"; a black soldier returning home was murdered; women were assaulted, beaten, and told to leave the county. There was a school burning, a church burning, and other similar incidents. In Selma, a woman was beaten by her employer with a club, leaving her "head cut in most shocking manner." In Montgomery, another person was burned by a policeman while being detained. For July 16 alone, there are eight incidents, mostly beatings of freedwomen, and one murder. One of my shocks at looking over the lists was the predominance of assaults on women.[51]

The epidemic of violence against African Americans got into northern papers and things came to a head.[52] In March 1867 Congress passed the Military Reconstruction Acts, upending much of the president's idea of Reconstruction. "Congress gave the federal government unprecedented power to reorganize the ex-Confederate South politically, imposed political disabilities on leaders of the rebellion, and most stunning of all, extended the elective franchise to southern black males, the great majority of whom had been slaves." The acts also called for the Union generals in charge of each of the designated five districts of the South to call for new state constitutional conventions to rewrite state laws a second time.[53]

In Alabama, the indignation over being awarded freedom without a way to make a living short of accepting slavery-like work terms came hand-in-hand with this new level of terror. By 1867, there was a great deal of political activity taking shape in the area where the Tarrants lived. People organized freedmen's conventions in order to build an African American agenda.

The issues raised in the freedmen's conventions of this period were wide-ranging and geared toward obtaining all the rights of citizenship for African Americans. While the old political system had been destroyed, no new system had been put in place. A look at a list of the proposals and demands of any of the black conventions held in states of the former Confederacy is still worth a review today, as many have been accomplished by law, but not in practice. African Americans across the South were particularly concerned with being able to testify in court, become jury members, and achieve equal justice before the law. They were also very anxious to ensure the right to vote and that the ballots be counted.[54]

In 1867, African Americans in Yazoo began to arm themselves and to organize politically. Charles and Albert Morgan had a chance to see the arming firsthand when they assisted in the building of a black church that was also to be used as a school. No local people would build it so the Morgans paid their own carpenters to do the work, and donated the lumber. Threats began to be heard immediately and a few days later the freedmen, the white carpenters, and mill hands (who had been in the army) started packing pistols. Another Morgan associate, who had been an officer with African American troops and then with the Freedman's Bureau, arranged for a squad of Federal troops to be sent to Yazoo to prevent any interference with the building of the school.[55]

That fall, blacks tried to vote, but because the local officials had not yet changed, they were threatened with loss of jobs and with violence. The Morgans' crop failed, as did most crops that year, but their sawmill kept them afloat. After they got a white woman from the North to teach at the school, they started to get harassed on the streets in town and told to "walk in the street with the niggers." In court one day after being arrested on a trumped up charge, Albert Morgan was even informed that he was not white. That more or less says it all when it comes to the true tenets of white supremacy—whiteness does not include disloyalty to whiteness. With the New Reconstruction mandates in place, and a new election required, Yazoo blacks and carpetbaggers renewed their organizing.[56]

At least two of the former Campbell slaves, who no doubt experienced their own instances of discrimination, were not persuaded that progressive politics would change their lot. Maryann wrote to Sarah Rush Owen in May 1867 from Ottomwa, Iowa, where they were evidently relocated after being freed by Union forces. This may be Lulu's "mammy" Mary, though I cannot be sure. The "Abb" she refers to is apparently the same man (spelled earlier as Ab) who went with the Campbells to the U.S.-Mexican War and the Civil War. The most striking feature of the letter is that these former bondmen were very anxious to find each other.

> . . . I was happy to hear from you all again and that you was doing well I am getting along tolable well considering the times I want you to write and tell me if you have heard from Phashivanna[?] since you wrote that last letter and if she is married or not and tell her that I should be happy to see her agin I would like to know where she is so that I could write to her I want to hear from you often it gives me pleasure to learn how you are . . . remember my love to all of them. and kiss Lulu three times for me. . . . give my love to Peggy and tell her when she hears from ben to send bain my love and tell him that I am yet alive we have not seen Ellen since we parted in Missouri the last we heard of her she was in St Louis Abb was ther [illegible] but could not find her
>
> Abb is well and goes a head in affairs just the same he did in Missouri and does not let polatics trouble him in the least we are

called primarily among the Collord people dimocrats Abb sends his love to you and wishes to see you.[57]

That same May, L. A. wrote from Valley Home to Sarah, but made no reference that spring (or summer) to the kinds of events Morgan details as going on in Yazoo County. During this period as the Campbells attempted to sell some properties and settle Louisa's estate, Leonidas became consumed with the estate matters, particularly claims that turned up supposedly signed by the younger boys deeding land over to various people. These all had to be answered in court in Missouri or Tennessee and generated quite a few letters. The next day he sent Sarah a paper regarding land deeded to her and picked up for the third or fourth time the issue of his old flame Fanny.

> As I have an oportunity of sending letters to the river, I write you a few lines . . . the floods have subsided & am through planting my Crop . . . Sam has gone, Have not, Heard from him since He left, do you hear from Missouri Now, I cannot get any . . . Information from those *Confounded* People whatever . . . do you Hear from Miss Fanny Smith, & is she married, I would advise Her to marry as soon as possible I got a Letter from Till Weaver [a cousin] last Fall & she wrote me, that Miss Fanny . . . said I that was the Meanest Man, she ever knew I was truly glad to know that she has recovered, the *Equilibrium* of her *Spirits* & expected to hear of her marrying very soon . . . [58]

Miss Fanny Smith did indeed marry, settling down in Springfield with a successful farmer and widower twenty years her senior named Lewis Crenshaw. They had five children together. Lulu had by then taken up residence in Tennessee and began sending letters from John Polk Campbell's family home, "Bird Haunt," and from Aunt Nancy's, replete with stories of the doings of the servants and of friends and family getting married. She attended the Columbia Institute there whose principal was Mrs. Leonidas Polk, wife of their cousin the "fighting bishop" of the Confederacy. Sarah Rush Owen was in Missouri. It took three years of effort involving a number of trips home to clear claims made on their property and regain control of the homestead. She stayed with a cousin on her first trip since her mother's death, finding the town much changed with lots of new homes, "some of them very handsome, but the most of them are pretty Cottages." She found there were nearly as many people still in the family home as the previous summer. A couple of weeks later, she wrote again, chiding her daughters for not sending letters, and saying that she would not return till September or October. In September, she sold the first lot cut out from her parents' land to one of the homestead tenants.[59]

In Tennessee, Sarah's kids were with two cousins named John and Patti at a mineral spa area called Boiling Spring. Patti wrote describing the young friends that Mary Frances and Lucy had been meeting (daughters of the former Confederacy), and about the latest hairdos on ladies from Nashville—"water falls on top of their heads." In September Sarah wrote to delay her return once more in order to collect several hundred dollars after renting out the family home for another year.[60]

Leonidas and Will in Yazoo, Mississippi, were faced with a local disaster. There are no letters from the Campbells on what damages they suffered but, despite Leonidas's hopes, the cotton crop of 1867 was "almost a total failure," as DuBois put it. The troubles were a carryover from the previous year.[61]

In 1866 nature compounded the problems of southern farmers. The weather alternated between periods of drought and heavy rain, stunting the crops. Battered by war, levees on the Mississippi, Red, and Arkansas rivers gave way, flooding prime cotton lands and drowning cattle and mules. Finally, the dreaded army worm attacked what cotton had survived. "Planters of thirty years' experience pronounce this the worst crop season within their knowledge," wrote a South Carolinian. In 1867, many of the same conditions, especially flooding and the army worm, returned, and the crop again proved disappointing.[62]

In September armyworms hit Yazoo and up the road from Silver Creek Morgan saw that within ten days their 600 rented acres looked "as though they had been swept by fire." Their sawmill saved the day. Several loads of lumber had already been shipped to Vicksburg, but another half million feet of lumber remained, along with "nearly a million shingles," and logs in the river.[63]

And they still had enough cotton and corn to pay the rent. There were no liens on any of their property, only the regular rent due months off. When the armyworms had moved on, the sheriff appeared and said that their colonel landlord had gone to court and claimed the Morgans were probably going to move all the property out and defraud him of his due rent. The sheriff had a writ to seize everything. He returned with subsequent writs to claim the crops. The sheriff got paid. Colonel White got an $11,000 sawmill for $100 and anything else he wanted for a pittance. The logs were broken loose and allowed to "float away." Despite many efforts at legal redress, they lost their shirts—$50,000 and probably little of it their own—and no one would rent them any land. Friends in the North asked were there "no *courts* in Mississippi?" But their African American employees "voluntarily came forward, each and every one, and forgave us what we owed them." I found it comforting to learn that Colonel White never could find anyone to work the farm after that and lost the crop and the rent.[64]

Unlike the Morgans though, a disastrous crop for the Tarrants would have meant their first year of farming for wages might be one without pay, or working shares of the crop where the share might be less than expenses. Much needed cash may have only come from those who worked outside of farming, like Mariah and Belle in the laundry business, and perhaps from Chloe sewing for the white women in town.

In 1867, the new Military Reconstruction was placing vote registrars all over Mississippi. The former Confederacy was divided into five military districts controlled by U. S. troops. Blacks in Yazoo began organizing themselves in the spring and when elections were held they were able to elect representatives to the new constitutional convention. Yazoo had 2,816 black voters and 1,014 white voters. A. T. Morgan, along with other black and white Republicans, saw the new Military Reconstruction as a chance for real change. Rather than trying to return to farming, Morgan took up the study of law, becoming a lawyer in several years, and began his career as a Reconstruction activist. In writing his book, Morgan had the honesty to write that, had he been asked two years earlier about giving the vote to blacks in the south, he would have said, "Sure, why not?" But had he been asked about doing the same for blacks across the country, he probably would have said yes only with some kind of "qualification" for voting. He had previously voted only once, "while lying in the trenches before Petersburg." His two years' experience in Yazoo had given him, he writes, "a more perfect knowledge of the true character of 'conquered' rebels—especially of slave-holding rebels. And in the same manner I had come to form a juster estimate of the character and capacity of the African in America." In 1867 the emergence of the black vote gave him hope.[65]

> . . . As a whole, our hands [workers at Tokeba] had demonstrated their possession of the very best qualities of natural manhood and woman-hood. . . . During those two years, of the plantation force of more than one hundred and twenty-five only one had been drunk; only one had been caught stealing . . . and concubinage had been utterly routed. . . .[66]

During 1867 under Military Reconstruction, African American men successfully registered and voted for the first time in history. In Mississippi, with federal control in place, 60,137 blacks registered, and 46,636 whites, many of whom did not vote. In Alabama new officials registered 61,295 blacks and 104,518 whites in 1867 and, according to DuBois, "of the whites, only 18,533 voted in favor of a convention." Many whites thought they could derail this process by staying home; African American voters carried the day. The day before the election in Yazoo, Morgan ran into many African Americans who said the planters told them the election was off. Once freedmen heard otherwise from Republicans, they spread the word. When African Americans showed up the next day to vote, according to Morgan, most whites had stayed home and those at the polls were trying to bribe or bully blacks not to vote. Those running the polling places checked off the name of each one who voted, "so that it was impossible to prevent their old masters from knowing the fact that such a one had voted. Therefore, all who would vote subjected themselves to such vengeance as their old masters might choose to inflict." In that county 1,800 people voted for the convention, three against, and Morgan's ticket of potential delegates won with just under 1,400 voting for them and less than 400 for their opponents.[67]

According to Foner, "[b]lack turnout ranged from about 70 percent in Georgia to nearly 90 percent in Virginia, and their vote was all but unanimous (three states failed to record a single black ballot against holding a convention)." In most of the ex-Confederate states, the majorities of the populations were black, and the reality of black domination at the polls became obvious to everyone. (When I covered elections in Alabama's Black Belt in the 1980s, the percentages of voter turnout were still twice what I was used to hearing in the North.)[68]

In November 1867 A. T. Morgan was elected, along with "an African American blacksmith named William Leonard; and the former Freedmen's Bureau agent [Charles] Clarke" as Yazoo's Republican delegates to the constitutional convention of 1868, which became known among the irreconcilables of Mississippi as the "Black and Tan" convention. In January 1868 the convention began meeting in Jackson, Mississippi. White kids at every stop hooted at Morgan and all the other delegates on the stage route to Jackson. He notes that the word "carpetbagger" had not been invented yet, or at least, had not reached Yazoo.[69]

These conventions have come to fascinate me because they are really the first time that the voice of those who had been enslaved is really heard. The widespread lampooning of blacks who were involved in Reconstruction politics as ignorant, unlettered, uncouth, and unfit for service did a lot of damage to African American political progress and to blacks in general. That was a particular focus of D. W. Griffith's later film *Birth of a Nation*, which gave encouragement to the Ku Klux Klan's reemergence in the early twentieth century. Griffith's version of righteous propaganda was very dangerous, but the period he chose for his first full-length film is still worthy of a serious film. Stymied by all the attempts to keep blacks out of power was the great statement about the potential of democracy made by the early constitutional conventions. African Americans who had been forcibly and legally kept from learning to read and write were suddenly heard on the issues of their very lives. They could be seen standing toe-to-toe with practiced politicians, and the moment revealed them to be incredibly aware of the significance of the task before them and the impact of the political maneuvering going on in the South. Like the vast majority of black voters today, who are seldom fooled by political rhetoric into voting against their interests, southern African Americans understood very clearly their relationship to the power elite.

In 1997 the Library of Virginia invited my family to the opening of its new building in Richmond. We were startled to learn that the library had included a quote from my Virginian great-grandfather, William Roscoe Davis, among those of other Virginians like Thomas Jefferson, Patrick Henry, and James Madison that had been carved into the walls of the main reading room. We were astounded, not least because we had never seen a quote from him written anywhere, nor his signature, which is replicated below the quote. We had no idea that the library had found him somewhere in their records of the Virginia Constitutional Convention of 1867–1868, at which he served as Doorkeeper. His quote said that if the black man can gain education, he would be able to take charge of gaining all else that is needed.

While a bondman, William Roscoe Davis had worked his free hours as a boat pilot and saved enough money to buy his family's freedom, but neither the owner, nor years in court had released them. He escaped the plantation where he was a bondman when slaveholders in Hampton fled Sherman's arrival, and was then able to rescue his mother, wife, and children from the plantations where they were held and take them to refuge as contrabands at Fort Monroe. He worked there for the Union army distributing tents, blankets, and food to other contrabands. Until 1997, I had never looked at the involvement of freedmen and women in Virginia in the politics of the postwar period. In that state Radical Republicans won control of the constitutional convention. And many freedmen who voted for the Radical ticket immediately lost their jobs. The convention, held from December 1867 until April 1868, had 105 delegates—thirty-three conservatives siding with planters, and seventy-two liberals, of which twenty-five were African Americans.[70]

Thomas Bayne, a dentist and minister from Norfolk, Virginia, who had been enslaved and escaped, has become one of my favorite discoveries from re-reading DuBois and Foner. Though he had rather traditional, anti-feminist views on women's engagement in political struggle, he had both the wit of the great African American orators ("When James K. Polk was running for President, I was running through the woods from my master.") and the rhetorical power that makes almost contemporary one of his speeches before the convention:

> Does the gentleman mean that the black men are not to have any rights in this country? Does he mean to set us free today and in fifty or sixty years to come, then to give us the right of suffrage? I want it distinctly understood that the old slaveholders' coach moves too slow for us. They design to enslave the blacks again if they can. They design to make him a slave by cutting him off from all opportunites for labor, by starving and oppressing him. Set the Negro free now and let him remain here. No, that is too much for him. He will enjoy it too much. A hundred years to come will be time enough for him to have these rights. In order to carry out their ideas and designs they have commenced just like they did with secession. They are preaching the danger of a war of races in this hall. They are preaching it in Congress, in the cities and over the country, in the streets, and on the seas, on the steamboats, in the cars, in the taverns, and everywhere. This war of races is being preached up constantly, but nobody preaches it up but that side of the House which hates the Republican Party and hates the Federal government. . . .[71]

According to DuBois, "The native press ridiculed the [Virginia] convention, calling it the convention of 'Kangaroos' and the 'Black Crook

Convention.'" It is still shocking to me to read of people like Bayne or my great-grandfather being called kangaroos. Nevertheless, this is exactly the reception Morgan got on his way to the more politely derided "Black and Tan" convention in Mississippi, and that the Republicans of Alabama were treated to in that state.[72]

8

Silver Creek (1868–1878)

One of the primary things the Morgans learned in Mississippi was something locals, both black and white, understood quite well: the personal and the political were not separate spheres. Despite the racism endemic to the slavery system, the struggle that took place in Yazoo and elsewhere was about power. Treatment dispensed to blacks who stood up was just as easily applied to whites who fought the irreconcilables. Fewer whites took the chance. This was a lesson undoubtedly learned years earlier when the Campbells came from Missouri as evidenced by their long survival there and their ties to important people in town. The Morgans probably thought it reasonable to assume that they could work for their political ends and still live in the town.

While Albert Morgan was in Jackson at the convention, his brother Charles rented rooms for them in a boarding house run by a widow, who was immediately sent a threat signed "K. K. K." No one else in town would rent to them. They got someone to rent an apartment for them near a livery stable, only to discover that "none of the hotels, restaurants, boarding-houses or private-houses, owned or controlled by whites," would give them food or service. An African American woman in Yazoo City offered to provide food at cost because they built the freedmen's school. Then the locals came after her and began spilling her food in the street. Thereafter, the freedmen and women devised a series of ruses by which food and other supplies were brought to them without notice. The Morgans' new home turned out to be directly above the meeting place of the Klan, perhaps better described as a place where they all got drunk.[1]

During the convention some white gentlemen even drew their guns on Albert, and Charles Caldwell, one of the amazing African Americans of Reconstruction Mississippi, confronted the men, along with his friends and their pistols, and the whites backed down.[2]

Shortly after that Charles Morgan was arrested and nearly lynched. He had pulled his gun when some young thugs tried to topple a raft-type ferry he was using and send him into the river. He had been organizing voting clubs with the Loyal League (also known as the Union league), which sent people fanning out across the South to inform freedmen of their voting rights. He was arrested for brandishing his weapon, tried, found guilty, and placed in the jail. The sheriff and all of his deputies happened to leave town that evening. The Morgans later learned he was to be taken from the jail and hanged, but everyone already knew that might be the plan because this was a familiar scenario in the South, and in fact whites were the primary lynching victims before 1865. An alert went out among freedmen who arrived by the dozen with sticks and clubs until there was a crowd demanding Charles Morgan's release. With this backdrop of the threatening appearance of armed blacks, a white businessman and the Freedmen's Bureau agent succeeded in getting Morgan freed.[3]

For locals, integration was rather like miscegenation, one drop of blackness was too much. Despite its nickname, the "Black and Tan" convention was mostly white. As DuBois points out, while it was "the first political organization in Mississippi with colored representatives," only seventeen of the one hundred delegates were black, even though thirty-two counties had black majorities. In this case, blacks were responsible, along with white Republican leaders, as they formed slates that were largely white. They were not yet, as DuBois writes, attempting to "use their numerical preponderance in order to put themselves in political power." This was part survival strategy, part generosity, I suspect, and would change. DuBois also remarks, "It characterizes the times to know that five of the [seventeen Mississippi] members afterward met violent deaths."[4]

In all of these southern constitutional conventions, there was a question about whether or not to strip the former Confederate elite of its voting rights and the right to hold office. Given what planters were up to in attempting to put themselves back in office, it is hard to view this disenfranchisement maneuver as purely a matter of retaliation against those who mounted an armed rebellion for four years. According to Morgan one of the most progressive features of the new Mississippi constitution was an anti-concubinage clause. He felt it could have long-term healing effects. The situation Morgan sought to redress was the fact that it was commonplace across the South for white gentlemen to have black families as well as white, but gave them no protection or security. Black concubines as Morgan encountered them after the war were forced to be available to the men on a twenty-four-hour-seven-days-a-week basis. Section 22, Article 12, provided immediate official recognition to families formed during slavery and to couples not allowed official state marriage, and likewise made interracial concubinage subject to recognition as marriage. Morgan, however, clearly underestimated how easily brute force and economic intimidation could keep concubinage alive.[5]

When Morgan went to northern Mississippi to help sell the constitution to citizens, he heard objections to this clause, not made from fear of being taken to court for legal recognition of children and support (which some women did pursue), not from fear of everyone knowing their business (everyone already did), but in outrage that "all the d—n [damn] nigro wenches in the country will believe they're just as good as the finest lady in the land . . . " and "the end of it all will sho'ly be the degradation of ouah own ladies to the level of ouah wenches."[6]

When it came time for all of this to be ratified by the popular vote, political wrangling resulted in few Africans Americans being nominated for the Republican ticket and in the rise of a newly invigorated group of Democrats—the Democratic White Men's Party of Mississippi. Conservative forces went to work on African American voters, and this time the white voters did not stay home. In Yazoo, Morgan reports, the KKK rode out to scare black voters; local merchants offered free goods, from food to shoes, to any freedman who would agree to be taken to the polls by a Democrat.[7]

W. H. Foote, one of those later assassinated for his good works, then only twenty-five years old and new to the county, rode on horseback to "rescue" black voters in the clutches of Democrats. In one place he ran into a band of thugs who had stopped a group of about 400 blacks headed for the polls. When they threatened to shoot him for interfering, he is said to have replied, "Shoot and be d——d [damned]!" He then turned to the freedmen, according to Morgan, and yelled out, "Men, this is our day. The new constitution is for our freedom as well as that of our former masters. If ye reject it, ye reject liberty. Follow me!" The freedmen rallied to him and went on to the polling place. As it was characteristic for men like Foote to be killed at night and in secret, he escaped with his life that day.[8]

Thanks to the assiduous work of men like Foote, the constitution passed in Yazoo County. It was, however, defeated across the state. There were charges from several quarters that the election had been won by "terrorism" and "fraud." When the constitution was finally ratified, the Rebels got back the right to vote but the constitution survived for twenty-two years. DuBois points to the most important elements:

> It did away with property qualifications for office or for suffrage; it forbade slavery; it provided for a mixed public school system; it forbade race distinctions in the possession and inheritance of property; it prohibited the abridgment of civil rights in travel; and in general, it was a modern instrument based on universal suffrage.[9]

Well, universal suffrage among men. Still, this constitution was not only a clarion call for people like Chloe to come to Mississippi, but even after it was rewritten in 1890, she still benefited from the specific 1868 inclusion of rights that we now regard as ordinary.

Where Chloe was living, the local Democratic Club of Marion, Alabama, greeted the idea of black elected delegates not only with scorn but called on the "white men of the South" to shun, in every way possible, anyone who took an official position under the Reconstruction acts of the Congress. DuBois found the blacks of Alabama somewhat worse off than those in Mississippi when it came to a leadership group with any education. Looking at his list I found: one assistant newspaper editor, a barber, a carriage driver, a doorkeeper of the House of Representatives, and four field hands, one of whom, Tom Lee, represented Perry, the Tarrants' county. Lee, who was known for moderation according to DuBois, was also a founder of the Lincoln School. On the other hand, James T. Rapier, of Lauderdale County, who had been educated in Canada, and was elected to Congress in 1872, was a force to be reckoned with, and some of his work became part of the constitution. Rapier is well worth further reading and, as it happens, John Hope Franklin and Loren Schweninger published a book this year tracing the amazing story of Rapier's family from the early 1800s to his time as a leader in Alabama. By coincidence, I learned from that book, *In Search of the Promised Land, A Slave Family in the Old South*, that a Campbell cousin, Andrew Jackson Polk of Maury County, Tennessee, (and brother of General Leonidas Polk) played a role in that family story.[10]

One of the most interesting proposals to come up in Alabama was one that would provide back pay for those months when former masters did not necessarily inform people they were free, and/or did not acknowledge the idea of wages. The black representative of Dallas County demanded that Negroes be empowered to collect pay from those who held them in slavery at the rate of ten dollars per month for service rendered from January 1, 1863, the date of the Emancipation Proclamation, to May 20, 1865. An ordinance to this effect was adopted by a vote of fifty-three to thirty-one. I'd love to know if anyone actually collected.

Looking at this ordinance in hindsight it is easy to imagine why families like the Tarrants may have hoped to obtain what would have been a handsome sum per household. The entire family—leaving out grandchildren and in-laws—included nine working adults. At $10 a month for twenty-nine months, they were owed $290 each, totaling $3,190. That was an amount worth waiting for because it could establish the family on their own property, and the impact is even clearer when looked at in today's dollars as purchasing power equal to $848,540. In today's dollars, that $10 in wages would be $2,656.20 per month, $31,874.40 for the year, not an exorbitant salary. Pooling their funds, the family would have had the power of transformation for the whole family in terms of their ability to negotiate their futures. To imagine the full power of the ordinance, had it been honored across the Black Belt of Alabama, is to envision a vast change. At the very least, it was probably sufficient inspiration for someone like Chloe to begin to assess what it would take to buy one's own land.

The delegate's suggested pay figure was based on real numbers for the time. Men and women were not paid equally, but $10 would be a good average to strike for the back pay. Domestic work brought higher pay. People were paid twice a year, once in January and again in August or October. Deductions from their pay were made for food, shelter, medical expenses, any family members who didn't work, sick time, damage to tools, or injuries to stock.[11] This system, which was bad enough, soon gave way to one in which workers began to accept shares of the crop as part of their payment. And various systems of credit from employers were set up. The combination became lethal after a failed crop, when debts took all the wages.

This ordinance was not for reparations, but back pay legally owed—solely for the period of twenty-nine months from the end of chattel slavery to the end of the war. Had back pay been awarded for even half that amount only to the four million living survivors of slavery for the terms of their time in bondage at the end of slavery, they would have been able to acquire land, education, and a solid footing in this country. Paying people then would have been a far simpler proposition—and less expensive—than the way in which reparations are envisioned today—in terms of profits gained, with interest—by firms that were built or prospered in connection to slave labor. Ironically, the idea was first used in the American slavery context by planters who wanted Congress to give them reparations, compensation for the dollar value of those people freed.

In Alabama, as in Mississippi and elsewhere, once delegates established a public school system, whites vigorously protested any move to make them integrated. In Alabama whites were also enraged that the convention refused to outlaw interracial marriage. "This Constitution was afterward repudiated by the convention of 1875, when the Negroes had been driven from political power," writes DuBois. "Nevertheless it was a more modern and democratic instrument than any of the preceding Constitutions of the state, and the new Constitution of 1875 retained many of its provisions. In both states, the continued increase in political engagement by African Americans gave inspiration to increased violence from the then young Ku Klux Klan."[12]

The crop cycle was beginning again by the time Leonidas wrote Sarah Rush Owen in February that he was about to start what he thought would be a successful planting season, optimistic despite the previous year. He wrote to his sister apologizing once more that on one of his trips to St. Louis he had not stopped to visit her and her family on the way. He pleads that he was on "business for our parties and had to go & come as quickly as possible." He reported that he would have to go to Springfield in May to the Circuit Court, and planned there to "present bonds" in a suit against him, and sell land that he had in that area. That year he sold land in Missouri in June, July, and October. He congratulated her on having her "dower interest set apart," most likely rescued from claims against her husband's estate, and hoped she would realize what it was worth. It appears that she hoped to sell a piece of land perhaps given at the time of her marriage. The Campbell siblings were still trying to extract themselves from their parents' estate issues, and, understandably, he complained, "I was never more sick & tired of a thing in my Life." He had managed to see his younger brother Sam in recent months but had not seen Will in two months.[13] In April the sixteen-year-old Will wrote to Sarah of events in Yazoo:

We had a large fire in Yazoo City about a month ago, which destroyed a great many buildings. I received a letter from Lulu two weeks ago. I answered it last Sunday. Brother Lonnie was over from the Creek last Wednesday; he is going up to Missouri in about six weeks. The water was very high, but it is now falling, so

I do not think that we will have an overflow this year. This year
Brother says that he has a very good crop of corn and cotton and
if the water does not come up that he will make a very good crop
this year. [sic] I am going to school and getting a long very well
with my studies. I heard that you were going again to Missouri to
live. Brother Lonnie says he will give me a trip up to see you all in
vacation. . . .[14]

According to Morgan, the crop did turn out quite well that year. Farmers in Yazoo County were recovering, though not to the levels enjoyed before the war. In 1860, the Mississippi cotton crop was 1.2 million bales
and even by 1870 the crop was still less than half that at 565,000 bales.[15]

On June 6, 1868, eighteen-year-old Chloe Tarrant married nineteen-
year-old James Curry of Marion, Alabama. They were married by W. H.
McIntosh, pastor of Siloam Baptist Church in Marion. Jim Curry's father
was Moses Kelley from South Carolina; although his mother's name is
unknown, he knew she was born in Virginia. Curry was a name probably
obtained by way of planter Jabez Curry, who had 165 people in bondage
in the county. After their marriage Chloe and Jim were working as domestic servants, probably for Mary Ann Tarrant. While some owners in
the area or their children, taught their house servants to read and write,
only Jim Curry became literate, probably after 1870.

In 1868 Chloe's brothers Allen, now twenty-four, and King, sixteen,
were no doubt full-time farm laborers. George Aaron, eight years old,
would have been in school, along with their sister Lucy, six. Andrew, the
youngest, was three years old and, one hopes, at home.[16]

From Mississippi, Leonidas wrote to Sarah to give her some tough-
minded advice on how to move out from her relatives in Tennessee and
set up her own household:

I regret you are so uncomfortably situated at "Aunts" & If I had
the Means would send you an amount sufficient to settle you
Comfortably. [sic] but I have not got the funds. And I can suggest
but one way for you to place yourself in a Position not to be Hu-
miliated and Have your feelings wounded and Hurt upon all occasions where persons so desire. that [sic] is move to Missouri
take possession of the Homestead, borrow Moneys to go to Keeping House or, rent out the Farm, & do the best you can Until a division of the Lands take place & then you can sell whatever
portion on all of your distribution share If you so desire. It is impossible for you to realize any Money on Property Here in the
South. Nor Can I *Hypothecate* [pledge the title] my [certain?]
Land Interests Here & raise two thousand dollars with it as a
loan, You can borrow Money in Missouri if, [sic] you wish to do
so. I Know it is objectionable, but I see no other alternative It
will be late in the winter before I can go up there & probably
not at all__ I do not yet know the Property out there is going
to be valuable I think, as the building of the Rail Roads is now
fixed fact . . . [17]

He also told her she could bring her family to Mississippi to live with
him. In what seems a bit of sibling pique, someone, presumably Sarah,
wrote on the back of his letter, "Nov 1868 Speaks of all Lands in Miss as
His." And she was right. The lands he could not get a loan on were inherited by all of John Polk Campbell's children and Lulu. Perhaps he had
borrowed on the land already. Still, as I mentioned before, he seems to
have already sold land in Missouri several times that year. Clearly,
Leonidas, now thirty-three, had considerable expenses as the family patriarch, and enjoyed an costly lifestyle as well. He was definitely getting
poorer as land values dropped after the war and, like most planters in Yazoo, he was on his way to being out of cash, at least by planter standards.
While he still valued the family land in Yazoo at $40,000 as his brother
had in 1860 (and it may have been worth less), his personal wealth in
1870 was $3,750 (at least $82,500 in today's dollars, so he wasn't broke).
That is still a far cry from the $70,000 that John Nathaniel had in the

bank in 1860. Younger brother Samuel, twenty-four years old, held only a $5,000 parcel in 1870 and $300 in the bank. If in 1868 Leonidas had only a similar sum, $3,000 to $4,000, he may not have, been comfortable with sending Sarah half to set up a home.[18]

And that is a lot of housekeeping. As one can move some households for that amount today, I am led to believe they were thinking of grander quarters than a three-bedroom cottage, though cottage is a word she sometimes used to describe her imagined home. What she did, however, was to stay put.[19]

Having said all that, according to A. T. Morgan Yazoo planters had considerable debt forgiven. Evidently, in the good old days, they had felt comfortable to go into a lot of debt, a habit that Leonidas maintained. "When the war broke out," Morgan writes, "nearly one-half of the planters and merchants of this county were in debt to the full amount of the cash value of their property in lands and slaves. . . . One-half of the remainder were in debt to fully one-half the value of their said property." Emancipation definitely wiped out a big chunk of collateral. (DuBois' numbers would put postwar property values in Mississippi at nearly half their antebellum value, just from the loss of slave property.) At the end of the war, the legislature passed a law to postpone debt collection. And then apparently northern creditors offered to settle debts, "some on a basis of one-half, some one-quarter. In some instances they forgave all."[20]

What did the Campbells make on their cotton? And how much did it cost them to raise it? Mary Campbell, John's wife, was the only person in the family who ever mentioned the price of cotton in the family letters. It was a meaningless number to me because the prices are given per pound, and I had no earthly idea how many pounds were in a bale. The average cotton bale seems to be between 400 and 450 pounds, though they can run quite a bit larger. According to Morgan, before the war the price of cotton was five cents to ten cents per pound; at the end of the war cotton was inflated, running at thirty-five to ninety cents per pound, then declining quickly. As of 1869, it was still at fifteen to ninety cents per pound. The Campbells claimed on a loan application in the 1880s to be able to make 1,000 bales of cotton; however, in 1871 Samuel mentions the figure of 100 bales during a bad crop year. That could mean the difference between

$60,000 and $6,000 using the 400-pound weight and the lowest price. I would guess crops had a mix of cotton grades or qualities and therefore a mix of prices per crop. "The average hire of a laborer to make the crop was fifteen dollars per month," according to Morgan, though elsewhere it was ten dollars. Hiring one hundred workers at the lower wage would come to $18,000 a year. (I have not tried to get figures for all the costs deducted from workers' wages which would lower this cost.) This makes cotton farming look much more like gambling than I imagined.[21]

When the Presidential election of 1868 rolled around, the Republican freedmen of Yazoo County and the Morgan brothers scraped up their few spare coins to have buttons made boasting a picture of Ulysses S. Grant. They wore them on the street and to work—in white homes and businesses. This must have horrified some of the "best citizens" of the county. Evidently W. H. Foote, now referred to among freedmen as *Mister* Foote, wore several of these and refused to step aside while walking on the pavement in town, when most moved out of the way of whites to avoid trouble. Those unfortunate enough to run into irate whites on a country road though risked a beating for wearing this accessory.[22]

The Yazoo Klansmen, thinking Grant would be defeated and the end of Reconstruction would come, began making noisy public demonstrations in town. They continued to prey on freedmen at night in their cabins, and paraded in the streets of Yazoo City banging pans, yelling, and blowing horns "until after midnight." But the parades so annoyed the good white folks in town that the local paper condemned it (while also supporting the aims of the KKK). The Grand Cyclops had to apologize.[23]

After Grant's election, Sarah Rush Owen heard from Joseph W. Farrier, a twenty-three-year-old white dry goods merchant in Springfield to whom she seemingly sold or rented part of the Campbell homestead land. (She does appear to have taken Leonidas's advice on that.) Farrier lived with two women who appear to be his mother and sister, a couple who may have been boarders or servants, and a mulatto boy by the name of Henry Farrier. He writes, "We had a very peaceble election us Rad's beat them right strait [sic] elong [sic]. I guess you have seen the news Papers and is [sic] equally as well posted as I am. I never hear Politics [sic] mentioned on the street since the election."[24]

The election of Grant was probably not happy news to Sarah, and it certainly was not to the white elite in Yazoo City. The Trinity Episcopal Church, according to one of its ministers, ceased "its mission among the black population of the county" and closed at least two of its missions in outer areas. The head of the Democratic Party and the various Klan Cyclopses went back to their day jobs, but not before one last stand outside the Morgan brothers' apartment. In a seemingly new choice of attire— black hoods and gowns—about forty Klansmen lined up outside and were ordered to stand at "parade rest" with weapons in hand. Evidently, after seeing light inside and realizing the little army that was often in the apartment was awake, they departed. Indeed the now finely tuned black warning system (in place since Charles was nearly lynched) had gone into action. A guard of freedmen silently assembled on the back stairs while the Klan marched outside, and they stayed throughout the night on the back stairs and porch and in the Morgans' rooms. Albert Morgan heard no more from the Klan till the next election, and says they never again bothered with disguises.[25]

As 1869 began Charles Morgan was appointed sheriff and tax collector of nearby Washington County by Adelbert Ames, then the new military district commander under Grant. Albert was elected as a state senator, and became head of the Yazoo County Board of Police, which was renamed the Board of Supervisors. As head of the board, he saw to the establishment of public schools in the county, the building of a new courthouse, (which is still there), and the repair of the jail and roads. "Mister" Foote was elected to the State House of Representatives. James Dixon, another African American, was appointed by Ames to the Board of Supervisors. Economically, "the years of 1868 and 1869 were exceptionally good ones, and both 'white' and 'black' were beginning to indulge in luxuries."[26]

In Missouri in 1869, John Nathaniel's widow, Mary, now thirty-two, had started another family with a new husband, William McKerall, a farmer and widower with two children. They set up their household in Springfield on the Danforth family lands, and Frances, their first child, was born in 1869. Mary must have met him in Texas. The only McKerrall in Texas in 1860 was William, who was in Waco with a young wife and son. His wife died sometime after the birth of their second child in 1862. I believe she was Aunt Nancy Sedbury's daughter Alice, who married a McKerall. So I would guess they met through Aunt Sedbury when they were both in mourning.[27]

Also in 1869, Sarah Rush Owen packed her children, Lulu, and her household goods into a mule-driven covered wagon and returned to Springfield. They arrived in December. This sounds rather colorful when there were trains to take, but she chose to come by mule wagon having realized she would need both the mules and the wagon at the farm in Missouri. Lulu was now twenty-one years old and had graduated from college. She had pined for the old home in Springfield since she was twelve and, finally making it back there, must have been somewhat horrified. Despite Sarah's three years of legal efforts to reclaim the property, there were a lot of strangers living on the place—a different family in each twenty-by-twenty-foot room. Sarah, Lulu, and the children had one room in which to camp—their grandmother's parlor—only after Sarah had gotten the Irish woman who was living there to move out by paying three months' rent for her at a boarding house. Their upstairs neighbor had butchered "five hogs and salted them in a corner of the upper hallway," and "the bloody water was dripping down the stairway," according to Sarah's daughter Lucy. They further discovered a sow and her pigs under the parlor floor. On their way into town, Mary McKerall had given them two hens, a rooster in a crate, and a coon dog, though they had brought a dog from Tennessee. They cooked dinner in the parlor fireplace and, after heated discussions with the children about leaving the dogs outside, they put the chickens in a corner, the dogs under the beds, and the four children and two women bunked down for their first night at home. During the night, they awoke to the sounds of donkeys outside trampling toward the warmth of the chimney; "the rooster crowed; Jack [their dog] growled; the coon dog barked and the old razor-back under the floor grunted, and scratched its back against the joists." In the morning, one of Sarah's children recalled, some of them planted seeds they had brought from Tennessee. They had to use shovels and water to get the mud out of the hallways. Gradually, the tenants moved on.[28]

After all that, Lulu's stay at home was somewhat short-lived. She ran into an old playmate of Will and Sam who was an officer in the U. S. Navy. She married Frances Henry Sheppard that year and moved to Annapolis. Lulu McKenny Sheppard gave birth to ten children, six of whom survived.[29]

In 1870 Chloe Curry, now twenty, and James Curry, twenty-two, and their baby, James Curry, Jr., less than a year old, had begun their lives as a young family. As domestic servants for Mary Ann Tarrant, their home was probably a cabin on her property. My grandmother's memoir suggests that Chloe may have been a cook in this household. Living with them, perhaps in the other half of a typical double cabin, were four other Currys: Sarah, twenty-three, and Victoria, twenty-eight, also servants, as well as two children, Manerva, six, and Lettie, four. It would be my guess that the other Curry women were Jim's older sisters, though they may simply have been freedwomen who took the name. Either Chloe or Jim could have been with the widow Tarrant for years. The black Tarrant women who might have been held by Mary Ann in 1860 were Caroline and Mariah. Of course, Caroline, Mariah, and Chloe could also have been on the farm of Mary Ann's brother-in-law, Larkin Tarrant. Not that it matters too much, but Mary Ann was about the same age as Chloe's mother, Caroline, as was Mary's husband, Felix Tarrant.[30]

Will Campbell was eighteen years old and in Springfield in the summer of 1870 visiting his sister Sarah and her children: Mary, fifteen, Felix, thirteen, Lucy, ten, and Jay, nine.

That year Leonidas and Samuel were in Yazoo, and the only other member of their household was a black farm hand. Neither had married, but Leonidas would soon do so. His bride was named Lucy, though she was not the wealthy young widow with two children by that name that turned his head in New Orleans in 1866. He chose Lucy McElhany, daughter of a family friend, Springfield banker Robert McElhany, and a woman the same age as two of his nieces—nineteen years his junior. This Lucy was also known as Lula or Lulie, and her banker father was well off, holding

$50,000 in land and $30,000 in personal assets in 1870. All of Leonidas's romantic interests seem to have had similar financial advantages. Her father, another Tennessean, lived near the Campbell homestead and had some connection to the Campbells' ongoing estate transactions. The McElhanys were politically well-connected. Lucy's older sister married a man named Sempronious H. Boyd, who had quite a career. Boyd, also from Tennessee, was by then in the U.S. Congress. He did everything from gold prospecting in California, leading a Union regiment at Wilson's Creek, to becoming mayor of Springfield. The local bar association has it that in 1865 he served as judge at the trial of "Wild Bill" Hickock after the first of his now famous gunfights. In the 1890s he would be appointed Minister Resident and Consul General to Siam by President Benjamin Harrison. Lore has it that his son became friends with the young king known to us by way of the musical, *The King and I*, but that king (Rama IV) had died by the time Boyd went there. Still, Lulie's house must have been alive with good stories. She and Leonidas were wed in 1871.[31]

Albert Morgan also got married, but hardly to such advantage. In 1870, at the age of twenty-eight, he married twenty-one-year-old Carolyn Victoria Highgate, an African American teacher from New York. She had come to the South after the war with her mother and a sister to teach in a freedman's school in Jackson, Mississippi. Not only was his choice somewhat daring for the time because of her race, but it was plucky when one considers the family of feminists into which he married. Carrie Highgate came from an unusual family by any standard of the day. She and her sister Edmonia had gone to Syracuse University. Carrie had been living in a black boarding house until she married and moved to Yazoo City. To say she was not welcomed into Yazoo society is probably unnecessary but I should point out that even if her color were not a problem—which it was—Albert Morgan was not welcome in Yazoo's polite society anyway.[32]

Carrie's sister Edmonia had taught in Virginia, New Orleans, and Mississippi during the years after the war. In New Orleans she fought against segregated schools, and experienced a white race riot against Unionists in which 48 were killed and 166 wounded. In 1870 she spoke before the last convention of the Massachusetts Anti-Slavery Society and warned abolitionists that attaining the legal end of slavery was only half the battle. She called for "Anti-Slavery" teachers who could teach not only the academic basics but also "that it is safe to do right" and who could work against "caste-prejudice, the twin sister of slavery." She argued her own version of the reparations issue:

> As to lands for freedmen, and other help proposed for them, all we can do is only a part of what the nation owes to the colored people. It is no gratuity. These men and women have earned more than all we can do for them; and not only is their state necessitous, but in the interior rural districts considerable numbers are yet held in positive slavery.[33]

A few months later, shortly after the Morgans had visited her on a honeymoon trip in the North, Carrie's sister was found dead in an abortionist's boarding house in McGrawville, New York. That year Edmonia had fallen in love with John Henry Vosburg, a married white poet whose wife was institutionalized. He said he could not marry her because of her color, owing to the fact that he was dependent on help from his family that would be denied if he married a black woman. Albert later heard the two had been secretly married, which in no way allayed his wrath against Vosburg over Edmonia's death.[34]

When Morgan reported to the capitol for the opening of the legislature in 1870, the composition of the Mississippi House and Senate had been historically transformed.

> The first Reconstruction legislature met at Jackson; January 11, 1870 . . . Negro membership in the new legislature was larger than in the convention. There were forty colored members, some of whom had been slaves before the war; but among them were some "very intelligent" men. Particularly, there was considerable representation of ministers. In the Senate, there were five colored members.[35]

DuBois is here quoting John Roy Lynch, a fascinating man who was there in 1870 as a representative from Adams County. Lynch later became Speaker of the House in Mississippi, and then was elected to the U.S. Congress. His illustrious political career continued from there, but he also wrote a book, *The Facts of Reconstruction* (1913), on which DuBois relied heavily for the chapter on Mississippi in *Black Reconstruction*.

Morgan expressed some dismay over one member of their local slate, but he was too discreet to give the name. The three state representatives from Yazoo were W. H. Foote, F. E. Franklin, and A. S. Wood. About the latter two I can only say that they were white. Morgan himself was the only state senator from Yazoo from 1870 to 1873. DuBois goes to some length to demonstrate that, despite all the fears of black domination in the papers, and despite the election of numbers of blacks in 1870, "Negroes never controlled Mississippi." Nor did the carpetbaggers.[36]

The backlash against the Republicans started in earnest in Alabama before it really began to take effect in Mississippi. By 1870 the Ku Klux Klan had focused its violence, with some particularly heinous assaults, in Alabama's Black Belt counties. One especially gruesome incident was taken to the governor by the Perry County representative Greene S. W. Lewis, but the sheriff simply told the governor it never happened. African American officials lost their seats all over the state "but black representation was completely removed in six counties. Black belt counties such as Sumter, Elmore, and Greene, where black voters outnumbered whites by more than two to one, did not elect black representatives in 1870."[37] In Alabama, the Democratic "Redemption" was on.

There are no Campbell family letters surviving from 1870 and only two from 1871. The first of these is a draft of a childhood letter from Sarah Owen's third child, Lucy Owen, who was about ten at the time. At the beginning of the year she wrote from the Wind Haunt plantation, in Tennessee, saying only that they had had a festival "for the confederate ded, [sic]" and $400 was raised. The other letter was sent by Samuel from Valley Home and is the only one from him that I have seen:

Dear Sister
I left the Springs the 16th, I did not receive your letter until the day before, I left, I left it to, [sic] Brother to have the case put off as

we talk over the matter before . . . I improved a great deal at the Springs, I don't know wether [sic] I will have to go back or not, Crops are generally bad on the Creek, I beleive [sic] we have as good prospect as any of the planters it has been a very bad year on the planters I think if we make a hundred bales we will [do] well considering such a bad year, Excuse this badly written letter.[38]

Seven months later, on February 4, 1872, Valley Home neighbor Nannie Hall, possibly the wife of a local planter, wrote to Sarah that Samuel Independence Campbell had died.

It becomes my painful duty to announce the death of your loved Brother "Sammy" at 11 1/2 oclock P.M. ___His illness was of short duration but very violent . . . Sam was taken with a chill on Wednesday which ran into *pneumonia*, he had every attention from friends & servants but all of no avail__ God had summoned him home We can but bow & say "thy will be done." . . . Your Brother L. is deeply affected__crushed he will indeed be lonely without him . . . [39]

When I think of the illnesses suffered by the Campbell brothers, as well as Louisa, Will, and Lulu, I've become convinced that during the war they all contracted malaria or chronic pulmonary problems that made them susceptible to bouts of pneumonia. Given the long-term nature of Samuel's bad health, one has to wonder if the illness was not something more chronic than pneumonia. Leonidas also suffered periodically from some illness that forced him to stay home and rest. As Albert Morgan's malaria often revisited him, Leonidas may had a similar ailment.

In 1872 Will was in a school down on the Gulf of Mexico in Pass Christian, Mississippi. He was twenty years old. In June he jotted off a petulant note to his seventeen-year-old niece, Mary Frances Owen, complaining that she had not written to him. He expected school to get out on July 26, at which time he would return home. He was most likely graduating. In any case, he took up permanent residence in Yazoo around that time.[40]

A former bondman of the Campbells wrote to Leonidas for help in August of 1872. The last page is missing, and therefore the author is unknown, but it may be representative of the kinds of problems the Campbells' "servants" faced after being put in freedmen's camps and then shipped off to various areas:

> i Seat my self to write to you as your old bodly [sic] Servant i have been wanting to write to you for a long time but i did not know where to write__ some times i heard you was in New Orleans and some times in Mo. and some times in Yazou City so i did not know where to write
>
> i have worked heard [sic] to buy me a little home but i have at last lost it, all by its attempts and i am now getting old and feelbe [sic] can't work and you will obligh me varry [sic] much if you will send me some money i have long wanted to come home but i did not have the means to come i am well at preasant hoping [these] few lines will find you the sam[e] we are all well at preasant we are to gather that was when we were taken except Hagar and we hav[e] not seen her since we parted at Hellines [Helena, AK] i have to walk with a cain [sic] now my children are all growe up and married i would like to see you all once more in this world but if i may never see you in this world i hope i may meet you in . . . heaven[41]

In Alabama Chloe had her second child, Carrie Vienna Curry. These may have been the first grandchildren for her parents, who themselves still had young children at home. Her younger brother George Aaron was only twelve, Lucy was ten, and the baby, Andrew, was only seven. The next year her sister Mariah married Zeno Tutt, also from Marion. They had a baby girl named Margaret, who was known most of her life as Meg.[42]

Leonidas was in Mississippi, where his wife Lucy gave birth to their only child, Robert Lee. He also made a will that year in which he left his twenty-one-year-old brother Will a plantation at Silver Creek called Ingleside, and gave to his wife all the "real and personal property" in "the States of Missouri Louisiana Mississippi or elsewhere." (The following year, for reasons unknown, he annulled the gift to Will.) In January of 1873 Will wrote to his cousin Fannie again:

> You must excuse me for not answering your letters . . . for I have been very busy and have had very little time to write, but will try here after to answer your letters more promptly__all though I expect to be kept pretty busy as "Brother" has a good many more hands on his Places this Year, he sent on to Alabama a few weeks ago and got fifty Hands and has about fifteen or twenty more coming on. . . . Last Sunday was Brother's birth day, Sister had a fine Turky and pig for dinner. . . . Brother is improving slowly sister and the Boy is very well, the Boy is as fat as a pig, cannot walk yet . . . [43]

In the letter Will also says he had gone to town and called on two young women friends of his, daughters of one of the most prominent men in town, a businessman who had just lost $140,000 in the Panic of 1873, which was followed by an economic depression. He does not mention his own family being hurt by the run on banks that occurred. Will no doubt did not realize it then, but the 1873 Panic provided more pressure on planters paying monthly wages and contributed to the spread of the practice of offering "shares" of the crop instead of wages. Within ten years of the end of chattel slavery, farms such as the Campbells' had a mixture of work arrangements from wages to sharecropping that would remain in place for decades to come.

Most important to me, of course, is that the letter is a direct link between Will Campbell at Silver Creek and Chloe Curry in Marion, Alabama, and offers a possible explanation for how the Currys got to Mississippi. Another Delta planter who sent a black squad leader from his plantation to Alabama to recruit workers paid nine dollars for railroad transportation for each worker who came to Mississippi. This fare took one from Selma, Alabama, to Vicksburg, Mississippi. If Jim and Chloe came to Mississippi because the fare was paid, it seems likely that they also had to leave the young children because a planter would not have wished to pay for children too young to work. In any case, word that money could be made in the Delta did reach Chloe's ears. The next year Chloe's third child, Ruth, was born, and the following year, Tommy. After his birth, her Alabama days came to a close. By the mid-1870s, many African Americans in Alabama had good reason to emigrate. At the end of the decade, thousands moved to Kansas as part of what is called the Exodusters movement. The economy in Alabama was still so bad that many African Americans there would starve for another year.

Some time before the birth of her last child Chloe Curry went to Selma and had photographs made of herself and each of her children. She also got photographs of her siblings and, I believe, her mother. When she and Jim moved to Yazoo County, they likely elected to farm in a way that gave them autonomy, which meant either sharecropping or renting ten or fifteen acres. According to my grandmother, they were working for Leonidas Campbell. Renting could produce the greatest income in a good year, but it had the drawback of having a fixed rental fee. The amount due had to be paid whether the cotton crop would cover it or not. Working shares was at first beneficial for blacks, but once planters discovered they made more steady money from extending credit to workers and collecting their debts than they did off the fluctuating numbers of cotton bales, sharecropping became a re-enslaving cycle for black farmers. Landowners also learned they could profit by charging high prices for equipment and mules to people like the Currys who would have come from too far to bring livestock.

So Chloe and Jim started out in a difficult situation, raising cotton as the prices were falling in the 1870s and most likely having to carry debt for supplies. Though the presence of Chloe's brother King and his family would have greatly aided them in making the transition, come the end of their first year, they were probably far from their dream of being able to build a home for their family. By 1880 they did bring their children to Mississippi. Most likely, they brought them to one of the standard plantation cabins such as they may have lived in all their lives.

Long before their children arrived, Jim Curry had begun to say that he wished to return to Alabama. Neal writes, "Jim did not care for plowing, wood cutting and other farm work." As he had been a household worker before, the backbreaking fieldwork in the Mississippi heat may have seemed all the worse. Given the political climate prior to the election of 1875, if that is when they came, their first few trips to the New Foundation church on the Silver Creek plantation must have provided them with an earful of the Republican organizing going on in the area, as well as the intimidation facing everyone involved. They would have experienced firsthand the violence that included Patterson's lynching. If they arrived the next year, which is also possible, they would have heard about the Patterson lynching and the related court case of the Silver Creek man accused of murder. The combination of trying to farm their acres on their own and the increasingly oppressive environment may indeed have made Jim long for home ground.[44]

For Chloe, the people she met at Silver Creek became lifelong friends and, as time went on and the children grew up, some also became kinfolk. More than anything else that is apparent after piecing together the many patches of fact that make up parts of Chloe's life, is that what was most important to her were family and the people with whom she lived and worked in Alabama and Mississippi. Even within her family, she remained closest to those who shared the same kind of life—rural, hard working people, who did not measure life by material goods. She spent all her efforts to see that family members were cared for, had land to work, and went to school. Mississippi gave her a home from which to make it possible for them to build lives.

If Chloe Curry did not know James Patterson personally, most of those close to her probably did; they were there before he came to Silver Creek and after he died. She would have known many who went to the Republican meetings he held. Patterson was a teacher for the black children and adults at Silver Creek, where he no doubt also farmed side by side with the Carters and all the people she knew. Morgan mentions people from Silver Creek coming to his home in town to ask about political events in the news. If Chloe did know Patterson, like Morgan, she may have felt that his death could not be forgiven. And perhaps she did know him. Still living there also were the family of William Thomas, said to have murdered a man at Patterson's behest. The only man by that name in Yazoo on the 1870 census was then forty-two years old and, like the man convicted of the murder, had a wife and two children.

The only James Patterson there in 1870 was the son of a man from Virginia, and both were farm laborers. However, as the newspapers of the day referred to Patterson as a "colored carpetbagger," and he was said to have asked for his money to be sent to his family in Ohio, I am tempted to think he came to the county sometime during the 1870s from elsewhere.[45]

In January 1876 Leonidas Campbell took James Patterson's seat in the State House of Representatives. As a Democrat officeholder he "redeemed" that seat for the Old South. Here is my dilemma: Was Leonidas running against Patterson that fall before the lynching? According to the 1868 Mississippi Constitution, state representatives had to run "every second year," so I expect they were both running, although I have not been able to verify that. Again, this is one of those areas where the lack of any family letters for the time period really hurts, and really makes me suspicious. If Leonidas was not running, did the Democrats affect some kind of appointment to fill the vacant Patterson seat? After the lynching, I can't imagine any of the people who lived and worked at Silver Creek voting *against* him, even if the election were honestly counted. All the same, I'm quite sure most just stayed home out of fear, as James Dixon said he did.

In December 1876 William Thomas was tried for the murder of the unnamed victim at Silver Creek. As the newspapers for the time are gone, except for the one article on his sentencing, I can't judge the facts presented. There is only this story of the women of Silver Creek turning out the courthouse. From the flabbergasted tone of the reporter, I have to assume this was a rare circumstance. My suspicions tell me that the relationship of the murder to the lynching made this a trial that Thomas's family might want to protest. Beyond that, I can only wonder, as I did at the beginning of this story, what Chloe, so new to the Delta, may have made of it all.[46]

According to a later letter from Sarah Rush Owen, Chloe had a grievance with Leonidas Campbell. She refers to it with disdain as a "perceived injury." I would love to know what that was, but my imagination provides a range of possible offenses from slight to significant to grim. Whatever her grievance was, even in Sarah's sequence of events, which would place it before Chloe moved into Will Campbell's home, Chloe made it known sometime around 1876.

If Leonidas ran for office and his black opponent was killed right in front of everyone, possibly every black person on Silver Creek would have had a beef with L. A. Campbell. In 1876 Colonel Campbell went to the legislature for part of the year, and he should have been there for part of 1877 as well. Chloe certainly would have had less contact with him.

Most curious though is the fact that there in Springfield, Missouri, Sarah knew about the anger of a black cook in Mississippi—this automatically elevates the matter. It is impossible to know if Sarah visited Mississippi in the 1870s, if it was then that she met Chloe, or if Leonidas wrote of such an issue in his letters. If Sarah's story is true, Chloe had her run-in with Leonidas sometime in her first two years in Mississippi.

At some point in the late 1870s, Chloe and Jim brought their children from Alabama to the Delta. There was some kind of school that operated on the Campbell land, and James Patterson taught there when he was not at the State Capitol. Chloe's three oldest children were going to school during this time.

If my grandmother knew any of this, she certainly buried it. Her own notes though are both innocent and coy. Reading them, I become convinced that either she was not told about the worst of the bad old days or saw them as too remote to describe. Those whom I have talked to who knew Chloe or her siblings said they did not talk about their time in slavery, and this period might also have been left untold. Additionally, my grandmother's image of Chloe and Will is one of contented companions who did not necessarily have race issues standing between them that their daughter could perceive. She specifically told all of us that blacks and whites understood one another quite well in the old days. Even if she looked at things with some kind of naiveté, the environment in which she grew up allowed the perpetuation of her early ignorance of racial bitterness.

My grandmother wrote a romantic description of the first meeting between Chloe Curry and Will Campbell. She did tell me that this was how they met but, even as she told it, she was reflecting a lifelong conviction that Will was smitten with Chloe the first time he saw her. She described him as a "tall black haired southern gentleman."

The 4th Sunday in each month was meeting day at the church which was about 15 minutes' walk from Chloe's house, here the country folks would come to worship, [sic] they came in droves—some walking, some in buggies, wagons and on horse back. It was feast day; they brought trunks and baskets and boxes of food. Always there were 3 services morning, afternoon, and nite [sic], Chloe would attend only one. On her way home one Sunday from morning service, she met Mr. Campbell, a white gentleman on a high spirited horse which he could scarcely manage. He had heard about Chloe and he knew at a glance it was she because there was something different about her. She curtsied in a most polite manner and continued walking when she reached her cabin he was there on the stallion. . . .

"What is your name," he asked. "Chloe," she replied. "My husband and I live here in this house." She wished he would go. He understood and with a look of amusement in his dark eyes, he straighten[ed] up in his saddle and rode away. She had looked at him blankly. He was tall and thin and did not look his 28 years. He was emaculately groomed wearing a soft white shirt with a diamond [cluster] pin but no tie. . . .[47]

Will was actually several years younger when he met Chloe. Georgia writes that the plantation "was allotted to him by his people who settled in that [delta] land many years before." People on the plantation, she says, called him Mr. Will or "Captain Boss," and she judged him to be kind to his tenants, patient, and someone who endeavored to teach them how to use the credit system sparingly so as to have money left at the year's end. She evidently knew he was from Springfield and that he came from a large family that was scattered "except one daughter Miss Sarah who remained there." She knew Sarah had married a Mr. Owens, who was "in the milling business." And she knew of the older brother "called Colonel Campbell" who had served in the Civil War, and that his "plantation of several thousands of acres" adjoined Will Campbell's. She would not have known L. A. though, having at best merely set eyes on him as a toddler.[48]

My grandmother describes Will Campbell as anxious in the early summer of the year Chloe came to work for him because he still needed more laborers for the harvest. She also says there was a steady stream of new workers coming in by summer. In fact before Georgia was born, the hiring was seemingly Leonidas's responsibility. She says Will relied on Uncle Henry Weaver to get the gin ready, a man who may have been a Campbell bondman before the war. In 1880 Weaver was thirty-nine years old, listed as a mulatto with a family that included his wife, Fanny, and four children. Neal writes that they stacked wood to fuel the gin in piles eight to ten feet high "in a circle around the gin house."

The big house where Mr. Will lived was over the fence from the gin. Aunt Lou was his housekeeper she had been with the Campbell family all of her life and was his nurse when he was born. She called him Babe and was very much devoted to him. Aunt Lou was beginning to get feeble, the work was too heavy for her because her duties were many. There were cows to be [milked], chickens, turkeys, geese and ducks as well as guineas to care for, a large vegetable garden too was on one side of the house

On the other side of the house was a long lane leading from the main road in front, down into the fields, it separated the big house from a large lot with several barns which sheltered the mules and horses and hogs, the upper part of the barns is where the corn and hay was stored. Mr. Will drove a buggy drawn by two firey [sic] horses he named Tom and Dick, but he rode a chestnut colored mare named Ginsey around the plantation. The field hands would know when was coming because he liked to sing his favorite songs were "Annie Laurie" and "Sweet Violets Sweeter Than All The Roses."[49]

Aunt Lou was most likely Lou King, born in Georgia and the same age as a woman named Louisa on the Campbell family slave inventory. She was a cook, had two children, ages sixteen and twelve in 1880, and was forty-nine years old. Georgia may have had the impression Lou was much older, because she knew her at a later time. On the other hand, there could be other causes for Lou King becoming feeble in middle age. She had, after all, traveled from Missouri to Mississippi at the outset of the war, and then either endured time in the contraband camps where disease was rampant, and relocation or perhaps sojourned to Texas with John Campbell and his family and then returned to Mississippi. In any case Neal says that the local physician, Dr. Carson, was coming by regularly to see Lou. Worried that Aunt Lou could no longer handle the work, Will decided to hire Chloe.

Mr. Will's mind went back to the day he saw the pretty little brown woman on the adjoining plantation. . . . He began to pace the floor of the long veranda which was a habit of his when he was worried and wondered if he should go to see her and offer her a job as cook. . . .

"Lou" he said "go up the road to Chloe's house and ask her to come down here I want to talk to her on some important business." Now Aunt Lou began to wonder, "what in the world could Babe want to talk to her about, she is too high strung to work for anyone." . . . She reached the house and found Chloe making cotton-picking sacks on her sewing machine, [sic] this Aunt Lou had never seen before because the colored folks would sit up late at nite [sic] sewing those long sacks up by hand with large balls of thread which they used for every kind of sewing.

After exchanging the time of day and asking about the health of each and family she gave Chloe the message. It was a pleasant surprise to Chloe but she dared not show it and told Aunt Lou to tell Mr. Campbell she would be down there Sunday. What a break she said to herself and with Jim worrying about going back to Alabama. She did not know and could not guess just what the nature of this interview would be. She was sure it would be about work, because that was all that had confronted her all of her life. September was hot down in the delter [sic] you would think summer was just beginning instead of ending. . . .[50]

Chloe probably chose a Sunday to go to Will's house because there was less work to leave. His home was some ways away, with the New Foundation church off the road between her place and his. My grandmother knew, of course, that for a black woman to go to see the "captain boss" alone when all the black people were in church was a situation full of hazard. And unfortunately, because Chloe had been in bondage, we can be certain she knew even more about the dangers facing black women on plantations.

Chloe did not go to church but instead put on one of her prettiest dresses and went to see what Mr. Campbell wanted. She opened the wide gate to [the] long cris[s]-cross fence painted white entering a large yard where calves and his riding mare grazed on bermuda grass then she came to a smaller yard where roses and violets were blooming and honeysuckle vines were running on a trelles [sic] at each end of the porch. She knocked on the door [sic] it was some time before someone came as she stood there looking down the long hall on to the walk way leading to the kitchen. Her heart almost sank within her, and she felt like running away. Finally, Mr. Campbell came to the door. He invited her in and said "All the niggers have gone to church, so I am alone." She could not find words to reply. He told her of the work situation and asked if she would like to cook for him and Mr. Dixon [a white man recently hired]. She felt so relieved because it was work she wanted and needed.

Every morning by day lite [sic] she was in Mr. Campbell['s] kitchen getting breakfast, she found many other things to do. It reminded her of the days she spent in the white folks kitchen in Alabama, but here it was different [sic] she was her own boss and she enjoyed the freedom and the plentifulness of everything. She enjoyed being praised and was planning each day how to improve conditions on the plantation. The colored folks began to look upon her as the mistress in the big house; she was well liked as well as feared because she was very frank and too brutally frank. Nites [sic] when she would go home she was too tired to listen to Jims [sic] complaints although she would always take him a pan of food which he never found any fault with. He read his bible every nite and was forever preparing a sermon which he never got a chance to preach.[51]

While my grandmother had the honesty to show how Will Campbell really talked, and how her mother put people off being brutally frank, she may also have indulged some wishful thinking as far as people regarding Chloe as mistress of the house. But Georgia's greatest leap over the facts comes with regard to the relationship that took shape between Chloe and Will. She omits whether they fell in love or one was seduced or if Chloe simply encountered that which she had perhaps first feared, sexual assault by "Mr. Will." And I can't really say what Georgia knew, though I feel sure she knew more than this:

> [Jim] was so dissatisfied he went back to Alabama and Chloe then moved into the big house. Things went along fine until she became ill with morning sickness then it became known that she was pregnant . . .

First, my grandmother's coyness at this point in the story is irritating even if understandably protective. It is not clear at all that Jim left Mississippi at this point. He was not with Chloe and her family when they were all in Marion in 1880, and he was there in Mississippi when the census taker arrived at Silver Creek later that summer. He was not only present but so were all their children, including the toddler Georgia, whose last name was given as Curry like all the rest. Georgia's very reductive sentence says things were fine until it became *known* that Chloe was pregnant. Yes, I guess that is the crux of the matter. There must have been quite a drama hidden by this phrase despite the fact that this kind of pregnancy was one of the most common of southern tales.

One of the jarring contradictions to my grandmother's somewhat rosy recollections is another family version of the story. King Carter's great-grandson, Rainer Wilson, who grew up in Yazoo City, was told that Chloe was Will's slave and then became his mistress. Though the first part is literally possible, I suppose, given the lack of documentation of her family in the 1860s, it seems highly unlikely. That she was his mistress is probably a good way to look at the romantic relationship, though Will never had a wife. Georgia and my father referred to Chloe as Will's common-law wife, which also works, though it masks the origins of such unions in the nineteenth century. But the slave-to-mistress story is important because it speaks volumes about how she may have been treated in that household, and how her Mississippi kinfolk interpreted her situation. Rainer told me that people in his family had seen the pallet on the floor where Chloe was forced to sleep in Will's house. The second time I talked to him, he said, "She was his maid, and then his mistress." Different terms but similar relationships. This is absolutely the most sensible way to look at Chloe's circumstances. Seeing events from that vantage makes her pregnancy an unremarkable event.

How Jim Curry would have reacted is hard to know. The only descendant of his with whom I have spoken did not know of his Mississippi family, only that he had once lived there. Many African American men raised these children of the plantation owners, just as William Roscoe Davis, my other great-grandfather did with his wife's firstborn. I would wager that most did the same. There are too many families in the records with black parents and mulatto children. In freedom, keeping a family together was no longer a privilege but, being so hard-won, it was a central desire most people tried to fulfill. And life was too difficult. Like farm families everywhere, they needed every able body. Still, by today's standards it is not surprising that Jim left Chloe after Georgia's birth—and on her divorce papers she reports his departure as occurring after the date of the child's birth. Yet using the modern yardstick again, it seems more likely that a man would leave if a relationship persisted between his wife and another man. If he had been tossed aside for another man, Jim Curry may have acted on another new privilege—being able to put several hundred miles between himself and the situation.

In Sarah's later vindictive letter she accused Chloe of being insanely jealous when it came to Jim, a matter I cannot begin to address, except to say that's also possible. The family stories harp on Jim in negative terms, so this was a new angle for me. It is believable to me also that such jealousy may have fed her impatience with his disinterest in the farm. However, if Chloe were frantic with jealousy, I suspect she would have sat with him through all those church services. Sarah imagined Chloe to have seduced Will, first of all, in revenge against Leonidas for some fancied injury and secondly, because she was jealous when it came to Jim. I don't quite know what to do with that one. That sounds like a very personal grievance against Leonidas, not a wage or labor dispute, and the fact that Sarah knew about it makes it seem more than a minor accusation. If Leonidas was given to sexually exploiting black women on his place, Chloe was in the age range he preferred.

Sarah still seems to have put the worst possible face on Chloe and Will's relationship, in direct contrast to my grandmother, who put the best possible face on it. In Sarah's favor is the fact that Will would seem to have been anything but a man of the world, and in Georgia's favor is the fact that I have no clear indication of any serious female attachments before my great-grandmother. Surely Chloe may have seen this single, possibly lonely man of her own age who was the last of a line of well-off landowners as her own private reparation. She may have seen in him protection for herself and provision for her children for the duration of her life. In the harsh calculations to which bondwomen were accustomed, survival was often the highest good.

And then she may have been enamored of Will Campbell. He may have been nicer, more courtly than her husband. Odds are good that he was less angry. Will may have been autocratic, privileged, and racist, I don't know. However, by middle-age he had observed how intelligent she was and took the time to teach her his end of the cotton business. This was a choice. Chloe may have been elated to have someone in her life who had a road map for the intricacies of citizenship, property ownership, making business work, whether farming cotton or raising livestock, all of which he knew well. She would have counted herself lucky to have someone there who in fact could make it possible for her to safeguard her interests from most threats except rising water and boll weevils, and who was a day-to-day example of how a free life is lived with the possibility of a long future.

As with all other events in Chloe's life, I can only read her actions. She stayed with Will Campbell the rest of his life. And he stayed with her for the rest of his life. I can only assume a genuine affection of some depth developed between these two people. And so, with a grain of salt handy, I give credence to my grandmother's version. She finishes the sentence that began "Things went along fine until she became ill with morning sickness" with the statement that Chloe wanted to go back to Alabama "where her parents and relatives lived to give birth to her baby. Mr. Campbell was very much worried and eager for Chloe to return." The year was 1878.[52]

9

Colonel Campbell's Constituents

Leonidas Campbell's entry into electoral politics was no *Mr. Smith Goes to Washington*. In a different place and time someone probably would have remarked to officials or the newspapers that a candidate running for office was lynched on the property of his opponent. Someone would have surely pointed out that the opponent had accused him of arranging a murder and yet the man never lived long enough to get to jail or to court. Leonidas simply issued a statement that J. G. Patterson had been taken by forces unknown on his way to jail. And lastly, why would a man like Leonidas have been eager to run against a popular incumbent (albeit a lowly farm worker), likely to win the majority-black electorate's votes? Maybe if he had reason to believe he could win.

Sadly, Campbell's actions fit rather neatly into the string of similar scenarios that were part of a coordinated plan to rid Yazoo County of all its Republican officers and candidates. I was shocked enough when I discovered the lynching in Morgan's book, but when the full breadth of the events of 1875 was clear to me I was greatly disturbed, so disturbed that I became uncomfortable with telling Will and Chloe's story without saying something about those who suffered along with Patterson, even if not on the Campbell farm. Leonidas Campbell's election to a seat in the State House of Representatives would have meant little to his fellow Democrats without the removal of the other black elected officials. In accepting the "honor" of running for his district, he agreed to be part of a vicious seizure of power.

How many lies were told to satisfy the questions regarding what happened at his farm, I do not know. It would be helpful to learn, for instance, if he testified in the trial of William Thomas, the man accused of committing the murder at Silver Creek. Events of the late summer of 2005, including Hurricane Katrina, prevented retrieval of the transcripts in Mississippi. If he did testify, perhaps he cleared up exactly how he came to decide that Patterson had arranged the murder. When a U.S. Senate investigating committee came to Jackson to make inquiries into the violent run-up to the election of 1875, many local Democrats refused to cooperate. I saw no testimony from Leonidas in the records. So, I believe he was a full participant in the deadly conspiracy.

The full story brings together the Yazoo County of the Campbells with the Yazoo County of Albert Morgan, which had seemed to be two separate worlds. The conspiracy started with an unthinking reaction to the election of a sheriff. Back in 1873 the local Republicans had done as well as they ever would in winning local offices. "Mister" W. H. Foote became Circuit Clerk, and the Board of Supervisors gained several Republicans, including S. G. Bedwell, a white Missourian who was Yazoo Postmaster, and Hilliard Golden, an African American farmer. Two African Americans, Walter Boyd and J. G. Patterson, went to the State House. The newly elected sheriff was A. T. Morgan. The job of sheriff involved being the county tax collector and, as such, had certain legal rewards. (And to be sure, there seem to have been some tax collectors who did well from the illegal rewards possible in the job.) The outgoing sheriff, H. P. Hilliard, a Republican and a Morgan ally who in fact had gotten the job through Morgan's influence, refused to give up his office. He had not only done well by himself financially but, having married a woman from local planter society, he had risen socially and, one could say, lost his politics. He did not contest the election but simply refused to leave when Morgan came to take office in January.[1]

Morgan said the evening before his first official day on the job he received an offer of $5,000 if he would allow Hilliard to stay on for thirty days. Morgan no doubt could have used the money but he came to work the next day and Hilliard showed up on the courthouse steps with twenty to twenty-five supporters. Morgan told all his deputies, three of whom were African American, to go back into the office and, according to his account, went out to meet Hilliard, followed by one black deputy who would not let him go alone. Hilliard and his men charged past Morgan into the courthouse. They broke into the office and one of Hilliard's men fired a gun. One of Morgan's deputies fired back. When Morgan got there he saw Hilliard "reeling away from the now open office door." What followed was a five-minute melee in which, Morgan says, all but one of Hilliard's men fled. One of Morgan's deputies was shot, and Hilliard was dead.[2]

I suspect Hilliard thought he could just go take back his office. The melee allowed the Democrats to arrest Albert Morgan for murder and put him and his deputies in jail. Morgan thought at the time that it was an attempt to recapture the local government but, if it was, it was improvised. Morgan was refused bail in order to keep him from being lynched by a mob, but of course this simply put him in danger of being lynched later from the jail. When word got out that a good southern Democrat had been put in charge at the jail, according to Morgan, blacks began "pouring into town." The black men, estimated at two or three hundred and armed with clubs and a few guns, caught the white mob unprepared. Had they had their militias organized they could easily have cleared the area with armed men on horseback, but they were unable to act. The freedmen stood there, against all entreaties, for two days straight.[3]

The temporary sheriff was removed and Morgan and his deputies were secretly taken out of the jail to Jackson, where he awaited trial. Morgan was tried and acquitted, having in fact shot no one, and returned to his office in July 1874. This is an important story because the murders of 1875 might never have occurred if the African American community had not made it clear that day that they had no intention of letting their votes be dismissed or allowing an official elected by them just removed from office by force.[4]

This has to have been a pivotal event for the Democrats, one that would have forced them to come up with their plan: to take the Republican leaders out one by one, at night, without unfriendly witnesses. They would never again risk having an armed black community in their streets.

After the Republicans had their victory at the polls, the Democrats had their "Taxpayers Convention" and came up with the infamous six-point plan to take the election by force and fraud if need be. The Mississippi Plan was adopted across the state (and in other states), and the "Redemption" of the old Mississippi was its goal. Rumors spread again of a "nigro insurrection" and the whites began systematically arming themselves and building their militias. On one occasion a steamboat from Vicksburg stopped at every landing in Yazoo asking for donations of guns to help the white people of Vicksburg against a black rising. The men got double-barreled shotguns and rifles. When Morgan boarded the boat to inquire about the collection of arms, the captain told him there was "a mob of nigros" waiting on a riverbank to take his ship. Neither story was true.[5]

By the summer of 1875, Democrats were openly promising to retake the government, "peaceably if possible, forcibly if necessary." On September 1 the Republicans met at a hall in Yazoo, where Democrats showed up and the now infamous shoot-out took place. By the end of the month so many armed white men were roaming the streets of Yazoo City that Governor Adelbert Ames decided to send two companies of militia there—one headed by the estimable freedman Charles Caldwell—but Ames changed his mind when he learned his troops would be seriously outnumbered. Thereafter, the most serious violence took place.[6]

James Patterson was lynched on October 20. Two months after the Silver Creek murders the *Clarion* admitted that Patterson had been lynched but claimed, "[I]t was all the work of colored people. Patterson and his accomplice were colored. and [sic] he was tried, condemned, and executed by colored men—two thirds of whom were, no doubt, Republicans."[7]

Morgan told the Senate Committee that no one believed that Patterson hired Thomas to murder anyone. To the contrary, he said, a group of ad hoc militiamen known as Dixon's Scouts had warned Patterson not to remain in Yazoo, that he was a marked man. Asked if he understood that blacks had lynched Patterson, Morgan responded: "I understood a statement to that effect was published in *The Clarion* some time afterward. . . . But it is believed that he was hung by Dixon's scouts and regulators."[8]

When Leonidas sent to town for help, one assumes, he sent to the sheriff's office. Yazoo's white Republican postmaster, S. G. Bedwell, testified on this point. (Bedwell himself had been threatened and left the county during most of the trouble, claiming to be ill.) Throughout his testimony, he said he did not know which whites were engaged in violence. Bedwell said of Campbell: "He claimed that there had been a murder committed there and that he wanted the matter looked into." While a deputy sheriff seemingly did go out there, it is interesting is that one of the militia groups showed up. The posse that came to Silver Creek was a bunch who wore blue ribbons identifying them as Dixon's Scouts. Asked if Dixon's Scouts went out on such missions often, Bedwell replied:

> I don't think they were very frequent. . . . The only time I can recollect of their going, was when this man Patterson was hung, and they were then sent for by Colonel Campbell.
>
> Q: Were they sent for before or after the hanging of Patterson?
>
> A: Before the hanging.[9]

If Campbell sent for the Dixon Scouts at all, whether in addition to the deputy sheriff or not, he would have been fully aware that the lives of the two accused black men on his farm would be in immediate danger. If in fact Leonidas was aware that Patterson had been told by the posse to leave Yazoo but had not left his farm, he, or others perhaps, may have deemed it time to make good on the threat. Morgan testified that Patterson was hiding.

> . . . I have information from Mr. Fawn that a colored man went to Patterson's hiding-place and decoyed him out upon the highway, where he was captured. . . . Several days preceding his death he had taken all the money and valuables he had, about $1,500, and put them on his person and had hid himself in the canebrakes, as he had heard that Dixon's scouts were

coming after him; that they had made such threats. They employed or purchased a colored man, one of his own race, to go and decoy him out from his hiding-place to the highway, after which they seized him and hung him and distributed the money among themselves. He was a member of the legislature, and I always thought him an honorable man; he was a peaceable, law-abiding man.[10]

Deputy Sheriff Charles Fawn, a white Republican, later told Morgan and Bedwell that a member of the posse admitted to the lynching after Fawn pressed him about what they had been doing at Leonidas's farm for two or three days. They first had to find Patterson, as Morgan said. The man reported, according to Bedwell's testimony:

We just took him out there and got him on top of a mule and put a rope around his neck and tied it to a limb of a pecan-tree and drove the mule out from under him; and in driving the mule out from under him it pretty near killed him; and to keep him from dying there with his feet on the ground we took hold of the other end of the rope and pulled him up; before we could get the knot untied he died, it was tied in such a bungling way.[11]

While Leonidas had reported that the deputy sheriff was overtaken by an armed body, he seems to have sent for the armed body himself. If the posse was worried about "prosecuting" and punishing murderers, why did they only hang the elected official? They could as easily have lynched William Thomas. Instead they brought Thomas into town to the jail. One report even said that Thomas was released almost immediately.

Bedwell testified that Patterson was hung near the residence of Colonel L. A. Campbell. He was hung where people could see him and as Morgan writes, "that his fate might be a warning to all other Republicans, his body was left hanging there until the buzzards came and picked it." Certainly, Campbell's true constituents were not those in the majority in his district—the African American farm laborers who worked for him and a handful of other planters—but rather the planter elite of Yazoo County. The elite had observed not only that blacks would vote in their own choices but that they also would defend their representatives if necessary. By letting Patterson's body hang outside his home, he had sanctioned the lethal wave of attacks on Republicans in Yazoo.[12]

Within a day of Patterson's murder, Horace Hammond was found hanged following a militia sighting in his neighborhood. The Yazoo *Democrat* reported that he died from hanging "by parties unknown."[13]

Then Charles Fawn, the man who had told Morgan and Bedwell what really happened at Silver Creek and who had received a written threat to his life, was gunned down in broad daylight by an unknown white man. Fawn, who helped Morgan escape, was a merchant in 1870 and, by 1875, a lawyer.[14]

Another African American, Augustus Taylor or Albert Augustus (the records conflict) was hung on October 25 by a group of African Americans forced to kill him, according to Chancery Clerk James Dixon. Born a slave in 1835, Dixon was a carpenter and a minister, and he too was threatened that fall. African American State Representative Walter Boyd was threatened but survived the election season. A black schoolteacher named McCoy who had been in Yazoo less than a year was run out for working on the election. African American Supervisor Hilliard Golden's home was burned down, likely at this same time.[15]

Hilliard Golden is believed by his family to have been brought from North Carolina to Mississippi. At the end of chattel slavery he became a very successful farmer, and one of the county's largest black landowners. His granddaughter Lily Golden, a Russian anthropologist, documented his experience. Hilliard Golden's son, Oliver, became an agricultural expert after attending Tuskegee Institute and serving in the U.S. army during World War I. In the 1920s he joined the Communist Party and married a Polish Jewish immigrant. In 1931 the couple fled race prejudice for the Soviet Union, where he worked in Uzbekistan.[16]

Whites warned Justice of the Peace Major Harris that if he left until after the election, no harm would come to him. Harris, most likely born in slavery and a mason by trade, was married with three young children. One night, on a warning that a band of whites was headed to his home, he fled to the northern end of the county and stayed in a canebrake until after the election, at which point he was told they knew where he was and were still coming after him. He then left for Jackson, where he stayed until the violence had run its course.[17]

"Every leading white Republican remaining in the county surrendered and published the fact over his own signature, and then sent word to me that they had done so in the hope of preventing further bloodshed, and of saving their own property and lives," writes Morgan. The effect of their signatures was to remove the Republican ticket from the ballot. Morgan also charged that the chairman of the county Democratic committee went into the U.S. post office and had mail addressed to leading Republicans burned. Though Morgan sent Republican ballots to his colleagues, they did not use them, having been told it would mean the life of anyone associated with the ballots if they appeared at the polls.[18]

One incident was particularly chilling. A few days before the election, the voter registration board was revising the registration lists, according to Bedwell's Senate testimony, "in the lower end of the county, [when] a party of colored men came over from Brannon Ewing's plantation, and wanted to register . . . and they were driven back." He says then that a rumor circulated at the village of Satartia, "a place of about four or five hundred inhabitants," that the blacks were going to murder the people of Satartia.

A company of white people organized and went down there; and they met a party of colored men and drove them into the river, and there is no telling how many were killed. I heard one man, who was wounded there, and who is now dead, say that from the number of cries and groans that came from the damned niggers, they must have got a bushel of them. And some man, writing a description of it, said that they were all driven into the river and jumped in like frogs. I think that was the word he used. I have been told that there were several killed at that time. . . . The supposition was that there were several killed. They disappeared anyway, and were never seen or heard of afterwards.[19]

It would seem that one crucial detail was left out of this account—the company would have been on horseback and firing guns. Chancery Clerk

Dixon gave his account of the same event saying that the blacks at the Ewing plantation were having a meeting the day before the incident.

> . . . the whites wanted to get up a riot to keep them from going to the club meetings, and they tried to turn them back, and some one fired on them, and the colored people fired into them, and one or two white men were wounded and one colored man, I think was killed in the shooting. The next morning this news had gotten to Yazoo City, and they went down with this armed body of men.
>
> He [the man Dixon knew] had seen a group of 15 or 20 armed men who were on horseback heading . . . down to Satartia. . . . There was an armed body of men from Yazoo City down there in the neighborhood of Satartia. . . . There was a line of boats running on the river there, and they stopped a boat. . . I did not go down myself, but I was told that they put on the boat all the men they could get around Yazoo City, and sent them down, and those who did not go by boat, went on horseback. . . .[20]

The image of the would-be black voters being hemmed in between the men on horseback and the armed men on the boat is truly horrifying. I cannot imagine one of these thugs ever even thinking of doing such a thing to their farm animals, but black voters? No question. Dixon reported that he was told the blacks in that neighborhood had run off.

Dixon also said one of the "militias" was reported near his own place one night when a Republican meeting was set for twenty miles outside of town. He saw another group with ropes heading to Wolf Lake, an area between Yazoo City and Silver Creek in the northwest of the county. Dixon said they told him they were after "a colored man there that was teaching school, and they were going out there to run him off, or take him . . ." This teacher had also been organizing Republican clubs. And lastly he reported that a man named Johnson was drowned near Satartia.[21]

By all reports, the ensuing election in November 1875 was very peaceful. The election numbers for Yazoo County were said to have included 4,007 voting for the Democrats, and 7 for the Republicans. Every single black voter was said to have voted Democrat. Mississippi had been "Redeemed." Reconstruction was over in Mississippi, and definitely in Yazoo County. But one other important African American remained to be assassinated that year, Charles Caldwell, of neighboring Hinds County. On Christmas Day Charles Caldwell, who defended Morgan at the capitol and, more importantly perhaps, was leader of a government militia that was to go into Yazoo during the election turmoil, was murdered "after being lured to have a drink at a local store by a white 'friend.'" [22]

Four black men who had held positions in Yazoo seem to have survived. Dora F. Wade, born free, was a teacher, appointed marshal of Yazoo City in 1870, and elected to the State House of Representatives from 1871 to 1873. William Leonard was born a slave in Mississippi and became a blacksmith. He was not in any office in 1875, but had represented the county in the so-called "Black and Tan" convention of 1868. And Houston B. Burrows was county treasurer. [23]

When S. G. Bedwell was asked by the Senate Committee how many African Americans were killed prior to the election, he said:

A: I should suppose there were some six, eight, or ten. Every few days while I was away I would read notices in the papers of darkies being hung here and there and elsewhere, and some disappearing. I could not state how many. It was variously estimated at from five to fifteen.

Q: That does not include those killed at the time they were driven into the river?

A: No, sir. [24]

The fourth African American official to survive would manage to continue holding office in Yazoo for a few years: "Mister" William H. Foote. Born free in Vicksburg and a barber by trade, Foote is listed in the 1870 census as a "mulatto," occupation "legislator," with a three-year-old son and a two-month-old daughter. He was in the State House of Representatives from 1870 to 1871, and at first seemed to me to "go along to get along." He changed his mind and later became a formidable figure in the county. Other positions he held were Constable and Clerk of the Circuit Court. He was threatened in all of his posts. In 1875 he was the secretary of the Republican Party county executive committee and was shot and wounded at the Republican campaign meeting that set off the Yazoo riot of that year. Several years later, while the county's last remaining African American office holder as deputy internal revenue collector for Yazoo City, he was arrested, jailed, and lynched in his cell by a white mob, along with two other black men, who were hung, one with the forced assistance of other blacks in the jail. When the jailer told Foote that he should quiet himself and get ready for death, Foote assured the man he was settled. He positioned himself near the door, and was able to grab some kind of object for self-defense. He knocked out the first man stepping into his cell and fought six others before they shot him.[25]

When Albert Morgan heard of Foote's murder he began to work on his book. He and his family had fled the Delta for Washington, D.C., where he lived in the home of Frederick Douglass and lobbied for government action on what had taken place in Mississippi. At the end of his book Morgan also remembers some other men of the region, men who survived the initial onslaught of 1875. Typical of my experience looking for information on lynching victims or victims of mob violence, I was unable to identify the first two men he names.

> Some of the survivors of the campaign of 1875 the [Mississippi] bulldozer has silenced by cajolery, some he has bribed to silence, some he has silenced by threats and some he has killed. But such as he could neither cajole, bribe, intimidate, nor kill, he has pursued with a malice, a cunning, and a persistency that has driven them from their homes and scattered them to the four corners of the earth.
>
> Chisholm refused to surrender or run, and the bull-dozer killed his daughter that he might make surer work with him. Gilmer refused, and he "filled him full of lead." Charles Caldwell refused, and he "shot him all to pieces," and wantonly slew him and all his children, from the elder son to the baby in the cradle. But why continue the list? I could add a hundred names more to it.[26]

In 1877 President Rutherford B. Hayes removed the last federal troops from the former Confederacy and African Americans lost the last protection they had outside of the widespread practice of keeping a gun in one's house. Needless to say the power structures of the slave-owning autocracy returned to full power, and Redeemers like Leonidas Campbell probably felt the greatest part of their task was done. But they did not let up. In the elections of 1878 Democrats took control of the U.S. House and Senate. Leonidas stepped out of politics and back to his first interest: making money from cotton. He had received his reward, but others did not.

> The county's nonslaveholders or postwar white newcomers who played key roles in the 1875 violent coup d'etat against the Republicans shared little of the victors' spoils. When some of them later tried to gain office by forming an interracial independents' movement in 1879, planters murdered them in broad daylight on the streets of Yazoo City.[27]

Leonidas continued to pursue the good life, and increasingly he fell back on selling parcels of land. Between August and October of 1876 he parted with three parcels in Missouri. After leaving office he came up with the idea of transforming himself into a cotton factor, which would allow him to collect the hefty shipper's fee he was paying someone else. He doubtless imagined his constituents in Yazoo could pay him too.

10

∽

High Water (1880–1932)

Georgia Campbell Neal wrote that when her mother Chloe Curry returned to Mississippi with her last baby, the black folks were "curious," and the few whites around were "amazed." This is a veiled allusion to the fact that Georgia looked white, having inherited few elements of her mother's black looks. She had the same serious demeanor as her mother; her face often stilled into stern or sad expressions with her lips tightly shut. As she grew, she took on her mother's build—short, of medium weight, with real hips, and a thick waist. But she looked like a Campbell—white, freckled with straight hair, and in one photograph she eerily resembles Will's older sister Mary Frances. I believe that fact alone must have really startled Campbells like Sarah Rush Owen the first time they saw Georgia.

Any amazement the white folks may have had at Silver Creek more likely was caused by the baby coming to live in Will's house, but this probably did not happen until some time after the summer of 1880. The baby, Georgie, as she was called, probably spent her days in Will's house with her mother during the first two years of her life along with her four-year-old half brother Tommy. But until Jim left, they seem to have gone to the Curry cabin in the evening.

Chloe went home to Marion with all of her children that summer of 1880. Her whole family was there. Her father, Edmond, then sixty-eight years of age, and mother, Caroline, fifty-three, were living on a place near a farmer named E. B. Woodfin from Virginia. Woodfin was living with his second wife and her parents, who were from North Carolina. Perhaps they were Caroline and Edmond's employers. I have been unable to establish a definite connection.

Chloe's sister Mariah, now thirty-two, and her husband, Zeno Tutt, thirty, were there, and they now had three children: Meg, seven, Edmond, five, and Chloe, four. Her brother King was there with his wife of three years, Belle, and their two daughters, Annie, three, and Katie, six months. Aaron, her twenty-year-old brother, and all the other men were farm laborers. Chloe's youngest siblings, Lucy, seventeen, and Andrew, fifteen, were still in school.

Sometime after Chloe's family was together in Marion, Jim Curry returned to Alabama for good. He does not seem to have taken any of the children with him but by fall they too were likely in Marion, living with her parents and going to the Lincoln School. One of the persistent unpleasant stories about Georgia's childhood is that she did not know she was "half-white" as folks put it to me. This really meant she did not know she was black. Rainer Wilson told me that Will Campbell forbid her to play with her cousins and other black children her age—that could have included her half sisters and half brothers and perhaps her uncle King's daughters, Annie and Katie, who were about her age. Georgia, of course, grew up with them anyway and knew well all of the other children and cousins all her life, so I know that her mother worked hard to counteract any such rules Will may have set up. I was told many years ago that she was treated as if she were a little white girl, and remained ignorant because Chloe's other children went to Alabama. She would see them in the summer, I was told. However, Wilson told me that in Mississippi not only were they not allowed to play with her, but they also had to do chores for her such as shining her shoes. While at least one person in my family is reluctant to believe this, I can say only it is evidence of a fact Georgia herself tried to explain to us—a tear in the fabric of the family was created by her color and more importantly, by her white father's presence in her life (as opposed to the common arrangement where the father never lived with his black children). The breach was two-dimensional: based on color and economic privilege. In this light, Chloe's decision to send her children to her parents seems the wiser of two difficult choices. Having already experienced unnatural separation in bondage, the separation may have been of less moment for her than for a contemporary parent. And it certainly would have been damaging to them to suddenly become second-class members of their own family.

Will's point of view is harder to grasp. As a man who grew up in the southern tradition—with mostly enslaved black playmates—he was depriving her of the joys of a childhood he himself knew. In the southern tradition, of course, such playmates were separated around puberty, but this goes a step beyond. It suggests he decided they had a different destiny, just as his enslaved friends had had. After that, one is left to wonder if he thought growing up as a white person would allow her to become a white person. I never got to ask her that question. It seems more likely that he didn't think it through but rather went on his instincts and, within limits, raised her as he was raised. And he may not have been concerned that Chloe's other children had to go to Alabama.

Sarah Rush Owen also did not worry about her children being separated from her. Relatives in Tennessee kept them many months of every year. And the boys, at least, seemingly never formed close relationships with her as a result. By the summer of 1880 she was a forty-two-year-old widow living on the family homestead with only her eldest son, Felix, twenty-two. Her eldest daughter Fannie, twenty-three, would marry George Bryan, superintendent at the Springfield Transfer Company in the next year. After her marriage, Fannie wrote to her mother, who was away from home again, to ask her to write Jay, the twenty-year-old baby of the family. Both Fannie and Lucy had joined a local "ladies club," and Fannie was particularly excited that the group was to study "architecture from ancient down to modern times." She was to give the first recitation on buildings of the Middle Ages. Their cousin, Laura "Lulu" Campbell, John Nathaniel's daughter, had married, had a child, and was already a widow at twenty-five years old.[1]

By 1880 Leonidas had left Grand Oaks and moved with his wife, Lucy, and son, Robert Lee, to Vicksburg where he now owned a house and an office. He was in a partnership with Sherman Parisot, a Yazoo steamboat operator. Parisot lost several boats during the Civil War, and afterward began another line, the "P-Line," which was successful. Parisot and Campbell called themselves "Cotton Factors and Commission Merchants." He had apparently broken off an earlier partnership. The farm stationery from 1880 to 1881 has two different headings: "L. A. Campbell, Grand Oak Plantation"; "Campbell & Gray, Dealers in General Merchandise, Grand Oak Plantation, Campbellsville, Miss." with "L. A. Campbell, Vicksburg and J. R. Gray, Campbellsville." In the latter case, when the stationery was used, Gray's name was scratched out, and the company name changed to "Campbell & Co."[2]

Had Leonidas tired of life in the hinterlands after his two years in the State House? Or was it simply a business move? I don't know. I am certain he would have preferred the social life of then prosperous Vicksburg, but he may have also been made uncomfortable by his unmarried brother Will's choice to have Chloe, a person white society would have regarded as a "concubine," and her child move into his home. I don't know if Will's friends such as the Harrison girls stopped receiving him. A few years younger than Will, they were still living in their father's home in Yazoo City at the time. His friends the Quackenboss boys had moved on to other parts, it seems. I found one of them running a grocery in Tensas, Louisiana, on the other side of the Mississippi between Vicksburg and Natchez. Will surely could have visited him and his family. The people in town that Leonidas likely socialized with would have included some of the Redeemers and probably no one inclined to entertain a man with a black common-law wife. Too bad Albert Morgan was run out of town.

My grandmother, on the other hand, was under the impression that black people began to regard Chloe as the mistress of the house, and believed that her own birth brought the twenty-eight-year-old Will joy he had never before known. Obviously, she felt loved by him, which was not often the case with biracial children of the time. Accepting Georgia as his daughter surely complicated or curtailed his social connections in the white community. On the other hand, Will was truly a full-time farmer and seemingly not one for sitting in cafes in town, so his day-to-day life was probably very much the same as it had always been.

Morgan found in the 1860s that the concubines of the local gentry were "at the head" of the African American social order and, he says, as such after 1868, "they appeared tolerably content and took advantage of the new constitution only for the purpose of enforcing their rights as heirs in cases where there were none having a prior right." Things began to change in the early 1870s, in part because of these very Reconstruction laws:

> Now that the concubine's position as a social leader of the colored people was not only in danger, but several of them in Yazoo had been "turned out of church" because they were "living in adultery" in the sight of man as well as of God, many of that class began to inquire whether there was any legal inhibition upon their marriage with "white sweethearts."[3]

This suggests to me that Chloe also may have paid some price in isolation, perhaps more so after her husband's departure. On the other hand, hardheaded realism is a staple in African American communities, and Chloe's situation was far from unusual. Other responses to the loosening of restrictions on interracial marriage and cohabitation in the 1870s that Morgan heard about ran the gamut. "One began the erection of an elegant new residence just south of our home . . . and allowed it to be given out that it was for his concubine . . . another gave money to his; another secretly married his; another satisfied his with promises." Some men opted to give up their "claims" on the women and, he reports, "the great mass 'bided their time.'" I actually looked for some of these possibilities in my own research, and found nothing like a secret marriage.[4]

If Will and Chloe had had any mind to marry, they were just dreaming. Chloe was not divorced for several more years, and it wouldn't have mattered if she were divorced. A state law banning interracial marriage was on the books by the time she moved into his house.

A creature called "Jim Crow" was born by the beginning of the 1880s, and many states, certainly led by the South, but in no way confined to the South, began to pass laws establishing segregation in all walks of life. The first of these appeared in 1881 and segregationists continued to conceive of new arenas for segregation, and new ways to restrict the enfranchisement of black men throughout the decade. So, though Albert

Morgan had made interracial marriage possible for himself and any others who dared in the 1870s, such partnerships were outlawed after my grandmother was born. In 1880 a revised state code declared "marriage between white persons and Negroes or mulattoes or persons of *one-quarter* [my emphasis] or more Negro blood as incestuous and void. The penalty was a fine of up to $500, or imprisonment in the penitentiary up to ten years, or both." In 1888 railroad travel was segregated, and in 1890 the new state constitution banned marriage between a white and "a negro or mulatto or person who shall have *one-eighth* or more of negro blood." Clearly they thought even one-eighth black blood would taint the white race. In Virginia in the previous century, Thomas Jefferson and the state legislatures had decided one-eighth black was a point at which someone could just be declared white (though that would not free a slave whose mother was a slave). Mississippi didn't play that. By the late 1800s, "one drop" was too much.[5]

By 1892 Chloe's pallet on the floor would have been necessary at least to keep up the pretense of living within the law. There was by then a law against sex across race lines, with the same penalties as intermarriage. One can guess that this law was aimed at black males rather than white ones, and yet the very existence of such a law would have encouraged the shunning of any man who openly cohabited with his dusky sweetheart. Perhaps the most edifying law, showing the lengths to which segregationists would go, was one that restrained freedom of speech: "Any person guilty of printing, publishing or circulating matter urging or presenting arguments in favor of social equality or of intermarriage between whites and negroes, shall be guilty of a misdemeanor."[6]

If I imagine another scenario entirely, for instance, Chloe having been the victim of a rape by some other person and Will merely befriending her, their situation in the world of Mississippi would have been exactly the same with regard to his place in his own race. If he himself were marginalized, as a homosexual, as another example, and their friendship was a shelter for both, their bond would still be suspect. Jim Crow, in effect, outlawed almost any variety of bond they may have shared. Once the trains and other public conveyances had become segregated, he could not ride around with a black girlfriend next to him in his buggy without giving the appearance of flaunting the intent of the new laws of the land. The many possible realities of human connection were quashed into invisibility in a narrowly conceived world that abhorred interracial sexual connections, even though forced miscegenation marked the South to its very core, and was central to the region's difference from other regions of the country.

Whatever Will may have felt to be proper or improper about his relationship does not appear in any of the surviving letters. And one can easily imagine that he would not take up the subject with his family. They may have brought it up with him, and I imagine Sarah had something to say, but I have no proof of that. I feel comfortable in assuming they would not have approved, and even more confident that they would have feared for him if he stepped beyond whatever standard of behavior was acceptable at the time.

Will wrote to his sister Sarah in May 1881 to console her and complain about her son Felix taking off and leaving her, apparently without notice. Felix seems to have gone to Texas, where he lived off and on until 1920. Her son took some of the equipment for horses and mules (including some that belonged to Will) and left her high and dry. Felix also left Will's colts for her to tend. Will offers to make amends to her for their care, and nevertheless thinks Felix will yet turn out alright. He further offers to give her other son, Jay, a job when the cotton crop is being weighed.

Will says that he has furnished and set up his home, the only clue he ever gives to having become newly domesticated. This may indicate that he moved into Leonidas's former residence, or that he moved into a new home of his own. He is clearly comfortable enough to urge her to visit.

> I am glad to hear that Springfield has at last took [sic] a start to grow & I do hope she will continue to do so & become a large place & I hope property will go up. when I thought of returning to Springfield it was only my intention to build my houses on my lot & if I can get off this summer I will come up & if every thing is as prosperous then as now I will have some put up, Jackson is now due me for Eight-Months rent . . . & you can collect it You

can do so & make use of same that is if you need the money, Now dont think I am to [sic] liberal for if you need the money & can collect do so, for you are perfectly welcome . . . I am fixed up very comfortably for house keeping & have gone to some expense but not to much so & I will be glad to have you come down & stay at any time & as long as you like there is nothing that would give me more pleasure than to have you come & I want you to stick to your promise, I will send [illegible] the money this week . . . [7]

The letter is signed with the nickname "Bud." One month later he wrote again, mostly about family news. He had just been apprised of the impending marriage between his niece Fannie and George Bryan.

. . . You will have to come & live with me for you will be all alone before you know it, Jack [Jay] will be the only one left & it will not be long before he will set out in search of some girl If Felix is married why is it that Jack didnot [sic] see his frau, he certainly stayed with Felix while he was down there [Texas] I am glad to hear he is getting along so well . . .

The Old Man [the seventeen-years-senior Leonidas] is up looking over crops & straitening [sic] out the "boys" in general he has been Complaining with his Ears has a rining [ringing?] in both of them . . . he is going to send Sister [L. A.'s wife, Lucy] & Lee to Ocean Springs [resort near Biloxi] for a month or two & he told me he had invited Fanny to come down & go with her & I think it would be a nice trip for Fan & it woud be a benefit to her, L. a. [sic] is going to New York on R. Road business & cant be with sister he will go sometime this month. . . . Tell Jack to hurry & come hunting is good & I will be glad to have him with me.[8]

Will's mention of Leonidas's early summer bout of ringing in the ears made me laugh—in horror—that at least two of us in my immediate family might have inherited this tintinitus (usually with vertigo) from the Campbells. The fact that I am related to Leonidas suddenly got real for me. The railroad business mentioned was part of a maze of railroad lines creeping up, down, and across Mississippi. By the late 1880s there were fifteen lines snaking through the state, many of which would not last long enough to be made famous by the Mississippi Delta Blues that taught America the names "Illinois Central" and "Yellow Dog." Two decades before Charley Patton sang of "going where the Southern meets the Dog," cotton farmers were trying to lower the costs of moving cotton by building lines like the Yazoo & Mississippi Valley line (the Yellow Dog), which came into Yazoo in 1884.[9]

Sarah Rush Owen did keep her word and came to Mississippi. She and her daughter Lucy seem to have traveled south by boat to Vicksburg in the beginning of 1882. In her papers I found an elaborate menu from a Mississippi steamboat trip. This may have been a souvenir from that journey or another, as that particular service, the Anchor Line, only started up that year, and one of the menu pages is from September. (Sarah probably did return to Mississippi that September.) Still, the menu, which covers six days of repasts, does give a glimpse into a bygone style of travel—and it's somewhat amazing considering that the meals were accomplished without refrigeration. The cover is pure antebellum nostalgia, pastoral scenes of Negroes hauling cotton by wagon along a riverside, or running to greet the steamboat as a young white damsel enjoys the scenery from a little knoll above. Vines are etched around the central design. These menus include one sheet of offerings, and another with blank spaces in which the diner would write her selections. While the choices of Red Snapper with anchovy sauce or turkey with baked macaroni are simple enough, one of the travelers filled the dessert section with every possible choice. Some dishes one isn't often served now include Braised Hogshead (which Sarah chose), tongue hash on toast or woodcock on toast for lunch, oyster soup, or graham mush for breakfast. They ate lots of seafood and fresh vegetables, Parker House rolls, and desserts made from fresh fruit.[10]

On January 6 Fannie wrote to Sarah somewhat in advance of her arrival. The post office name at Silver Creek had changed by then from Campbellsville to Green Hill. The letter casts doubt on whether Sarah and Lucy actually left Vicksburg and went to Will's farm. If indeed they did, this could have been the first occasion in which Sarah encountered Chloe. Since Sarah knew of Chloe's anger at Leonidas from several years before, I suspect they met in the 1870s.

> . . . Was glad indeed to get both and am happy to hear you are both enjoying yourselves so much.__
>
> I wrote you two letters to Green Hill which I suppose from your letter you have not yet received. Please have uncle Will forward them to you and answer as soon as possible. Jay wrote to you last Sunday and sent the letter to Green Hill also.
>
> Only two cases have died yet with Small Pox but several have it. Every body has been vaccinated; but a great many vaccinations did not take. Mr Bryan's arm has been very sore while mine did not take at all. . . . All the cases are confined as yet to negroes and a low class of persons. . . .[11]

If two of her children had written to Silver Creek, clearly they expected her to visit there. When Fannie wrote she had already heard from both Sarah and Lucy, so her suggestion to have Will forward the mail leaves room for speculation that Fannie was informed the two women would not be going to see Will. The change of plans is curious given the distance traveled from Missouri to Mississippi.

In the spring, the rivers and creeks overran the levees and fields, and Will sent a book to Sarah with the following inscription: "Rush Campbell Owen From W. A. Campbell, Who rescued it, this book, from the flood of 1882, Yazoo Co. Mississippi."[12] Despite the loss suffered from the high water, the most lasting damage of that spring was a loan taken out in March by Leonidas against the land. He signed three deeds of trust for the loan, which was obtained from a New Orleans bank with a local Yazoo man as trustee. In May Will was obliged to sign over his share of the land to Leonidas to facilitate the loan. The bank required repayment in three notes when the crop came in that year: $5,368 due November 15, 1882; $5,416 due December 15, 1882; and $5,444 due January 1, 1883. If the sum went unpaid, a 10 percent interest rate kicked in. The deal involved shipping the cotton crop to New Orleans to the bank's agents and letting them sell it.[13]

On September 7, while staying with his wife and son at the Southern Hotel in St. Louis, Leonidas Campbell died after an illness of short duration. On his deathbed he made an oral will, asking his wife to write it down. In court papers submitted by Lucy Campbell in Vicksburg, she reported that in "his last sickness and a few hours before his death [he] said to me in the presence of our son Lee—tell Will—meaning W. A. Campbell his brother. I give him 'Grand Oak Plantation' meaning his plantation on Silver Creek Yazoo County Miss. I want him to treat you as his Sister and be kind of Lee. and to look after your business for you." The document was signed by Lucy Campbell, and witnessed by her brother-in-law, Sempronious Boyd (the gentleman who befriended the king of Siam).[14]

Lucy and her son moved back to Springfield. In Mississippi Will was faced with the prospect of having to raise the money to pay the loans and save the farms. Some portion of the debt was paid (the amount was illegible on the documents I've seen), and the debt persisted through the next year.

What emerged from the probate process was more debt. Leonidas had property and equipment at Valley Home, Grand Oak, and another place called Grosvenor worth $15,039. He owed $23,920 to the 148 farm workers, seemingly all African American, and including Chloe's brother King. He also owed $22,943 on five farms and the house at Grosvenor. (I could not determine if this last figure included the $16,000 in bank loans against the land.) And he owed $7,750 on a joint loan with someone else. At best, this is a total of $54,613 and, at worst, $70,613.

He also owned stocks worth $17,655 in several Vicksburg wharf enterprises and the P-Line Steamboat company owned by his partner, Parisot. However, he had signed over what seems to have been more than half of these to his father-in-law Robert McElhaney and Mississippi planter Samuel L. Woolridge. Lucy had to sell some other shares in these companies, as well as streetcar stock. Her father, who administered the estate, sold almost $8,000 worth of land in Missouri and paid $10,000 alone to the Springfield Bank (probably his bank).[15]

In 1884 the debt in Mississippi was still unpaid and the land was forfeited and put up for auction in Yazoo. Samuel L. Woolridge received the deed on Feb. 4, 1884. The description of the land included "the property referred to as L. A. Campbell Plantation, Alluvia Plantation, Valley Home Plantation, Grand Oak Plantation." Woolridge belonged to a longtime Mississippi planting family. (One of the Woolridges who was a former Confederate officer gave Yazoo County its first free African American. After the Civil War, he had a law passed so he could free his valet Dave Woolridge for valor at Bull Run. That freedman, who Morgan said was "nearly white" and a cripple, was used to stir the rumors of a black rising. Morgan wryly notes that Dave pronounced Negro like a "real gentleman," meaning "nigro.") Will continued to live there and plant cotton. The rivers overflowed again that spring but perhaps did no great damage.[16]

Somehow, Will was able to buy back some portion of the land. There are no records of a purchase from Woolridge, but that doesn't mean there was no private transaction. My assumption is based on the fact that in 1885 Will and his nephew Erskine Argyle Campbell, John Nathaniel's eldest son, made a loan application to Shattuck & Hoffman, factors and commission merchants in New Orleans. Erskine kept a draft of the application. The description of the land offered as collateral is basically the same land they always had. Woolridge deeded at least some of Grand Oak over to a George S. Irving in 1886, from whom Will bought it back that same year.

The following notation on the loan application was written in answer to the question of who owned title to the land: "Bk Ky W. A. & E. A. Campbell." This suggests to me the two men, and the first two initials suggest something like a Kentucky bank. The application also asked if ownership had ever been "disputed or in any way questioned," to which there was the response: "Yes but this transaction settles it." Even as they were in this process, Leonidas's partner Parisot sued Will and Erskine, saying that he had bought a slice of land running across two of the sections in March of the previous year and it had not been surrendered to him. I never saw any other paperwork for this case in Mississippi, so perhaps it was thrown out. Lastly, there were several thousand dollars in taxes due the next spring. They applied for $50,000, to be repaid over five years, which I assume they did receive. Some of the same terms that L. A. faced were in force, like shipping the crop directly to the factors in New Orleans, but the application shows that the two men must have decided that the only way to make cotton farming work by then was to increase the amount of land being farmed by many more acres.

The application sheds a light on the state of the farm in the era when my grandmother was a child there. The land, for instance, still at 7,900 acres, by then had 2,800 acres cleared and 5,100 others, including 1,750 "subject to be tilled." This last group was what they called "deaddried," meaning men had gone into the woods, sawed the trees, and let them die and drop on their own. Later they would remove the trunks and clear the ground. By then 3,300 acres had been fenced, a luxury John Nathaniel did not really have. There were three steam-powered cotton gins, two grist-mills, and no insurance policy, although they promised to insure the gins and the cotton in storehouses.

I don't know if they achieved these goals, but the two men proposed to jump from planting 400 acres (producing 820 bales) as they did in 1884, to planting 2,800 acres. They felt sure from that planting they could turn over 1,000 bales to the New Orleans firm. For their first repairs, they intended to build new cabins for workers and put new roofs on existing ones. At the time they had 264 hands, all of whom worked on shares or wages.[17]

Richard Wright wrote that sharecroppers were advanced "one mule, one plow, seed, tools, fertilizer, clothing, and food, the main staples of which are fat hog meat, coarsely ground corn meal, and sorghum mo-lasses." Wright, who was born in 1908 to sharecropper parents, writes a devastating account of the hidden costs charged to sharecroppers:

The Lords of the Land assign us ten or fifteen acres of soil already bled of its fertility through generations of abuse. . . . Because they feel that they cannot trust us, the Lords of the Land assign a "riding boss" to go from cot-ton patch to cotton patch and supervise our work. We pay for the cost of this supervision out of our share of the harvest; we pay interest on the cost of the supplies which the Lords of the Land advance to us; and, because ill-ness and death, rain and sun, boll weevil and storms, are hazards which might work to the detriment of the cotton crop, we agree to pay at harvest a "time price," a sum payable in cotton, corn, or cane, which the Lords of the Land charge us to cover a probable loss on their investment in us.[18]

Writing six decades after the brutal fall of Reconstruction, Wright describes whippings, lynchings, and men dragged bleeding through the streets. He concludes with a description of what was wrought by the end of Reconstruction's short reign:

> And we cannot fight back; we have no arms; we cannot vote; and the law is white. There are no black policemen, black justices of the peace, black judges, black juries, black jailers, black mayors, or black men anywhere in the government of the South. The Ku Klux Klan attacks us in a thousand ways, driving our boys and girls off the jobs in the cities and keeping us who live on the land from protesting or asking too many questions.[19]

In 1884, Albert T. Morgan published his memoir of the Reconstruction years, *Yazoo: or, On the Picket Line of Freedom in the South*. He declared that since the coup to oust the Republicans in Yazoo, "colored men there have been whipped, hunted by hounds, and killed, and their mothers, wives, daughters and sweethearts have been reviled, seduced, raped, while Yazoo law gave them no redress."[20]

While he was still writing the book, *The Vicksburg Herald*, having learned of it, warned the readers:

> After nearly ten years of secretive silence, [Morgan] . . . pollutes the atmosphere of public opinion by the most atrocious slanders. . . . Like the man who secretes this horrid and horrible menu of infamy and falsehood, this book should be stamped indelliby with a mark like that set on Cain, that all the world might know that here is . . . an assassin-like murder of all the good men of Mississippi . . . [21]

Talk about a bad review! Since he hadn't finished the book yet, Morgan added it to his manuscript. He moved with his wife and six children to Kansas, in the footsteps of the black Exodusters, and tried to make a go of it farming.[22]

In Alabama Chloe's younger sister Lucy Tarrant finished the Lincoln School in 1884. She was the first in the Tarrant clan to gain a high school education. In Mississippi Chloe sued Jim for divorce and obtained a decree in 1885. Jim Curry married again in 1886 or 1887, and began another family. He married a woman named Sallie Laird, a former bondwoman, for whom this was also a second marriage. Their first child was born about 1889. They had six children, three of whom survived to adulthood. Two generations of this family are described in Minnie and Andrew Billingsley's *Climbing Jacob's Ladder* as an example of the black families of the period who concentrated their efforts on education, family, and community. Jim worked as a house servant, according to that account; on the 1910 census he reports that he was a laborer who did odd jobs, and his wife is listed as a cook for a private family. He was an occasional preacher at the Berean Baptist Church of his youth. His eldest son, Irving Curry, attended Lincoln, and of Irving's eight children, the seven who survived were all graduates of the school.[23]

Georgia Neal says that about this time—the mid-1880s—Will reluctantly agreed that she could go to Alabama to go to school like the other children. This seems a shrewd decision on Chloe's part, if indeed Will Campbell insisted on Georgia living in a cocoon in which she remained ignorant of the fact that she would be an African American no matter what her appearance. The decision was a profound one for my grandmother. If Will Campbell's race, wealth, and access to power would be frustrating for Georgia to emulate, even the small class-based difference being created between Georgia and her own family was harmful. Chloe's decision that her Campbell child should live in a black farming home and go to school with other children of freedmen and women would allow Georgia to learn values apart from those taught by privilege. Chloe seems to have been all about leveling the playing field, not escaping it. And my grandmother became a Race Woman.

I don't remember if Georgia told me specifically that she went to the Lincoln School; it has always just been my assumption that she did.

The school's surviving records only include graduates from the high school. Despite many efforts to find their old enrollment records I was unable to do so. By sending Georgia to Alabama Chloe saw to it that all of her children were together, not just for summers but for at least four years. In Alabama, Georgia also had the privilege of getting to know her grandparents, a situation that sadly I did not know in time to learn about from her. Georgia lived with Edmond and one of Chloe's sisters, either Lucy, if she was not at college, or possibly Mariah.

Mariah's first marriage ended sometime before the early 1890s. Over the years, as the eldest Tarrant child, she became head of the family in Alabama, as well as its heart. Janie Bassett described her as "a little lady, who looked like an Indian." Chloe, she said, "didn't look as Indian." Obviously, people who knew them did believe there was a Native American element to their ancestry. Bassett said Mariah was a very cheerful, good-natured woman who did not go out to work but ran her laundry business at home, and took care of her family's house all of her life. Bassett came from the country to Marion to go to Lincoln. She lived next door to Mariah with Meg Tutt, Mariah's schoolteacher daughter. Janie stayed there from childhood until she finished high school. People in town, she said, called her "Maggie Tutt's gal." She delivered baskets of laundry for Mariah to women around town. Evidently Mariah, who was often called Marie or Maria, was rather particular about her name. At church some referred to her as Marie Tutt, and after services she would complain that her name had not been called, as if she had not been recognized at all. Georgia worshipped the aunt she lived with, whether Lucy or Mariah, and thought her very kind and loving and the most beautiful woman she'd ever seen, according to her memoir.

Georgia's comment at this point in her story that her grandfather and an aunt were heads of the house is my only clue that my great-great grandmother Caroline Tarrant may have passed. When exactly Edmond and Caroline Tarrant died is still a mystery. Alabama did not start issuing birth and death certificates until 1908, and by reports from those I've talked to in Marion, the early freedmen seem to have been buried at farms outside of Marion. A manager of the local African American funeral home whose business dates back to Reconstruction told me they have no records from that time. The Tarrants were all, except Lucy, born too early and in the wrong business (farming) to show up on the records of the Social Security Administration.

Once Georgia started going to school she gained the nicknames "half-white," "no nation," and the like. She used to say she was constantly taunted about having a white father. She told me that her half sisters and brothers called her "Chloe's White Child," which later gave her the idea for the title of her book. She writes that during her years in Alabama she came to want to look like everyone else in her family, to have brown skin and nappy hair. Having gotten this late introduction to race and the baggage that accompanied births such as hers in the South, she says she became angry, in the way that a child might. She grew to resent her father, and later, she says, to hate him.

When her mother came and got her for the last time and brought her home to Mississippi, she was quite changed and felt she could not adjust to being back home. She remained angry that her father was white and for some time resisted his attempts to regain her affection. She writes that he lavished her with presents and provided "everything that she wanted to gain her confidence and love." The odd ways of race in the Delta must have compounded this sense of conflict. Georgia remembered riding the twenty miles to town in a buggy with her father, but reminded her grandchildren that Chloe could never be seen with him even in this manner or at public gatherings. Even so, it seems odd that Campbell would have made any assumptions about Georgia's color making it acceptable for him to publicly acknowledge his attachment to her. I think he knew better. But he did it anyway. The white-looking children of black concubines were common sights in a southern town at that time, and the towns themselves were too small for anyone to mistake my grandmother's identity.

In 1889 Leonidas Campbell's widow, Lucy, died, leaving her son a handsome fortune according to Springfield accounts. In May of that year, Will wrote one of the only remaining letters of the period to his nephew Erskine saying that it was so cold even then that he built a fire, and the crops were badly in need of rain.[24]

In 1890 the first of Chloe's children to finish high school, Carrie Vienna Curry, graduated from Lincoln. She returned to Mississippi to live. In September Sarah Rush Owen went to visit Will, and wrote to her son:

> My Dearest Jackie,
> This is the first opportunity I have had to send a mail, We reached Yazoo City about 10 o clock Monday . . . left the city at 7 and reached home about five. Found the swamp pretty bad owing to recent rains but roads on the creek lovely It is still warm here but I hope cooler with you, the winter astonishes every one and I can not help grieve over your loss. All the meat that has been killed in the Creek has spoiled and as the corn crop was poor they can fatten no more hogs.
> Will has not killed [livestock] and he is still picking cotton and ginning.[25]

During the flu season of that year, this son, born John Jay Owen, died of the disease. A local newspaper article states that he had been running the Owen Coal and Lumber Company and that it was at this juncture that Sarah Rush Owen stopped running her farm fulltime to run the business. This seems a bit pat, as someone had to keep her husband's concern going when her children were young. In 1892 Sarah Rush Owen lost her daughter Mary Frances Bryan, age thirty-seven. Mary's husband, George, had died three years earlier. Sarah would raise Mary's two children, now ages eight and five. Judging from a chapbook of vignettes that Owen published in 1901, *Anemone's People*, she was by then working in the office of the coal and lumber business every day, as well as making rounds once a month or more to collect rents from those living on her property who by then were African Americans. Owen took to writing fiction in the 1890s, and this phase of her life, shortly before and after she sold the business around 1905, is the background of her writings.[26]

Published for the sixty-fourth anniversary of the founding of Springfield, *Anemone's People* is dedicated to the city's teachers, as well as a dozen individuals, mostly men identified only by their last names, three women, and the single-named Musick, the former slave who helped her mother during the war. The somewhat odd feature of this thirty-nine-page collection is that the two main vignettes are about African Americans, complete with dialect. This gave me a clue to the many clippings from the 1880s and 1890s in Owen's files, newspaper samples of newly-minted African American folklore (what I would call fake folklore), and cartoons with black characters. She collected this antebellum nostalgia—as if to study faintly humorous sketches of the alleged antics of someone's former bondmen, or African Americans encountered in a white person's travels. (As the dialect of most of these works often lacks authenticity, to replicate the genuine—or the fake—would take some study.) The writings she clipped are hardly Mark Twain, more like imitation Uncle Remus stories. In her own work, Owen does not attempt parable in quite the same way, and certainly does not write humor, but she does seem to have been preoccupied with what the freedmen and women were making of the opportunity to fend for themselves. She also seems to compare their choices to her own as a widow with a dozen mouths to feed.

The last sketch in the chapbook is interesting; as its subject is the white landlady's discovery of her own selfish heart. After refusing a beggar at her office with the remark, "I have been a widow for forty years; have never asked for bread yet," she realized, "This was an untruth. Every day of her life she had asked for bread, and it had been given her." She writes several more accounts of staring down someone in need and refusing them—a woman asking to pick up chips in the lumberyard to use for fuel, for instance, where the favor might have been granted with no effort and no loss. That night she went home and had an epiphany in which she realized her own "smallness," seeing she had been "visited by angels unawares" and "had not taken them in."[27]

Her novella, a work of some length and without a title so far as I can tell, seems somewhat indulgent and even a bit silly to a contemporary reader, relying as it does on the return of an old love who has become the handsome prince on the white horse, so to speak, being both rich and the heir to a title in the homeland Scotland. The story's chief value is in the light it shines on her early life as a young married woman, and on her later role as the parent of her grandchildren. The children in the book are about the age of Mary Frances' offspring when they became orphaned or her daughter Lucy's children at the turn of the century.

In this work, she engages in a lot of sentiment over the loving and loyal servants. Her sense of the race that had once been held in bondage by her family is very similar to the ideas about African Americans written by her niece Lulu. However, there is one phrase in the book that provided me a hearty laugh. Sarah notes that a set of beautiful new clothes was being expertly packed by the maid Jane, "who caresses the rich silks and gloats as only a southern Negro can over finery." I do know quite a few southern Negroes who are the last authorities on "finery."[28]

Owen's most arresting adventure was an extended tour of the coal mines in the East. One assumes she felt the need to learn more about the coal industry sometime after taking the reins of the business in Springfield. I find this very daring of her. She gives an account of going "first to Jelico in the East Tennessee mountains, through Kentucky, up the Kanawha, New River, Pittsburg, Piedmont, George's Creek, Cumberland, and into the anthracite region. She had bought Piedmont and hard coal for years; had been ever anxious to see it on its 'native heath.'"[29]

In the 1890s A. T. Morgan also set out for mines—the silver mines of Colorado, where he hoped at last to make some money to support his family. Farming in Kansas had not worked out for him, so he left his family in Topeka and went west. His four daughters took up singing to make money, and when the youngest son died in 1894, Morgan's wife went on the road with their other son, Bert, to manage the careers of the daughters. His mining adventure did not turn out successfully. Morgan visited them but was too ashamed to ever live with them again. His family was also ashamed of him, not owing to his penury but because he was too open about his interracial marriage. They had decided it was easier to be white.

Thereafter, their lives were plagued by tragedy. After one daughter died in 1898, the musical act the children created broke up, and they scattered to seek lives in the white world. Although Albert managed to live a relatively respectable life as a white-collar railroad employee in Indiana, three of his daughters suffered broken marriages, and two of them—after their African American ancestry was revealed publicly—ended their lives as inmates of insane asylums. His youngest daughter Nina Lillian, who took the pen name Angela, gained some fame as a writer in the 1920s, but only after carefully covering up all traces of her Mississippi birth and the true identity of her parents.[30]

The tragedy in this is compounded when one reads his words, as nearly the last thought in his book is of the situation of black women:

How dare you consent, as you have been doing for two centuries, that every woman of African blood shall not hope for a higher life? How dare you consent, as you have been doing for two centuries, that while your daughter may not marry a "nigger," nor yet be the mistress of one, your son may make my daughter his concubine, though he shall not marry her?[31]

In the early 1890s, probably 1892, Georgia Campbell went off to school again, this time in Jackson, Mississippi, about fifty miles from home. She attended the Mary Holmes Seminary, a school for African American girls. She spent two years at Mary Holmes, during which, she said, "a gleam of happiness began to creep" into her life.[32]

The dangers facing African Americans in the South were not only considerable, but on the rise. That September, when Georgia went to Jackson, a man, his wife, his mother-in-law, and an acquaintance of theirs were lynched by a mob on suspicion of poisoning a well from which a white family got sick. No investigation was ever completed in the man's case, and the women were immediately cleared of any connection to the suspected poisoning. The man who was their friend was never subjected to any inquiry at all. In June of that year a young white woman in Memphis made it into the papers because the Woman's Refuge, where she had gone to have a baby, made her leave when the baby turned out to be black. "She is the mother of a little coon," said *The Memphis Ledger*. She was forced to leave and go to the city hospital and the newspaper voiced outrage that she would not "reveal the name of the Negro who had disgraced her," which would have likely been his death sentence. Two years later a man named Ready Murdock was lynched in Yazoo for attempted rape. A black woman of Mississippi, Ida B. Wells, exposed these cases in the black press.[33]

An array of repressive measures had been taken to keep African Americans in check since the beginning of Reconstruction. DuBois discusses the early efforts during Reconstruction to keep arms out of the hands of African Americans, and the connection made by the mid-1870s between having a job and giving up the vote. He writes, "[f]rom 1880 onward, in order to earn a living, the American Negro was compelled to give up his political power." Even though only black men were entitled to vote, it goes without saying that these proscriptions applied to whole families when it came to political activism. New laws designed to purge blacks from the rolls of eligible voters were enacted across the South. "To make assurance doubly sure, the 'White Primary' system was built on top of this, by which the 'Democratic' party confined its membership to white voters of all parties. The 'White Primary' was made by law and public pressure the real voting arena in practically all Southern states." Oppressive taxes were also compelled. Funds for public schools were distributed unequally to the advantage of schools for whites. Children were often kept in the fields and school terms were kept short. DuBois also makes a compelling argument that a criminal class was purposely developed among black males so that they could be forced into work gangs.[34]

> Since 1876 Negroes have been arrested on the slightest provocation and given long sentences or fines which they were compelled to work out. . . . The normal amount of crime which an ignorant working population would have evolved has been tremendously increased. Young criminals and vagrants were deliberately multiplied and this in turn made an excuse for mob law and lynching. Colored women were looked upon as the legitimate prey of white men and protection for them even against colored men was seldom furnished. . . . Practically all men went armed and the South reached the extraordinary distinction of being the only modern civilized country where human beings were publicly burned alive.[35]

The year Georgia headed off to Jackson, Ida B. Wells, a native of Holly Springs, Mississippi, who was in bondage as a child, published an editorial against lynching that began an antilynching crusade that gained an increasingly loud voice from then till the turn of the century. Wells, whose parents were active in the community, attended Rust College but left in 1878 when her parents and a brother died in the yellow fever epidemic. She became the provider for her five younger siblings. Moving to Memphis, she took up journalism and, when three friends were lynched for opening a store opposite one owned by whites, she decided that someone had to speak out against a scourge that was becoming common across the South, especially in Mississippi. Because her editorial scoffed at the ubiquitous charge of black-on-white rape, her newspaper was destroyed and her partner barely escaped with his life. (She was out of town, and did not return for thirty years.) Among other things that Wells reported was the fact that in 1892 "241 men, women, and children across twenty-six states were lynched." Of these, 160 were African Americans, "which represented an increase of 200 percent over the ten-year period since 1882, when the number of African Americans lynched was fifty-two." Five of these victims were women, and two were fourteen and sixteen years old, a girl and a boy. Wells made a systematic study of lynching cases, their alleged causes and trends. Her work continues to be the basis of contemporary records of lynchings of that period. If you look up lynchings in Mississippi, the records begin with the first cases she that recorded.[36]

Women like Wells, who were the age of Georgia's aunt, Lucy Tarrant, were gaining education and going into African American communities to teach and serve families still establishing a foothold in the economy, and they were beginning to become leaders. Education produced, within a generation after slavery, teachers throughout the black South. Lucy married a man named General Grant Walker in 1893, and the next year gave birth to her first child and began teaching at the Lincoln School. Georgia went to Nashville, Tennessee, to Fisk University in 1894 or 1895. She writes that one of her half sisters was there for two years at the same time. Her half sister Carrie married that year, so perhaps it was Ruth. Georgia was thrilled by Fisk and seems to have come into her own as a young woman while there. She made peace with her origins and recalls that it was a joy to return to Mississippi. In the university's earliest days as a freedmen's school, students ranged in age from children to seniors and, in Georgia's day, it was still not unusual for students younger than today's college age to attend. Georgia was probably fifteen or sixteen at the time, though she claimed to have gone there at twelve. After a year, she went to Rust College in Holly Springs, Mississippi, another African American institution nurtured in part by Ida B. Wells's parents. Wells's father had been a trustee of the school.

While Georgia was away Will lost his nephew Robert Lee Campbell, Leonidas's son, who died at age twenty-one in Springfield. The History Museum sent me a picture of him as a child seated on a fur rug. It had been signed to his uncle "Pony"—Sempronious Boyd. A label on the picture reads: "Lee descended from two of Springfield's best families and was left an orphan at sixteen, inheriting a great deal of money. It was said of him, 'Lee was probably the best known young man in the city. His income was large and his liberality [sic] equalled his income.'" Perhaps Robert gave it all away, or just was left somewhat poorer than people thought. I actually looked at his probate records because of the quote on this photograph as the source of his wealth was not readily evident, given the poor shape of his father's finances when he died. His mother did come from a wealthy family, yet the inventory of all his wordly goods yielded only a couple of trunks of moth-eaten women's apparel that probably belonged to his mother, a few pieces of her gold jewelry, and some pieces of sterling and plate silver. He had two or three lots of land that were sold. His grandfather, Robert McElhany, administered his estate, coming up with $208.63 in bills, and $226.90 in assets, leaving a positive balance of $18.27. McElhany did protest that some of Robert's assets were seemingly gone to places unknown.[37]

The next year, Will lost another nephew, Erskine Campbell, known as Argyle, the young man who had helped him save the Yazoo land. Argyle was thirty-nine with a wife and two children, and died in Kansas City, Missouri.[38] As the twentieth century opened, Will found himself one of the last of his generation of Campbells. Only his sister Sarah and John Nathaniel's widow, Mary McKerall, remained of that generation. Besides these three, only Lulu McKenny Sheppard could also remember the 1850s and 1860s, when the Campbells had settled into prosperity after the days of pioneering, trekking to Mexico and California, going to the Gold Rush, and turning southward after King Cotton. Those who were born in the 1860s would never really remember the war, with its horrors and privations, the swamps and malaria, the cannons firing into men, and bayonets tearing at them amidst piteous screaming. And even these four knew probably very little of bloodshed for, like the children of bondmen and women, they lived with people who likely spoke little of the worst.

In the summer of 1900, the census taker who came to Silver Creek discreetly recorded that Will lived alone on his plantation. In October Will Campbell made a will; he had contracted consumption sometime that year. He spent several months of 1901 in the dry air of Texas in hopes of regaining his health.[39]

On July 31, 1902, Will Campbell died at his home on Silver Creek at two in the morning. He was fifty years old. Georgia left school and returned to Yazoo. A local paper referred to him as one of the "oldest citizens" on Silver Creek, though I think what was meant was that he was one of the most long-term residents and from "an old and honored Missouri family." The young man from Missouri had, in middle age, become a member of one of the oldest families of the county, a true honorific of the South. Thereafter the newspaper runs into a vale of error, mistaking his brother John for his father and getting some of the dates wrong:

> Mr. Campbell, with his brother, the late Col. Lonnie Campbell, settled on Silver Creek in the year 1869, and from that time to this was actively engaged in looking after his plantation interests, covering many miles of the richest farming lands in the Delta. Campbellsville, on the Sunflower River, was named after the family. . . .
>
> His last minutes on earth were very quiet and peaceful. He dozed off into a sleep and went to meet his Maker.
>
> The remains, accompanied by a number of Silver Creek friends, were conveyed to Yazoo City and interred in the City cemetery.[40]

Sarah Rush Owen came to his funeral, but Chloe did not attend, or as my grandmother put it, it would not have been acceptable for her to attend. I imagine it was not acceptable for my grandmother either as she also did not attend. Pretty soon, it also became unacceptable for some of Campbell's most trusted hands to work at Silver Creek when word got out that Will Campbell had left all of his land to Chloe Curry. My grandmother told of her mother and herself being left alone at the plantation. Some of the black workers left out of fear, she said. Fear, of course, that trouble would follow because Will's family or just "the white folks" would not find the terms of the will acceptable. And indeed, the will seems to have shaken Sarah Rush Owen, who must have assumed she was Will's only remaining heir. She must have even assumed that he could have no other heir that a court would recognize.

My grandmother's story was that Sarah contested the will and they went to court. She said the people at court had known Will for years, had known he lived with Chloe, and knew him to be of sound mind when he made his will. And she said, they ruled in Chloe's favor. I have to say, I always found this extraordinary, just because it was Mississippi. In Yazoo City, my friend Arnim, an attorney, and I went through every file bearing any of the pertinent names and found only that Chloe had come to court and presented the will. Nevertheless, the land became Chloe's. One of the Confederate veterans in town had signed the papers as an official of the court. Family stories have it that she gave some piece of it to Sarah, but I have no way of knowing if that is so. In 1915 a suit was brought against Owen for two parcels of land that were claimed by a Yazoo man who said he bought them years earlier but had no proof. He had paid the taxes though, and she had not, so he was awarded the land. Sarah never appeared in court about the matter. Will must have sold or lost portions of the land to Leonidas's debt. The land Chloe inherited was likely the northern end of the Campbell property.

After Will's death Sarah evidently made some gesture or offer to help pay Will's debts. I do not know what those debts were or if Sarah made the offer before knowing the contents of his will. She certainly would have known there were debts on the land. Sarah changed her mind about helping. As was often her habit, Owen made a draft—actually two drafts—of the letter she wanted to send and kept them in her files. Writing on stationery from the Owen Coal Company ("Dealers in Coal and Wood, Breeders of Registered Berkshire Hogs") on August 16, 1902, she addressed Barnett and Perrin, Chloe's attorneys in Yazoo City. I have no doubt that this was the most unusual letter she ever wrote, straining as it does to contain some overpowering emotion not evident in any others that I have read:

> And yet I believe in her—
>> That she will Make the run,
> And come in a nose
>> Ahead of her woes

Barnett & Perrin
　Gentlemen:
Yours in regard to Chloe Curry's interrogation received__I admit that my proposal was Quixotic__ No one can pay my Brothers "Just debts" but her self When she blindly and ignorantly (I hope) debautched him to revenge her self on Col Campbell for a fancied injury__ and upon her husband of whom she was insanely jealous__ she assumed debts that miners can not pay

> The debts to an outraged Community—
> The debts to wounded and defiled kindred—
> The debts to her outraged children;

Whom she has taught[?] to hang over her like vultures with extended talons and distended mouths clamoring for the carrion with which she has for years fed them and greater than all the debt she owes to him for his blighed [blighted], outraged and tortured life—
　Cut off from his Kind his shade follows her—
　When her flesh shall fall away from her and her bones are knoted [sic] and twisted with Pain she will cry for that second birth that men call death—only to find she is herself made a manifest spirit capable of double suffering__Given her choice to fight [above, something like "through them," largely illegible] her way back to innocence or sink into deeper degradation__ The time is past when I could have helped her__Rush Campbell Owen

[p. 2]

> "The unknown Steersman whom
> men Call God stands at the Wheel"

Mssrs. Barnett & Perrin

Yazoo City, Miss

    Gentlemen:

My answer to Chloe Curry's interrogation is No. I could not ever interfere with her paying all[double underline] of My Brothers "Just Debts"—

    My offer was Quixotic

> I b'leave in her
> That she will make the run—
>   come out a nose
>   A head of her woes.
> The unknown Steersman, who men call God
>   stands at the Wheel—[41]

This is certainly one of the most uniquely venomous letters I've ever seen. Given all the Campbell family mythology, which Sarah herself had a strong hand in spreading, that contended the Campbell relationship to people of color had been entirely benevolent, it strikes me that Sarah would have found Chloe's assertion of right to the inheritance lacking in gratitude. Anyone so venal as to assert her right to inherit instead of Sarah clearly knew no humility, a trait Sarah associated with her own bondpeople and servants. Chloe would have been found wanting in those qualities of loyalty and devotion that Sarah valued, and therefore this freedwoman must have been the author of her own success, and her own consequent damnation. Sarah took an almost hysterical exception to Chloe's ability to act on her own behalf, to exercise power over her own life—powers that set Sarah herself apart from many of her peers.

Yet, in tangling with Chloe she put herself in direct confrontation with Chloe's considerable familial and experiential legacy—a sense of the empowerment of women, a worldview that made family and "village" primary, a preference for decision-making rather than dependency, and a dogged determination born of already knowing what one can endure.

While this letter informed me that Chloe inherited, at this point, not only the land but like Will, the debts, the challenge Sarah attempts to cast at Chloe played to this freedwoman's strengths, not her weaknesses. This is one contest in which the formidable Sarah was outmatched. If all Chloe had to do was stay there and raise cotton and pay those debts, Sarah would be waiting a very long time for Chloe to be crushed under the weight of it and repent, or pray for death, or whatever wish Sarah was trying to articulate in her letter. As folks used to say, "ain't no days like that."

The debts turned out to be about $22,000. The spring before he died, Will had basically put up the land he had recovered for three loans. The land was in deeds of trust to Jeptha F. Barbour, grandfather of the present governor of Mississippi, Haley Barbour. There is an irony in an illiterate former bondwoman assuming the debts of a planter, and having to run his plantation to pay them. Of course, having made his will two years before, Will had time to tell Chloe how the debts could be handled. I feel certain that my grandmother's story of Chloe having to find workers to get the crop out that fall holds a drama that tells who Chloe was perhaps more than any letters she might have left. As Georgia wrote, work "was all that had confronted her all of her life." The day Sarah's letter came was no different.[42]

I can picture the harvest that fall. If she could not hire enough hands within the month, there were still numerous people who would have helped. I can see the Carters, her brother's family, coming—King, Belle, and Annie, if she was there, Katie and Sam Woolfolk, and teenaged Willie Carter; Chloe's son Tommy, if he was still there; her daughter and son-in-law Carrie and Peter McConnell. The faces of her photo album, workers around Silver Creek come to mind: Clay Crawley, Louisa Benton, George Campbell, Rosa Hall, Martha White, and Jerry Thomas, faces of Mississippi. And those others, more than one hundred, that she must have hired or cajoled to return. I see the relief in their faces as the walls of the gin slowly became surrounded by white lint, white lint packed and climbing, hiding the planks of the building that exhaled steam as the gin ground on in its work. That first harvest, whether 100 bales or 600, was an incredible victory over slavery, starvation, the loss of loved ones, and the terrible odds against many. It was a triumph for the bond between Chloe and Will and the promises people make to live on, to keep going what has been built, and to take care of those who need help. It's the victory we have when we get another day to do the work that is ours to do, when we are allowed by good fortune to press body, mind, and soul to a task we have actually chosen. Chosen, not by force of a whip, but by our own determination to win another day. And this victory was sweet because a freedwoman would know so well the difference between a chance and no chance at all. A freedwoman would know survival alone can be a triumph.

Whether Chloe slept in a bed that night or on a pallet on the floor, or just laid on the porch because it was still hot, doesn't really matter. She knew so much that no woman in her family had known for more than one hundred years—she knew at fifty-two years old that whatever was to be made of the rest of her life would be in her own hands. Even if the time turned out to be short, that life was hers to create. She knew that her children would have food on the table and an absolute chance to survive. That she probably didn't do anything different the day after the land became hers is almost shocking to imagine these days, not something one would expect of people any more. It means she knew who she was, and maybe today, while no one lacks for dreams, we do lack that sight that each of us is, in some way, already there, where we are supposed to be.

She paid the debts and in March of the next year, when one tract of the land was put up for auction, Chloe Curry had the highest bid. Each year for the next sixteen years, Chloe would obtain loans from several different institutions, putting up deeds of trust as she had with Barbour the first year. They were all paid.[43]

Georgia Campbell married a young man named William Knight and went off to Nebraska to pharmacy school. I wrote to Creighton University to find out about her records and was referred to a college outside of Omaha that has the old records of the Fremont College of Pharmacy. The archivist wrote me a kind letter saying she found Georgia was unusual both for having been a married woman student and because she took courses more often chosen by men. The courses she probably meant were physics, botany, chemistry, calculus, a range of pharmaceutical sciences, and pharmaceutical Latin. She did very well, though calculus kicked her butt. Included in the package were photographs of the school and articles featuring women students. One article was about the increase in the cost of student's meals in 1911—from roughly seven-and-a-half cents to nine-and-a-half cents. This was after my grandmother's time there but still pretty amusing to read. For the seven-and-a-half-cent price at breakfast one got fruit, oatmeal, toast or pancakes (syrup and butter), and coffee. The same amount would buy a lunch of roast, stew, meat pie or fish, potatoes, a green vegetable, pudding, bread, and coffee; or a supper of baked beans, "hog and hominy," macaroni and cheese, yeast rolls, salad, tea biscuits, and tea or coffee. None of the Nebraska stories in the papers impressed me with my grandmother's fortitude nearly as much as visiting Nebraska in 2004 during Black History Month—February, that is. There was a blizzard the second day I was in Omaha, and two days later I had to travel to Lincoln across a vast icy plain littered with overturned SUVs. Having just barely learned about my grandmother's time there in the 1900s, I was unable to imagine living there at the turn of the last century.

Georgia and her husband opened a drugstore in Oklahoma, probably in Guthrie, and soon after, her husband was killed in a holdup. Chloe sent one of Georgia's cousins and lifelong friends to live with her and help her through the ordeal. She stayed there a while and then came home to Yazoo. In Mississippi she fell in love with a young man I think she knew when she was young. Augustus Garfield Barbour was by then a tailor in Memphis, with dreams of moving North. They married, and my mother, Willie Louise Barbour, known as "Billie," was born in Yazoo. They moved to Chicago, and Georgia worked in a drug store there.

In 1905 Sarah Rush Owen, then sixty-eight, gave up the coal business. Her son, Felix, who raised horses and lived in Gainesville, Texas, for some years, was likely the person who found out what it meant to have oil coming up in the spring water. He died in Missouri in 1936 and left mineral leases in Texas as part of his estate. Sarah's youngest daughter, Lucy, lived with her husband, children, and Sarah in the family homestead. Lucy's husband, John P. McCammon, became city attorney in the late 1880s and later, a corporate attorney. Lucy had a daughter named Lucy McCammon, who remembered riding with Buffalo Bill as a little girl. She became a teacher and, God bless her, built theaters in Chicago, Evanston, and at Bloomsburg State College in Pennsylvania. She died in 1991.[44]

Despite the efforts of many to gain some legal protection against lynching, during the first years of the twentieth century it never happened. In Springfield in 1906, the year after Sarah retired, a mob of at least 3,000 whites lynched three African American men from a tower in the center of town. Two of the men were accused of rape but acquitted by the coroner's inquest, and the third man was in the jail on an unrelated charge. The mob demanded them anyway, and they were killed. Roaming rioters went after other African Americans around town, and people fled. While in 1890 blacks made up one third of the town's registered voters and held offices in the county, a week after the lynchings, a third of the black population had left permanently. Others continued to move until the town's black populace was down to 1 or 2 percent. It has remained much that way ever since.[45]

In 1910 Chloe was living at Grand Oak. Her brother King and his family were next door. During this period Chloe continued sending family to Alabama to go to school. She sent at least one of King's daughters, if not all three, to get an education beyond the segregated, barely-funded local public schools that were only open when the cotton crops did not demand all hands. She sent King's granddaughters Dora and Annie Lillie to the Lincoln School. Dora became a teacher and Annie Lillie worked at a Chicago university. Chloe's nieces, Mariah's daughters, went to Lincoln and both became teachers: Meg taught in a country school in Alabama and Chloe became superintendent of rural schools in Perry County. Chloe's niece Myra Walker, daughter of Chloe's baby sister Lucy, went to Lincoln and became a teacher in Mobile, Alabama. Chloe educated everyone who was willing. Every child of all the Tarrant freedmen and women became literate.

My grandfather, Augustus Barbour, went to World War I in 1917. When he returned he became one of the roughly fifty African American policemen in the city of Chicago at that time. I never knew anything much about him really except that he had gone to World War I, was later a policeman, and left my grandmother for another woman. I learned that he was born in Greenville, Mississippi, only after receiving from my brother a birth certificate my mother had had made as an adult. I had found Barbour on several census records and gathered that he was born in 1882, but some records said he was from Mississippi and some said Tennessee. The state of Illinois sent me his death certificate on which his widow said he was from Holmes County, Mississippi. And not having remembered I would receive the information, I was surprised to see on the death certificate the names of another set of my great-grandparents. My Barbour great-grandmother was born Sarah J. Davis in Mississippi. She was listed on most census records as a mulatto. I found one woman of that description living at age seventeen in Holmes County, Mississippi, which sits on the northern border of Yazoo. Georgia said she had known Augustus when she was young, that he was a "neighbor boy." In 1880 Sarah Davis married Edward Barbour, an African American twelve years her senior. In 1900 they were living in Memphis where he was a bartender. His mother was from Mississippi and he seems to have been born in West Virginia or Louisiana, and died before 1910, probably in his fifties.[46]

My grandmother confused the issue by saying that Augustus was "half-white" like herself, and he and his brother Edgar (the only members of that family I've seen in photos) certainly would not have struck me on a glance as black people. So, if Augustus's father was someone white, I don't know.

When Augustus returned from the war, Georgia and my mother were boarding with a black couple at 4527 Wabash Avenue. The wife was from Nebraska, and perhaps one of Georgia's fairly numerous black friends from Omaha, whom she went to visit over the years. Augustus moved back in with his mother and brother, who were in an apartment at 4542 Wabash Avenue. Perhaps their relationship did not survive this transition after the war, or fell apart later, I'm not sure. Sometime in the early 1920s, Georgia and Billie moved to Kansas City, Kansas. She opened the Dunbar Drugstore there. In 1923 she sent my mother to college at the Sargeant School, now part of Boston University. I was told she gave her a raccoon coat, and bought her a car.[47]

Maybe some wisdom came to Sarah Rush Owen late in life. If she continued to view race and class as fixing a person's place in life, she was in other ways not typical of her times. Confederate though she was, she dedicated her novel to Walt Whitman and the people of the "coal trade." In middle age she had an unaccountable affinity for Eastern thought and her own version of Transcendentalism. Her writing makes passing references to Confucius, Brahma, and Buddha, and being in the "one-moment-ness." Her great-granddaughter Jane McCammon remembers visiting the home in Springfield and seeing Sarah, who was regarded as "the Scarlett O'Hara in the family." McCammon would have been very young when she last saw Sarah, but she recalls Sarah asking for someone to prepare her some sassafras tea. A southerner to the end, she died in 1925 at eighty-eight years of age.

Albert T. Morgan never changed his stripes at all. He gave up on the major political parties, became a Socialist, at least for a while, and never gave up the dream that Reconstruction provoked him to dream. He writes at the end of his book:

> It will not always be true that "the heart which responds to the call of duty finds no rest except in the grave." Have patience—wait. The forty years in the wilderness are passing away.
>
> Some day the telegraph, the telephone and the printing press will assemble the world in one congregation, and teachers will appear to instruct all in the language and justice of truth.[48]

In the 1920s Chloe was still on Silver Creek and in her seventies. In fact, it is interesting that she was still there because in 1919 she struck a deal with Jeptha Barbour and another gentleman named R. J. Coker to sell them the northern end of the land. They assumed her last loans, totaling $6,700, and were to pay her about $50,000 in yearly installments through 1924. (These sums would be worth a little more than ten times those values now.) One or two tracts of the land Barbour bought went to a third buyer, who declared bankruptcy by 1922, and Chloe bought it back from him. That she was able to do all this, navigating her way through deals that left behind a stack of paperwork two inches thick on my desk, is phenomenal. For a woman who could not read, she sure could count.[49]

This was Will Campbell's other legacy to Chloe. He not only left her all his land and money, but he shared his knowledge of how to work the annual cycle of debt, planting, harvest, and payments, an established habit of saving and the savvy to go about getting back land lost to various bumps in the road. And he left her his lenders along with his debts. Having paid the first debts to his creditors, she became a good risk and they became her lenders. And she passed on the knowledge; Georgia was a very sharp businesswoman. Both Will and Chloe had numerous family connections to which they felt responsible. When Sarah Rush Owen complained that Chloe had raised her children to hang on to her, as if after carrion, she had lost sight of the fact that every male in Sarah's family helped pay her bills and take care of her. She had a different style of raising her children than Chloe, who may have been very anxious to keep hers near after the forced exiles of slavery and Reconstruction. All of Chloe's family lived close to each other; this perhaps was simply something Sarah could not understand. Aside from the love he must have had for her, Chloe's most lasting gifts from Will were the huge advantages of stable money and property, rare commodities for freedmen and women. She would naturally become a central figure in the struggle they all waged in order to keep afloat, and they would emulate her. This too, then, is a choice made by Will Campbell for Chloe Curry's family.

Will had been the last patriarch of his line, the first resort for help, and though perhaps shunned because of his common-law wife, he continued to offer to shoulder the burdens carried one after another by his elder brothers. In these actions Will and Chloe took I hear what they talked about on the porch at night.

Perhaps she went back to Alabama after 1924, but I know if she did stay on in Yazoo, she would definitely have "retired" after 1927, having sold her land and taken care of her children.

In the most recent picture I have of her, she is standing in a lane on her farm flooded by high water. She has pulled up her coat and skirts to her knees to show how high the water had risen or, perhaps, how low it had fallen.

A phenomenal and ruinous flood took place in 1927. "The Mississippi River and Yazoo Rivers began to rise alarmingly in April," states a Yazoo history. Then word of flood waters came from north of the county, by way of refugees fleeing areas already hit, and I would guess, the radio. Sack levees were built up but this was the Great Flood of 1927.

In the first days of May, levees from Greenville to Yazoo City began break-ing. The Delta was under water and its entire population was displaced. A refugee camp was established at Satartia and another, accommodating up to ten thousand people from all parts of the Delta, was set up north of Yazoo City. . . . [City officials, with the aid of boats from the Gulf Coast began] picking stranded residents from rooftops, trees, Indian mounds, and cotton gins. Yazoo City was without electricity for over a month. The city in the Delta portion was covered with water standing three to five feet deep . . . [50]

Photographs show what could be acres of cotton bales floating in Ya-zoo City. A local paper reported:

Houses were swept from their foundations . . . and many persons were swept out by the flow of water, clinging to pieces of furniture, housetops, and cotton bales.

The terrific force of the water at the collapse of the levee could be heard for miles. The inky blackness of the night with no light to direct the work of rescuers, . . . [the] swirl of waters carrying all before it, the shriek of whistles apprising all of the catastrophe, all combined to make a story that we pray will never again affect our city. [51]

The great Mississippi flood of 1927 swamped homes over 27,000 square miles, or as Chana Gazit's documentary *Fatal Flood*, put it, "an area about the size of Massachusetts, Connecticut, New Hampshire and Ver-mont combined. For two long months the water would remain above flood stage, leaving hundreds of thousands of people displaced from their homes." Many have put the number of homeless at one million. Until the horrific devastation of Hurricane Katrina in 2005, this was the worst natural disaster in U.S. history. It was so destructive and deadly in the Delta that it is easy for me to imagine the receding waters as an occasion for Chloe to have her picture taken showing how deep the water still stood on her land. And it is an appropriate last image of my great-grandmother.[52]

The lives of blacks were harder hit than others, both due to the location and the condition of their homes. Evacuation camps were set up, but when tents arrived there were no floors and people had to eat with their hands, standing or squatting, and sleep on wet ground. Most insulting though was that the National Guard patrolled the camps and, once there, no one could leave. Thousands of livestock were dragged dead or alive downriver.

Many blacks never made it to the camps and were stuck living on the levees. There were also charges that they received inferior food. Evacuees would only be released with a written request from the Red Cross. The guard was also used to force black people to work—unloading food supplies for humans and livestock, moving containers of water, cleaning buildings, and many other tasks. In various places in the state blacks were beaten and whipped with gun straps. At the camps they waited in long lines for inoculations. In the few photos I've seen, everyone in the area traveled in shallow bayou bateaux. In the Holly Bluff near Silver Creek, and where Chloe's daughter and grandchildren lived, cattle were stranded atop the ancient Indian Mound, the only dry ground around. The disaster had wide-ranging effects on the country, from helping to put Herbert Hoover into the presidency, to forcing government control of the Mississippi, to promoting the rise of Huey Long to governor of Louisiana, and prompting a migration of thousands of sharecroppers to the North.[53]

Some record executives, smelling an opportunity, had a contest for the best blues song about the flood. Big Bill Broonzy recalled that they sent an array of blues artists down to the Delta with the promise that whoever created the best song would get $500. He remembered going, "me and Jim Jackson, Charlie Jackson, Blind Lemon Jefferson, Bessie Smith, Ida Cox, Ma Rainey, and this guy they called Barbecue Bob, and Shorty George. . . . The one that Bessie wrote, it had more feelings to it. . . ." And as he put it, "Bessie Smith got the 500 dollars," for "Back Water Blues."[54]

Funny thing is she had already recorded the song in February of that year. I don't know if that was prescience or the contest was just publicity, but the song was a great hit.

A year later the Red Cross was still feeding thousands of people. Thousands of African Americans left, and even that was difficult. Many had to sneak to the train stations at night, or walk to the next station after their own town to avoid being hauled back to the plantations where they worked.

Some planters even began to figure that getting a crop with only 50 percent of their workforce would be a fortunate outcome. In Washington County, where the first levee broke and the use of the National Guard was perhaps most egregious (under the insistence of powerful planter and former Senator LeRoy Percy) half of the black population left. This episode then was part of the second wave of the African American migration north. While 522,000 blacks left the southern states in the Great Migration between 1910 and 1920, the time when my mother and grandmother went to Chicago, in the 1920s 872,000 more left the South.[55]

And in Chloe's life this was also true: By the late 1920s another set of Chloe's kin were just old enough to make the decision to stay or go. While Chloe's parents and siblings had stayed close to the land, many of the next two generations migrated to Chicago, Kansas City, or further west. For some in the Delta, having to start over after 1927 may have been the last straw. In any case, I've decided that if I were Chloe, that would do it for me.

For those who stayed, rebuilding must have been both backbreaking and heartbreaking. Chloe would have been faced with starting over at seventy-seven years old. And she had likely lost some of her children by then: I found no trace of Jimmy, Jr. after 1880, no indication of what became of Ruth after about 1895, no record of Tommy after 1910, and none for Carrie after 1920. In any case, some time before 1931, she gave the family members left in Mississippi land enough for all of them to live and farm. As Rainer Wilson put it, "She was magnificent. She gave everyone education and land—not money—education and land." The money she gained from selling the rest she gave to Georgia, the child who would never live close to the land like the others. In the late 1930s Georgia moved from Kansas City, Kansas, to Kansas City, Missouri, and opened the Royal Drugstore in the black community. She married a man from Georgia, J. McKinley Neal, who went to school and learned pharmacy and helped her in the business. In 1948 he became the second African American elected to the Missouri State House. If she knew about the Colonel's route to the State House over the body of James Patterson, she may have had some satisfaction that "Mac" was elected by the black folks of Kansas City, and actually took his seat and kept it for decades.

Georgia Campbell Neal died in Kansas City in 1971 after starting her memoir of Mississippi. My grandmother lived ninety-four years, and, free-thinker that she was, she asked to be laid away in her favorite red suit. Georgia had brought a bed to her home in Kansas City, the bed that belonged to her parents on Silver Creek. Those of us who visited there have all probably slept on that bed made of heavy, carved Mississippi wood, with dark, brown-black finish. I slept in it the week Georgia died. The silver dollar that was to be my only bequest from her was minted around the time Chloe converted that land into money for her daughter. But, of course, Georgia left me her mother's epic tale.

Chloe went back to Marion, Alabama, and lived on a farm she had bought or already owned there. Maybe it was a place she had gotten for her parents. She raised her own food and, according to Janie Bassett, she hardly ever wore shoes. A small woman, she really never gained weight in old age, but remained much the same as in years past. During her last years, some of her grandchildren came to live with her and went to school at Lincoln.

Sundays she rode her buggy into town to her sister Mariah's house, about three miles away, and visited before going to church at Berean Baptist. Janie braided her hair up for church. Mariah still took in laundry and had frames set up in the back yard for blocking lace curtains for white ladies in the town of Marion. The two sisters continued to get along well and enjoyed each other's company. Chloe only dressed up and put on good shoes on Sunday. After church, Janie says, she nodded off to sleep on the way home and the horse took her back. "The horse would just go right in the gate and walk up to the house." When she died in 1932 at eighty-two, she left to a grandson one last piece of Yazoo land, the bed she had in Alabama, and her Winchester rifle. This, I believe, is the story her daughter Georgia wanted told, and I am honored to have survived to do that for her. What is inside me now is as vast as the eye can see standing up in a Delta cotton field after every plant has been picked. I walk with fluffy white lint under every step.

Epilogue

In this age, redemption has more than one meaning. To redeem once meant to reform, repair, restore. I grew up with a childlike but haunting sense that I understood the line, "I know that my Redeemer liveth," and I am still moved by these words, especially when sung. Now, its first meaning is to buy back, repurchase, get back, win back, and in some senses, to cash in. In this age of fundamentalism, many perhaps hope to be redeemed in the Christian sense, to be cleansed, born again. Yes, we all need rebirth in grace. But whenever humans set about "redeeming" society, dangers appear for all.

The people encountered in this story, so many of them, were un-Redeemable, with a capital R.

They could not be Redeemed by a system—a way of life—that grew more vicious toward them with each year after the Civil War—more ruthless in its depictions of them and even its memory of them. The freer they became, the more they turned up in popular papers in grotesque cartoons, parodied for wearing the latest styles, for making money, for going to a race track, or dancing, for protesting the horrid conditions in which they lived. In consequence, they turned up on the end of more ropes, with gasoline poured over them, wood set burning beneath them, and their heads propped up for photographs that would become postcards.

Their very existence stood in defiance of every norm known in mainstream media, and so they were limned as less and less human. The freedpeople, penniless, and uneducated as they were emerging from a condition of chained servitude, became a rebuke, smart or ignorant, well dressed or in rags, to the idea of a white America, built by white Americans, for white Americans. They should be honored as a group just as the "Greatest Generation" of World War II has been honored. Towns throughout the South should display the names of people who were killed because they voted or asked for fair terms for their labor. Women, children, and men should be honored. For long before the marchers of Selma showed people across the globe what America can be like to its own citizens, before Native Americans succeeded in teaching this society how it had been built, freedmen and women tested Americans' character and bore the brunt of our culture's inability to give up white racist laws, traditions, habits, attitudes, and privileges. They were grand and epic people.

The African American people of Yazoo County, Mississippi, at the time of this particular story acted with the kind of magnanimity, courage, and heart that we all use to define the seldom seen greatness of human beings. The whites who stood with them showed this same humanity, and acted out of a willingness to battle white supremacy that is rare, and not much honored either. These people were the Mandelas, Kings, Parks, and Hamers of another time, and yet they were the ones buried secretly in the woods and bayous, and never mentioned again on the public streets of where they had lived.

In their wake came the realization that the abolition of slavery had left us standing on a brink, at a way station for full citizenship—waiting for our votes to all count, for work to come to those who seek it without the mark of slave ancestry putting us at the back of the line. This place of waiting is described eloquently and in great detail by W.E.B. DuBois in *The Souls of Black Folk*. When he was writing that 1903 publication, he was able to know the people of whom I write now—they walked the streets with him.

Away back in the days of bondage they thought to see in one divine event the end of all doubt and disappointment; few men ever worshipped Freedom with half such unquestioning faith as did the American Negro for two centuries. To him, so far as he thought and dreamed, slavery was indeed the sum of all villainies, the cause of all sorrow, the root of all prejudice; Emancipation was the key to a promised land . . . [1]

And so, yes, freedwoman is a term with meaning still and I cast my lot with those who wished to redefine the possibilities for their people, and saw victory as certain in the last years of the nineteenth century.

There are many generations of us now who in some degree, small or large, have benefited by their labors and yet are still poised at the gate of a society of mutually recognized humanity. As more and more people in this society become their own personal dot-coms, packaging themselves, and as more people step up to buy them for lack of anything else new to purchase, still others will gather at this gate where the rest of us abide.

The word freedwoman, or freedman means partially freed, not free. To fully understand its meaning, we need to ask ourselves: having been a slave, having tasted ten years of legal freedom, made a family, built a living, could I stand up when the lynch mob comes and go to my death because I would vote? These are stories we have to dig out in bits and pieces and reconstitute for ourselves, our children, and our increasingly needed sense of community, in order to rebuild the world sanely.

Richard Wright wrote powerfully of the generations trapped after the rise of Jim Crow in *12 Million Black Voices*:

> Each day when you see us black folk upon the dusty land of the farms or upon the hard pavement of the city streets, you usually take us for granted and think you know us, but our history is far stranger than you suspect, and we are not what we seem.[2]

To some extent, we are not what we seem to ourselves as well. Finding our own strange stories is a kind of psychic toil. For me to find what was whole and what was broken, the whole story needed to be stitched from what I had. Some of the pieces are missing, abandoned like odd pieces of clothing or furniture when people move from place to place. They are stories though. These shards of history and narrative have eluded the record books; they were stories, or questions that should have been asked, or letters that should have been saved. Researching family history in this country puts you face to face with that foundational American habit of leaving the past behind for a new self, new wealth, new chances, and all their complications. We have now another chance to reflect on the view in the mirror.

As I was making changes to the copyedited manuscript of this book, Hurricane Katrina hit the Gulf Coast. In the weeks since I have seen many stories comparing this most incomparable of disasters to the Great Flood of 1927 in search of previous events through which to see a disaster that not only nearly wiped a small but major city off the map, dislocated a million people, but was also hitting hardest an African American community. When I saw the desperate people crowded outside the New Orleans Superdome after days of being trapped by the ruinous flood, I saw the packed hulls of slave ships, the contraband camps, the so-called Freedmen's Camps of places like Selma where our families begged for food. And yes, the flood of 1927, when we were trapped on the levees.

I saw Chloe and all her family. I saw myself, there with these people so unnecessarily reliving horrors tragically too familiar to our communities.

And the thousands stranded in New Orleans, then evacuated to dozens of states are the Katrina Diaspora.

Even in this age of so much instant communication, two thousand children have been lost to their families for weeks now, and it resembles nothing so much as the first days out of bondage. Katrina exposed that this country still has many freedmen and women, not free yet, but trapped by poverty and obvious now to all, a poverty that discriminates. And even as they were trapped there, they were demonized, depicted as criminal and depraved, out of sheer habit, an absolute, unthinking, unquestioned habit nearly a century and a half since African Americans walked out of slavery. This is particularly painful, not only because New Orleans is one of the ancestral homes of this unique culture, but because most of those exiled from that town by the storm and the failure of levees, evacuation strategies, and shelter plans were born there, have their roots there and indeed are the descendants of the very people who survived slavery. They are the descendants for whom segregation was invented, for whom racial profiling was created, for whom the aghast and racialized cries of newsmen were aimed. And of these descendants of our enslaved generations, a CNN anchor said last week, "and they are so poor, and so black."

Within days we were witness to a dislocation one-fifth the size of the Atlantic slave trade—which took place over more than 200 years. And all those conveniences of modern social organization that would mitigate its effects for most of us—phone, Internet, cars, gasoline, and family with ample housing—do not apply to this country's poor. For them, getting lost may mean not being found any more easily than in 1865 when people went on foot and in wagons following word of mouth leads to find where family members may have been sent.

What is needed is another Reconstruction, not just of an American city and its shipping, oil, and tourism industries, not just of the Gulf Coast and lower Mississippi Delta but also of the inequities we had a chance to make right before. The Katrina Diaspora deserves a Reconstruction that aims for justice, that refuses to dismiss the mistakes of history, a suffering that has now spanned generations. They deserve a Reconstruction that is not Redeemed by politics, greed, or the habit of putting up with the suffering of people who live in places like New Orleans' Ninth Ward, the places closest to sea level and disaster.

Getting grounded in what one's people went through is not to determine what one will be, but to gain powerful reminders not to throw away what has been done, given, prayed, and paid for in human experience.

The privilege I feel for finding my own particulars is enormous. But learning the specifics has made me clear that the beauty and joy of those whose names were lost in the past, and those whose names we never learned this month is ours to save. They must not be Redeemed, cashed in, or "reformed" because we did nothing to save even one small bit. So many freedmen and women are waiting. They are scattered around us, and there inside. I heard a Nigerian dance master say what he tells his students: "I am giving it to you, don't break it in your time." That is our charge.

Notes

CHAPTER 1

1. Toni Morrison, *Playing in the Dark: Whiteness and the Literary Imagination* (Cambridge: Harvard University Press, 1992), 52.

CHAPTER 2

1. Georgia Campbell Neal, Manuscript of notes for a memoir. Davis Papers 1.

2. Ibid.

3. On the original 1857 Mississippi black codes: Albert T. Morgan, *Yazoo: or, On the Picket Line of Freedom in the South: A Personal Narrative* (Columbia: University of South Carolina Press, 2000). On the provisions of the 1865 black codes in Mississippi: W. E. B. DuBois, *Black Reconstruction in America, 1860–1880* (Cleveland: World Publishing, 1968); Eric Foner, *Reconstruction: America's Unfinished Revolution, 1863–1877* (New York: Harper & Row, 1988). To read the act itself: http://www .toptags.com/aama/docs/bcodes.htm [accessed Sept. 8, 2005].

4. Mississipppi population in 1860: 353,899 white, 437,404 African American. DuBois, 431.

5. W. A. Campbell to Mary Frances "Fannie" Owen, January 19, 1873, Item # 92–56–24–66, History Museum for Springfield-Greene County, MO: Sarah Rush Owen Papers (HMSGC).

6. John C. Willis, *Forgotten Time: The Yazoo-Mississippi Delta after the Civil War* (Charlottesville: University Press of Virginia, 2000), 33.

7. Neal, 1–2.

8. Neal, 7.

9. Harriet DeCell and JoAnne Prichard, *Yazoo: Its Legends and Legacies* (Yazoo City: Yazoo Delta Press, 1988), 15–19.

10. DeCell, 98.

11. DeCell, 96.

12. Neal, 7.

13. Neal, 5.

14. Neal, 4.

15. Ibid.

16. Clayton E. Jewett and John O. Allen, *Slavery in the South, A State-by-State History* (Westport: Greenwood Press, 2004), 164.

17. Neal, 2.

18. Neal, 3.

19. Neal, 3–4.

20. Morgan throughout the book.

21. Morgan, xxxviii–xxxix.

22. DuBois, 494; Morgan, 445.

23. Morgan, 445.

24. DeCell, 336.

25. Morgan, 454.

26. Morgan, 468–469.

27. Morgan, 474–475; Foner, 559–560.

28. Morgan, 477–501.

29. Ibid.

30. Morgan, 483; DeCell, 342.

31. Senate Report, *Mississippi in 1875: Report of the Select Committee to Inquire into the Mississippi Election of 1875*, 44th Cong., 1st Sess., Rep. 527, 2 vols., 1649–1651.

32. Eric Foner, *Freedom's Lawmakers: A Directory of Black Officeholders During Reconstruction*, rev. ed. (Baton Rouge: Louisiana State University Press, 1993), 167; Senate Report, 1677.

33. Morgan, 482, 484.

34. Morgan, 486, 492.

35. Senate Report, appendix; DeCell, 423.

36. *Mississippi House Journal*, January 4, 1876, Roll Call; *House Journal*, January 2, 1877, Roll Call, MDAH.

37. *Yazoo City Herald*, December 15, 1876, 3.

CHAPTER 3

1. U.S. Bureau of the Census, Federal Census, 1880, Alabama and Mississippi.

2. Greene County Archive Center, Springfield, Missouri, Probate Records, folder #1469, file #007909.

3. U.S. Bureau of the Census: Federal Census, 1820–1860, Alabama; 1850 and 1860 U.S. Federal Census Slave Schedules. These are used throughout. Also, Jordan R. Dodd, comp. Alabama Marriages, 1809–1920 (Selected Counties) [database online]. Orem, UT: MyFamily.com, Inc., 1999 [accessed Sept. 8, 2005].

4. www.rootsweb.com/~alperry/a2zbio.htm; Official site of Marion, AL; Alabama Women's Hall of Fame website [accessed June 14, 2004].

5. Ibid.; also, "Sowing Seeds of Hope, Living Missions: History of the Baptists in Perry County," Perry County & the Alabama Cooperative Baptist Fellowship, www.pinebelt.net/~sshope/history.html [accessed Sept. 8, 2005].

6. Dodd [accessed Sept. 8, 2005].

7. Andrew Billingsley, *Climbing Jacob's Ladder: The Enduring Legacy of African-American Families* (New York: Touchstone, Simon & Schuster, 1992), 213–215.

8. Walter Minchinton, Celia King, and Peter Waite, eds. *Virginia Slave-Trade Statistics, 1697–1775* (Richmond: Virginia State Library, 1984); also U.S. Census 1810.

9. www.libarts.ucok.edu/history/faculty/roberson/course/1483/suppl/chpVII/CaesarTarrant.BlackPatriot.htm [accessed Jan. 7, 2005]; the Virginia Historical Society also has some information on Tarrant.

10. Andrew K. Frank, *The Routledge Historic Atlas of the American South* (New York: Routledge, 1999), 42.

11. www.archives.state.al.us/teacher/creekwar/creek2.html [accessed Oct. 22, 2004], p. 2; and www.worldstatesmen.org/US_NativeAM.html [accessed Sept. 8, 2005], 10.

12. *The New York Times* published an interesting article April 13, 2005, by Emma Daly on the reactions of students at Pennsylvania State University who took a similar DNA test. The testing was conducted by a professor who gave them percentages of each race in their genetic mix—52 percent African, 48 percent European, etc. Unfortunately, they only quoted African American students and none of the whites who, according to their teacher, each wanted to be part black, "because it would upset their parents."

13. There is an excellent account of the events in the Futa Jallon region that led to so many from that area being caught up in the Atlantic slave trade in Michael Gomez's *Exchanging Our Country Marks: The Transformation of African Identities in the Colonial and Antebellum South* (Chapel Hill: University of North Carolina Press, 1998). See Ch. 5, "Societies and Stools: Sierra Leone and the Akan." The greater value of this fascinating and astute book though is in its discussion of the cultures brought here in the Middle Passage and how they blended with each other and the dominant Euro-American culture.

On Temne agricultural practice, see: Judith A. Carney, *Black Rice: The African Origins of Rice Cultivation in the Americas* (Cambridge: Harvard University Press, 2001).

14. Gomez, 93.

15. Gomez, 92.

16. Gomez, Ch. 5.

CHAPTER 4

1. Campbell genealogy and a family photo indicating Will's date of birth, HMSGC, Owen Papers. Notes from the family Bible of John Campbell and Matilda

Golden Polk Campbell (owned by Lucy McCammon). This set of notes includes the various versions of the death of John Campbell of Virginia (1768–1816) and was sent to me by a Campbell relation in Illinois. The papers included information from Sheppard, a Campbell descendant in Missouri, and his wife, who wrote that Campbell's will of 1816 indicated "he was going with a load of goods by river barge to New Orleans to try and regain his health." On another document, Sheppard says, without citing a source, that Campbell "was killed in a riverboat explosion" on the Mississippi in 1816. Lastly, family papers say both that the Springfield, Missouri, gravestone of the elder John Campbell states, erroneously, that he died in 1812 in the War of 1812, and that the gravestone of John Polk Campbell says that his father died in the Battle of New Orleans in 1815. The date of the above-mentioned will contradicts the possibility of death in a battle in either 1815 or 1812.

2. "Told at the Dinner of 1907," *Greene County History: Personal Recollections of Early Settlers*. Springfield-Greene County Library, Springfield, MO, secs. 41–44. http://thelibrary.springfield.missouri.org/lochist/index.cfm [accessed Sept. 9, 2005]. Recollections of Sarah Rush Owen; also: "Pictorial and Genealogical Record of Greene County, Missouri: Together with Bibliographies of Prominent Men of Other Portions of the State, Both Living and Dead," Springfield-Greene County Library, Springfield, MO, 350–353; 380–383, at the same website.

3. *Springfield Press*, June 15, 1929. Springfield-Greene County Library Center, Local History Department.

4. "Told at the Dinner of 1907," secs. 41–44.

5. *Springfield Press*, June 15, 1929.

6. *Springfield Leader and Press*, October 6, 1944, Docia Karell's Column, Springfield-Greene County Library Center; "John Polk Campbell and Louisa Cheairs Campbell," Local History Website of the Department of History, Southwestern Missouri State University, Biographies, Springfield-Greene County History. http://history.smsu.edu/FTMiller/LocalHistory/Bios/jpcamp.htm [accessed Sept. 9, 2005].

7. *Encyclopedia of North American Indians*, Houghton Mifflin, online; I reviewed many of the sites operated by individual Nations, and I recommend visiting those sites, which are also rich in genealogical information. http://college.hmco.com/history/readerscomp/naind/html/na_000107_entries.htm [accessed Sept. 9, 2005].

8. Frank, 38–39.

9. On this sojourn I consulted with Diarmid Campbell, historian of the Clan Campbell Society, who said the standard Scots-Irish designation in the Missouri papers may have indicated a sojourn in Ireland after leaving Scotland.

10. Campbell genealogy, HMSGC.

11. "Cheairs Family History, copy of Uncle Nathaniel Cheairs Letter." HMSGC, Owen Papers.

12. *Springfield News Leader*, June 16, 1929.

13. *Springfield Leader*, June 3, 1932.

14. Greene County Archives & Record Center, Springfield, MS, Records of the Circuit Court 1836, John P. Campbell, 31.

15. U.S. Bureau of the Census, 1850.

16. Marion County Chamber of Commerce: www.jefferson-texas.com; Local Cass County GWTW-theme-song playing, souvenir-vending websites: www.scarletto hardy.com; www.scarlettohardy.com/bandb.htm; and best of all: www.scarletto hardy.com/TarainTexas.htm [all accessed Sept. 9, 2005].

17. Originally in William Elsey Connelly's, *Doniphans Expedition and the Conquest of New Mexico and California*. (Kansas City, MO: Bryant & Douglas Book and Station- ary Co., 1907); also: "Told at the Dinner of 1907," sections 41–44. http://thelibrary .springfield.missouri.org/lochist/index.cfm [accessed Sept. 9, 2005].

18. Ibid.; and: Connelly, 451–452. "On the 14th, Major Campbell and Forsythe, with 38 men, left Chihuahua, with the view of returning to the United States by way of the Presidio del Rio Grande, and thence across the plains to Ft. Towson on Red River. Without meeting with any very serious opposition from the indians [sic], or other cause, this party reached the frontiers of Arkansas in safety, where separating, they returned to their respective homes."

19. Connelly, 452–453.

20. U.S. Census, 1850; U.S. Department of the Interior, Bureau of Land Manage- ment, http://www.glorecords.blm.gov/PatentSearch/Results.asp?QryId=59723.48 [accessed May 7, 2003].

21. *Springfield Leader*, June 3, 1932.

22. John Polk Campbell to Louisa Campbell, September 4, 1851, HMSGC, Owen Papers; Item # 92–56–24–22.

23. John Polk Campbell to Louisa Campbell, October 28, 1851, HMSGC, Owen Papers; Item # 92–56–24–23.

24. Ad & quote: Patricia Leigh Brown, "New Signpost at Slavery's Crossroads," *New York Times*, December 16, 2004.

25. Louisa Cheairs McKenny Sheppard, *A Confederate Girlhood* (Unpublished manuscript, 1892; HMSGC, Owen Papers; also at University of North Carolina, Chapel Hill), 19.

26. Ibid., 2.

27. Ibid., 5–6.

28. On Nathaniel Cheairs: Cheairs-Hughes Family Papers 1636–1967. Tennessee Department of State, Tennessee State Library & Archives, Archives & Manuscripts Unit, MS Accession Number 88–21, location XVIII-G-3, 4. On Rippavilla: http:// rippavilla.org/ [accessed Sept. 9, 2005].

29. Brown, *New York Times*.

30. U.S. Slave Schedules, 1850 and 1860.

31. [Sarah] Rush Campbell Owen, *Anemone's People*. Springfield, MO: Jewell Publishing Co., 1901. HMSGC, Owen Papers, 29.

32. Jewett, 7, 26, and throughout.

33. Frank, 42.

34. Morgan, xxi–xxii.

35. Jewett, 161.

36. U.S. Slave Schedules, 1850 & 1860; and Campbell family slave inventory, HMSGC, Owen Papers.

37. Sheppard, 7.

38. J. N. Campbell to Mrs. Nancy R. Perkins, 22 October 1853, HMSGC, Owen Papers; Item # 92–56–24–40.

39. 1850s Correspondence, HMSGC, Owen Papers.

40. Hunting For Bears, comp. Missouri Marriages, 1766–1983 [database online] (Provo, Utah: MyFamily.com, In., 2004) on Ancestry.com [accessed Sept. 9, 2005].

41. Sarah Rush Owen, untitled novella, chapter entitled "Bab is Sick," 11.

42. Owen, novella, chapter entitled "Madame is Forced to Speak," 4.

43. Ibid, 8.

44. Ibid, 9.

45. http://www.brentwood-tn.org/library/Brentwood%20homesE.htm.

46. J. N. Campbell to Mrs. Nancy R. Perkins, April 21, 1855, HMSGC, Owen Papers, Item # 92–56–24–41.

47. J. N. Campbell to L. A. Campbell, April 2, 1857, HMSGC, Owen Papers, Item # 92–56–24–25.

48. Owen, novella, "Bab is Sick," 4–13.

49. Owen, novella, "Madame is Forced to Speak," 9–10.

50. Greene County Archives & Records Center: Campbell v. Sproul, 1856, Box 149, S/F010; Campbell v. Owen, 1859, Box 144 F01123.

51. U.S. Bureau of the Census, 1860; Willis, 8.

52. L. A. Campbell to Thomas Campbell, Dec. 3, 1856, HMSGC, Owen Papers, Item # 92–56–24–24.

53. J. N. Campbell to L. A. Campbell, ca. 1860, HMSGC, Owen Papers; No item # visible.

54. J. N. Campbell to Louisa Campbell, January 20, 1861, HMSGC, Owen Papers, Item # 92–56–24–21.

55. Stephanie M. H. Camp, *Closer to Freedom: Enslaved Women & Everyday Resistance in the Plantation South* (Chapel Hill: The University of North Carolina Press, 2004), 36–37, 53.

56. Camp, 51–52.

57. Notice of Runaways posted by Louisa Campbell & G. P. Shackelford, ca. June 3, 1861, HMSGC, Owen Papers, Item # 92–56 [remainder illegible].

CHAPTER 5

1. Sheppard, 7–8.

2. Ibid.

3. Ibid.

4. Ibid., 8–9.

5. James M. McPherson, *Battle Cry of Freedom: The Civil War Era* (New York: Ballantine, 1989), 290–291.

6. Ibid., 291.

7. On the Campbells: Confederate Service Records, Missouri State Archives (MSA).

8. Mary Danforth Campbell to Sarah Rush Owen, July 28, 1861, from Bethel, MS. HMSGC, Owen Papers, Item # 92–56–24–39.

9. Ibid.

10. McPherson, 350; Sheppard, 9–10.

11. Sheppard, 11.

12. Ervin L. Jordan, Jr., *Black Confederates and Afro-Yankees in Civil War Virginia* (Charlottesville: University Press of Virginia, 1995), 186.

13. McPherson, 351; Sheppard, 10–11.

14. McPherson, 352; Sheppard, 11.

15. Sheppard, 11–12; *Springfield Leader*, June 3, 1932; *Springfield News and Leader*, September 26, 1937.

16. Jordan, 58.

17. McPherson, 355, 291.

18. Sheppard, 12.

19. McPherson, 354.

20. Sheppard, 12; On D. D. Berry & family: "The Richest Man in Greene County," Robert Neumann, Director, Greene County Archives, Greene County Historical Society Bulletin, Vol. 58, #2, May–August, 1997. Copyright 1997.

21. Sheppard, 13–15; *Springfield Leader*, June 3, 1932.

22. Ibid., 16.

23. Ibid., 10.

24. Alice Fahs. *The Imagined Civil War: Popular Literature of the North and South, 1861–1865* (Chapel Hill: University of North Carolina, 2001), 22.

25. Shepppard, 15.

26. Missouri's Union Provost Marshal Papers: 1861–1866, Campbell, Greene, Springfield, 10-02-1862, Reel #F1185; Sheppard, 24.

27. *Springfield Leader*, June 3, 1932.

28. Ibid.; Sheppard, 23–24; Missouri Union Provost Marshal Papers: 1861–1865, Items dated 9-14-62, 9-18-62, 9-19-62, 10-24-62, 10-30-62, 11-14-62, 11-15-62.

29. "1862: 'A Continual Thunder,'" by William L. Shea, in Mark K. Christ, ed. *Rugged and Sublime: The Civil War in Arkansas* (Fayetteville: The University Press of Arkansas, 1994), 22.

30. William D. Baker, *History and Architectural Heritage of Searcy County* (Little Rock: Arkansas Historic Preservation Program, no date given), 13–17; Sheppard, 24.

31. Sheppard, 17.

32. Campbell genealogy, HMSGC; U.S. Bureau of the Census 1860; Connelley, 453.

33. Cheairs-Hughes Family Papers; www.state.tn.us/sos/statelib/techsvs/manud/88–021.pdf [downloaded Sept. 10, 1999].

34. Christ, 24–26.

35. Ibid., 26–28; McPherson, 404.

36. Christ, 29–31.

37. Christ, 27-37; McPherson, 405.

38. Christ, 37–38; McPherson, 405; Philip Katcher, *Battle History of the Civil War, 1861–1865*. (New York: Barnes & Noble Books, 2000), 34–35.

39. Sheppard, 17.

40. Camp, 17–18.

41. Ibid.

42. McPherson, 497.

43. www.pinebelt.net/~sshope/history.html; ADAH, Alabama governors: www.archives.state.al.us/govs_list/g_moorea.html; and ADAH on flag designer, Nicola Marschall: www.archives.state.al.us/marschall/german.html [both accessed April 29, 2005]; www.americancivilwar.com; http://www.lib.niu.edu/ipo/iht429748.html [accessed Sept. 11, 2005].

44. Christ, 37–38.

45. McPherson, 406–409.

46. Ibid., 410.

47. Ibid., 413.

48. J. N. Campbell's military records, MDAH; McPherson, 416; National Park Service: http://www.cr.nps.gov/history/online_books/hh/10/hh10e.htm [accessed Sept. 11, 2005].

49. McPherson, 417.

50. G. N. Beaumont to Louisa Campbell, June 30, 1862, HMSGC, Owen Papers, Item # 92–56–25–1; Thomas Campbell military record.

51. McPherson, 513; James R. Arnold and Roberta Weiner, *The Timechart of the Civil War* (St. Paul: MBI Publishing Company, 2001), 43; Sarah Rush Owen to Nancy Perkins, August 18, 1862, HMSGC, Owen Papers, Item # 92–56–24–44.

52. Sheppard, 18.

53. Ibid.

54. Picket Guard Pass for Louisa Campbell, September 10, 1862; Owen Papers, Item # 92–56–19–6; McPherson, 522–523; J. N. Campbell military record, MDAH.

55. J. Matthew Gallman, ed., *The Civil War Chronicle: The Only Day-by-Day Portrait of America's Tragic Conflict as Told by Soldiers, Journalists, Politicians, Farmers, Nurses, Slaves, and Other Eyewitnesses* (New York: Crown Publishers, 2000), 250.

56. Sheppard, 18–19.

57. *The War of the Rebellion: A Compilation of the Official Records of the Union and Confederate Armies*, [OR], Making of America Collection (Ithica, NY: Cornell University); OR, (Washington: Government Printing Office, 1891) Series 1, Vol. 22, Part 1, Ch. XXXIV, 178; OR, Series 1, Vol. 22, Part 1, Ch. XXXIV, 206–207.

58. McPherson, 580–582.

59. Bruce Catton, James M. McPherson, *The American Heritage New History of the Civil War* (New York: MetroBooks, 2001), 263.

60. Gallman, 261, 269–270.

61. January 25, 1863, Pass to cross Union line, HMSG, Owen Papers; Item # 92–56–19–7; McPherson, 586–587.

62. J. N. Campbell's military medical records, February 27, 1863, MDAH.

63. Sheppard, 20–21.

64. McPherson, 617; Col. G. F. Neill to Congressman O. R. Singleton, April 4, 1863, military records of J. N. Campbell, MDAH.

65. http://www.civilwarhome.com/forrestcampaigns.htm; http://americancivil war.com/statepic/tn/tn015.html [both accessed Sept. 9, 2005].

66. http://www.civilwarhome.com/vandornbio.htm; http://www.springhilltn.org/history.htm [both accessed Sept. 9, 2005].

67. Sheppard, 22–23.

68. Ibid., 24–25.

CHAPTER 6

1. Catton, 317.

2. Thomas A. DeBlack, "1863: 'We Must Stand or Fall Alone,'" in Christ, 74–84; OR, Series 1, Vol. 22, Part 1, 178; On Marmaduke's Expedition into Missouri: OR, Series 1, Vol. 22, Part 1, 205–207.

3. Christ, 84.

4. Patricia J. Williams, *Open House: Of Family, Friends, Food, Piano Lessons and the Search for a Room of My Own* (New York: Farrar, Straus, Giroux, 2004).

5. Sheppard, 26.

6. Sheppard, 27.

7. U.S. Department of the Navy, Naval Historical Center Homepage, On-Line Library of Selected Images: http://www.history.navy.mil/photos/sh-usn/usnsh-e/eastport.htm; http://www.history.navy.mil/photos/sh-usn/usnsh-c/covngtn.htm [accessed March 13, 2005]; Sheppard, 27–28.

8. Sheppard, 27–28.

9. Ibid.

10. Ibid.

11. Ibid., 29.

12. Bill Shea, "Regional Summary: Northeast Arkansas," Vol. 3, Spring 1985, www.arkansasheritage.com/in_the_classroom/lesson_plans/civilwar/NEArkansas summary.pdf

13. Noralee Frankel, "Breaking the Chains, 1860–1880," in Robin D. G. Kelley and Earl Lewis, eds., *To Make Our World Anew: A History of African Americans* (New York: Oxford University Press, 2000), 231.

14. "'Contraband Camps' Help Former Slaves Establish New Lives," *The Arkansas News*, Spring 1985, 1–3. [accessed March 13, 2005]; http://www.oldstatehouse.com/educational_programs/classroom/arkansas_news/detail.asp?id=689. Department of

Arkansas Heritage, Homepage, "African-Americans: Civil War," 2. [accessed March 13, 2005]. http://www.arkansasheritage.com/people_stories/africanamericans/page2.asp [accessed March 15, 2005].

15. *The Arkansas News*, Spring 1985, 1–3.

16. Leslie Schwalm, "A Complicated Story," University of Iowa homepage http://www.uiowa.edu/homepage/news/annual_report99/02_schwalm.html [accessed March 18, 2005].

17. Leslie A. Schwalm, "'Overrun with Free Negroes': Emancipation and Wartime Migration in the Upper Midwest" *Civil War History*, Vol. 50, No. 2 (2004) 145–174. http://www.findarticles.com/p/articles/mi_m2004/is_2_50/ai_n6148034 [accessed March 16, 2005], 2–3.

18. http://www.infoplease.com/ce6/society/A0813151.html/ [accessed March 13, 2005].

19. McPherson, *Battle Cry of Freedom*, 784–785.

20. Ibid., 786.

21. Ibid., 783–787.

22. Sheppard, 29–31; 1860 Slave Schedule.

23. Sheppard, 32.

24. Ibid., 32–33.

25. Ibid., 32–35; National Park Service, Battle Summaries, American Battlefield Protection Program, Little Rock: www.cr.nps.gov/hps/abpp/battles/ar010a.html [accessed April 1, 2005].

26. OR, Series 1, Vol. 22, Part 1, Ch. XXXIV, 533–534.

27. Ibid., 534.

28. On Marmaduke: http://www.missourilife.com/peop016.shtml [accessed March 31, 2005].

29. Sheppard, 36–38.

30. Ibid., 39–40.

31. OR, Series 1, V XXII, Part 1, 724–725, 731–732 [accessed March 31, 2005]; National Park Service, American Battlefield Protection Program, Pine Bluff: www.cr.nps.gov/hps/abpp/battles/ar011.html [accessed April 1, 2005]

32. Ibid., 724–725.

33. Ibid., 1055; MSA, Confederate service record, L. C. Campbell.

34. Cheairs-Hughes Family Papers, 4; Lizzie Campbell to Sarah Rush Owen, January 2, 1864, HMSGC, Owen Papers, Item # 92–56–24–45.

35. L. A. Campbell to Sarah Rush Owen, Dec. 9, 1864, Item # 92–56–25–2, HMSGC; Owen Papers; MDAH, Confederate service records of J. N. Campbell; gravestone photo furnished by John Polk Campbell. Sheppard wrote of Louisa's trip to Arkansas at the time of the Battle of Poison Spring: "She had intended to go on to Mississippi to see Uncle Jack, who was now an invalid, but this was not possible. He died just before the close of the war and she never saw him again after the time we left him on the plantation in '63," Sheppard, 46; YCC, Will of J. N. Campbell.

36. L. A. Campbell to Sarah Rush Owen, Dec. 9, 1864.

37. OR, Series I, V XXXIV, Part 1, 832; Sheppard, 46.

38. Sheppard, 46.

39. Ibid.; Daniel E. Sutherland, "1864: 'A Strange, Wild Time,'" in Christ, 115.

40. "The Camden Expedition of 1864," by William D. Baker, Little Rock: Arkansas Historic Preservation Program; http://www.arkansaspreservation.org/pdf/publications/Red_River_Campaign.pdf; Christ, 116.

41. Christ, 116.

42. OR, 828.

43. OR, 820. On the murder of African Americans, see Ira Don Richards, "The Battle of Poison Spring," *Arkansas Historical Quarterly*, V XXVIII (Winter 1959), 349: "Much has been said concerning the massacre of Negro troops at Poison Spring. Reports of Union officers engaged in the fighting frequently mention that wounded negroes were shot down without mercy. The surviving evidence tends to support this assertion. While no Confederates reported a 'massacre,' General Cabell did state that 'Morgan's regiment killed at least eighty Negroes.' Morgan did not participate directly in the fighting but was stationed between Poison Spring and Camden in the path of the fleeing Negro troops. It also seems significant that the Confederates reported the capture of only four Negroes." Also, Sheppard, 46.

44. McPherson, *The Negro's Civil War*, 221–223.

45. Ibid., 256.

46. Sheppard, 46–47; 1860 slave schedule.

47. Christ, 119; on Second Kansas: Transcribed from Report of the Adjutant General of the State of Kansas, 1861–1865. V 1. Topeka, Kansas: The Kansas State Printing Company. 1896. http://skyways.lib.ks.us/genweb/archives/statewide/military/civilwar/adjutant/2col/history.html [accessed April 24, 2005]

48. Provost Marshall Papers, 7–18–1864, F1185; 7–21–1864, F1185.

49. Sheppard, 47.

50. OR, 952.

51. Sheppard, 44–45; L. A. Campbell to Sarah Rush Owen, August 13, 1864, HMSGC, Owen Papers, Item # 92–56–24–29.

52. Sheppard, 46.

53. McPherson, *Battle Cry of Freedom*, 787; OR, 720; Christ, 134–135.

54. McPherson, *Battle Cry*, 787; Christ, 134–136.

55. McPherson, *Battle Cry*, 787.

56. McPherson, *Battle Cry*, 788.

57. L. A. Campbell to Louisa Campbell, Dec. 9, 1864, HMSGC; Owen Papers; Item # 92–56–25–2.

58. M. A. Campbell to Sarah Rush Owen, Undated Letter Fragment, HMSGC, Owen Papers, no item number.

59. Sheppard, 49.

CHAPTER 7

1. Arnold, 63; Battle summaries, National Park Service: http://www.cr.nps.gov/hps/abpp/battles/a1007.htm.

2. Ibid.

3. Gallman, 509.

4. http://college.hmco.com/history/readerscomp/civwar/html/cw_011201_selmaalabama.htm [accessed Oct. 29, 2004].

5. Macmillan Compendium, *The Confederacy, Selections from the Four-volume Macmillan Encyclopedia of the Confederacy* (New York: Simon & Schuster Macmillan, 1993), 423; http://www.wordiq.com/definition/Nathan_Bedford_Forrest.

6. Elijah Evan Edwards. Journals. Elijah Evan Edwards Papers. Archives & Special Collections, Roy O. West Library, DePauw University, Accession #(UM87–102, (UM88–72) Folder 4, March 21, 1865–1866 September 1865.

7. Steven Hahn, *A Nation Under Our Feet: Black Political Struggles in the Rural South from Slavery to the Great Migration* (Cambridge: The Belknap Press of Harvard University Press, 2003), 83.

8. Edwards, 264–265.

9. Ibid., 266, 273, 275.

10. Ibid., 288.

11. Ibid., 290.

12. Ibid., 300.

13. Richard Bailey, *Neither Carpetbaggers Nor Scalawags: Black Officeholders During the Reconstruction of Alabama, 1867–1878* (Montgomery, AL: Bailey Publishers, 1993), 2; Neal, 11; Edwards, 323.

14. Edwards, 299, 322.

15. Alice Fahs, *The Imagined Civil War: Popular Literature of the North & South, 1861–1865* (Chapel Hill: University of North Carolina, 2001), 185–186.

16. Edwards, 300.

17. Ibid., 300–301.

18. 1860 slave schedule.

19. Edwards, 309–312.

20. Ibid., 318.

21. Ibid., 325; www.pinebelt.net/~sshope/history.html, 2.

22. Edwards, 349–354, 359.

23. Sheppard, 51–52.

24. Sheppard, 52; http://www.geocities.com/Athens/Aegean/6732/files/look_solomon_union.html [accessed Sept. 12, 2005].

25. Morgan, 434–435.

26. Sheppard, 52.

27. Kelley, 239; Hahn, 130–154.

28. Hahn, 150.

29. W. E. B. DuBois, *Black Reconstruction in America, 1860–1880* (Cleveland: World Publishing, 1968), 489.

30. Morgan, Introduction by Joseph Logsdon, xix–xx.

31. Morgan, 55.

32. Hahn, 146.

33. Hahn, 149, 155–156; Morgan, xxxiv.

34. Sheppard, 52–53.; Louisa "Lulu" McKenny to Sarah Rush Owen, January 18, 1866, HMSGC; Owen Papers; Item # 92–56–24–4.

35. Bailey, 3.

36. http://www.lagrangetn.com/history.htm [accessed Sept. 12, 2005].

37. L. A. Campbell to Sarah Rush Owen, January 29, 1866, HMSGC, Owen Papers; Item # 92–56–24–11? [illegible].

38. L. A. Campbell to Sarah Rush Owen, March 20, 1866, HMSGC, Owen Papers; Item # 92–56–24–14.

39. L. A. Campbell to Sarah Rush Owen, April 4, 1866, HMSGC, Owen Papers; Item # 92–56–24–13.

40. *Springfield News Leader*, June 16, 1929.

41. Sheppard, 53–54; Louisa "Lulu" McKenny to "Auntie" [Sarah Owen], May 13, 1866, HMSGC, Owen Papers; Item # 92–56–24–8.

42. Sarah Rush Owen to "Fannie," June 17, 1866, HMSGC, Owen Papers, Item # 92–56–24–51.

43. L. A. Campbell to Sarah Rush Owen, July 16, 1866, HMSGC, Owen Papers; Item # 92–56–24–52; August 8, 1866, L. A. Campbell to Sarah Rush Owen, HMSGC, Owen Papers, Item # 92–56–24–12.

44. U.S. Bureau of the Census, 1860; Decell, 422; Betty C. Wiltshire, *Yazoo County Mississippi Pioneers* (Carrollton, MS: Pioneer Publishing, 1992), 210; Reverend Robert G. Certain, "Trinity Church: A Sesquicentennial History of the Episcopal Church in Yazoo, Mississippi." (Publisher not given) Ricks Memorial Library, Yazoo City, Mississippi, Accession # 282.26.249 ccr, 85-01388, 21; Receipts from L. A. Campbell, Guardian report, 1866, YCC.

45. www.pinebelt.net/~sshope/history.html.

46. Hahn, 171.

47. Morgan, xxxvii.

48. Ibid., xxxix.

49. Ibid., xxxiii.

50. John C. Willis, *Forgotten Time: The Yazoo-Mississippi Delta after the Civil War* (Charlottesville: University Press of Virginia, 2000), 28.

51. www.freedmen'sbureau.com [accessed March 13, 2005].

52. Hahn, 156–157.

53. Ibid., 163.

54. Ibid., 122–127.

55. Morgan,103–104.

56. Ibid., xlii; 113.

57. "Maryann" to Sarah Rush Owen, May 4, 1867, HMGC, Owen Papers; Item # 92–56–24–54.

58. L. A. Campbell to Sarah Rush Owen, May 16, 1867, HMSG, Owen Papers; Item # 92–56–24–15.

59. Louisa "Lulu" McKenny to Sarah Rush Owen, July 14, 1867, HMSGC, Owen Papers, Item # 92–56–24–5 and Item # 92–56–24–3; Sheppard, 54–55; Sarah Rush Owen to "My Dear Child," July 23, 1867, HMSGC, Owen Papers, Item # 92–56–24–56; Sarah

Rush Owen to a daughter, August 5, 1867, HMSGC, Owen Papers, Item # 92–56–24–57; Greene County, MO, Archives and Record Center, Deed index.

60. Patsy[?] to Sarah Rush Owen, August 7, 1867, HMSGC, Owen Papers, Item # 92–56–24–58 ; Sarah Rush Owen to Aunt [Perkins], September 6, 1867, HMSGC, Owen Papers, Item # 92–56–24–33.

61. DuBois, 434.

62. Foner, 140–141.

63. Morgan, 122.

64. Ibid., 122–128, 134.

65. Ibid., xlii, 129–131.

66. Ibid., 132.

67. DuBois, 434; Morgan, 149.

68. Foner, 314; DuBois, 490.

69. Morgan, 157.

70. DuBois, 541.

71. Ibid., 543.

72. Ibid., 541.

CHAPTER 8

1. Morgan, 159–164; 167–175.

2. Ibid., 176–179.

3. Ibid., 181–194.

4. DuBois, 436.

5. DuBois, 438; Morgan, 205.

6. Morgan, 212.

7. Ibid., 207.

8. Ibid., 208.

9. DuBois, 436–440.

10. Ibid., 490–491. I know not everyone will be interested in this history, maybe even because it is so unfamiliar, but for those who are, I really recommend reading about J. T. Rapier of Alabama, James Lynch of Mississippi, and Thomas Bayne of Virginia.

11. Bailey, 6–7; DuBois, 492.

12. DuBois, 493–494.

13. [Cut off/ seems to be] L. A. to Sarah Rush Owen, February 27, 1868, HMSGC, Owen Papers, Item # 92–56–24–16.

14. W. A. Campbell to Sarah Rush Owen, April 26, 1868, HMSGC, Owen Papers, Item # 92–56–24–63.

15. DuBois, 432.

16. The marriage date was 1868 on their divorce papers, 1869 in Alabama Marriage Book 1867–1876, Lic. # 170; U.S. Census Bureau of the Census, 1870.

17. L. A. to Sarah Rush Owen, Nov. 8, 1868, HMSGC, Owen Papers, Item # 92–56–24–17.

18. U.S. Bureau of the Census, 1860 & 1870; Loan application by L. A. Campbell, March 17, 1882, Book AD, 484, Chancery Clerk, Yazoo County.

19. L. A. to Sarah Rush Owen, Nov. 8, 1868, HMSGC, Owen Papers, Item # 92–56–24–17; 1860 and 1870 census.

20. DuBois, 432; Morgan, 409.

21. Morgan, 411.

22. Ibid., 230–232.

23. Ibid., 234–236.

24. Joseph W. Farrier to Sarah Rush Owen, November 13, 1868; HMSGC, Owen Papers, Item # 92–56–24–35.

25. Certain, 21; Morgan, 244–246.

26. Morgan, 260, 411.

27. U.S. Bureau of the Census 1860.

28. *Springfield News Leader*, June 16, 1929.

29. Sheppard, 55; U.S. Bureau of the Census, 1860–1900.

30. U.S. Bureau of the Census, 1870 & family records of the Bush family of Mobile, AL: http://www.ebcal.com/family/genealogy/bush_parental_ancestry/a1.htm #i582.

31. U.S. Bureau of the Census 1870; website of the U.S. Congress, biographies; Holcombe's History of Greene County, Springfield-Greene County Library, Local History Section: http://198.209.8.180/lochist/history/holcombe/grch30pt2.html [accessed June 27, 2004]; Springfield Bar Association history: http://www.smba.cc/SMBAHistory.cfm [accessed June 15, 2005]; Campbell genealogy, HMSGC.

32. Dorothy Sterling, ed., *We Are Your Sisters: Black Women in the Nineteenth Century* (New York: Norton, 1984); On the whole family, especially Edmonia: 294–305; U.S. Bureau of the Census 1870; Morgan, xix.

33. Sterling, 294–305, quote, 301.

34. Ibid.

35. DuBois, 440.

36. Ibid., 441. DuBois quotes Lynch on this subject: "No colored man in that state ever occupied a judicial position above that of Justice of the Peace, and very few aspired to that position. Of seven state officers, only one, that of Secretary of State, was filled by a colored man, until 1873, when colored men were elected to three of the seven offices, Lieutenant-Governor, Secretary of State, and State Superintendent of Education. . . . Of the ninety-seven members that composed the constitutional convention of 1868, but seventeen were colored men. The composition of the Lower House of the State legislature that was elected in 1871 was as follows: Total membership, one hundred and fifteen; Republicans, sixty-six; Democrats, forty-nine; colored members, thirty-eight; white members, seventy-seven; white majority, thirty-nine."

37. Bailey, 169, 171.

38. Lucy Owen to "Irene," February 26, 1871[?], HMSGC, Owen Papers, Item # 92–56–24–18; S. I. Campbell to Sarah Rush Owen, July 30, 1871 [unclear on orig.], HMSGC, Owen Papers, Item # 92–56–24–36.

39. Nannie Hall to Sarah Rush Owen, February 4, 1872, HMSGC, Owen Papers, Item # 92–56–24–37.

40. W. A. Campbell to Mary Frances "Fannie" Owen [1855–1892], June 12, 1872; HMSGC, Owen Papers, Item # 92–56–24–65; I found an Episcopal school that may have been where he attended in Pass Christian, but it no longer exists, so I was unable to check for records.

41. Unknown Freedman to L. A. Campbell, August 26, 1872, HMSG, Owen Papers; Item # 92–56–24–10.

42. U.S. Bureau of the Census, 1870; Alabama Marriage Book 1867–1876, 463.

43. W. A. Campbell to Mary Frances "Fannie" Owen, January 19, 1873, HMSGC, Owen Papers; Item # 92–56–24–66.

44. Neal, 2.

45. Morgan, 492; U.S. Bureau of the Census 1870.

46. *Yazoo City Herald*, December 15, 1876, 3.

47. Neal, 6.

48. Ibid., 8.

49. Ibid.

50. Ibid., 9–10.

51. Ibid., 11.

52. Ibid., 12.

CHAPTER 9

1. Morgan, 371–381; DeCell, 423–425.

2. Morgan, 379–384.

3. Ibid., 384–400.

4. Ibid.

5. DeCell, 316, 336; Morgan, 437–440.

6. Morgan, 457, 475–481.

7. Ibid., 483.

8. Senate Report, 1776.

9. Ibid., 1650, 1653.

10. Ibid., 1776.

11. Ibid., 1650.

12. Morgan, 483–484.

13. Ibid., 482.

14. Ibid., 478; U.S. Bureau of the Census, 1870.

15. Senate Report, 1651, 1677, 1678; Foner, *Freedom's Lawmakers*, 63–64; Morgan, 482.

16. Foner, 88; Lily Golden, *My Long Journey Home* (Chicago: Third World Press, 2002), 1–4.

17. U.S. Bureau of the Census, 1870; Foner, 97–98; Senate Report, 1678.

18. Morgan, 485.

19. Senate Report, 1651, 1654.

20. Ibid., 1676.

21. Ibid., 1677.

22. Morgan, xlv; Foner, 36.

23. Ibid., 219, 131–132; Senate Report, 1683.

24. Senate Report, 1654.

25. Foner, 76; Morgan, 494–498.

26. Morgan, xlvii.

27. Ibid., 505.

CHAPTER 10

1. U.S. Bureau of the Census, 1880; Mary Frances Owen to Sarah Rush Owen, January 12, 1881, HMSGC, Owen Papers, Item # 92–56–24–38.

2. DeCell, 108; 7 May, W. A. Campbell to Sarah Rush Owen, June 4, 1881, letters, HMSGC, Owen papers, No item numbers.

3. Morgan, 361.

4. Morgan, 362.

5. http://www.jimcrowhistory.org/scripts/jimcrow/insidesouth.cgi?state =Mississippi [accessed July 11, 2005]; http://americanradioworks.publicradio.org/ features/remembering/laws.html [accessed July 11, 2005]; http://www.orig.jackson sun.com/civilrights/sec1_crow_laws.shtml [accessed Sept. 12, 2005].

6. Ibid.; jimcrowhistory.org.

7. W. A. Campbell to Sarah Rush Owen, May 7, 1881, HMSGC, Owen Papers, No item number.

8. W. A. Campbell to Sarah Rush Owen, June 4, 1881, HMSGC, Owen Papers, No Item number.

9. DeCell, 351.

10. Bill of fare, St. Louis and Vicksburg Anchor Line (2 pgs.), HMSGC, Owen Papers, No item number.

11. Mary Frances Owen to Sarah Rush Owen, January 6, 1882, HMSGC, Owen Papers, Item # 92–56–24–20.

12. Signed book cover, 1882, HMSGC, Owen Papers; Item # 92–56–24–39.

13. Loan documents, March 20, 1882, Book AD, 360, Chancery Clerk, Yazoo City, MS.

14. Probate of L. A. Campbell, October 10, 1882, Book AD, 19, Chancery Clerk, Yazoo, MS.

15. Greene County Archives & Records Center, Probate Records of L. A. Campbell, #007909, File #1469.

16. Deed to Woolridge, February 4, 1884, Book AF, 72, Chancery Clerk, Yazoo City, MS; Morgan, 58.

17. Loan application from W. A. and E. A. Campbell, 1885, collection of John Polk Campbell.

18. Wright, 40.

19. Wright, 43–44.

20. Morgan, 505.

21. Ibid., 506.

22. Ibid., xlvii.

23. U.S. Bureau of the Census, 1900 & 1910; Billingsley, 312–316.

24. Campbell genealogy, HMSGC; W. A. Campbell to Erskine A. Campbell, May 20, 1889, Collection of John Polk Campbell.

25. "Rush C. Owen" to her son Jay "Jackie" Owen, Sept. 1, 1890, HMSGC, Owen Papers, No Item number.

26. Campbell genealogy, HMSGC; Springfield Leader, June 3, 1932.

27. Owen, Rush Campbell [Sarah Rush Campbell Owen]. *Anemone's People* (Springfield, MO: Jewell Publishing Co., 1901). HMSGC, Owen Papers, quote, 36.

28. Owen, Untitled novella, Chapter entitled, "The Invitation," 12.

29. Ibid., chapter entitled "Madame's Trip," 1.

30. Morgan, xlvii.

31. Ibid., 511.

32. Neal, 13.

33. Jacqueline Jones Royster, *Southern Horrors and Other Writings: The Anti-Lynching Campaign of Ida B. Wells, 1892–1900* (Boston: Bedford/St. Martin's, 1997), 111, 150.

34. DuBois, 694–699.

35. Ibid., 698–700.

36. Royster, 10, 14–15, 87.

37. Greene County Archives, Probate records of Robert Lee Campbell, #102741, File #1687.

38. Campbell genealogy, HMSGC.

39. U.S. Bureau of the Census, 1900; W. A. Campbell, 1901, Chancery Clerk, Yazoo City; "Death of Mr. W. A. Campbell," *Yazoo Sentinel*, August 7, 1902, 8.

40. Ibid.

41. Sarah Rush Owen to Barnett & Perrin, Folder "1900–1921," HMSGC, Owen Papers; No Item number.

42. Deeds of Trust, W. A. Campbell to J. F. Barbour, Book BK, 651, Chancery Clerk, Yazoo City.

43. Deeds of Transfer, 1903–1919, Chancery Clerk, Yazoo City.

44. *Springfield News & Leader*, April 4, 1954, D1; *Springfield Leader*, June 3, 1932; Information on the younger Lucy McCammon is on pages 2–13 of the biography of Alvina Krausse at: www.bte.org/about/alvina_krause.htm [accessed Sept. 12, 2005].

45. Fischer Cherye, "Racism in Springfield," *Z Magazine* (June 9, 2004; http://www.zmag.org/content/showarticle.cfm?ItemID=5682 [accessed Sept. 12, 2005]).

46. U.S. Bureau of the Census, 1880–1910; Death Certificate, State of Illinois, Department of Public Health, Division of Vital Statistics.

47. U.S. Bureau of the Census, 1920.

48. Morgan, 512.

49. Deeds, Curry to Barbour, Book DL, 458, Chancery Clerk, Yazoo City.

50. DeCell, 382.

51. Ibid.

52. http://www.pbs.org/wgbh/amex/flood/filmmore/fr.html [accessed July 10, 2005].

53. John M. Barry, *Rising Tide: The Great Mississippi Flood of 1927 and How It Changed America* (New York: Touchstone, 1997), 313; 315–316.

54. http://www.geocities.com/BourbonStreet/Delta/2541/blbbroon.htm.

55. Barry, 416–417.

EPILOGUE

1. W. E. B. DuBois. *The Souls of Black Folk* (New York: Fawcett, 1961), 18.

2. Richard Wright. *12 Million Black Voices* (New York: Thunder's Mouth Press, 1988), 10.

Bibliography

ABBREVIATIONS

ADAH   Alabama Department of Archives and History
HMSGC   History Museum for Springfield-Greene County, Springfield, MO
JPCP   John Polk Campbell Papers
MDAH   Mississippi Department of Archives and History
MSA   Missouri State Archives
OR   The War of the Rebellion: A Compilation of the Official Records of the Union and Confederate Armies
SGCL   Springfield-Greene County Library, Springfield, MO
YCC   Yazoo Chancery Clerk's Office, Yazoo City, MS

ARCHIVES AND MANUSCRIPT COLLECTIONS

History Museum for Springfield-Greene County, Springfield, MO
    Sarah Rush Owen Papers
Springfield-Greene County Library, Springfield, MO
    Personal Recollections of Early Settlers
    Holcombe History of Greene County
B. S. Ricks Memorial Library, Yazoo City, MS
    Yazoo City History Collection

PRIMARY SOURCES

Campbell, William Argyle to Erskine Argyle Campbell. Letters. Private papers, John Polk Campbell.

Cheairs-Hughes Family Papers 1636–1967, Tennessee State Library and Manuscript Unit, S Accession #88–21, location XVIII–G-3.

Edwards, Elijah Evan. Journals. Elijah Evan Edwards Papers. Archives & Special Collections, Roy O. West Library, DePauw University, Accession # (UM87–102), (UM88–72) Folder 4, March 21, 1865–September 6, 1865.

Morgan, Albert T. *Yazoo: or, On the Picket Line of Freedom in the South: A Personal Narrative.* Columbia: University of South Carolina Press, 2000.

Neal, Georgia Campbell. Manuscript of notes for a memoir. Thulani Davis Papers.

Owen, Rush Campbell [Sarah Rush Campbell Owen]. *Anemone's People.* Springfield, MO: Jewell Publishing Company, 1901. Sarah Rush Owen Papers, History Museum of Springfield-Greene County.

_____. "Madame's Trip to Eastern Coal Fields, By Anemone." Unpublished short story. Sarah Rush Owen Papers, History Museum of Springfield-Greene County.

_____. Novella manuscript, possibly untitled. Sarah Rush Owen Papers, History Museum of Springfield-Greene County.

Sheppard, Louisa Cheairs McKenny. *A Confederate Girlhood*, unpublished manuscript, 1892. Sarah Rush Owen Papers, History Museum of Springfield-Greene County; also available at University of North Carolina, Chapel Hill, Southern Historical Collection #1632.

GOVERNMENT DOCUMENTS

State of Alabama, Department of Archives and History. Marriage certificates, census records. Montgomery, AL.

State of Alabama, Department of Public Health, Center for Health Statistics. Death certificates. Montgomery, AL.

Chancery Clerk's Office. Court documents and land records. Yazoo City, MS.

Dodd, Jordan R, comp. Alabama Marriages, 1809–1920 (Selected Counties) [database online]. Orem, UT: MyFamily.com, Inc., 1999. Original data: Early American Marriages: Alabama, 1800 to 1920.

Greene County Archives and Records Center. Deed index, probate records, and Campbell legal cases. Springfield, MO.

Jackson, Ronald V., Accelerated Indexing Systems, comp. Mississippi Census, 1805–1890 [Database online]. Provo, UT: Ancestry.com, 1999. Compiled and digitized by Jackson and AIS from microfilmed schedules of the U.S. Federal Decennial Census, territorial/state censuses, and/or census substitutes.

Social Security Administration. Social Security application record. Baltimore, MD.

State of Mississippi, Department of Archives and History, Archives and Library Division. *Records of Mississippi State House of Representatives; The Official and Statistical Register of the State of Mississippi*, Centennial Edition by Dunbar Rowland; Confederate Service Record of J. N. Campbell; Confederate Grave Registration of J. N. Campbell.

State of Missouri. Missouri State Archives, Confederate Service Records of L. C. Campbell, S. I. Campbell, T. P. Campbell.

U.S. Bureau of the Census. Federal census for: 1850, 1860, 1870, 1880, 1900, 1910; 1850 and 1860 Slave Schedules. National Archives, New York, NY.

United States Congress. Senate. 44th Cong., 1st Sess., Report No. 527, 2 vols. *Mississippi in 1875: Report of the Select Committee to Inquire into the Mississippi Election of 1875*, Columbia University.

The War of the Rebellion: A Compilation of the Official Records of the Union and Confederate Armies. Cornell University, Making of America Collection; Washington, D.C.: Government Printing Office, 1891.

SECONDARY SOURCES

Books

Arnold, James R., and Roberta Weiner. *The Timechart of the Civil War*. St. Paul: MBI Publishing Company, 2001.

Arnoldi, Mary Jo, Christraud M. Geary, and Kris L. Hardin, eds. *African Material Culture*. Bloomington: Indiana University Press, 1996.

Bailey, Richard. *Neither Carpetbaggers Nor Scalawags: Black Officeholders During the Reconstruction of Alabama, 1867–1878*. Montgomery: Bailey Publishers, 1993.

Baldwin, Cinda K. *Great and Noble Jar: Traditional Stoneware of South Carolina*. Athens: University of Georgia Press, 1993.

Ball, Edward. *Slaves in the Family*. New York: Farrar, Straus and Giroux, 1998.

Barry, John M. *Rising Tide: The Great Mississippi Flood of 1927 and How It Changed America*. New York: Touchstone, 1997.

Beardsley, John, et al. *The Quilts of Gee's Bend*. Atlanta: Tinwood, 2002.

Berlin, Ira, et al, eds. *Free at Last: A Documentary History of Slavery, Freedom, and the Civil War*. New York: The New Press, 1992.

Billingsley, Andrew. *Climbing Jacob's Ladder: The Enduring Legacy of African-American Families*. New York: Touchstone, 1992.

Camp, Stephanie M. H. *Closer to Freedom: Enslaved Women & Everyday Resistance in the Plantation South*. Chapel Hill: The University of North Carolina Press, 2004.

Campbell, Will. *Providence*. Atlanta: Longstreet Press, Inc., 1992.

Carney, Judith A. *Black Rice: The African Origins of Rice Cultivation in the Americas*. Cambridge: Harvard University Press, 2001.

Catton, Bruce, and James M. McPherson. *The American Heritage New History of the Civil War*. New York: MetroBooks, 2001.

Christ, Mark, ed. *Rugged and Sublime: The Civil War in Arkansas*. Fayetteville: University of Arkansas Press, 1994.

Clinton, Catherine, ed. *Southern Families at War: Loyalty and Conflict in the Civil War South*. New York: Oxford, 2000.

Connelley, William Elsey. *Doniphan's Expedition and the Conquest of New Mexico and California*. Kansas City, MO: Bryant & Douglas Book and Stationary Co., 1907.

Current, Richard Nelson. *Those Terrible Carpetbaggers: A Reinterpretation*. New York: Oxford University Press, 1988.

DeCell, Harriet, and JoAnne Prichard. *Yazoo: Its Legends and Legacies*. Yazoo City: Yazoo Delta Press, 1988.

DuBois, W. E. B. *Black Reconstruction in America, 1860–1880*. Cleveland: World Publishing, 1968.

———. *The Souls of Black Folk: Essays and Sketches*. New York: Fawcett Publications, 1961.

Earle, Jonathan. *The Routledge Atlas of African American History*. New York: Routledge, 2000.

Fahs, Alice. *The Imagined Civil War: Popular Literature of the North & South, 1861–1865*. Chapel Hill: University of North Carolina, 2001.

Faust, Drew Gilpin. *Mothers of Invention: Women of the Slaveholding South in the American Civil War*. New York: Vintage, 1997.

Foner, Eric. *Reconstruction: America's Unfinished Revolution, 1863–1877*. New York: Harper & Row, 1988.

———. *Freedom's Lawmakers: A Directory of Black Officeholders During Reconstruction*, Rev. ed. Baton Rouge: Louisiana State University Press, 1996.

Frank, Andrew K. *The Routledge Historic Atlas of the American South*. New York: Routledge, 1999.

Franklin, John Hope. *Reconstruction After the Civil War*. 2nd ed. Chicago: University of Chicago Press, 1994.

Franklin, John Hope, and Loren Schweninger. *In Search of the Promised Land: A Slave Family in the Old South*. New York: Oxford, 2006.

Fry, Gladys-Marie. *Stitched from the Soul: Slave Quilts from the Antebellum South*. Chapel Hill: University of North Carolina Press, 2002.

Gallman, J. Matthew, ed. *The Civil War Chronicle: The Only Day-by-Day Portrait of America's Tragic Conflict as Told by Soldiers, Journalists, Politicians, Farmers, Nurses, Slaves, and Other Eyewitnesses*. New York: Crown Publishers, 2000.

Gardner, Sarah E. *Blood and Irony, Southern White Women's Narratives of the Civil War, 1861–1937*. Chapel Hill: University of North Carolina Press, 2003.

Genovese, Eugene D. *Roll, Jordan, Roll: The World the Slaves Made*. New York: Pantheon, 1974.

Golden, Lily. *My Long Journey Home*. Chicago: Third World Press, 2002.

Gomez, Michael A. *Exchanging Our Country Marks: The Transformation of African Identities in the Colonial and Antebellum South*. Chapel Hill: University of North Carolina Press, 1998.

Gutman, Herbert G. *The Black Family in Slavery and Freedom, 1750–1925*. New York: Pantheon, 1976.

Hahn, Steve. *A Nation Under Our Feet: Black Political Struggles in the Rural South from Slavery to the Great Migration*. Cambridge: The Belknap Press of Harvard University Press, 2003.

Jewett, Clayton E. and John O. Allen. *Slavery in the South, A State-by-State History*. Westport, CT: Greenwood Press, 2004.

Jordan, Ervin L., Jr. *Black Confederates and Afro-Yankees in Civil War Virginia.* Charlottesville: University Press of Virginia, 1995.

Jordan, Winthrop. *Tumult and Silence at Second Creek: An Inquiry into a Civil War Slave Conspiracy*, rev. ed. Baton Rouge: Louisiana State University Press, 1995.

Katcher, Philip. *Battle History of the Civil War, 1861–1865.* New York: Barnes & Noble Books, 2000.

Kelley, Robin D. G., and Earl Lewis, eds. *To Make Our World Anew: A History of African Americans.* New York: Oxford University Press, 2000.

Leslie, Kent Anderson. *Woman of Color, Daughter of Privilege: Amanda America Dickson, 1849–1893.* Athens: University of Georgia, 1995.

Litwack, Leon F. *Been in the Storm So Long: The Aftermath of Slavery.* New York: Vintage Books, 1980.

Macmillan Compendium. *The Confederacy, Selections from the Four-volume Macmillan Encyclopedia of the Confederacy.* New York: Simon & Schuster Macmillan, 1993.

McMurry, Linda O. *To Keep the Waters Troubled, The Life of Ida B. Wells.* New York: Oxford University Press, 1998.

McPherson, James M. *Battle Cry of Freedom: The Civil War Era.* New York: Ballantine, 1989.

_____. *The Negro's Civil War: How American Blacks Felt and Acted During the War for the Union.* New York: Ballantine, 1991.

Minchinton, Walter, Celia King, and Peter Waite, eds. *Virginia Slave-Trade Statistics, 1698–1775.* Richmond: Virginia State Library, 1984.

Mitchell, Michele. *Righteous Propagation: African Americans and the Politics of Racial Destiny After Reconstruction.* Chapel Hill: University of North Carolina Press, 2004.

Morgan, Philip D. *Slave Counterpoint: Black Culture in the Eighteenth-Century Chesapeake & Lowcountry.* Chapel Hill: University of North Carolina Press, 1998.

Morrison, Toni. *Playing in the Dark: Whiteness and the Literary Imagination.* Cambridge: Harvard University Press, 1992.

Piston, William Garret, and Richard W. Hatcher III. *Wilson's Creek: The Second Battle of the Civil War and the Men Who Fought It.* Chapel Hill: University of North Carolina Press, 2000.

Roediger, David R. *The Wages of Whiteness: Race and the Making of the American Working Class*, rev. ed. London: Verso, 2002.

Royster, Jacqueline Jones. *Southern Horrors and Other Writings: The Anti-Lynching Campaign of Ida B. Wells, 1892–1900.* Boston: Bedford/St. Martin's, 1997.

Singleton, Theresa A., ed. *"I, Too, Am America": Archaeological Studies of African-American Life.* Charlottesville: University Press of Virginia, 1999.

Spear, Allen H. *Black Chicago: The Making of a Negro Ghetto, 1890–1920.* Chicago: University of Chicago Press, 1967.

Sterling, Dorothy, ed. *We Are Your Sisters: Black Women in the Nineteenth Century.* New York: Norton, 1984.

Vlach, John Michael. *The Afro-American Tradition in Decorative Arts.* Athens: The University of Georgia Press, 1990.

Wharton, H. M., ed. *War Songs and Poems of the Southern Confederacy, 1861–1865.* Edison, NJ: Castle Books, 2000.

White, Deborah Gray. *Ar'n't I a Woman? Females Slaves in the Plantation South.* New York: Norton, 1999.

Williams, Patricia J. *Open House: Of Family, Friends, Food, Piano Lessons and the Search for a Room of My Own.* New York: Farrar, Straus and Giroux, 2004.

Willis, John C. *Forgotten Time: The Yazoo-Mississippi Delta After the Civil War.* Charlottesville: University Press of Virginia, 2000.

Wiltshire, Betty C. *Yazoo County Mississippi Pioneers.* Carrollton, MS: Pioneer Publishing, 1992.

Wright, Richard. *12 Million Black Voices.* New York: Thunder's Mouth Press, 1995.

Yafa, Stephen. *Big Cotton: How a Humble Fiber Created Fortunes, Wrecked Civilizations, and Put America on the Map.* New York: Viking, 2005.

Yazoo Herald. *A Pictorial History of Yazoo County.* Yazoo: Heritage House Publishing, 1996.

Yellin, Jean Fagan. *Harriet Jacobs: A Life.* New York: Basic Civitas Books, 2004.

Articles

Baxter, William A. "History and Architectural Heritage of Searcy County." *Little Rock: Arkansas Historic Preservation Program,* undated.

Richards, Ira Don. "The Battle of Poison Spring." *Arkansas Historical Quarterly* XXVII (Winter 1959): 338–349. http://peace.saumag.edu/swark/articles/ahq/camden_expedition/poisonspring338.html [accessed April 10, 2005]

Saxton, Alexander, "Blackface Minstrelsy," as reprinted in Bean, Annemarie, et al, eds. *Inside the Minstrel Mask: Readings in Nineteenth-Century Blackface Minstrelsy.* Hanover: Wesleyan University Press, 1996. pp. 67–85.

Schwalm, Leslie A. "'Overrun with Free Negroes': Emancipation and Wartime Migration in the Upper Midwest." *Civil War History* 50, no. 2 (2004): 145–174.

Vaughn, Carol Ann, "History of Baptists in Perry County." *Sowing Seeds of Hope, Living Missions* [online]. http://www.pinebelt.net/~sshope/history.html. [accessed September 8, 2005].

Acknowledgments

I started this book while recovering from a bout of bronchitis after a trip to Thailand, India, and Nepal. It was primarily a spiritual pilgrimage to sites where the Buddha lived and taught, especially the impoverished village of Bodh Gaya, where he attained enlightenment. I started the year 2001 twice, sleeping through New Year's Eve once in Bangkok and then again over the Pacific Ocean. From that time I have been face to face with the fact that one's life is just not in one's own hands. In the first three weeks I found two great-great-grandparents whose names I had never known, Louisa and John Polk Campbell. In June, after becoming the City/State Editor for the *Village Voice* in New York, I stopped working on this book without realizing it. My first task at the *Voice* was to prepare coverage for what turned out to be the biggest municipal election in city history. I stayed late many nights and was looking forward to going back to a regular schedule (and working on the book at night) after the primary on September 11, 2001.

The primary never took place that day. Life in New York became dramatically different and the long work hours not only continued but also became days of trying to make sense of an event that was not only tragic but complex in its effects. The woman who lived across the hall from me was working on a floor where one of the planes hit the World Trade Center, and she just disappeared. At work they handed out masks for us to wear over our noses and mouths because we were inside the "frozen zone" downtown where the air was dusty. I walked a good part of the way to work from wherever trains stopped each day, crossed the barriers manned by the National Guard, and then entered utterly empty streets. One evening on the walk back, a woman jumped into rush hour traffic from a building on Park Avenue South. Many of us stood on the sidewalk sobbing. I came to rely on daily Zazen meditation to keep myself together. Late at night, I researched the Campbells.

In June 2004, almost three years to the day since I came to the *Voice*, I was just as suddenly gone. I was laid off in a meeting that took no more than four minutes. When I went to my desk, the email was shut down. On my way home I got a phone call asking if I could get on a plane to Mississippi the next morning. I said, "Sure." I went to speak to a group of former civil rights workers who had returned to commemorate the fortieth anniversary of the deaths of murdered activists Michael Schwerner, James Chaney, and Andrew Goodman. From that day to this I have been a captive of Mississippi and its memories.

During the Christmas holidays that year my landlords informed their tenants that the building had been sold and gave us thirty days to get out. I did not get another place in that time, so I put everything in storage and moved in with family for several months. The book became my job and home and, other than my dogs, the only solid reminder of my old life. Before finishing, I moved again, and I have yet to finish unpacking.

As a result of all that I have many people to thank, first of all "family," some very newly found: Janie Bassett, Jennie and Raymond A. Brown, John Polk Campbell, the late Annie Coleman, Minnie Curry, Violy and Collis H. Davis, Donna Davis, Dr. Clifton Howell, Joseph Jarman, Jane McCammon, John P. McCammon III, Louis Massiah, Alondra Nelson, Jill Nelson, Denise and Roderick Randall and their computer-savvy children, Dawn Saito, Charles Stone III, Louise and Chuck Stone, Bill Warrell, Reverend Rainer Wilson, George C. Wolfe, my agent, Faith Hampton Childs, the Brooklyn Buddhist Association meditation group, and the Mindfulness Sangha that grew out of the former 96th Street Sangha, especially the founding members, A.J. Fieldler, Sharon Combs, and Rae C. Wright.

For responding to my calls for scholarly assistance I am indebted to Christine Clark-Evans, Eric Foner, Michael Gomez, Steven Gregory, Walter Johnson, and Robin D. G. Kelley.

I am also grateful for the honor of a 2002–2003 fellowship from the Charles H. Revson Fellows Program on the Future of the City of New York at Columbia University and to Karen Vrotsos, Program Manager, for her tireless assistance. Thanks also to the New York Coalition of One Hundred Black Women for the 2003 Legacy Award.

I owe much gratitude for research assistance to the staff of the History Museum for Springfield-Greene County, Missouri, especially Shauna Smith, and Tracie Holthaus; the staff of the Missouri State Archives; the staff of the Alabama Department of Archives and History; Richard B. Bernstein and Heights Books, Brooklyn, New York; Linda Butler, DePauw University, Greencastle, Indiana; my kinsman, Diarmid Campbell of Argyll, Scotland, and the Clan Campbell Society of North America; Iris Doksansky, Archivist, Midland Lutheran College, Fremont, Nebraska; John Ellzey, Ricks Memorial Library, Yazoo City, Mississippi; Noreene E. Girard, Chancery Clerk, Yazoo City, Mississippi; Trish McKelroy, Legal Document Researcher, Oxford, Mississippi; Robert Neumann, Greene County Archives & Records Center, Springfield, Missouri; and Elizabeth Wells, Samford University, Birmingham, Alabama.

At *The Village Voice* Ward Harkavy, Stacie Schwartz, LD Beghtol, and Alex Press helped me immeasurably on an article that was my first attempt to shape this story. I also want to thank Nat Hentoff, who has championed me unreasonably since my first feature article thirty years ago.

Thanks to my editor, Liz Maguire, Vice President and Publisher at Basic Books, for her patience and insight, and to Jo Ann Miller, Vice President and Editorial Director, as well as Chris Greenberg. Thanks to Louise Stone for last-minute proofing.

During the time I was working on this book a number of people passed who have been important to me: Rev. Gyoko Saito, my Buddhist teacher, a rebel in the finest sense, and a man of immeasurable wisdom; Lester Bowie and Malachi Favors Maghoustus, two of the great ones, who inspired me and honored me with their friendship; Jack Newfield and Ron Plotkin, two journalists who taught me a lot and encouraged me; Clarita Adams Watkins, my cousin and lifetime friend; and my cousin Joan Eileen Davis, my first friend and my "other" sister.

Lastly, two people in particular kept me going: My aunt, Lenne Davis, who continues to teach me how to live in this world and who provided assistance of every kind, chief of which were love and listening. My friend of thirty-eight years now, Arnim Johnson, Jr., drove all over Mississippi, read legal papers, called, emailed, encouraged, cajoled, and nagged me to keep at it. He read some of the books I used, helped with research, sent money, packed boxes, and read every word. I am privileged to have him as a friend. *Namu Amida Butsu.*

—*Thulani Davis*

Index

Ab (bondman), 81, 99, 102, 136, 138, 186
Academy of the Visitation (St. Louis), 178
African American history, Grand Narrative of, 3
African Ancestry (firm), 60
Africanism/Africanness, 9, 10, 13, 14, 164
Agra, Zaluma, 44
Alabama, 2–4, 22, 31–32, 49, 65, 85, 91, 161–162, 168, 172, 173, 175, 181, 185, 190, 194, 198–199, 215, 253
    backlash against Republicans in, 211
    Constitution, 200–201
    Democratic Club of Marion, Alabama, 198
    Department of Archives and History (ADAH), 44
    Ebenezer Church, 159
    Elyton and Montevallo, 159
    Jefferson County, 49–50, 53
    Marion, 18, 20, 43, 49, 50, 53, 54, 159, 180–181, 198
    Montgomery, 162, 184
    Perry County, 43, 50, 53, 115, 167, 180
    Selma, 160, 164, 165, 169, 184
Alabama Baptist, The, 52
Alexander II (Czar), 176
American Missionary Association, 180
Ames, Adelbert, 34, 206, 230
Anderson, "Bloody Bill," 154, 155

Anderson, Marion, 74
Anemone's People (Owen), 256–257
Ann (bondwoman), 81
Architecture, 26. See also Housing/homes
Arkansas, 106, 108, 115, 121, 152
    Helena, 127–128, 133–134, 139
    Little Rock, 140, 141
    Poison Spring, 147, 152
Armyworm, 188, 189
Aunt Nellie (bondwoman), 131

"Back Water Blues," 275–276
Ball, Edward, 130
Band of Angels (film), 111
Barbados, 14, 55, 61
Barbour, Augustus Garfield, 269, 270–271
Barbour, Edward, 271
Barbour, Haley, 267
Barbour, Jeptha F., 267, 272
Barbour, Willie (Billie) Louise, 269, 271
Barnett and Perrin attorneys, 264–266
Barron, John, 50, 52, 53
Barron, John Thomas, 51
Barron, Julia Tarrant, 50–51, 52, 53
Barron, William C., 50
Bassett, Janie, 254, 277
Bayne, Thomas, 193
Beaumont, G. N., 117
Beauregard, Pierre (General), 116, 117

315

Bedwell, S. G., 228, 231, 232, 234, 236
Berean Baptist Church, 52, 55, 169, 253, 277
Berry, Daniel Dorsey (Major), 101, 102, 106, 139
Berry, Letitia Danforth, 101, 107, 140
Billingsley, Andrew, 54, 253
Birth of a Nation (film), 191
Black Codes, 21, 32, 40, 182–183
Blackman, June, 157
Blackman, Wallace, 101
Black Reconstruction (DuBois), 10–11
Boone (Captain), 160
Bowser, Pearl, 31
Boyd, Sempronious H., 209, 249, 262
Boyd, Walter, 228, 233
Broonzy, Big Bill, 275–276
Brown, John, 82
Bryan, George, 241, 246
Buell, Don Carlos (General), 116
Bureau of Refugees, Freedmen and Abandoned Lands, 31. *See also* Freedman's Bureau
Burrows, Houston B., 236
Bushwhackers, 82, 96, 106, 133, 137–138, 155
Butler, Benjamin (General), 100

Cabell, William (General), 149
Caldwell, Charles, 196, 230, 236, 237
Camp, Stephanie, 92
Campbell. Constantine, 77
Campbell, Elizabeth "Lizzie" Berry, 145
Campbell, Erskine Argyle, 250, 262
Campbell, Ezekiel Madison, 106
Campbell, James Cheairs, 93
Campbell, John, 69, 73
Campbell, John Nathaniel, 77, 78, 84, 85–86, 90, 97, 99, 103–104, 106, 111, 116–117, 118, 119, 121, 122–123, 132, 145, 153, 156
    children of, 120, 241
    death of, 146
    letters of, 88–89, 91, 92
    personal wealth of, 203–204
    resignation from army, 123, 146
Campbell, John Polk, 69–70, 72, 73, 74, 85, 90
    charged with kidnapping, 75
    death of, 76–77, 79, 155
    myths surrounding life of, 78
Campbell, John Polk (author's third cousin), 128–130
Campbell, Junius T., 99, 105, 152
Campbell, L. C., 110, 121, 145
Campbell, Leonidas Adolphus Cadwaller, 22, 24, 34, 77, 85–86, 90–91, 124, 146, 153, 155–156, 157, 169–170, 175, 176–177, 179–180, 187, 212, 238, 246
    and Chloe Curry, 217–218
    in Confederate forces, 97, 99–100, 106, 117, 120–121, 141, 144, 147, 148–149, 152
    death of, 249
    elected to state legislature, 39–40, 40–41, 217, 227
    letter of advice to Sarah Rush Owen, 202–203
    and lynching outside home of, 35, 36–37, 227, 231, 232–233
    marriage and son of, 208–209, 262
    move to Vicksburg, 241
    personal wealth of, 203
    will of, 213, 249
Campbell, Louisa Cheairs, 69, 73, 75, 78, 79, 80–81, 89–90, 93–94, 95, 96, 98, 100, 101, 105–106, 107, 124–125, 140, 147, 151, 157, 170, 177
    crossing Union lines, 106, 119, 122
    eviction from her house, 104–105
    death of, 178–179
    and "servants" taking care of her children, 143
    travel to Arkansas with Will, Lulu, and bondpeople, 128, 130–134
Campbell, Lucy, 208, 241, 249, 255
Campbell, Mary Danforth, 84, 97–98, 104, 107, 156, 204, 206, 239
Campbell, Mary Frances. *See* Sprouel, Mary Frances
Campbell, Robert, 72, 151
Campbell, Samuel I., 96, 97, 99–100, 106, 117, 119, 124, 132, 138–139, 140, 147, 152, 156, 157, 176, 180, 208, 211–212
    death of, 212
    personal wealth of, 204

Campbell, Sarah Rush. *See* Owen, Sarah Rush Campbell

Campbell, Thomas P., 96, 97, 99–100, 101, 102, 104, 106, 117–118
  death of, 118

Campbell, William Argyle, 16, 17, 19, 27, 40, 80, 111–112, 240
  birth/early life of, 20, 69, 74, 81, 93, 94, 95, 96, 99, 103, 107, 119, 125, 130–131, 140, 142, 143–144, 152, 153, 157, 170, 176, 208, 212, 220, 241
  death and will of, 263–266
  letters to Sarah Rush Owen, 201–202, 245–246
  and Louisa Campbell's death, 178–179
  photo album of, 16, 17–18, 70, 97, 180
  and will of Leonidas Campbell, 213, 214
  See also Curry, Chloe Tarrant, and William Campbell

Carlton, Eli, 149–150

Carpetbaggers, 12, 27, 33, 186, 191, 211, 217

Carter, Bell, 46, 267

Carter, King, 22, 46, 202, 215, 249, 267, 270

Casualties. *See under* Civil War

Catton, Bruce, 121

Censuses, 19, 44, 45–46, 48, 49, 51, 53, 57, 77, 84, 175, 181
  racial descriptions in, 46–47

Cheairs, Louisa Terrill. *See* Campbell, Louisa Cheairs

Cheairs, Nathaniel IV, 82–83, 84, 94, 108, 155

Cherokee Native Americans, 71, 72, 109

Chicago, Illinois, 269, 270, 276

Chickasaw Native Americans, 71

"Chloe's White Child" (Neal), 16, 80

Choctaw Native Americans, 3, 8, 45, 46, 71, 147

Christ, Mark, 110

Christmas Insurrection Scare of 1865, 174

Civil War, 4, 11, 68, 94, 95–110, 112, 113.
  See also individual states
  African Americans in federal forces, 121–122, 144, 145, 147–148, 149–151, 152, 174
  Battle of Bull Run, 98

Battle of Gettysburg, 127

Battle of Lexington (Missouri), 102

Battle of Pea Ridge, 110

Battle of Poison Spring, 147, 152

Battle of Selma, 160

Battle of Spring Hill and Battle of Franklin, 155

Camden Expedition, 147

casualties, 110, 116, 121, 127, 128, 145, 148, 149, 154, 160

defections of federal officers, 97

end of, 157, 161, 162

Fort Sumter, 93

Marmaduke's Expedition, 120–121, 127, 154

plundering in, 154, 155, 162

See also Reconstruction period

Clan Campbell Society of North America, 72

Clarion, 36, 230

Clarke, Charles W., 183, 191

Clark-Evans, Christine, 169

Clay, Buriel, 4

Clayton, Powell, 144–145

Climbing Jacob's Ladder: The Enduring Legacy of African-American Families (Billingsley), 54, 253

Clothing, 17, 59, 86, 170, 172, 219, 258

Coal, 256, 258

Coker, R. J., 272

Coleman, Annie Lillie, 46

Colonels, 9, 22, 67

Concentration camps, 134, 137

Concubines, 12, 60, 190, 197, 242, 243, 255, 259

Confederate Girlhood, A (Sheppard), 80, 130.
  See also McKenny, Louisa Cheairs (Lulu)

Confederate States of America (CSA), 97, 106

Connelly, William Elsey, 76

Constitutional conventions (state), 185, 190, 191–192, 193, 194, 196–197

Contraband camps, 134, 135, 165, 192

"Contraband's Return, The," 166

Corbett, Margy, 180

Corn, 26, 28, 90, 147, 148, 202
  corn harvest festival, 118–119

Cotton, 2, 4, 19, 22, 25, 26, 49, 50, 58, 69, 85, 90, 155, 202, 225, 238, 247, 248–249, 251, 278
  cotton gin invented, 57
  crop failures, 186, 188–189
  prices, 204–205, 215
  and yearly cycle, 28–29
Covington, 132–133
Cowan, George, 159–160
Creek Native Americans, 58
Crenshaw, Lewis, 187
CSA. *See* Confederate States of America
Curry, Chloe Tarrant, 15–16, 51, 53, 67–68, 115, 144, 171, 181, 189, 200, 239–240, 272–273, 277–278
  birth, 43, 45
  children of, 46, 213, 215, 218, 256, 276
  daily chores of, 29
  death of, 278
  and education of Tarrant children, 270, 276
  at end of war, 160
  first journey to Mississippi, 18, 20, 21, 22, 23, 42, 214, 215
  as illiterate, 20, 202, 273
  jealousy of, 224
  and Leonidas Campbell, 41, 217–218, 224, 248
  marriage of, 202
  photo album of, 16, 17–18, 43–44, 47, 49, 53, 267
  siblings of, 44, 202, 213, 215, 240, 249, 270. *See also* Tarrant family (African American)
  and Temne people, 60–61
  and William Campbell, 42, 214, 218–219, 221–225, 242–243, 273
  and William Campbell's will, 264–268
Curry, Jabez, 202
Curry, James, 15, 20, 23–24, 42, 46, 51, 53, 202, 208, 215, 216, 240
  as preacher, 30, 222, 253
  and pregnancy of Chloe Curry, 224
  second marriage of, 54, 253
Curry, Minnie, 54, 55
Curry family (African American), 11, 208. *See also individual members*

Curry family (white), 53
Curtis, Samuel R. (General), 108, 135

Danforth, Josiah Finley, 70
Danforth, Letitia. *See* Berry, Letitia
Danforth, Mary A. Roane, 84. *See also* Campbell, Mary, *and* McKerall, Mary
DAR. *See* Daughters of the American Revolution
Daughters of the American Revolution (DAR), 73–74
Davidson, John W. (General), 140
Davis, Andrew, 7
Davis, Arthur, 7, 9
Davis, Jefferson, 106, 117, 160
Davis, Lenné, 67
Davis, Sarah J., 271
Davis, William Roscoe, 7, 192–193, 224
Deaths of African Americans, 34–35, 38–39, 149–151, 160, 162, 164, 168, 183, 184, 196, 198, 233, 234–235, 236, 237, 238, 252, 260, 279–280. *See also* Lynchings
DeCell, Harriet, 25–26
Democratic Party, 32, 33, 39, 120, 197, 198, 206, 229–230, 238
  shoot-out with Republicans, 230
  and White Primary system, 260
Dixon, Henry M., 39
Dixon, James, 206, 233, 234–235
Dixon's Scouts, 230–231
DNA testing, 60, 65
DOC. *See* Daughters of the Confederacy
Dodd, Phil, 159
Doniphan, Alexander (Colonel), 76
Douglass, Frederick, 122, 237
Dred Scott Case, 89
DuBois, W.E.B., 10–11, 173, 188, 190, 193–194, 196–197, 198, 201, 210, 260, 280–281

Easter, Calley, 75
Eastport, 132–133, 134
Education, 6, 20, 37, 61, 86, 119, 153, 156, 170, 171, 175, 178, 180, 182, 185, 199, 200, 253, 256, 261, 268–269, 270, 271
Edwards, Elijah Evan, 160–161, 161–162, 163, 164–165, 165–166, 167–169

Edwards, John C., 76
Ellen (bondwoman), 101
Emancipation Proclamation, 119–120, 121,
    135, 168, 199, 204, 281
Ewing, Thomas (General), 138
*Exchanging Our Country Marks: The
    Transformation of African Identities in
    the Colonial and Antebellum South*
    (Gomez), 62
Exodusters movement, 215, 253

Facts of Reconstruction The (Lynch), 211
Farrier, Joseph W., 205
"Fatal Flood" (documentary), 274
Fawn, Charles, 231, 232, 233
Feminists, 209
Firearms, 32, 33, 34, 173, 185, 196, 229, 230,
    234–235, 238, 260
Fisk University, 261–262
Flooding, 83, 90–91, 122, 123, 188, 248, 273.
    See also Mississippi, Great Flood
    of 1927
Florida, 91, 114, 172
Foner, Eric, 27, 191
Foote, W. H., 33, 38, 198, 205, 206, 211,
    228, 236
Forrest, Nathan Bedford (General), 18, 118,
    124, 145, 149, 159–160
Fort Donelson (Kentucky), 108
Foster, Stephen, 167
Franklin, F. E., 211
Franklin, John Hope, 199
Freedman's Bureau, 31, 66–67, 172–173, 175,
    183, 184, 191, 196. *See also*
    Freedmen/freedwomen
Freedmen/freedwomen, 5–6, 21, 32, 33, 46,
    47, 114, 133–134, 162, 165, 172, 192,
    205, 280, 281, 282, 283
    back pay for, 199–200
    dangers facing women, 181–182, 184,
        221, 260
    freedmen's conventions, 185
    as laborers, 135–136, 166, 181–182, 183,
        214, 219–220
    and rebel atrocities, 164
    soldiers shot when captured/wounded,
        149–151
    squads of, 181, 182

uprisings, 173, 174, 230
    See also Deaths of African Americans
Fremont, John C. (General), 100, 101
Fremont College of Pharmacy, 268–269
Fulbright, William, 70
Futa Jallon jihad, 62

Gazit, Chana, 274
Georgia, 62, 91, 114, 172, 191
Golden, Hilliard, 39, 228, 233
Gomez, Michael, 62, 64
Grand Oak plantation, 22, 24, 31, 249,
    250, 270
Grant, Ulysses S. (General), 108, 116, 122,
    205, 206
Gray, J. R., 242
Great Migration, 275, 276
Greene, Colton, 144, 148–149, 152
Griffith, D. W., 191–192
Guerrillas, 137–138, 154

Hahn, Steven, 174, 181
Hairston, Jester, 111
Haley, Alex, 64–65, 66
Hamilton Belle, 134, 140
Hammond, Horace, 38, 233
Harris, Major, 233
Hayes, Rutherford B., 238
Hickok, "Wild Bill," 109
Hicks, A. M., 40
Highgate, Carolyn Victoria and Edmonia,
    209–210
Hilliard, H. P., 228–229
Hood, John Bell (General), 155
Hoover, Herbert, 275
Housing/homes, 26, 27, 74, 83, 84–85, 87,
    97, 135, 188, 204, 208, 215, 275
Howard College (Alabama), 52
Hudson, R. S., 40, 182
Hurricane Katrina (2005), 275, 282–283
Hyatt, Oceana, 180

Impressment of goods, 123
Indian Removal Act (1830), 71. *See also*
    Trail of Tears
*In Search of the Promised Land, A Slave
    Family in the Old South* (Franklin and
    Schweninger), 199

Interracial marriage, 200, 243, 244, 258
Iowa, 134, 136, 186
Irreconcilables, 32
Irving, George S., 250

Jackson, Andrew, 71
Jackson, Claiborne Fox, 96
James, Jesse, 82, 154, 155
Jarman, Joseph, 59
Jayhawkers, 82, 137–138
Jazz, 6, 14
Jeffers, William L., 141
Jefferson, Thomas, 8, 12, 244
Jewett, Milo P., 52
Jim Crow, 243–245, 281
Johnson, Andrew, 183
Johnston, Albert Sidney (General), 108, 116
Jordan, Ervin, 99
Judson College (Alabama), 52

Kansas, 82, 138, 155, 215
    First Kansas Colored Infantry regiment,
        147–148
    Kansas City, 271, 277
    Second Kansas Colored Infantry, 152
Kelley, Moses, 202
Kickapoo Native Americans, 70, 71, 77
King, Lou (Aunt Lou), 220–221
King, Richard, 4
Knight, William, 268
Ku Klux Klan, 12, 160, 191, 195, 196,
        197–198, 201, 205, 206, 211, 252

Labor contracts, 21, 173, 174, 183, 184
La Grange Military Academy
        (Tennessee), 176
Laird, Sallie, 54, 253
Land mines, 102
Lane, James, 148
Lee, Robert E., 127, 157
Lee, Tom, 199
Legal cases, 87, 89–90, 250, 264
Leonard, William, 191, 236
Levees, 122, 188, 248, 274, 275, 276, 282
Lewis, Greene S. W., 211
Lincoln, Abraham, 91, 98, 101, 157, 162, 180.
        See also Emancipation Proclamation
Lincoln School (Marion, Alabama),
        180–181, 199, 253–254, 261, 270

Link (bondman), 138–139, 140, 143, 147,
        151, 157
Liza (Davis ancestor), 7–8, 61
Long, Huey, 275
Louisiana, 85, 91, 275
    New Orleans, 170, 176–177, 282, 283
Loyal League (Union League), 196
Loyalty oath, 106, 118, 135, 157
Lynch, John Roy, 210–211
Lynchings, 11, 35, 36–37, 38, 40, 67, 184,
        216, 217, 227, 230–231, 232, 237, 259,
        260, 270, 279, 281
    crusade against, 261
    of whites, 196
    See also Deaths of African Americans
Lyon, Captain Nathaniel, 96, 97, 98

Madagascar, 6, 61
Mail service, federal, 103
Marmaduke, John (General), 141, 144, 145,
        147, 177. *See also* Civil War,
        Marmaduke's Expedition
Martial law, 100, 114
Masons, 134
McCammon, Jane, 272
McCammon, Lucy (granddaughter of John
        Polk Campbell), 70, 73, 269–270.
        See also Owen, Sarah, children of
McCammon, Lucy (great-granddaughter of
        John Polk Campbell), 269–270
McCulloch, Benjamin (General), 106, 109
McElhany, Lucy, 208–209. *See also*
        Campbell, Leonidas, marriage of
McElhany, Robert, 249, 262
McIntosh, W. H., 52, 53, 202
McKenny, Elnathon D., 79, 143
McKenny, Louisa Cheairs (Lulu), 79–81, 86,
        93, 95, 96, 99, 101–102, 105, 107,
        110–111, 114, 119, 152, 157, 161,
        170, 175, 208, 262
    dislocated shoulder and illness,
        142–143
    marriage and children of, 208
    nanny of (Mary), 120, 136–137,
        186–187
McKenny, Talitha, 79
McKerall, Mary, 262. *See also* Campbell,
        Mary, *and* Danforth, Mary A. Roane
McKerall, William, 206–207

McKissack, William II, 82
McPherson, James M., 98, 114–115, 117,
    137, 138, 149, 150, 153, 154
Memphis Ledger, The, 259
Mende people, 64
Middle Passage, 48, 62, 63
Migrations. *See* Great Migration
Military District of the Trans-Mississippi,
    106, 115, 157
Military Reconstruction Acts, 184,
    186, 189
Mills (Colonel), 98
Mississippi, 2, 15, 32, 49, 73, 77, 91,
    156, 169, 181, 189, 261
    Black and Tan convention in, 191, 194,
        196–197
    Black Codes in, 182–183
    Constitution, 198, 217, 243, 244
    Corinth, 116, 117, 119
    Democratic White Men's Party of
        Mississippi, 197
    election of 1875, 33, 35, 38, 39–40, 42,
        228, 229, 230, 233, 235
    Farmington, 117
    Great Flood of 1927, 274–276, 282
    Jackson, 169
    legislature in 1870, 210, 211
    Natchez, 79, 83, 85
    National Guard, 275, 276
    property values in, 204
    Reconstruction legislature and laws,
        21–22
    Satartia, 234–235, 274
    slave population increase in, 85
    State House Journals of 1876/1877, 40
    The Mississippi Plan, 32–33, 230
    Vicksburg, 83, 122, 124, 127, 169, 174,
        230, 241, 247, 252
    Washington County, 276
    Yazoo City/County, 31, 34, 85, 170, 171,
        173, 174, 180, 185, 188, 190, 195–196,
        197–198, 201–202, 205–206, 209, 211,
        212, 227–237, 238, 260, 265, 274, 280
Mississippi River, 103, 115, 124–125, 128,
    133, 134, 138, 139, 151, 152, 188,
    274, 275
Missouri, 73, 74, 81–82, 93, 100–101, 102,
    137, 155, 169, 186–187
    Fort Davidson, 154

History Museum for Springfield-Greene
    County, 74
Kansas City, 276, 277
Missouri State Guard, 97, 106
St. Louis, 154, 170, 175, 178
See also Springfield, Missouri
Mitchell, R. B., 33
Montgomery Advertiser, 165
Moore, Andrew Barry, 115
Morgan, Albert T., 27–28, 32, 34, 35, 37,
    173–174, 181, 182, 183, 185–186,
    189, 190–191, 196, 197, 204, 205,
    206, 216, 234, 237, 243, 244,
    252–253, 272
    daughters of, 258–259
    marriage of, 209
    as sheriff in Yazoo County, 33, 171,
        228–229
    testimony at Senate Committee,
        230–231, 231–232
Morgan, Charles, 173–174, 183, 185–186,
    195, 196, 206
Morrison, Toni, 9
Mulattoes, 47, 171, 220, 224, 271
Mumbo Jumbo (Reed), 134
Murdock, Ready, 260
Musick (bondman), 105, 140, 257
Muskogee Native Americans, 71

National Archives, 66–67
Native Americans, 24, 58, 59, 66,
    71, 155, 254. *See also*
    individual groups
Naval Historical Center of the Department
    of the Navy, 132
Neal, Georgia Campbell, 15, 17, 20–21,
    58–59, 63, 253–254, 259, 261,
    263–264, 273
    after death of William Campbell,
        268–269, 276–277
    death of, 277
    marriage of, 277
    physical appearance of, 239,
        240, 255
    writing of, 15–16, 18, 23, 29–30,
        30–31, 215, 218–223, 239
Neal, J. McKinley, 277
Nebraska, 268–269
Neill, G. F. (Colonel), 123

New Foundation Church (at Grand Oaks), 31, 216
1959 (Davis), 56

Oklahoma, 59, 72, 269
Open House: Of Family, Friends, Food, Piano Lessons and the Search for a Room of My Own (Williams), 129
Order of American Knights (Sons of Liberty), 138, 153
Owen, Jabez (father), 87
Owen, Jabez (son), 84, 87–88, 90, 107
Owen, Sarah Rush Campbell, 41, 70, 76, 84, 87–88, 89, 97, 107–108, 118, 130, 143, 145, 153, 179, 187, 201, 202–203, 205, 207, 217, 218, 241, 273
  chapbook and fiction of, 256–258, 272
  children of, 89, 179, 208, 211, 212, 241, 245, 247, 256, 269
  death of, 272
  and will of William Campbell, 264–266

Panic of 1873, 214
Parisot, Sherman, 25–26, 242, 249
Patterson, James G., 35–38, 39, 93, 216–217, 228, 230–231
Percy, LeRoy, 276
Perkins, Nancy Cheairs, 84, 128
Peters, Jessie Helen McKissack and Dr. George B., 124, 139
Phelps, Mary Whitney, 108, 177
Photo album. *See under* Campbell, William Argyle; Curry, Chloe Tarrant
Pickens, Lucy Holcombe, 176
Plundering. *See under* Civil War
Polk, Andrew Jackson, 199
Polk, James K., 73, 76
Polk, Leonidas, 142
Polk, Matilda Golden, 73, 74
Polk, Mrs. Leonidas, 187
Pottery, 49, 58, 62
Prentiss, Benjamin (General), 128
Presidential election of 1868, 205–206
Price (Colonel), 138–139
Price, Sterling (General), 94, 97, 106, 108, 117, 119, 138, 153, 154, 155

Quantrill, William Clarke, 137–138, 154, 155
Queen of the Confederacy, 176
Quiltmakers, 58

Railroads, 246, 247
Rape, 7, 9, 60, 67, 115, 171, 252, 260, 261, 270
Rapier, James T., 199
Rations, 27, 84, 165, 175
Reconstruction period, 21, 31, 184, 191, 205, 210, 243, 252, 260
  Redemption period, 10–11, 38, 211, 230, 236
  See also Military Reconstruction Acts
Reed, Ishmael, 134
Religion, 3, 14, 52, 113, 163, 168–169, 178
Reparations, 200, 210, 225
Republican Party, 32, 33–34, 35, 38, 190, 193, 194, 196, 205, 216, 227, 228–230, 234
  shoot-out with Democrats, 230
Rice farming, 62, 72
Richmond Whig, The, 166
Riverboat landings, 25
Roach, Max, 14
Robinson, Benjamin (Sergeant), 149
Roots (Haley), 66
Rust College (Mississippi), 262

St. Francis River, 139, 140
Samford University (Alabama), 52
Sargeant School (Massachusetts), 271
Scalawags, 33
Schwalm, Leslie, 136
Schweninger, Loren, 199
Secession, 91, 104
Secret societies, 64
Sedbury, Nancy, 145
Seddon, James, A., 150
Segregation, 243, 244, 283
Sharecropping, 23, 27, 40, 214, 215, 275
  hidden costs charged to, 251–252
Sheppard, Louisa McKenny, 79, 80, 208. *See also* McKenny, Louisa Cheairs (Lulu)
Sherman, William Tecumseh, 116, 172
Sierra Leone, 14, 60, 61, 62, 64
Sigel, Franz, 98, 109–110

Siloam Baptist Church, 52, 169

Slavery, 3, 10, 18, 25, 52, 54, 55, 56, 62, 63, 66, 72, 75, 83, 91, 129, 165, 200, 209–210, 281, 283
  body servants, 99
  and intimacy, 12, 112–113
  legacies of, 112
  Mississippi slave population increase, 85
  Missouri divided concerning, 81–82, 93, 104
  Natchez slave market, 79
  rations during, 27, 84
  runaways, 81, 92–93, 94, 100, 112, 114, 115
  slave censuses of 1860, 19. *See also* Censuses
  slaves confiscated by northern troops, 100, 114
  slaveships from Barbados to Virginia, 61

Slaves in the Family (Ball), 130

Smith, Bessie, 275

Smith, Fanny, 105, 177, 179, 187

Smith, Kirby, 148

Songs, 110–111, 131, 167, 168, 220
  about Great Flood of 1927, 275

Souls of Black Folk, The, (DuBois), 280–281

South Carolina, 49, 57, 58, 62, 65, 91
  Port Royal, 114–115

Spencer (Major), 98

Springfield, Missouri, 65, 69, 70, 72, 78, 94, 104, 121, 170, 177, 206, 207, 208, 218, 245
  lynchings in, 270
  Southern sympathizers in, 95–96

Sprouel, Mary Frances (Mary Frances Campbell), 79

Sprouel, Dr. Samuel, 90

Steele, Fred (General), 140, 141, 147, 151

Stone, Louise Davis, 16

Sultana (steamboat), 25

Sweeney, Thomas W. (General), 98

Tarrant family (African American), 11, 19, 43, 65, 169, 172, 175, 189, 199–200
  Allen, 45, 202
  Andrew, 46, 202, 213, 240
  Caroline and Edmond, 44, 45, 48, 51, 52, 55, 56, 57, 60, 182, 208, 240, 254

  children in, 45–46, 47, 48, 240, 253
  George Aaron, 46, 202, 213, 240
  King. *See* Carter, King
  Lucy Ann, 36, 202, 213, 240, 253
  Mariah, 44, 45, 189, 208, 240, 254, 277
  See also Curry, Chloe Tarrant

Tarrant families (white), 48, 49–50, 53, 55, 56–57, 65–66, 159. *See also individual members*

Tarrant, Caesar, 56

Tarrant, Carter, 55, 57

Tarrant, Carter (Rev.), 57

Tarrant, Colonel Felix Noble, 50–51

Tarrant, Francis, 55, 57

Tarrant, Julia Ann, 50–51

Tarrant, Larkin Young, 50, 52, 208

Tarrant, Leonard, 49, 50

Tarrant, Lucy, 55, 57, 261

Tarrant, Mary Ann Smith, 50–51, 202

Tarrant, Richard, 55, 57

Tarrant, Sampson, 56

Tarrant, William, 55

Tarrant, W. R., 50

Taylor, Augustus, 38, 233

Temne people, 14, 60–61, 62–64

Tennessee, 49, 70–71, 73, 176, 187, 188
  Forge Seat historic landmark, 87, 88
  Fort Pillow, 149–150
  Memphis, 103, 259, 261
  Rippavilla Plantation in Spring Hill, 82–83, 84, 155
  Shiloh, 116, 117
  Stones River, 121

Texas, 4, 49, 65–66, 73, 89, 91, 146, 152, 153, 169
  Cass County, 75–76
  Waco, 143, 145

Thomas, William, 36, 41, 216, 217, 232

Thurmond, Strom, 10

Trail of Tears, 3, 59, 72

Trinity Episcopal Church (Yazoo City), 206

Trinity School for Boys (Yazoo City), 180

Tucker, John, 55

Turner, Nat, 7, 112

Tutt, Meg (also Maggie), 240, 254

Tutt, Zeno, 45, 213

12 Million Black Voices (Wright), 281

United Daughters of the Confederacy, (UDC), 80
U. S. Congress, 35, 36, 184, 236, 238. *See also* Morgan, Albert A., testimony at Senate Committee
U.S.-Mexican War, 51, 76, 81

Van Dorn, Earl (Major-General), 106, 109, 110, 115, 124, 139
Vicksburg Herald, The, 252
Virginia, 2, 3, 7, 9, 10, 48, 49, 55–58, 65, 191, 192, 244
    constitutional convention in, 193–194
    cotton farming in, 57–58
    Fortress Monroe, 100, 193
    Hampton, 55, 57, 100
    Library of Virginia, 192
    Richmond, 123, 192
Vosburg, John Henry, 210
Voting, 4, 11, 13, 21, 33, 184, 185–186, 189–191, 196, 217, 260, 280, 281. *See also* Mississippi, election of 1875

Wade, Dora F., 236
Walker, General Grant, 46, 261

Walker, Lucius (General), 141
Walker, Myra, 270
Walker, Thomas, 167
Weather, 28, 89, 92, 93, 108, 109, 119, 175, 188
Weaver, Uncle Henry, 220
Wells, Ida B., 260, 261, 262
White, J.J.B. (Colonel), 174, 189
White Leagues, 34
Whitney, Eli, 57
Williams, Patricia J., 129
Willis, John C., 183
Wilson, James Harrison (General), 159, 164, 180
Wilson, Rainer, 46, 223, 240, 276
Wood, A. S., 211
Woodfin, E. B., 240
Woolridge, Dave, 250
Woolridge, Samuel, L., 249, 250
Wright, Richard, 251–252, 281–282

Yazoo, or on the Picket Line of Freedom in the South (Morgan), 27–28, 237, 252, 272. *See also* Morgan, Albert T.
Younger gang, 155